The New Economy and the Modern South

WORKING IN THE AMERICAS

UNIVERSITY PRESS OF FLORIDA

Florida A&M University, Tallahassee
Florida Atlantic University, Boca Raton
Florida Gulf Coast University, Ft. Myers
Florida International University, Miami
Florida State University, Tallahassee
New College of Florida, Sarasota
University of Central Florida, Orlando
University of Florida, Gainesville
University of North Florida, Jacksonville
University of South Florida, Tampa
University of West Florida, Pensacola

WORKING IN THE AMERICAS

Edited by Richard Greenwald, Drew University; Timothy Minchin, LaTrobe University; and Ralph Armbruster-Sandoval, University of California–Santa Barbara

Working in the Americas is devoted to publishing important works in labor history and working-class studies in the Americas. This series seeks work that uses both traditional as well as innovative, interdisciplinary, or transnational approaches. Its focus is the Americas and the lives of its workers.

Florida's Working Class Past: Current Perspectives on Labor, Race, and Gender from Spanish Florida to the New Immigration, edited by Robert Cassanello and Melanie Shell-Weiss (2008)

The New Economy and the Modern South, by Michael Dennis (2009)

The New Economy and the Modern South

Michael Dennis

Foreword by Richard Greenwald and Timothy Minchin

University Press of Florida
Gainesville/Tallahassee/Tampa/Boca Raton
Pensacola/Orlando/Miami/Jacksonville/Ft. Myers/Sarasota

Printed in the United States of America. This book is printed on Glatfelter Natures Book, a paper certified under the standards of the Forestry Stewardship Council (FSC). It is a recycled stock that contains 30 percent post-consumer waste and is acid-free.

14 13 12 11 10 09 6 5 4 3 2 1

Library of Congress Cataloging-in-Publication Data
Dennis, Michael, 1967–
The new economy and the modern South / Michael Dennis.
p. cm.—(Working in the Americas)
Includes bibliographical references and index.
ISBN 978-0-8130-3291-7 (alk. paper)
1. Southern States—Economic conditions—20th century. 2. Virginia—Economic conditions—20th century. 3. Business enterprises—Virginia. 4. Industrial promotion—Virginia. I. Title.
HC107.A13D56 2009
330.9759—dc22 2008033605

The University Press of Florida is the scholarly publishing agency for the State University System of Florida, comprising Florida A&M University, Florida Atlantic University, Florida Gulf Coast University, Florida International University, Florida State University, New College of Florida, University of Central Florida, University of Florida, University of North Florida, University of South Florida, and University of West Florida.

University Press of Florida
15 Northwest 15th Street
Gainesville, FL 32611-2079
http://www.upf.com

Dedicated to Frank V. Dennis, my father, who probably disagrees with most of what's written here, but has nevertheless served as my example of dignity through work, sacrifice, and commitment.

Contents

Foreword

Michael Dennis's *The New Economy and the Modern South* joins a small but growing body of literature that tries to ground globalization in local space, to slow it down in real time and analyze it in the concrete rather than the abstract. For Dennis the local is Virginia during the past twenty years. Political elites in state and federal government allied with business interests adopted an aggressive style of free market ideology. Nowhere did this ideology advance as quickly or solidly as in the American South. "Virginia's experience," according to Dennis, "illustrates what was at the core of the American experience in the late twentieth century: the loss of political control by working-class people. That was a southern story, but it is also the national experience. Virginia's recent history has never been more thoroughly American." The story of job losses, anti-union campaigns, and the rise of conservative Republicans is now America's story. What we see in the Virginia of the late twentieth century is an "ideology that combined traditional southern conservatism and libertarian economic thinking to sanction the supremacy of the market in social affairs."

Dennis presents a tour de force of political economy that will influence generations of scholars interested in globalization and its complex relationship to the local, the South, and of course the modern working-class life. What makes his analysis so penetrating is that he never loses sight of the importance of power, even when discussing resistance from the bottom up. His is not a hopeless history. Rather, by locating the theater of opposition to globalization in the local, he provides a sophisticated model for future scholars. His rich use of a variety of sources and voices allows him to provide an understanding of race, class, and power in the modern South.

Richard A. Greenwald
Timothy Minchin
Series Editors

Acknowledgments

This book wouldn't have happened without the dedicated assistance of a battalion of librarians at Acadia University, most notably, Darlene Sweet, Wilma Meyer, and Patricia Gallant. They hunted down request after request and searched high and low for material that proved invaluable in the long run. I thank them sincerely. Minor T. Weisiger and the staff of the Library of Virginia provided indispensable assistance in the early stages of research and in the latter stages of editing—thank you. Dan LeBlanc, formerly president of the Virginia AFL-CIO, offered tremendous insight into the labor movement and political culture of the Old Dominion, and I wish to express my gratitude for his assistance here. I'm tremendously grateful to Eli Bortz, who patiently guided this project to completion, navigating more than a few treacherous obstacles, some of the author's own making. Meredith Morris-Babb of the University Press of Florida expressed enthusiasm and support for it right from the beginning and ensured that it saw the light of day. Marthe Walters skillfully guided it through final revisions and accommodated changes that improved the final product. I'm grateful for her assistance. For his expert copyediting and sharp eye for detail, I would like to acknowledge Eivind Boe.

For their constructive, insightful criticism of the manuscript, I'd like to thank John Dale and Richard Greenwald, both of whom spent considerable time shedding light on some of the dark corners of an earlier draft. W. Fitzhugh Brundage is exonerated from any and all of the ideas enclosed here, but his example, wisdom, and friendship have been indispensable throughout. Gratitude is also in order to Bruce Matthews, former dean of Arts and Sciences at Acadia, who provided critical financial assistance and consistent moral support during the process. Barry Moody, Bob Perrins, David Duke, and Vern Provencal of the Department of History Classics have been supportive colleagues and sharp critics from start to finish, and I'm supremely grateful. Drew Swanson and Leah Blain also deserve a special note of gratitude for their editorial and bibliographical contributions at a critical stage of the project. I'd also like to thank Bruce Nissen of *Labor Studies Journal* and Craig Phelan of *Labor History* for guiding two revised chapters into print and for helping me to clarify my arguments. Gratitude is in order as well to David R. Goldfield, who looked at a few chapters early on and provided necessary corrective guidance. To Melanie and Michael Jr., I would like to extend a sincere expression of affection for their consistent support. It made all the difference.

CHAPTER 1

The South in the Era of Market Dominance

The strange paradox of our times is that despite America's fabulous wealth, most people's lives are shadowed by economic anxieties and real confinements, the wounds that market ideology has imposed.

William Greider, "The Future Is Now"

On the forefront of global economic relations since the seventeenth century, Virginia and the South were at the center of American global integration in the 1990s. This is the main story of the region in the fading years of the twentieth century, and is likewise that time frame's dominant story for the whole American experience. Virginians, like most average Americans, were drawn into the flow of economic changes that fundamentally altered their sense of possibility and eroded the moderate economic security they had achieved in the post-war era. Market ascendancy and the subsequent decline of the social contract decisively influenced their hopes for the future.

This is not simply another chapter in the contested story of globalization. In fact, the globalization trope distracts attention from the most significant development of the era: the rise of an ideology that placed the unfettered marketplace at the center of American life. As momentous as this development has been, it belongs in turn to a series of much longer and more profound changes, those which economic historian Karl Polanyi identified over sixty years ago in *The Great Transformation*. Transfixed by the threat of fascism and a world convulsed by depression, then war, Polanyi set out to explain the titanic forces that shook the modern era. Underneath the clash of chauvinistic imperialism, totalitarian dreams of domination, and the shock of international economic collapse lay the modern era's seismic shift toward marketplace dominance. The "origins of the cataclysm," he wrote, were in "the utopian endeavor of economic liberalism to set up a self-regulating market system" that would dissolve the social bonds of state, community, and religion alike.[1] Through an anthropological investigation of tribal clans and tradition-bound societies, he arrived at the startling conclusion that "man's economy, as a rule, is submerged in his social relationships." People do not have a natural and irresistible affinity for the marketplace, as Adam Smith suggested. In traditional societies governed by the norms of folk culture, the market had functioned as an ancillary feature of social interaction. It was subordinate to the relations defined by community standards, traditional conventions, and social institutions. "The economic system was submerged in general social relations," Polanyi submitted. It was "merely an accessory feature of an institutional setting controlled and regulated more than ever by social authority."[2]

While Polanyi's historical recollections may have exaggerated the harmonious character of exchange in traditional societies, his argument was powerful: the market economy had yet to become the omnipresent phenomenon it would in the industrial era. It had yet to become the principal mechanism through which societies and people within a given society interacted. It had yet to exalt individual self-interest over the social and cultural connections that dignified the human predicament.

The industrial revolution, of course, changed everything. For Polanyi, however, this was not simply a matter of machines over humanity or the degrading condition of work or even the growing class chasm between workers and owners. Instead, the industrial revolution launched the drive for the "self-regulating market," even while industrialists benefited considerably from state assistance in achieving it. The process was complex, but the objective fairly clear: the achievement of "conditions which make the market the only organizing power in the economic sphere."[3] The principles of "reciprocity" and "redistribution" that had once governed the market and ensured social cohesion disintegrated as the profit imperative swept up land, production, labor, finance, and exchange. Free trade, an inflexible gold standard, and a ruthless labor market replaced the checks and balances that had once protected Western society against the corrosion of unrestricted competition.[4]

For all of its overarching generalizations, Polanyi's bleak vision of market dominance captured the dynamics at work in the Gilded Age. So too did his analysis of the response to these developments. The juggernaut of industrialization produced a protracted struggle in which progressive middle-class reformers and workers collaborated to restrain the self-regulating market. The "labor question" that loomed over the Gilded Age like the sword of Damocles was finally addressed when labor unions and state intervention began to limit unrestricted competition. Aiming to "rehabilitate the lives of men and their environment" and "give them some security of status," the regulatory onslaught "necessarily aimed at reducing the flexibility of wages and the mobility of labor, giving stability to incomes, continuity to production," and something approximating full employment. In the United States, that interventionist movement reached its height in the form of the New Deal, the series of reforms that the Roosevelt administration and its liberal allies in Congress advanced in response to the economic catastrophe of the Depression. Extended in the post-war years, it helped sustain a high level of prosperity by contributing to real wage growth and higher productivity, countering vicious cyclical downturns, and investing in social institutions that expanded the middle class and raised the standard of living.[5]

The enormous spending on the Cold War national security state also contributed to prosperity, a development that benefited the South even while southerners rediscovered the political benefits of railing against Big Government. It was a kind of military Keynesianism that both Democrats and Republicans could support. Of the top ten destinations for military investment, the South has five of them, and Washington, D.C., is the sixth. By 2000, 47 percent of all military personnel on active duty were serving in the region. Virginia did extremely well in the military bonanza. By 2000, five southern cities enjoyed military investments of over $2.25 billion—Norfolk and Arlington were two of them. Even in the last decade of the twentieth century, the South's share of the military was expanding considerably. In 1994, the eleven states of the former Confederacy received 32.3 percent of federal expenditures on military contracts. By 2000, that investment had grown to 51.8 percent, with Texas and Virginia reaping increases of almost 50 percent. Not without reason do historians Charles S. Bullock III and Janna Deitz conclude that federal military spending drastically improved the South's economic conditions while simultaneously reducing regional distinctiveness. Federal authority also played an invaluable part in advancing the cause of racial equality by extending the reach of national law into areas of southern life that had long been governed by the dictates of white supremacy. Despite the rhetoric of southern conservatives determined to slash social spending and liberate corporate potential, the federal government had become the indispensable ally to the South.[6]

Even in the latter years of the twentieth century, the national security state remained surprisingly vibrant. The interventionist program that permitted a limited form of social democracy to flourish did not. The acquisitive individualism and unmitigated competition that had troubled Polanyi so much and which precipitated the American economic collapse of the 1930s had returned. The South would become the site of its greatest achievements and the home of its most devoted supporters. Military Keynesianism aside, southern business and political leaders championed a new economic order that bore all the signs of Polanyi's "self-regulating market." What few advocates of the New Economy South anticipated is that the region would foster its own, fledgling answer to the problem of market dominance. "To separate labor from other activities of life and to subject it to the laws of the market," Polanyi ruminated, "was to annihilate all organic forms of existence and to replace them by a different type of organization, an atomistic and individualistic one."[7] That was the challenge facing working-class southerners, white and blue collar, in the late twentieth century. A surprising constellation of reformers would begin to address that challenge at the height of the New Economy era. In the latter days of the waning twentieth century, it seemed as if social democratic reform had been revived.

* * *

Advocates of the self-regulating free market hoped that, if left unmediated by state action and untrammeled by public control, it would become the dispenser of material improvement and the arbiter of social values. That ideology achieved considerable success in the 1990s, as state and federal governments pursued an agenda that sought to eradicate deficits, suppress inflation, deregulate financial and labor markets, drastically reduce public spending, and expose the United States to a new regime of unrestricted capital mobility and free trade agreements.

That ideology advanced most rapidly in the American South, where it came up against fewer obstacles and fewer opponents than anywhere else in the United States. Virginia is important, then, not only because of job losses and gains from declining textile mills and rising high-tech investments. It is significant not simply because of the inexorable march of religious conservatism and the meteoric rise of its Republican leaders. It is important because its experience in the 1990s exemplified the ascent of an ideology that combined traditional southern conservatism and libertarian economic thinking to sanction the supremacy of the marketplace in social affairs. It did more than exemplify, though. Through its business-development strategies, its participation in international trade agreements, its celebration of an ethic of market-oriented individualism, and its cultivation of an ethos of global competitiveness, it led these changes. The promise of democratic regeneration that briefly flourished during the era of the civil rights movement dissipated as lines of race and class division sharpened in the booming

1980s. Virginia's experience illustrates what was at the core of the American experience in the late twentieth century: the loss of political control and economic stability by working people. That was a southern story, but it was also the national experience. Virginia's recent history has never been more thoroughly American.

Virginia was born in the era of global commercial expansion. Investment in tobacco, rice, cotton, and slaves made the southern colonies a major thoroughfare in the movement of transnational capital during the Age of Exploration. That pattern continued as the region traded in commodities and lives, accumulating the capital and the political determination for independence. In the aftermath of the Civil War, the South developed an "isolated" labor market dependent on commodity crops and low-wage, secondary industrialization typified by the textile industry.[8] Economically peripheral, the South was never insulated from the cruel vagaries of international capitalism. The fluctuations in the international cotton market had a dramatic impact on the livelihoods of hundreds of thousands of southern sharecroppers and tenants. The technologically deficient, low-skilled industries that relocated to the South in the early twentieth century had a lasting impact on the region's character. Its failure to develop a skilled labor market, a diversified economy, an advanced educational system, and the public infrastructure necessary for development plagued the region even after the fall of Jim Crow.

Yet despite the legacy of racial segregation and commodity crop agriculture, the South did change—and dramatically. Federal intervention during the Great Depression in programs ranging from public utilities to public works programs whittled away at regional stagnation. Government spending on public infrastructure, transportation systems, and manufacturing facilities during the Second World War modernized the regional economy in a fashion unimaginable to the boosters of the New South. Migration out of the rural South into the urban North and South drastically altered the character of the region's labor market.

Growing northern and foreign investment injected capital into the region while continued military spending lifted the South out of its agrarian torpor. The image of the South changed in response. From poverty and cultural isolation, the dominant theme shifted to the South's rapid economic development, the abandonment of the region's exploitative agricultural system, and its replacement by industrial growth. Textile mills, furniture manufacturers, and petrochemical producers flourished in the low-wage, anti-union South.

Most importantly, it was the place where African Americans organized to overthrow a repressive system of racial control that had its roots in slavery. In response to the political changes of the World War II era and as the result of the concentration of African Americans in urban centers, the drive for racial equality coalesced. Political and economic factors destabilized the system of racial control that developed after the Civil War, but black civil rights activists ultimately compelled the federal government to dismantle it. In the aftermath of the demise of Jim Crow, the growth of the Sunbelt South, with its transplanted industries and bustling urban centers, loomed largest. The emergence of a competitive political system was heralded as a major development. So too was the supposed integration of southern institutions and public spaces.

While Jim Crow faded into the past, the region's conservatism did not. The South never did undergo the kind of democratic revolution that would have allowed working-class blacks and whites to address their common economic challenges.[9] Yet racial stratification did diminish, particularly for middle-class blacks who enjoyed greater social mobility and access to public service sector jobs. African Americans did begin to enjoy the economic benefits of Sunbelt industrialization. Integration moved ahead, and blacks and whites did mix, at least superficially, in the South's public places and work spaces. Yet these years also witnessed a political transformation that would dramatically alter the social landscape of the South. Blacks established a political presence in the region, but it was in a Democratic party that conservative whites rapidly abandoned. In the 1980s, the Republicans gained a 50 percent increase of support among southern white conservatives. A full 60 percent of white conservatives supported the Republicans in 1988. By 1996, the Republicans had the support of 37 percent of all southern voters.[10]

The South's racial divide persisted into the 1990s, conspicuously evident in the conflict over public historical memory. In Virginia, that debate over the past focused on a controversial proposal to erect a memorial of Arthur Ashe on Monument Avenue, effectively "integrating" the pantheon of Confederate heroes in downtown Richmond.[11] It was also manifested in a debate over a proposal for Confederate history month, which Governor Jim Gilmore finally endorsed in 2000, as well as over the adoption of a Confederate counterpart to Martin Luther King Day. Commentators focused on the rise of the conservative right and the South as the staging grounds for a Republican Revolution. Closely related to this fixation was the assertion that the South was exporting its values to the rest of the country, producing the "southernization" of America at a time of cultural uncertainty. The South was a uniquely—even morbidly—religious region where evangelical efforts to purge sin and assure salvation permeated the cultural atmosphere. Stock car racing, country music, anti-establishment, "good-ole boy" individualism, local autonomy, and family traditions still apparently set the region apart. While most historians and journalists focused on southern cultural distinctiveness, the persistence of regional economic liabilities, or persistent racial antagonism, others began to address the decline of manufacturing from international competition. Even here, however, commentators chose to emphasize the region's continuing appeal to automobile manufacturers, the proliferation of jobs in its service sector, and the explosive growth of dynamic cities like Charlotte and Atlanta.[12]

Historians have expended considerable energy exploring the cultural dimensions of the South's past out of a legitimate recognition that there is no homogenous South, no culturally unified Dixie. No less important, commentators on the South in the late twentieth century have drawn necessary attention to the divisive and incendiary debates over the representation of the past in the present. In doing so, they have corrected a vision of the southern past defined by white racial mythology. They have also identified the central place that culture and historical consciousness have acquired in the enduring struggle over the meaning of slavery, the Civil War, and the aftermath of Reconstruction. In place of a mythologized southern past they have fashioned a history of the region shaped indelibly by ethnic and racial diversity. By riveting our attention on gender dynamics, cultural conflict, debates over the legacy of Confederate symbols, the mythology of the Civil War, historical memory, and race as the key dividing lines in the modern South, historians have explored dimensions of southern life that earlier analysts had simply ignored or deliberately obscured. Instead of searching for the region's "central themes" or documenting conventional politics, historians have turned their gaze to the volatile intersection of identity, power, and history in the region's unique and troubled experience.[13]

In an era of corporate downsizing and the decline of the social security state, though, the primary focus on cultural identity obscures some of the paramount issues. The primacy it has achieved in historical analysis reflects the late-twentieth-century struggle to expand the reach of American democracy to previously subjugated and subordinated groups. As vital as these movements were to the redefinition of American democracy and as compelling as they remain today, they are part of a larger picture of social crisis that intensified in the last two decades of the previous century. Southern historians need to devote more attention to the experience of economic insecurity that defined the lives of most working-class southerners in the late twentieth century. Rejecting the liberal consensus appropriate to an era of near monolithic anti-communism, historians of the post–civil rights era uncovered the lines of acrimonious cultural and racial division in the southern past that white supremacy had supposedly subdued. Those racial and cultural tensions have by no means disappeared. If anything, they have intensified in an era of economic polarization, school resegregation, and official color-blindness. Even so, they are inseparable from the social forces that are now propelling black, white, and Hispanic workers together as never before. That is not to suggest that working-class southerners achieved some unifying consciousness or racial modus vivendi that historians have somehow overlooked. Neither is it to suggest that the intense debates over Confederate history months, African American heritage, and Confederate flags flying atop state buildings were meaningless distractions from the real story. Throughout the late twentieth century, the realities of racial subordination and privilege continued to mediate the experience of class. It is, however, to suggest that those electrifying debates often failed to address the socioeconomic tremors rumbling beneath the feet of black, white, and Hispanic workers in the New Economy era. In large part they failed to address underlying economic inequalities because Americans lacked a language for discussing widening class disparities in a meaningful way. Additionally, it is to remind historians that the material circumstances, the daily realities, and the future prospect of production have always been central concerns of working people. Identity, culture, tradition, and religion mediate those experiences, but they do not displace them. Questions of racial and cultural identity cannot be disentangled from socioeconomic class and thrown away in the interest of getting at the "real" problems. At the same time, though, the often stridently divisive "culture wars" of the 1990s cannot be considered the alpha and omega of that era's zeitgeist.[14]

Sociologist Todd Gitlin has pointed to the illusions inherent in a type of intellectual inquiry that substitutes culture for politics and economic power: "The thirst for consolation explains the rise of academic cultural studies during precisely the years when the right held more political power for a longer stretch than at any time in generations." Yet that "thirst" has led to additionally arid endeavors. Cultural studies cannot substitute for an analysis of the material conditions and ideological conventions that govern the lives of working people. "If we wish to do politics," Gitlin advises, "let us organize groups, coalitions, demonstrations, lobbies, whatever; let us do politics. Let us not think that our academic pursuits are already that."[15] The "academic pursuit" I present here is not an exercise in partisanship or policy analysis. It does, however, adopt a critical perspective on the ideology and practice of business dominance in southern life. It asks whether or not average southerners benefited from an agenda that made capitalist accumulation the centerpiece of American social and political life. It suggests that the market dominance which fixated Karl Polanyi has returned to the United States and is conspicuously evident in the South, along with all of its attendant social consequences.

As valuable as the post-modernist turn has been in alerting us to the connection between language and power, discourse and authority, it should not replace our concern with the objective economic conditions that invariably influence the lives of working people. Addressing the question of poverty in an era of market liberalization, historian Jacqueline Jones warned against it being reduced to a "post-modern phenomenon." Jones discouraged historians from turning the lives of the poor into a "text" to be examined by "detached 'readers' who see in those lives only irony and contradiction." The experience of the poor is not a "discourse" that is "subjective and relative," but something lived and endured by real people. Ignoring that objective reality for scholarly abstractions eliminates the possibility that historical inquiry can advance social justice.[16]

Some of this post-modernist temperament is evident in the most recent studies of southern globalization. For James Peacock, an anthropologist who has studied globalization and the South, "Globalism creates diversity as people, things, and ideas migrate here. . . . Globalism is not just capitalism. . . . it is also an attitude, an identity."[17] While the semantics of globalization might be subject to debate, there is little question that the most significant impact of international integration has been economic disruption. Working people measure their lives first in terms of financial security, family stability, and community cohesion. That means that for average southerners, if not for academics, the exigencies of capitalism has indeed been the centerpiece of globalization. As the editor of the recent collection *The American South in a Global World*, Peacock is principally concerned with the impact of globalization on identity, not the livelihoods of working people. To give but one example of the problems inherent in this approach, consider Peacock's second hypothesis, that the South's "opposition to the nation is giving way to a sense of integration with the wider world." For Peacock, the "overriding concept is identity," not market integration or class disparities. This "Copernican Revolution" of international awareness, however, is but a half-revolution at best.[18] International consciousness did not displace the South's embrace of a national political party that disparaged international agencies like the United Nations, abdicated environmental responsibility, and seemed to posit Christian fundamentalism as the standard for global morality. Nor has international consciousness provided much consolation for southerners suffering job displacement and downward class mobility.

Contributors to *The American South in a Global World* do not exclude economic transformations, of course; at least one scholar underlines the deleterious economic consequences of global integration, and the present work incorporates those insights. Yet the burden of the discussion is on identity, cultural interaction, and transnational movements of people and information. The movement of migrant workers should not be confused with globalization, however; it is what an earlier generation described as immigration. Immigration has indeed diversified and enriched the South and is now one of the most contentious issues in the region. It is important, therefore, to separate the private enterprise program out from these other developments, since fusing them allows historians to obscure the deliberate nature and negative consequences of business dominance. The escalating influx of migrant workers from Latin America into the United States, for instance, should raise troubling questions about the veracity of claims made on behalf of recent free trade agreements. Corporate globalization has been considerably less sanguine for the region, for the nation, and for working people than cultural exchange, and it is time that historians began to address this.

To offer a critical perspective on corporate-led globalization is not to enter automatically in to a "screed," as some commentators would suggest.[19] Economic or class perspectives are disparaged as throwbacks to an ideological age. Culture, identity, and language, by contrast, are not only academically fashionable but edgy, critical, and intellectually respectable. Yet since post-modernists disparage objectivity as a simplistic if not pernicious relic of a rationalistic past, and since a considerable number of historians have fallen under the thrall of post-modernism, which dismisses material conditions as a critical factor in social analysis, we are often left with a history that dances awkwardly around the most important forces at work in the lives of working-class southerners, not to mention Americans in general. Historians have become increasingly uncomfortable with social class and the economic factors that shape the social order. It is as if they have decided to cling to E. P. Thompson's injunctions to explore working-class culture while leaving his material concerns almost completely behind.

In the context of a discussion of the New Economy, this has often translated into an unwillingness to examine the social impact of the free market system. The bias is unfortunate, but it is particularly strong in southern history. Despite the indispensable attention paid to gender and race in the southern experience, historians of the American South tend to avoid class—let alone class antagonism—while burying economic factors so deeply in discussions of cultural storm and stress that we lose sight of them altogether. Southern labor and industrial historians are the notable exception, but their perspective seems to be a minority opinion in the analysis of the region's last forty years.[20] In looking at globalization, historians have emphasized the positive over the negative, the cultural benefits of open borders, the long-term benefits or, conversely, uncertainty about its consequences due to insufficient historical perspective. As a general rule, they have stressed the commonsense inevitability of it all. There may be cracks in the edifice, some bugs to be worked out in the system, but overall, market integration has benefited the South.

This would seem to be the position of James Cobb and William Stueck, who submit that none of the authors in their collection believe that "globalization in the southern United States has shown itself to be the hydra-headed monster its critics seem to describe." Accepting "inequalities of wealth" as the inevitable result of market integration, Cobb and Stueck champion globalization. To do otherwise would be to "reject the simple realities of capitalism," the "only modern economic system that has demonstrated the capacity over time to improve the lot of those whom it exploits." Of course, no other "modern economic system" has benefited quite so extensively from state assistance, coercive and otherwise. In the American context, no other economic system has benefited from the ideological authority granted it by media, political, and intellectual elites who ensured an inextricable link between capitalism and "freedom." Their criticism sets up a familiar dichotomy, reminiscent of the Cold War, when one could either choose the liberating winds of free market capitalism or the stifling oppression of state communism. There was nothing in between. What Cobb and Stueck overlook, however, is that the United States enjoyed its greatest economic success at precisely the time that it was the most regulated, the most protected, and the most socially democratic. It is not simply a question of wealth inequality, as the authors suggest, but a question of whether or not meaningful democracy can be sustained in a region and in a country that permits these inequalities to grow unabated.

This is what many critics address—the relationship between free market integration and economic democracy at home. While some have offered little more than strident denunciations lacking historical perspective, others have advanced a model of globalization that is fair, decent, and responsible. They have offered the vision of a world governed by active citizens rather than simply by business leaders and their political allies.[21] Cobb and Stueck turn to Africa, a favorite example of what neoliberal proponents believe has gone wrong with international trade, to make their point. It is "the least globalized continent" but also the "poorest, sickest, and most strife ridden as well." Their logic is dubious, considering that no mention is made of the legacy of colonialism, imperialism, slavery, and international political intrigue. Surely these developments were earlier chapters in globalization? Their collection would seem to imply as much, studded as it is with chapters on the South in the currents of global integration before 1950. Despite claiming that "globalization cannot be fully understood as simply the march of indomitable economic forces," the authors leave little room for any other conclusion. To challenge those economic forces is to challenge the "simple realities" of capitalism.[22]

Similarly, *The American South in a Global World* suggests that globalization is a "process" that acts like an "asteroid" or a "hurricane," striking different regions in disparate ways. Despite the apparent inconsistency between the image of clinical processes and natural forces, the combination of the two reveals quite a bit about prevailing perspectives. Committed to a free market ideology, even liberal academics wish to suggest that globalization is inevitable ("process") but also destructive ("asteroid"), at once rational but invariably disruptive. What most academic proponents of globalization seem to miss is that real people in positions of power make decisions that are anything but inevitable but which often carry devastating consequences for other real people.

For the most part, Cobb, Stueck, and Peacock overlook the operation of this business imperative in some of the most important developments in the South of the past fifty years. They underplay the impact that unregulated capitalism has had on democracy in the South and in the United States. Free markets are not abstract, disembodied, ideologically neutral "realities." Instead, they are political arrangements that provide for the advancement of the few, sometimes the many, but often at the expense of most. Have some southerners benefited from expanded trade in the past several years?

Certainly they have. Have *most* southerners—that is, the working class—benefited from the political program to reduce democratic controls on transnational capitalism? Can that be determined simply by weighing the balance sheet of per capita income, high-tech jobs, and rates of investment? On both counts, no. That is why it is important to retrieve the discussion of American political economy from the ether of globalization. Questions about work, power, and democracy are tied up in transnational flows of capital, of course, but they are not captive to them. They are not decided by anonymous and irrepressible forces. They cannot be extricated from a discussion of the political decisions generated in the United States during this era of decline.

The purpose here is not to obscure the social improvements that have flowed from—for example—foreign relocation of automobile production to the South. Nor is it to adopt some reductionistic model that disposes with ethnicity, religion, race, and ideas in explaining the southern experience. It is certainly not to question the benefits that have accrued to the region from cultural exchange and ethnic diversity. An increasingly borderless South exposed to new ideas, customs, and values is a necessarily more humane South. A region steeped for the longest time in provincial isolation can only benefit from the kind of cross-cultural fertilization that comes in a world bound together by advanced communications, mobile workers, and the exchange of ideas and perspectives that flow from those developments.

The purpose is, however, to point out that the developments we associate with globalization belong to a larger discussion of democracy. That discussion must include economic conditions and power, a point which southern historians familiar with Reconstruction should readily concede. They are part of a larger story about the distribution of wealth and power in the region during the final years of the twentieth century. Global integration has not simply been a historical inevitability, but the result of a complex interplay of political, economic, and ideological forces. Some of those forces have been the product of human will in the interest of agendas that have little to do with cultural pluralism. One of the most important lessons drawn from the civil rights movement is that relations of power, not local culture or regional identity, determine who benefits in a liberal democratic society. As for the historiography on globalization and the South, the burden of it has suggested that there have been few alternatives to the present, few "roads not taken" for contemporary Americans. Even the idiom of "globalism" implies something benign, cosmopolitan, and therefore normative. The effort here is to correct that view, in part by identifying the material, economic interests at stake in market integration. In part, the objective is to identify those groups and individuals who challenged the assertion that market principles should be exalted over other categories of social value. Outside of the echo chamber of mainstream politics, southerners from a variety of racial backgrounds offered the cooperative, humane principles of the New Deal tradition as a challenge to the claims of marketplace primacy in American life.[23]

This historiographical detour is necessary, but not the ultimate destination. The aim is not to engage in interpretive fisticuffs, particularly since this study leans so heavily on these very historians who have so productively ploughed the fields of the South's recent past. Instead, the objective is to illuminate the experiences of people who are often forgotten in scholarly discussions on globalization. At the same time, we need to uncover the ideologies that have often flown under the flag of individualism, freedom, and the "right to work." It is important to point out that the easy ideological assumptions that governed their lives in those years have been absorbed by commentators who report them back to us as commonsense truths. That is why it is important to separate immigration, the flow of information, the development of new technology, and the beneficent cultural exchanges of modern life from corporate globalization. The latter has not been value neutral or inevitable. Economist William K. Tabb describes it as the promotion of free markets in order to allow "capital to further dominate labor by structuring exchange in such a way that nonmarket criteria of fairness and equity are inapplicable, and democratic control and social regulation are beyond the pale."[24] Addressing corporate globalization's corollary, neoliberalism, economist Jeff Faux argues that it is a "vision of society in which competition for wealth is the only recognized value and virtually all social decisions are left to unregulated markets."[25] It is this vision of a society geared to the dictates of the marketplace which historians have tended to neglect. It is a vision which has left a decisive imprint on Virginia, the South, and the United States.

If anything, the pivot of this discussion is the connection between political ideology, economic self-interest, and public policy. The corollary to this point is that the South cannot be examined in isolation from the economic and political forces that transformed the United States in the late twentieth century. Given these points, it should come as no surprise that southern distinctiveness is not the focus of this examination. Instead, we explore two paths that historian Gavin Wright has recently suggested are critical for understanding the South in modern America. Despite the fundamental changes that the civil rights movement wrought in the architecture of the South, the economic prospects of the region did not improve significantly following the 1970s. From that period until the present, average real wages for the southern working class declined or remained static. Income disparities grew wider and wider for American workers, southern workers, black and white workers, male and female workers. Wright's central claim, and our departure point, is that these developments are "national or global in character, beyond the control of southern state politics with or without the Voting Rights Act. *But they have hit the South with unusual force,* as they have coincided historically with the retreat or demise of New Deal labor market institutions and policies" (emphasis added). While Wright underestimates the influence of state leaders in facilitating those changes and ascribes these developments to seemingly anonymous forces, the critical insight remains. The South did not encounter corporate globalization and trade liberalization on its own. The region was particularly susceptible to the search for "flexibility" in capitalist production, but it was not alone. What we confront, then, is the paradox of a region that is on the forefront of market integration, often plays the role of peripheral region for capitalist development at the core, but is increasingly swept along by forces that act aggressively on itself and the rest of the nation.[26]

If the South was not simply the victim of anonymous social forces, neither was it a victim of economic geography. The deepening insecurity of southern workers did not simply reflect the South's traditional status as a peripheral region. It belonged to the world of international trade and investment, it experienced the benefits and losses of capital mobility, and it bore the brunt of trade policies designed to take advantage of workers even cheaper than southerners. Political considerations had always governed southern economic life. Political ideology, however, took on a new and powerful significance in the late twentieth century. Southern traditions of minimal government regulation, the decentralization of power, anti-unionism, favoritism to business elites, and uncompromising individualism gained new authority in the 1990s. This was largely the case because they harmonized with the economic objectives of corporate capitalism. The South "rose," if you will, in large part because its political economy fit the needs of companies that sought to reengineer themselves back to profitability. This was not simply a matter of exporting southern cultural values; this was a case of southern political leaders and American business elites defining the national mood, the ideological milieu, the political economy of late-twentieth-century America.

To bring us back to the ground of southern experience, we need to think about the most pressing realities of southern life in the 1990s. As momentous as it continued to be, the question of racial integration could no longer be separated from the economic landscape of the South. This is *not* to suggest that racial inequality had disappeared. Despite considerable economic and political progress since the black freedom movement, the problem of racial inequality remains. The resegregation of southern schools and the consequent impoverishment of public schools attended by blacks, the loss of industrial jobs for African Americans, the superficial mixing of black and white social spheres, the acceleration of "white flight" from urban centers, and the persistence of residential segregation in supposedly integrated communities defy the claim that the region has transcended its past.[27] By the end of the century, however, the disparities in black and white economic influence, the judicial and legal bias against African Americans, ranging from the higher rate of incarceration to racial profiling of young blacks, and the astonishing poverty levels among blacks in the inner city could no longer be treated separately from the economic changes transforming the nation. Of course, Martin Luther King, Bayard Rustin, and a coterie of civil rights activists had made the connection between racial oppression and class stratification long ago. King had acted on that insight when he launched the Poor People's Campaign and fatefully traveled to Memphis in 1968 to support the black sanitation workers' strike there.[28]

Moreover, the experience of black and Hispanic workers in the late twentieth century was increasingly determined by economic uncertainties that afflicted working- and middle-class whites as well. Ironically, while working-class blacks endured what many considered a new era of segregation, the experience of economic insecurity brought them closer to working-class and many middle-class whites than they had been since the Great Depression. Of course, racial difference continued to mediate the way that southerners encountered the workplace, the public sphere, and social affairs. To a considerable degree it still determined who experienced the greatest economic decline and the least amount of political influence. African Americans endured the highest levels of economic uncertainty, sometimes in the form of abject poverty but usually in low-wage, tenuous employment. Yet economic uncertainty—the kind that reminded people of the existence of class—seared the consciousness of average southerners, regardless of race and ethnicity. The point is that questions of racial inequality and identity could not escape the shadow of economic instability. The decline of the social contract conditioned the experience of race in modern America. The diminishing strength of the social contract was the defining experience of the twilight years of the twentieth century.

It was the loss of a core of security that troubled southerners and Americans the most. Journalist Edward Luttwak encapsulated the mood of the era: "The problem in question is the unprecedented sense of personal economic insecurity that has rather suddenly become the central phenomenon of life in America, not only for the notoriously endangered species of corporate middle managers, prime targets of today's fashionable 'downsizing' and 'reengineering,' but for virtually all working Americans except tenured civil servants—whose security is duly resented."[29] The diagnosis applied no less to southerners than to their northern brethren. The erosion of middle-class stability; the intensification of production for people still employed in manufacturing and the loss of thousands of jobs for those who were not; the escalating attack on trade unions, together with the nebulous but persistent sense that the bottom had fallen out of the American social responsibility state—all profoundly affected working southerners. That means that southerners also participated in the social contract as it developed out of the New Deal era. It means that class distinctions, which on the one hand became more rigid for those in the working class and more ambiguous for those in the offices of northern Virginia, mattered enormously.

Although Social Darwinism made a raging comeback in the 1980s, social class did not disappear from American life. Generations of African American slaves, free black victims of Jim Crow, white sharecroppers, and plantation patricians have attested to the existence of class in the South. But so too could striking meatpacking workers in Minnesota, striking mine workers in Pittston, Virginia, striking air traffic controllers across the country, and just about anyone who had to walk past curtained-off "executive" class flyers to reach their destination in coach.[30] Despite nominal upward mobility, the lingering effect of the Cold War's anti-progressive ideology, the consumer ethos which permeates every corner of American life, and the conservative media bias against organized labor ensured that class distinctions persisted in the American experience.[31]

In the South as much as the rest of the country, those class distinctions were drilled into the concrete experience of work. There, class lines were built on more than income or patterns of consumption. They were reflections of power. Declining and stagnating wages expressed the limited control that southerners exercised in the workplace and over their economic future. Yet class distinctions have been manifested well beyond the shop floor. In the legislative assemblies of Virginia government, in the media and its treatment of the New Economy, in the quadrants of higher education that promoted new styles of managerial control, and in the boardrooms of government agencies responsible for economic policy, the influence of socioeconomic class distinctions has been profound.

That does not mean that business has always had its way and that workers are uniformly exploited—or virtuous. What it does suggest is that social class was an intrinsic feature of the New Economy South. In fact, those class distinctions became sharper and more troubling in the 1990s than they had been since the 1930s. Class had not disappeared from American life, although powerful interests were determined to consign it to a contentious but distant past or deny that it had ever been a reality in the first place. The friction generated by rationalization of work in the 1990s, from corporate downsizing to workplace speedups, provided some of the evidence that class relations persisted. While the diminished ability of employees to oppose the will of management transmitted the erroneous impression of workplace harmony, the tension fostered by the drive to "reengineer" the workplace suggested that class conflict had not disappeared.[32]

Like most Americans, the majority of southerners of this period could count themselves as members of the working class. They were the men and women who occupied jobs in manufacturing but more often in the service industry. Despite the frequent assertion that workers in southern manufacturing, hotels, hospitals, and office-buildings were "unskilled," they were anything but. Anyone who has driven a ten-ton, double-axle, standard-shift truck (as I have) or cleaned away the detritus of hotel guests while expeditiously folding, primping, and preparing for the next ones will understand that point. They will also understand that, as economist Michael Zweig explains, the working class "share a common place in production, where they have little control over the pace or content of their work, and aren't anybody's boss."[33] Like their counterparts in the North, Virginians of the working class were not only store clerks at the Piggly Wiggly or textile workers in dying southwestern towns. They were also data entry clerks, administrative assistants, bank tellers, call center attendants, security guards, and salespeople. Unlike the middle class, which exercises a measure of independence in the workplace, working-class people do not. Doctors, lawyers, accountants, and architects enjoy salaries but also power and autonomy in the production process that even well-paid auto workers do not.

These distinctions are questions of degree, but they matter immensely when measuring who exercises power. No less significant is the degree of authority and economic influence wielded by the ownership class. Corporate executives, members of boards of directors, substantial shareholders, chief financial officers, and investment managers constituted the capitalist class, however quaint or dogmatic that may sound to our postmodernist ears. They were the top layer of this social structure in the late twentieth century, a reality that applied as much in the American South as anywhere else. Income was not the determinant of class but often a reflection of the power that a given class could exert in the American social system. Relations of power and authority, not styles of consumption, were central to class.[34] Never far from these were the fundamental questions of dignity and meaningful independence. These have been the objectives of social movements in the South since the Populist uprising of the 1890s. One hundred years later, they became the animating impulse of a resurgent labor movement.

The most important development in recent southern history is the ascent of the marketplace as the regulating institution of public life. Unable to significantly influence economic decisions, control the production process, and communicate their interests in the political sphere, southern workers saw their sense of security in American society erode dramatically. That loss of security reflected the rising influence of a marketplace presided over by concentrated capital. It also reflected the unprecedented cultural authority of business. A new business ethos dominated American life. It sunk particularly deep roots in the South, where it benefited from years of antagonism to democratic reforms but also where it encountered little effective opposition.

At the end of the Cold War, in the midst of a gripping recession that pummeled Virginia, southerners and Americans confronted opportunities but also dangers. The opportunities flowed from the promise of directing resources from a wasteful standoff with the Soviet Union into social investments. The dangers flowed from economic policies that drastically reduced state protection of vulnerable working Americans. Virginians, like southerners, stood at a critical juncture in the American experience. The New Deal state—which had been under assault since the 1970s—threatened to topple completely as Democrats rushed to the political center in a desperate effort to replicate the Republican message.

This coincided with the intensification of international market integration, which took on new and ominous significance during the recession of the early decade. Virginia's Republicans, business leaders, and champions of a New Economy capitalized on the opportunity. Promoting free markets, corporate reengineering, and a radical form of entrepreneurial individualism, they offered a blueprint for the post–Cold War era. They responded to fears of global integration by assigning blame to "tax-and-spend liberals," who allegedly did not understand the requirements of business competitiveness. They promised to deliver southerners from job loss and stagnating wages by harnessing the supposed potential of the unfettered marketplace. Southerners, like most Americans, would be transformed into savvy investors. At the same time, they would be reengineered into newly productive, technologically proficient "associates." New Economy pundits marketed Virginia and the South as an economic frontier for businesses seeking relief from labor unions, environmental regulation, and intrusive social policy.

While the South had traditionally been more conservative on fiscal and social issues since the nineteenth century, conservatism was not a southern monopoly. What made Virginia and the South important in this period was that the ideology that championed unrestricted trade and free markets over social protections faced so little opposition there. The South did not have a monopoly on the belief in the primacy of the marketplace. It was not the only place where elites celebrated the benefits of business-led social policy. It did, however, throw up considerably fewer obstacles to the philosophy of free market supremacy. It offered comparatively less resistance than other regions of the country to a rehabilitated Social Darwinism, one that made gaping exceptions for state support of capital ventures while insisting that working-class southerners were on their own in the struggle for "competitiveness." Bereft of strong labor unions, deficient in grassroots organizations that could articulate a democratic agenda, and marred by uneven economic growth in the Sunbelt era, market fundamentalism advanced aggressively in the South.

Southern Democrats offered little opposition and less of an alternative to the free market libertarianism of the Republicans. In fact, the southern Democratic president of the 1990s championed the New Economy and the wonders of dissolving trade barriers. Examining the economic changes that were transforming America in the 1990s, journalist Edward Luttwak zeroed in on the impact they were having on public life: "What is missing is anything resembling a social perspective. In fact it is simply taken for granted that economic efficiency must never be compromised in the slightest to suit the needs of society." This, ultimately, defined the American zeitgeist of the late twentieth century. The defining ethos of American life was the veneration of market principles and economic efficiency over a "social perspective." That development, which had been emerging for some time but which only crystallized in the 1990s, is the period's single most significant legacy. The South and, in particular, technology fixated Virginia, fostered that ethos. The South provided a crucible for the alchemy of globalization, traditional Jeffersonian individualism, economic libertarianism, and an evangelical persuasion that fit comfortably into the new Social Darwinism.

While they celebrated the promise of a New Economy, Virginia's neoconservatives demonstrated how much they owed to the past. Technological innovation would be built upon the traditions of limited social investment, low wages, anti-unionism, indifference to the legacy of racial discrimination, and government non-interference. The New Economy in the South looked remarkably like the old one. Despite the overtones of continuity, the recession of 1990/1991 triggered a crisis that business used to legitimize the new Social Darwinism.

The crisis also forced the major parties to define themselves on key economic and social questions. They had to clarify their ideological perspectives. The recession gave the Democrats an opportunity to reinvigorate the social democratic strains of the New Deal. It also afforded the Republicans the chance to consolidate their power on the basis of the new business ethos. The mainstream political parties may have failed working southerners, but the crystallization of the business ethos catalyzed progressive forces in the South. A revitalized labor movement and initiatives for racial justice, economic democracy, and living wages percolated up from the grass roots. Once again, outside pressures forced mainstream political leaders to respond. More importantly, reform organizations in Virginia began to assemble a protean social democratic agenda that pointed the way toward working-class revitalization. Corporate restructuring and economic uncertainty created a common ground for black, white, and Hispanic workers. It created opportunities for genuine progressive reform across the boundaries of race and culture. By the end of the decade, those opportunities seemed to be gathering momentum.

Instead of generalizing about developments in the South and how they related to national developments, this study focuses on Virginia. The former home of the Confederacy, a state steeped (and some would say mired) in tradition and historical consciousness, Virginia had always straddled the line between two worlds. Tradition, both in the sense of self-conscious gentility and unspoken social hierarchies, coexisted alongside the state's proximity to national power. Immersed in a world of international commerce, Virginia was also strangely isolated by a political culture defined by slavery and class stratification. If Virginia's economic diversification and geographical proximity to the North protected it from the volatile race relations in the rest of the South, its sense of immutable hierarchy placed it in the front ranks of resistance to the civil rights movement. That combination of self-conscious, carefully constructed tradition and the state's exception from some of the most tragic episodes in the history of the New South allowed Virginia to claim a southern heritage without the burden of southern pathologies. State leaders could turn to Virginia's pantheon of colonial luminaries and use them as examples of an American yet distinctively southern tradition. The essence of that tradition was limited government. That was the key to Virginia's resistance to the civil rights movement in the 1950s. In periods of disruptive social change, Virginia's political and economic elite could sanctify their actions with the revolutionary iconography of the state's past. In Virginia, the ideological inheritance of the nation's republican past could be dusted off and presented as something uniquely southern, specifically Virginian, but unmistakably American. When state leaders invoked the ideals of individualism and minimal government to justify the New Economy, they did so with a measure of ideological authority that Virginia's past was peculiarly qualified to confer.

Virginia is important for reasons beyond ideology, however. Military contracts won by solicitous politicians and the state's proximity to power made select regions of the state prosperous in the 1970s and 1980s. Military spending brought job opportunities and tax dollars to the people of Norfolk, Hampton Roads, Radford, and other cities lucky enough to land a base. Military contracts courtesy of Ronald Reagan's massive buildup, technological investment, and the growth of a high-tech sector made Virginia into a showcase of southern economic dynamism. Virginia's political and corporate elite began to package the state as a model of technological progress. The recession of the early 1990s and the reduction in military spending following the Gulf War dealt a powerful blow to the state's vaunted prosperity. It also revealed the social divisions that had lingered beneath the glittering surface of 1980s affluence. More importantly, it accelerated the effort to sell the state as a Silicon Dominion, a technological El Dorado at the top of the South, where the virtues of traditional southern labor practices harmonized with the rhythms of the New Economy. Despite the buoyancy of the 1990s, Virginia's experience demonstrated that chronic uncertainty at the center of the drive to market Virginia in the age of global capitalism.

The vibrant economy of the 1980s also fundamentally altered the demography of the state. Between 1980 and 1988, northern Virginia, including the cities of Arlington and Alexandria in Fairfax County, grew by 23 percent to a population of 1.4 million.[35] The state's population exploded again in the 1990s, adding 889,000 to the census rolls. A full 558,000 of those, or 63 percent of the total, ended up in places like Fairfax, Loudoun, Prince William, and Chesterfield Counties, the northern areas that defined the state's economic and political character. Those counties would provide the foundation for the Republican insurgency in Virginia.[36] Yet the ethnic composition of those migrants was not as homogenous as many commentators believed. Half of the 14.4 percent increase in the state's population during that frenetic decade was from racial minorities. The Hispanic population grew by 106 percent while whites only accounted for 5.6 percent of the increase. In Fairfax County, northern Virginia, 86 percent of the population increase came from Hispanics, Asians, and African Americans.[37] Virginia might exalt its traditions and conservatism, but the changing ethnic composition of that state challenged the foundations on which they had been built. In fact, political and corporate elites utilized Virginia tradition as a *response* to the challenges of immigration, racial conflict, and economic dislocation, a bulwark against dislocating change.

The larger significance is that Virginia was in the throes of dramatic changes that reflected both the southern and the national experience. It exemplified the economic and social forces that were undermining regional distinctiveness. It was a microcosm of resistance to the social contract inherited from the New Deal era. The state also captured the sense of opportunity and promise that had served as a galvanizing myth in the American experience. Looking at Virginia in the 1980s, we peer into a time capsule of the American—not just southern—encounter with globalization and the decline of the New Deal order. We grasp the forces that propelled the conservative Right to political influence. We gain a stronger sense of the insecurities that gripped working Americans at time when media and a legion of corporate pundits heralded the arrival of a new, promising economic order.

Virginia is important not because it was the most economically blighted of the former Confederate states. Many Virginians made gains in the 1990s, new tax dollars flowed into its coffers, high-tech investment dramatically increased, and per capita income surged ahead of other southern states. Rather, it is important because it exhibited the full range of insecurity and inequality generated under the rubric of a New Economy. It showcased the rise of a self-conscious New Economy elite and an ideology of free market supremacy that became dogmatic in the 1990s. At the crossroads of southern influence in national life, high-tech development, and New Economy politics, Virginia also provides an ideal site for examining the impact of these developments on average Americans. Despite claims of unprecedented growth, the latest era of free market euphoria could not exceed the productivity, growth, and security of the period when government regulated the private sector. It could not parallel the period in American history when the federal government set the pace for investing in the public interest.[38]

In focusing on Virginia, we remind ourselves that the South was at the juncture of the old and new economies. That was also the case in the seventeenth century, when the region stood at the forefront of a new commercial order based on slavery. If we would like to understand the political, economic, and social factors that transformed the United States in the age of global integration, then we should start in Virginia. There, the drive to reengineer the workforce, market the state to business investors, ratify supposedly beneficial trade agreements, counter union organization, and reduce social protections in the name of market freedom achieved special prominence. Those efforts generated a fledgling response that would remind southerners of another tradition from their past, one in which the commonwealth figured more prominently than self-interest.

CHAPTER 2

Reengineered and Rewired

Downsized Business and the Insecure Worker

The dominant theme of the 1990s was the explosive potential of advanced technology. It was a theme that wove its way through silicon enclaves from California to Massachusetts. Pundits heralded the microprocessor as the solution to the nation's productivity woes and the catalyst to a new day of business efficiency. The most effusive proponents believed that technology was forging a wired, integrated, harmonious world out of the ashes of the corporate hierarchies of the past. Operating out of flattened organizations that prized innovation and workplace flexibility, corporations were supposedly reinventing the workplace and restoring productivity.[1] Yet these high-tech regions were in the traditionally liberal Northeast and Northwest. In Virginia, the former capital of the Confederacy, the high-tech phenomenon played out against a background of social and political conservatism. Virginia welcomed the New Economy, but on its own terms. The synthesis of technological futurism and political conservatism would quickly influence the national character of American society in the late twentieth century.

In the 1980s, Virginia was on the forefront of a new wave of capitalist economic expansion. Searching for relief from taxation, state regulation, and unionization in the Northeast, venture capitalists and established companies relocated to the South.[2] Companies were eager to reverse the downward slide of profitability, and the South seemed to offer an environment in which they could reinvent themselves. Corporate executives and owners looked for locations in the United States that would allow them to transform their operations into globally competitive, "lean and mean" enterprises. Pro-business Virginia became a haven for many of those companies. While Mexico and Southeast Asia became magnets for manufacturers seeking low-skilled labor, Virginia offered familiarity, political conservatism, and a slack but relatively skilled workforce. Its political elites were also favorably attuned to the central tenets of the New Economy. Virginia, in fact, had been practicing for the New Economy for some time.

And what exactly was new about this New Economy? It certainly was not technology, which had been transforming American manufacturing since the Gilded Age. The expansion of computer technology accelerated the work process and reduced the workforce, but it did not revolutionize the process of making and distributing goods. What was new was that business leaders convinced the American public as well as policymakers that institutional changes were necessary in order to accommodate an Information Economy. Proponents of the New Economy argued that in order for companies to fully exploit the new technology, they had to strip away the hierarchical arrangements of an earlier business model. Corporate bureaucracies had to be replaced by adaptability and innovation. Instead of peaceful coexistence with businesses in the same field, companies had to be aggressively competitive. Instead of attachment to old product lines, companies had to be prepared to change gears quickly.[3]

Champions of the New Economy had more in mind than new product lines, though. At the center of the reengineered corporation was the demand for reduced labor costs. The euphemism that change management consultants employed was "flexible" labor. According to the doctrine of flexibility, labor forces had to be streamlined, companies had to be willing to dismiss employees at a moment's notice, and contingent workers had to replace full-time employees. Labor unions and workplace regulations obstructed flexibility. They added costs, disrupted production, and thwarted innovation. Governments also had an obligation to facilitate the New Economy. Proponents claimed that governments had to deregulate the telecommunications, finance, and labor markets. To maximize competitiveness, they had to minimize labor regulations. They had to privatize public companies and dismantle the social welfare state. The core idea was to limit government intervention in the marketplace and foster maximum competitiveness. This, at its most basic, was flexibility.[4]

In effect, advocates of a New Economy were calling for an updated version of the 1980s downsizing strategy. According to historians David Kotz and Martin Wolfson, the New Economy represented the "pro-business, free-market, and anti-labor agenda that corporate America had been pushing since the late 1970s." New technology and business competitiveness did not, in fact, require the subordination of labor. That policy reflected the collective decision to pursue the most mercenary yet least effective long-term strategy toward profitability. "The road not taken," as Kotz and Wolfson argue, "regards workers as assets rather than as expenses, seeks cooperation with unions, invests in worker skills, and focuses on quality as well as costs."[5] Instead, the road taken in the 1990s was toward tenuous work at less pay and fewer benefits. Technical and professional experts continued to command high-paying salaries, but flexibility demanded the growth of contract labor. The expansion of contract labor also aggravated the income disparities that had grown unabated since the 1970s.[6]

Despite the claims that the New Economy would democratize the workplace, liberate employees from the drudgery of routine, and allow them creative control over production, it fostered uncertainty and an environment in which business prerogatives went unquestioned. Longer hours, fewer workers, and persistent job insecurity became the norm. It also accelerated the de-skilling of the workforce. According to economist Doug Henwood, the function of the New Economy was largely ideological and "disciplinary." It was meant to convince young workers to accept the primacy of business profitability. It inculcated the idea that insecure, self-denying work was the norm. Young workers would accept this state of affairs in the expectation of a significant return on their investment of time and risk. What is important to understand is that the strategic jargon about reengineering was inseparable from the prevailing ideology in the United States. The "social philosophy," as Henwood puts it, that influenced economic policy in the 1990s was "hard to distinguish from that of 100 years earlier, though publicists and graphic designers have made it look more dazzling than it was in Herbert Spencer's day."[7] What was old was indeed new again, and the South was its main harbinger. If it was the prevailing social philosophy, Virginia and the South played a decisive role in fashioning it for a modern audience.

In Virginia, the epicenter of the New Economy was northern Virginia, north of the Rappahannock River, in the counties circling the national capital. Arlington, Alexandria, Fairfax, and Loudoun Counties became vibrant satellites of Washington, D.C. Federal government contracts in telecommunications and information technology drew companies to the city and to the contiguous Fairfax County.[8] By the 1980s, the corporate headquarters of airlines and other major interests were relocating to Fairfax. Internet, software, and business service ventures soon followed. Private investment fueled technological development, but state funds provided indispensable assistance. While mouthing the platitudes of state independence, Virginia consistently provided generous assistance to the high-tech sector. In 1984, under the leadership of Governor Charles Robb, construction started on the $30 million Center for Innovative Technology. Illustrating the fusion of government and business interests in the Reagan era, the center would become a "broker" between private enterprise and the state. Higher education would be a key partner and beneficiary of high-tech capital investment. Proximity to the Kennedy Center, exclusive private schools, the persistently magnetic attraction of Washington, and the sense that northern Virginia was uncomplicated by the racial frictions of larger metropolitan areas made this region a center of elite white power in the state.[9]

The proliferation of retail outlets and major shopping centers like the ostentatious Tysons Corner Center convinced Fairfax's parvenu that northern Virginia had arrived. By 1995, northern Virginia featured 1,115 high-tech firms employing some 125,000 workers. That was nearly 16 percent of all the jobs in the region, earning a whopping $5 billion annually. With taxable aggregate income reaching $10 billion, Fairfax alone contributed the heftiest taxes of any county in the Dominion in 1990. The historical contrast could not have been more powerful: the South's economic future seemed to have arrived in the region where the Confederacy first spilled blood to preserve the past.[10]

Business elites and journalistic pundits soon began projecting a tone of New Economy hubris. Armed with high-tech hyperbole, they sought to redefine the Virginia brand. Business boosters talked about "emancipating" Fairfax County from peonage to Washington. They would push its development as a "world-class center for business." Local business champions claimed that systems integration, aerospace, bio-chemical, and telecommunications ventures were liberating the city from Washington's "orbit" and forging Northern Virginia into the state's gateway to the "global economic nexus."[11] Columnists at *Virginia Business*—the bullhorn for private enterprise and an influential champion of free market orthodoxy in the state—were at pains to differentiate Fairfax from Loudoun, Alexandria, and Arlington. Fairfax was becoming an independent economic entity but also a community, they argued. With acronym-brandishing companies such as BDM, AT&T, and Electronic Data Systems along with Sprint, Mobil, and America Online locating in Fairfax, the region was making its mark. With median household incomes shooting up to $69,402 by 1997, it was easy for regional leaders to convince themselves that the Digital Dominion had arrived.[12]

It was also easy to believe that northern Virginia *was* Virginia. Local elites imagined that the rising tide in Fairfax would lift boats from Martinsville to Hampton Roads. Virginia boosters placed as much emphasis on image as on substance. Fairfax, like the rest of the state, had to position itself as a business-friendly, high-tech nirvana. As journalist Paula Odin exclaimed, "Fairfax's high tech gloss puts a sheen on Virginia's image. The

Old Dominion still suffers from a deep-South stereotype. By touting Northern Virginia's high-tech reputation, economic development strategists aim to change those lingering misperceptions."[13] Northern Virginia would also promote synergy between business, government, and higher education. Business elites would utilize public resources to expand private business opportunities. They would make the area south of the Potomac a model of southern development in the New Economy.

A class-conscious business elite soon emerged in northern Virginia. Journalist Andy Taylor identified a corps of leaders who were making the Tower Club in Tysons Corner the preferred lair for leading local powerbrokers. It displaced Richmond's antiquated Commonwealth Club and Washington's Metropolitan Club as the locus for Virginia's powerbrokers. Real estate developers Albert J. Dwoskin and John T. "Til" Hazel Jr., attorney Carrington Williams, defense contractor John Toups, and George Mason University president George W. Johnson lodged themselves on the board of the Tower Club. Williams and Hazel then launched the Virginia Initiative in 1990, a vehicle for promoting the business agenda of northern Virginia.[14]

In meetings and cocktail parties, the Virginia Initiative forged links between business and government. While the initiative paid homage to southwestern Virginia, where factory closings and international competition hit the hardest, it failed to relocate high-tech firms from Fairfax to Roanoke and beyond. The Virginia Initiative, like the Tower Club, represented the political and economic interests of an increasingly rootless business class. As journalist Andy Taylor warmly observed, "The Tower Club is emblematic of Fairfax's fission from Washington. The county's prosperity has produced a cohesive, and extremely powerful, business elite that finds it more worthwhile to dine and shmooze with one another than to hobnob with Washingtonians." These self-conscious millionaires were not reluctant to spend conspicuously to promote their interests. In the gubernatorial election of 1989, the Fairfax elite lavished money on Republican Marshall Coleman, outdistancing contributions from any other Virginia county or city.[15]

In an economy in which information was capital, the Fairfax business elite understood the benefits of higher education. They established close relations with George Mason University, which evolved into a training ground and advocate for the high-tech industry. Liaisons between GMU and the high-tech industry assumed a formal shape through the George Mason Institute, which sought to coordinate higher education and public policy. Northern Virginia's economic players gained additional leverage not only through massive lobbying campaigns (discussed later) but through subtler, no less powerful methods. The Fairfax County Economic Development Authority and the Center for Innovative Technology gave business elites avenues for influencing public policy. The high-tech sector could not dictate public policy, but it could speak with a unified and persuasive voice. Documenting the transplantation of Novadyne Computer Services from Southern California to northern Virginia, journalist Jason White attributed the move to the area's information technology resources and proximity to Washington. White acknowledged that the move expressed the ambition to join a business community that "exercises tremendous influence on public policy."[16] As journalist James A. Bacon described them, the Fairfax business elite exuded a "capitalistic" spirit "driven by enterprise and innovation." They had become a "powerful economic and political force." A new entrepreneurial class for a bold, free-market-oriented economic order had arrived.[17]

Champions of Virginia's high-tech sector realized that in an intensely competitive economy, effective marketing was the key to attracting new investment. Yet the element of southern continuity was remarkable: industrial boosters lauded Virginia's traditional hostility to unions, low wage rates, limited social services, and minimal taxation. At the same time, they promised that Virginians understood the merits of hard work. As *Virginia Business* explained in 1995, the South positioned itself as a magnet for northern businesses seeking to restore profitability: "Probusiness Southeastern states have been capturing much of that outflow because they offer lower wages, cheaper insurance, lower taxes and less-stringent regulations."[18] Maryland relocation consultant Brad McDearman explained that the draw for northern business was the region's pristine free market environment. Virginia had successfully resisted the kind of influences that had leveled the economic playing field in the North: "For a long time manufacturing firms have had a rough time with the costs, the regulatory climate, taxation and the general state attitudes in the Northeast. . . . The South has aggressively gone after that."[19] In the high-tech industry, where wages were above the national average, promoters stressed the state's commitment to assisting business as well as the spin-off benefits of high-tech jobs.[20] Yet they were also eager to remind fleet-footed businesses of the state's enduring commitment to traditional southern economic practices.

For all of the hubris about an independent northern Virginia, however, it still relied extensively on Washington for its economic survival. High tech thrived in Virginia not simply because it offered low taxes and microchip critical mass. It thrived because of its connection to the powerbrokers and purse strings in Washington. Here, then, was one of the central contradictions in the southern version of the New Economy. On the one hand, advocates of economic development called for low taxes, minimal labor regulations, and an unfettered marketplace. On the other, they looked to the state for assistance, financial incentives, and business opportunities. Evidently, technology boosters were no more committed to a free market economy than their Gilded Age predecessors. State intervention was repugnant when it restrained business in favor of labor, the environment, or the consumer. Otherwise, it could be very helpful indeed.

The New Economy strategy was not nearly as new as some of its champions believed. The South had been using it to attract northern manufacturers to the region since the late nineteenth century. Inexpensive labor, low taxes, municipal bonds, and assurances of a pro-business climate had lured railroads and textile manufacturers to the New South. The program to sell the region as a repository of cheap labor and low taxes accelerated in the 1930s, particularly in Mississippi, where the state launched the "Balance Agriculture with Industry" program. The BAWI authorized a state industrial commission to assist local governments in securing land and production facilities for new companies. It also provided state support for local bond issues to underwrite the construction of factories and manufacturing facilities. The program spawned imitations throughout the South, as states mortgaged their futures to attract northern and foreign business investment. For the most part, what they gained were low-skill, labor-intensive, and resource-extractive operations that flourished in a climate of political conservatism and racial control.[21]

Minimal government and a docile working class continued to dominate Virginia's marketing strategy in the late twentieth century. What changed was that the Virginia creed had become the national creed. In an era of massive corporate restructuring and global capitalist competition, Virginia's strategy sounded remarkably like those found above the Mason-Dixon line. Struggling to replace the jobs lost in the tobacco, textile, and furniture industries, southeastern states superimposed the New Economy template on the South. Technological innovation was grafted on to low wages and minimal taxes. It was sold in the globalizing, pro-business idiom of the 1990s. In effect, Virginia's business leaders updated the image of the South as a bastion of anti-unionism and political conservatism. Donning the cloak of the microchip revolution, Virginia clothed its traditional practices in the attire of global competitiveness.[22]

Virginia's boosters fashioned a marketable image, but it was not simply smoke and mirrors. The state delivered the goods in terms of manufacturing wage levels below the national average, minimal government activism, and legal impediments to unionism. State leaders crafted a brand name grounded in the idea that Virginia was a place that meant business, a claim that Virginia leaders had been making for years. Historian James Cobb points out that in the 1960s, Virginia advertised itself as "the first corporation in America" and the place that "Brought Profit to America." Now, in the 1980s, state boosters would update the claim by invoking the image of technological progress and innovation. The constant struggle in the new campaign was to balance the benefits of a mythologized history against the liabilities of its image as a quaint, gentrified, but ultimately regressive backwater.[23]

Marketing the state required the cooperation of workers, journalists, and political leaders. "Selling the commonwealth is just like selling any other product," journalist Mary Helen Frederick proclaimed in 1995. "Persistence and personal relationships pay off." A multimillion-dollar marketing campaign backed by tax breaks and financial incentives also helped. By 1995, the state Department of Economic Development (which that year was renamed the Virginia Economic Development Partnership) had amassed a $6.5 million budget which supported offices in Frankfurt, Tokyo, and Botswana. Each served to convince international investors that "the commonwealth is a good place to do business." Encoded in this expression was the idea that Virginia, like the South, was a place where workers were compliant and business dominated the social agenda. Economic policy was in the hands of technological innovators and forward-looking entrepreneurs. Any complaints by workers about the social costs of the updated development strategy only betrayed their failure to adjust to changing realities. Failing to be "flexible" now carried overtones of moral inadequacy.[24]

Similarly, government leaders were expected to defer to the wisdom of corporate mavericks who were leading the United States out of the quagmire of an old industrial economy. Virginia was selling itself as "The Bottom Line State," Frederick cheered. Through consumer magazines and trade publications, the Old Dominion promoted its "pro-business climate," its right-to-work law, "its low workers' compensation and unemployment insurance rates," and a corporate income tax rate that had not increased since 1972.[25]

The high-gloss sales job was not limited to northern Virginia. As journalist Jim Gallant noted, "the southern piedmont is selling its conservative, pro-business attitude," perpetuating a southern tradition that stretched back to the New South boosterism of Henry Grady and Richard Edmonds.[26] The difference was that southern business promoters were now able to borrow the mantle of high-tech innovation. The kind of social responsibility envisioned in Lyndon Johnson's Great Society reforms could now be portrayed as an impediment to business competitiveness in a global economy. They could present Virginia as a place that respected business efficiency, technological advancement, and the primacy of free market principles. Southern business conservatism had become hip.

Yet companies wanted more than a business friendly environment. Northeastern corporate leaders were drawn by the willingness of southern states to offer tax concessions, infrastructure projects, reduced environmental regulations, and additional financial incentives. This theme would dominate the economic development strategies of the late 1990s (and will be examined in a later chapter), but it was clearly taking shape in the late 1980s. Mark Kilduff of the Department of Economic Development suggested that incentives sent the message that the state was hospitable toward business. Oddly enough, state intervention in the form of tax breaks and subsidies also assured companies that government regulation would not get in the way of business development. After considering locations in California and the merits of staying in New Jersey, an aquarium manufacturer decided to move the operation to the Roanoke Valley. The plant's general manager couched the decision in terms of the community's efficiency and "cooperation." Yet the key factor seemed to be the city government's offer of financial assistance. By paying for improvements to the plant location, Roanoke demonstrated "a sense of partnership."[27] James Bradshaw, director of the Franklin/Southampton County Economic Development Commission, was less coy. "When you get down to the last two or three [sites], everybody asks 'What can you do for me?'" The veneer of business partnership and community involvement was thin. Corporate welfare had made an astonishing comeback in the South. Rural, de-industrializing towns were willing to bet that giveaways in the present would lead to prosperity in the future.[28]

The marketing campaign appealed to northerners for a variety of reasons, not least of which was the desire to escape the social turbulence of the urban Northeast. Economic boosters used code words to suggest that in Virginia, businesses would find a reliable, non-unionized, politically inert workforce. Economic developers presented the state as an oasis for cost-cutting companies. They identified and exploited the anxieties that drove northeastern business leaders to relocate.

James Bacon, editor of the high-profile and influential magazine *Virginia*

Business, believed that he had diagnosed the forces at work in the shift of manufacturing to the Southeast. The flight of capital to the South was nothing new, of course; it had been going on since the late nineteenth century. But James Bacon was convinced that business relocation was undergoing a "qualitative change." Sophisticated investment banks, accounting firms, multitasking law firms, and corporate headquarters were making the former capital of the Confederacy an attractive prospect. Business facilities and capitalist infrastructure were not the only magnets; lower taxes and "productive work forces" were readily available. The recession of 1990/1991 only exacerbated the conditions plaguing northern businesses. It was not just high taxes and a stagnant economy that clouded the northern business atmosphere but the "politics of envy." According to Bacon, the economic vitality of the 1980s, with its leveraged buyouts, junk bonds, and massive real estate deals, masked the underlying structural problems afflicting the industrial Northeast. In contrast, Bacon believed that Virginia offered a sea of political tranquility for businesses beset by interest-group politics and social turmoil:

> The anti-business coalition of organized labor, limousine liberals and radical Elements of the gay, feminist, and minority movements have deep roots in the Northeast. Even if voted out in a tax revolt, as in Massachusetts after the Dukakis disaster, liberalism is a political Frankenstein, always capable of returning to life. *No such threat exists in Virginia.*[29] (emphasis added)

For business elites, the South offered respite from the culture wars. It was an oasis of freedom from the social welfare state and the kind of "special interest populism" that infected the decadent Northeast. Extolling the "pro-business" virtues of Virginia, Bacon identified the larger framework governing economic power in the United States: "In the final analysis, the problem is political. Rather than regarding business as a healthy element of society, Northeastern liberals blame it for all manners of ills from racism to sexual chauvinism, from the rape of the environment to the exploitation of the working class." More than information technology, Virginia offered to protect companies in their effort to improve shareholder returns and curb the influence of labor.[30]

Business pundits also strove to reassure investors that the political climate favored business dominance. Bacon tried to convince *Virginia Business* readers that the election of the African American Douglas Wilder to the governorship and the ascent of Mary Sue Terry to the attorney general's office did not threaten Virginia conservatism. He found support from one political scientist who insisted that the state was becoming more "libertarian," not more liberal. It was consistently hostile to government intervention and social legislation. Bacon took comfort from another political commentator who believed that Virginians objected to governments regulating the "moral fabric" of their society. The evidence was in the 1989 election. That year, Douglas and the Democrats never questioned the state's prohibition on public sector unions, the principle of a balanced budget and line-item vetoes, and the state's anti-union "right-to-work" law. Unlike the Northeast, where "special-interest constituencies" such as the NAACP championed a radical agenda of racial equality, local African Americans accepted the status quo. They even signed on for the Persian Gulf War of 1990. The critical difference in the Old Dominion was that blacks and workers had not formed a "mutually reinforcing phalanx." Unlike northeastern liberals, who were driven by a "Puritan desire to achieve moral redemption through good acts," Virginia's elite considered the maldistribution a product of "natural" laws. African Americans were politically inert, the environmental movement was polite and ineffective, the "extreme gay-righters"—as political scientist Mark Rozell put it—were nonexistent, and the labor movement largely neutralized. "What most distinguishes the political economy in Virginia is that the wealthy elite is solidly pro-business and conservative." The limousine liberals were mostly non-Virginia transplants safely quarantined in Charlottesville and pockets of northern Virginia. With a weak and isolated liberal movement, the state was open to uninhibited business growth. "The priorities of economic growth and fiscal conservatism stand unchallenged," Bacon proclaimed. With a political environment like that, Virginia was definitely open for business.[31]

While high-tech synergy and tax subsidies were critical to Virginia's business development strategy, claims about the Virginia work ethic dominated its marketing plan. The emphasis on the work ethic reflected the fear that Americans would be left behind in the global race for market share if they did not increase their productivity rates. Beginning in the 1980s, corporate managers tried to convince employees that streamlining their operations required longer hours, unconditional commitments to company objectives, and greater insecurity. Now, employees labored under the stress of dismissal, one of the many consequences of "flexibility." Programs designed to generate employee productivity were often used to justify overwork. In the drive to increase competitiveness, companies adopted the "teamwork" strategy, a method that promised increased output but also threatened to undermine employee job control. Teams gave companies a mechanism for extracting innovative ideas from workers without compensation. Through "innovative" business strategies that eliminated middle management positions, rationalized operations, and consolidated departments, businesses increased productivity. They simultaneously enhanced worker anxiety.[32]

While computer technology dramatically increased business efficiency in certain areas, it eliminated thousands of jobs and increased employee vulnerability. Almost 20 percent of switchboard and telephone operators became "redundant" through the introduction of labor-saving technology. Automated answering machines and dazzling new software applications allowed companies to eliminate a range of salaried positions. Secretaries, bank tellers, payroll department personnel, clerical supervisors, administrators, sales representatives, and office managers became redundant in the early years of the 1990s. Electronic data interchange (EDI), which coordinates purchasing and shipping information and reduces the labor demand for moving goods to market, liquidated an estimated $73 billion from the $220 billion annually spent on health care administration. Rising productivity was tied to a new business regime of profitability through corporate streamlining. Before the 1990s, companies routinely kept employees on during recessions. They reasoned that in the long term it would build worker loyalty, retain talented people, and increase productivity. In the 1990s, that long perspective disappeared as employers scrambled to "trim the fat" and "reengineer" for cost effectiveness. Employees had always been an asset and a cost. In the era of corporate downsizing—an era that demanded higher stock prices—employees were increasingly seen as only a cost. Those who kept their jobs were made to feel fortunate for having them; those who lost them were assured that they had advanced the greater cause of global competitiveness. Short-term profitability took the place of pragmatic but mutually beneficial obligations.[33]

An equally distinctive feature of the reengineered company was lean production. Faced with capital deficiency in the post-war period, Japanese manufacturers adopted methods of accelerated, cost-effective production that became the model for North American corporations in the recession-stunned 1980s. Japanese lean production depended on neutralizing organized labor and maximizing management's control. Through extended hours, escalating work routines, low wages, and a hierarchical chain of production, Japanese manufacturers updated Ford's mass-production system without abandoning the logic of Taylor's scientific management.[34]

Through a practice known as *kaizen*, or "constant improvement," corporations institutionalized the idea that workers were accountable for increasing production efficiency. The idea was to standardize manufacturing beyond what Ford and Taylor had imagined and increase managerial control over production. Workers were expected to produce a variety of goods and perform a multiplicity of tasks using the same capital resources. In the process, they would submit to increasingly restrictive production schedules. As sociologist Kim Moody suggested, though, lean-production flexibility really meant borrowing worker knowledge about achieving efficiency and adding it to computer automation, contracting-out, manufacturing speed-ups, shift extensions, and part-time employment. While lean production became the popular solution to the productivity woes of the 1980s, there was little evidence that it achieved the kind of productivity leaps its proponents claimed.[35]

What manufacturers adopted was "management by stress," and the South was at its leading edge.[36] The search for flexibility was part of a larger drive for a market-oriented political order that emerged in the 1980s but coalesced in the following decade. It included the use of contingent and part-time employees, the vigorous assurance of an environment hospitable to business, resistance to unionization, and the utilization of convict labor and undocumented immigrants. These strategies were indistinguishable from the campaign to dismantle government social programs and hold the line against tax increases. At the same time that proponents of market dominance assailed interventionist government, they provided assistance to military contractors and key corporations through lavish public spending.[37]

The process of lean production operated on the assumption that persistent "stretching" of the production process through the elimination of workers and materials would increase efficiency. Business advocates promoted it even while they applauded their fellow citizens' resilient "work ethic." Using the tactics of Just-In-Time delivery, team production, "quality management," multitasking, outsourcing, job flexibility, and task rotation, managers imposed a cost-reduction regime that simultaneously reduced the security and autonomy of workers. Organizing workers into teams became a popular method of implementing lean production. Yet teamwork was not an innocuous innovation. Teams provided a method for extracting valuable knowledge from workers while standardizing the process and exercising greater control. Although the production reforms sounded innovative, most companies ended up abandoning them, either because there was too much internal resistance or because the reforms had achieved their goals.[38]

According to studies of the auto industry in Japan in the 1990s, companies disbanded teams when its members had disclosed the insights that management wanted. In other cases, managers simply ignored the teams when they were determined to push through major changes. Human resource specialists added a process known as "functional flexibility" to the industrial arsenal in the 1990s. Aimed at reducing costs, it required the restriction or removal of job descriptions ratified by union agreements. The effort to rotate jobs and send workers into frenzies of "multitasking" innovation was part of the continuing saga of workforce de-skilling. It was also part of a concentrated attack on union-negotiated rules that provided a measure of employee independence. Teams and quality circles played a critical ideological role in expanding management authority over production. As Kim Moody explained, the quality campaign was designed to "tie the workers and the union to the goals and objectives of the corporation—to inculcate the ideology of partnership in competitiveness. The widespread practice of 'job control' unionism in the US is one reason why teams are universal there."[39]

Managers added flexible schedules to functional flexibility. Round-the-clock plant operations were designed to increase production without adding to the labor force. Similarly, companies used overtime to extend the workday without hiring additional workers and paying additional benefits. It also complemented corporate downsizing. That was the case when NYNEX began automating its Switching Control Center in 1989. While integrating digital switching between 1989 and 1994, the labor complement declined from sixty-five technicians and three clerks to twenty-seven technicians and one clerk. Doing more with less had never sounded more futuristic.[40]

Nor did this exhaust the list of cost-reduction strategies dressed up in the 1990s managerial idiom of cooperation and empowerment. Perhaps the most insidious was Total Quality Management (TQM). The central idea in this program was that managers and laborers should take responsibility for maintaining quality control. Salespeople dealing with customers as well as line workers handling equipment were given the latitude to address problems without consulting their bosses. The classic example, used over and over by defenders of TQM, was the lowly assembly worker who could submit an invoice for the purchase of parts under $100. The rhetoric of empowerment was strong, but the power imbalance between workers and management only increased. As Michael Mandel explained, workers and lower-ranking managers bore a disproportionate responsibility for problems that emerged during production. What they did not have was the authority to alter the production process: "The problem is that the transferred responsibility under a TQM system increases the pressure on workers and managers. They know their job is on the line if they screw up."[41] Workers were told to join the culture of risk-taking, but they had no promise of enjoying the benefits of increased productivity. Nor could they shield themselves from the consequences of innovations gone wrong. Outsourcing as well as the use of part-time, temporary, contract, subcontracted, non-union labor, and homework added additional insecurity to this volatile mix.[42]

It was against this background that state business boosters tried to convince business prospects that Virginia was uniquely suited to the demands of the New Economy. They also wanted to warn managers and workers that growth in the New Economy hinged on doing more with less. The campaign began early in the decade, at the Forty-second Virginia Conference on World Trade. Richard G. Holder of the Reynolds Metals Company told some four hundred businesspeople that the fall of the Berlin Wall meant the rise of a globally integrated economy in which outsourcing and fleet-footed businesses were a reality. Like most globalization champions, Holder offered a mixed message of painful costs and long-term rewards. While "economic prosperity" might take a while to arrive, he was certain that it would, since "increased globalization means increased business, no matter how you look at it." Yet prosperity through globalization depended on increased productivity, since "Corporations are looking anywhere and everywhere for the best values of labor, supplies and services."[43] The message was clear: Virginia would have to join the national movement for massive restructuring and cost reduction. Global competitiveness depended on it.

Although Holder provided no evidence that the American economy had in fact become drastically more globalized, his rhetorical strategy had the ring of daunting truth. In the economic downturn of 1990, as managers joined manufacturing workers in a wave of corporate downsizing, people were listening to the message of survival through rationalization. In an era of diminished expectations, increasing productivity seemed to justify any number of sacrifices that fell on the shoulders of American workers. The ambivalent tone soon gave way to alarm, as educational elites, business leaders, and government officials grappled with the economic recession of 1990/1991. Virginia secretary of education James W. Dyke called for an educational "crusade" in the state lest it be "left in the dust" of progress.

Sounding a theme that would become commonplace in the 1990s, Dyke argued that America's educational system was woefully unprepared for the rigors of the global economy. But he also explicitly tied educational reform to productivity, making a connection that countless business boosters would make throughout the era. "Virginia must set higher educational and productivity standards or risk being unprepared to compete in the international arena." Dyke's recommendations included some of the typical features of the conservative school-reform agenda of the 1990s, including standardized testing, core curricula, and closer cooperation between business and schools. "The future owners of businesses are sitting in our classroom today," Dyke claimed.[44] He may have been deceiving himself about the opportunities for social mobility, but he offered progressive proposals to reduce the disparity between rich and poor areas. He also advocated schooling alternatives for those who would never see the inside of a college classroom. While pundits fixated on productivity, companies sought to restore business profitability. Both seemed to require layoffs, speedups, wage controls, and longer hours.

Academics also advocated government programs to educate workers for the global economy. Daniel Nelson, a business entrepreneur and a professor of international relations at Old Dominion University, issued a clarion call for state-level leadership in the drive for global competitiveness. Citing statistics showing Virginia's mediocre performance in per capita foreign investment and exports, Nelson called for a council to foster business cooperation between Mid-Atlantic states and attract investment to the region. In the idiom of business reengineering, Nelson demanded "globally applicable" and "world class" skills as well as an ambiguous "global education" that would enhance the state's "competitive edge." Higher education had a critical role to play, not in sustaining the traditional humanities or expanding scientific research but in promoting computer skills and business-friendly expertise. The university's key social function was in making the state globally competitive. The millennial tones so characteristic of 1990s journalistic sermons on the New Economy resonated in Nelson's *Virginian-Pilot* article. His recommendations, the paper urged, "ought to be at the core of any platform for putative Virginia leaders in the final years of this millennium. Whoever becomes Virginia's next governor must 'think globally' as never before." Then, the dire warning: "To fail in such strategic vision will deprive the commonwealth of resources essential to the fight against crime, urban decay, unemployment," and other social ills.[45]

Dyke's and Nelson's warnings were probably inspired in part by the conclusions of a General Assembly joint subcommittee on the state's labor force in the new decade. The report featured what would become standard rationalizations of restructuring in the era of global competition. First, the crisis: "productivity growth has been slowing dramatically for many years," which precipitated a flurry of studies on engineering the workforce to meet the demands of the twenty-first century. The premise was one that would govern economic policy throughout the 1990s: low-wage, low-skilled jobs were disappearing, presumably shifted overseas to developing nations. The trend was inevitable, and Virginians had little choice but to retool for the high-tech economy. That meant reengineering education to provide highly skilled workers for Virginia's demanding businesses. Since attracting qualified workers from other companies to fill the demand would have the effect of "driving up wage scales and reducing price competitiveness"—an unthinkable proposition in the New Economy era—schools would have to emphasize practical training.[46]

A governor's advisory committee was more alarmist but equally committed to pedagogical utilitarianism. According to this collaborative study, which Secretary Dyke co-chaired, the "rapidly emerging global economy is creating a new environment with formidable new challenges." Virginia had to "set higher educational and productivity standards for its workforce or risk being unprepared to compete in the international arena." The overarching conclusion was that Virginia students had to approximate "world-class standards" in order to participate successfully in a global economy. What that translated into was a recommendation for "performance-based evaluations"—standardized testing, which would eventually become law under a Republican governor. Under Democratic governor Douglas Wilder's leadership and on the committee's recommendation, the government implemented the Virginia Business-Education Partnership Program to coordinate policy between the two sectors. Democrats and Republicans were of the same mind: education meant training for the global marketplace.[47]

By the 1990s, business and journalistic champions of the New Economy had become convinced that integration into the global marketplace would solve America's social problems. As we will find out later, Republicans would soon domesticate the forces of corporate globalization. They did so by insisting that the ethic of competitive individualism, government nonintervention, reduced social services, and free market fundamentalism could shield Americans from the ravages of competition. The Democrats also championed global integration but could not provide a set of rubrics that promised to guide Americans in an era of change. Instead, Republican rhetoric and Democratic indifference toward the working class made the party look like the authors of trade agreements that damaged American manufacturing, eliminated jobs, and allegedly discriminated against white male workers. Before those developments took place, the immediate question was whether or not Virginians would support a costly program to advance the cause of global competitiveness. What was certain was that Dyke, Holder, and Nelson were speaking for those who believed they had seen the globalized future and were convinced that high-tech production was the answer.

As American manufacturers adopted lean production, Virginia's business champions announced the virtues of a workforce that never watched the clock. It was the "pro-business climate and good labor force" that brought John Mastroianni and his Massachusetts-based electronics company to Bedford County. Before transplanting the operation to the Old Dominion, the Massachusetts entrepreneur decided to go slumming in the countryside. Hanging around in bowling alleys and bars, inconspicuously talking with the locals after donning the appropriate denim uniform, he found people who "didn't view hard work as an alien notion." Yet journalist Ann C. Penn and by extension Mastroianni made it clear what they meant by "hard work." Rather than some timeless American ideal, one that complemented religious freedom or free speech, "hard work" in the business nomenclature meant willingness to adapt to the requirements of lean production. As American businesses adjusted to "survive in a global marketplace," Penn asserted, they scoured the southern countryside for "people with a positive attitude toward work." And what constituted a negative attitude toward work? Attachment to workplace protections won through collective bargaining or shop-floor conventions that gave employees a measure of control over production. "Managers want employees who are motivated and adaptable, not plodders determined to stick to rigid, out-dated rules and procedures."[48] Companies were looking for workers either willing or compelled to abandon job-control protections.

Central Virginia's Region 2000, an economic development alliance, adopted the work ethic angle as a selling point after it showed up in the research of an independent analyst. Countless regional development agencies must have used the same analyst, since one after another claimed that their region offered an exceptional work ethic in the 1990s. Business boosters were certain what the work ethic rubric meant. If deriving satisfaction from one's labor, controlling the work process, and contributing value to the final product traditionally defined the work ethic for skilled laborers, farmers, and industrial workers, the business version of the work ethic in the 1990s emphasized docile compliance. Instead of skilled control, business pundits stressed "honesty, sincerity" and "respect for management goals and objectives" as the defining characteristics of the work ethic in globalizing America. In addition to these tranquilizing virtues, business leaders championed "dependability, loyalty, and pride in one's work." Business pundits demonstrated little awareness of the tension between "pride in one's work" and the "management goals" of lean production. Scott Sink, director of the Virginia Productivity Center, reinforced Penn's defense of the ethic of worker submission. "The flexibility of our work force and workers' ability to work smarter as well as harder will determine whether the United States remains competitive."[49] Yet Sink's version of the work ethic seemed to suggest submission to managerial authority more than dignified self-reliance.

For Penn, Scott, Mastroianni, and the business boosters of Virginia, the responsibility for success in the global race for lean production lay squarely on the shoulders of American workers. Economic success was defined in terms of work rationalization rather than the manufacturing of superior products. Success in the competitive marketplace became a question of how much pain the pampered, overpaid American worker could absorb. Business apologists invoked the disembodied forces of global capitalism to justify policies that promised renewed prosperity while increasing the insecurity of working people. It was all so mechanical and beyond anyone's control; one could either adapt or face extinction.

Transplant companies did more than move to Virginia; they began adopting the lean-production system once they arrived. Once on the ground in Bedford County, Mastroianni's Galileo-Electro-Optics abandoned the hierarchical supervisory structure and adopted the team system of organization.[50] Those teams were expected to hire their own members and monitor their productivity, effectively installing a system of internal rationalization that would have made a Puritan divine smile. Galileo also eliminated plant supervisors and time clocks, creating an environment in which teams could never be certain whether they had measured up to efficiency expectations. Under this system, employees would be more inclined to work beyond the time limits of their shift. Workers were also authorized to shut down the production line if they suspected that a defective piece was about to be shipped. Needless to say, employee productivity increased, double the national average, according to Mastroianni, when measured by average sales per employee.[51]

At EDS Design and Sales, "enthusiastic" workers participated in a quality system that underlined their own vulnerability. In the business equivalent of a penitential rite, workers were expected to "account for his or her scrap." It was not simply a case of identifying problems and correcting them; employees had to measure the market value of their mistakes. According to EDS vice president Mark Gignac, having the scrap reports "forces us to track mistakes and to deal with weaknesses that we knew were there. Now we can put a dollar value on those mistakes."[52] The human cost of intensified supervision was less clear. The adoption of lean-production techniques emphasizing total quality suggested that productivity and autonomy were mutually exclusive.

Employers and their journalistic allies championed a set of ideas that stigmatized regulations protecting employee job control. In their views, workplace rules and employee independence were obstacles to progress. Speaking on behalf of business innovators throughout the Old Dominion, journalist Mary Helen Frederick argued that "as American industry replaces assembly line stiffs with work-team technicians, adaptability becomes a crucial virtue."[53] Ann Penn joined the fun, ridiculing the "Johnny Paychecks of the world" who frivolously worried about wages and benefits.[54] Productivity became the dominant trope of business innovators, the antithesis of employee job control and workplace democracy. Breaks, moderate pacing, vacation time, sickness, individual space: these had little place in an era of global competitiveness. Instead of creating a more productive, healthy, secure, and reliable workforce, breaks and workplace regulations became impediments to efficiency. In effect, business apologists created a convenient narrative in which union regulations and reciprocal obligations belonged to an unproductive and archaic industrial era. Innovation, quality, and providing the lowest price at any cost became the future of American business. According to the managerial ideology that dominated in Virginia in the early 1990s, those objectives required anxious workers.

Companies often measured the employee work ethic by their willingness to log uncompensated overtime hours. For Adjustable Steel Products, a Lynchburg transplant from New York, employee willingness to sacrifice their personal time encapsulated the Virginians' superior work habits. "One packing employee came into the Lynchburg plant one weekend because he couldn't sleep. . . . The employee didn't have insomnia—he was fretting about some parts he hadn't loaded on a truck. He wanted to catch the truck before it left the plant." Either disingenuously or naively, the management of Adjustable Steel interpreted this manic episode as an example of hardworking, conscientious Virginians putting the interests of the company before themselves. It was "very impressive," according to Treasurer Chuck Sommerfeld, the kind of thing that would have never happened in Long Island. "The attitude in New York and in many other parts of the country is, 'I punch a clock—everything else is the boss's problem.'" Fear of losing one's job, the depth of inner rationalization, the sense that one could never be certain that their job was secure, the atmosphere of recession anxiety in the early 1990s: none of these factored into Adjustable Steel's assessment of its employees. Instead, it reflected the superior work ethic of Jefferson's agrarian descendants.[55]

The curious combination of new management strategies and praise for the Virginia work ethic was not limited to Lynchburg. While O'Sullivan Industries' plant manager Gary Schnipke praised the "real good work ethic" of the farmers who had surrendered the tractor for the assembly line, he suggested that the company would continue to "upgrade," "improve," and implement new processes. Evidently, the stellar work ethic of Virginia's farmers—"entrepreneurs," as Schnipke described them, models of Jeffersonian self-reliance—was not enough; new management strategies would also be necessary. In Danville, the highly automated Nestlé factory sought out workers with "good communication skills" and "problem solvers" who were willing to "learn a new process." Pliable workers who had not become entrenched in union job-control practices were ideal for Nestlé, since it was determined to "run in team-oriented fashion with high employee participation."[56]

Northern companies were not simply relocating to the South for lower wages and taxes; they were seeking out a labor force susceptible to "management by stress." At Nestlé, prospective hires were put through a battery of information sessions, plant tours, and seminars designed to make certain that workers understood the "team work concept" before they joined. Nestlé's management hoped to implement a "team-oriented work culture" that would increase productivity and give the company that "competitive edge." The C-K Company pursued lean production by moving aggressively toward automation and a "participatory form of management." What this meant was workers taking responsibility for setting up and maintaining machines. To advance the transition from Fordist manufacturing to New Age quality production, the company offered its workforce the opportunity to take basic computer training at Danville Community College. Plant manager J. Allen Oxford should not have been surprised that "Every one was interested in taking the course." Suffering from the downsizing of the early 1990s, the media demand for constant "re-training," and the subtle company message that workers who didn't "upgrade" probably would not hold their jobs, employees at C-K had little choice but to submit to training that ironically accelerated the de-skilling of the workforce. Like Nestlé, C-K was determined to impose the team system on production. More than "speed orders through the plant," the team program would "eliminate managerial barriers to efficient production," meaning conventions protecting employee job control, break times, and the pace of production. It was clear that C-K was intent on exploiting the Total Quality Management system to its fullest advantage. The company would do more than hire mere manual laborers; it would "harness the know-how of everyone in the plant," a transaction that promised little respect for worker autonomy.[57]

The selling of Total Quality Management was closely tied to the selling of Virginia as a low-wage, surplus-labor, anti-union state. In the town of Blacksburg, Virginia, in the southwest, in an area known as the New River Valley, the new management strategies gained ground against desperately underemployed workers. Corning, Inc., began operating the facility in Blacksburg in 1989, after having abandoned the region five years earlier in search of a better deal. This time, Corning pursued a new, quality-oriented strategy in which production employees managed the factory. Here was another reengineered factory operating without foremen and supervisors. "Employees work in teams, convening before each shift to discuss problems and goals and to receive updates from the previous shifts." While the company apparently paid their two hundred unionized "associates" fairly well in 1993, the beginning of the boom years, they extracted considerable control over them in return.[58]

At Celco in the New River Valley, the company negotiated a three-year contract in 1992 that included an agreement from the Amalgamated Clothing and Textile Workers Union to initiate "worker involvement," a polite term for total quality management. "There's not a lot of room for error these days," human resources manager Pam Shiflet insisted. Nor was there very much room for worker control in the drive "to be on the leading edge." The Corning and Celco agreements illustrated precisely how far labor unions had moved toward embracing the philosophy of Total Quality Management. While unions acquiesced out of powerlessness or the slim hope that a measure of substance underlay the quality movement rhetoric, business pundits made its fundamental motives quite clear. They also exposed the material realities that made the ascendancy of TQM possible. "Low payrolls reflect rural Virginia's modest wages, high productivity and weak unions," observed journalist Jane Gerring. In this pro-business environment, "Factory managers don't have to tussle with *unreasonable* shop stewards when they want to adopt work teams or other new management concepts, as many local employers are doing" (emphasis added).[59]

According to *Virginia Business*, Stanley Hardware in Henrico County was "unlike the typical American factory" where workers watched the clock. Employees were organized into production teams, paid salaries rather than hourly wages, expected to perform a variety of jobs, and permitted to set their own schedule. According to one employee, workers enjoyed greater "freedom" than under the old system. Yet the "freedom" that workers may very well have gained or at least hoped to achieve through "total employee involvement" operated against their long-term interests. The principles of quality management were diametrically opposed to the principles of union representation, a point which Mary Helen Frederick made clear in her discussion of Stanley Hardware: "There's no law that says you can't do this in a union shop, but it's a lot harder where union and labor and management have a tradition of conflict and mistrust and where *rules get in the way*" (emphasis added). The advantage, according to Frederick, was that Virginia had an exceptionally low level of unionization, "so such impediments rarely stand in the way of implementing new approaches."[60] Even if some workers embraced the promise of greater variety in their work routines and the acquisition of new skills, the reality stood in sharp contrast to the rhetoric. Proponents of teamwork and flexibility clearly understood that it was antagonistic to job control and employee autonomy, the very principles which union "rules" were designed to protect. While companies utilized the rhetoric of business reengineering and global competitiveness, they operated according to the traditional imperatives of corporate capitalism. The economic crisis of the 1990s gave proponents of neoliberalism the opportunity to present those business imperatives as incontrovertible truth and as positive social objectives.[61]

The quality movement was an essential feature of the New Economy in the South. It was becoming the standard fix for companies in search of competitiveness, the mantra of post-recession capitalism. It also illustrated the escalating impact of corporate globalization on the American South. Never a region immune from global trade patterns or colonial economic ventures, the South was now becoming a frontier for the quality management movement. This was in part a reflection of the lower rates of unionization in the South as well as the influx of northern and foreign companies into the region during this new wave of Sunbelt growth. As Ann Penn described it, "The precepts of the quality management movement are becoming standard language on the shop floor." Having introduced something known as the "Crosby Quality Process," Hubbell Lighting of Christianburg, Virginia, described the 1990s as "the decade of quality." Plymouth, Inc., which manufactured school supplies, transplanted itself from New Jersey to Radford, reducing its wages by a dollar an hour and eliminating $180,000 in union-negotiated benefits. Paradoxically, while companies like Corning applauded the "superb" work ethic in the New River Valley, they implemented Just-In-Time and TQM methods designed to stretch workers to the breaking point. Virginia was reengineering itself as a place for business innovation, which in the 1990s carried the additional implication of non-unionized, lean production.[62]

An essential objective of the new management philosophy was to absorb the employee into the company's market survival plan. Through training seminars, teamwork initiatives, profit-sharing arrangements, and the rhetoric of quality-driven customer service, companies tried to instruct workers in the virtues of the bottom line. Business owners convinced themselves that southern workers shared the same objectives. Surveying company managers in the Region 2000 area of central Virginia, journalist Ann C. Penn reported that supervisors and employees "trust[ed]" each other and "work[ed] toward mutual goals." Unlike the union-ridden, clock-watching workforce in the rest of the nation, workers in Virginia saw "nothing exceptional" in putting in "extra effort." According to Penn, it was "simply part of doing the job right."[63] If we are to take the comments of one union leader at face value—a questionable proposition considering that he was talking to *Virginia Business*—the workers and management at Corning shared a "common goal—the best interest of Corning and the employees." According to this union president, "there's a lot of trust and mutual respect between company leaders and union leaders." His comments may suggest that the union and the company had reached an accord, that profitability and the recognition of a common enemy in intensifying competition had erased the adversarial relations between management and labor. But the president of Local 1022 of the American Flint Glass Workers Union may also have inadvertently expressed the full measure of organized labor's capitulation to the business agenda. Considering the recent recession and the rising fear that American jobs would be lost to low-paid foreign workers, that might be the most plausible interpretation.

Like their northern counterparts, southern companies tried to bind their employees to the company's overarching objective of increasing share prices and profitability. Vigorous cost-cutting was the key to winning employees over to the program of increasing profitability. At Taylor Brothers, Inc., in central Virginia, the company sought increased loyalty through an Employee Stock Ownership Plan (ESOP). According to Bob Taylor, the program converted employees to the management worldview. Equipment and plant material damage declined; the trucks were better maintained; employees expressed concern about minimizing labor costs and seemed willing to spend more time on the job. "One of our older employees, who has been with the company for 20 years, will come back on a Saturday to see if we have enough people to work." Equally touching anecdotes of employee dedication came from Intertape Polymer Corporation, a company transplanted from the high-wage, unionized Quebec, Canada. According to journalist Ann C. Penn, the workers from Pittsylvania County exhibited a willingness to learn and a "quality-conscious attitude." This attitude was on conspicuous display when workers stayed longer than their shift required. "Sometimes we have to run them off," noted plant engineer David Bennet. Again, though, a solid work ethic was not enough. Rural devotion to hard work had to be directed into "working smart," which could only come by using "new philosophies" to forge a "new work force."[64] The consistent theme was "flexibility" and the willingness to adapt. Despite the rhetoric of workplace cooperation and democracy, management continued to determine the shape of those adaptations. Profit-sharing arrangements certainly did promise a greater sense of entitlement for workers while teamwork and job diversity held out the hope of a more stimulating and rewarding work environment. Employees may very well have been motivated by profit sharing. What continued to elude them was any genuine degree of control over the companies for which they worked.

Companies diligently persuaded workers that they had to further the objectives of global competitiveness and lean production. Jobs were a fortunate blessing that could be easily revoked if employees lost sight of company profit margins. Of course, conscientious employees who define themselves through their labor had been the mainstay of industrializing America. No doubt many of these found their way into the mills and factories of central Virginia in the 1990s. Yet southern workers also labored under the shadow of personal misfortune through job loss and regional economic stagnation. If profit sharing motivated some, the possibility of losing their tenuous grasp on security in the era of radical de-industrialization was no less imperative. The worker who came in on Saturdays probably had his job security on his mind at least as much as the company's profit and loss statements.

What is remarkable about the enthusiasm for the Virginia work ethic was the compartmentalization that went into explaining the investment influx in the state. In the very same articles celebrating the enigmatic Virginia work ethic and worker receptivity toward quality management, business pundits highlighted the factors that really propelled worker "flexibility." In southwest Virginia's New River Valley, a region that had grown dependent on manufacturing during the Second World War, the recession of the early 1990s struck with devastating force. In 1990, AT&T eliminated its microelectronic operations in Pulaski, tossing as many as 4,000 people out of work in the process. Post–Cold War military spending reductions also had an impact on the area. In 1989, the Radford Army Ammunition Plant, which produced explosives, cut its payroll by more than half, putting 2,500 people out of work. By 1991, the unemployment rate in the area had reached 9.7 percent.[65] In the storm of early '90s downsizing and reengineering, places like southwest Virginia offered a safe harbor of low wages and a fertile field for new management techniques.

For companies like Rene Composite Materials, Virginia offered relief from paying the living-wage rates in Quebec. Joining other automobile manufacturer and suppliers, including Volvo and BBA Friction, Rene Composite relocated to southwest Virginia in search of lower labor costs. As journalist Belinda Anderson reported, "Unemployment back in Quebec was so low that the company couldn't do any additional business there." Setting up shop in Giles County, the company hired fifty people to work for the paltry wage of $6.50 an hour.[66]

In Richmond and Norfolk, where relatively high wages and low unemployment prevailed in 1991, the problem was selling the labor market's hidden benefits. Don't be deceived, journalist Mary Helen Frederick assured business prospectors: Richmond was still the kind of place where corporations would find a docile labor force. The statistics did not capture the inscrutable Virginia "work ethic." Nor did they account for lower rates of absenteeism, unionization, work stoppages, and "workers' enthusiasm for change." Virginia had a well-educated workforce, with PhDs and computer technicians aplenty in Fairfax. But it also had an underemployed workforce that did not show up in traditional measurement of unemployment. Alfa-Laval Thermal, based in New York but originally from Sweden, found this comforting. The company was determined to lower production costs, so it undertook a study of sixty-five prospective cities, one of which was Richmond. The problem was that the average salary for manufacturing employees was $29,000, far too high to suit the company's needs. Yet business consultants convinced the company that the figures were inaccurate. The salary rates were driven up by a small number of high-paying, stable jobs in the city's flagship companies. "If you factor out Philip Morris, AT&T and Reynolds Metals, Richmond's average pay drops 'like a stone,'" Frederick writes, quoting a consultant. "'We don't have to pay anywhere near those numbers.'" Quite simply, the labor market favored a business agenda, a point which economic developers were at pains to stress. High unemployment numbers were good news for companies searching for a "larger pool of available labor, lower wages and a lower cost of doing business." Technology might have been a driving factor in the New Economy, but the old rules still applied, and business boosters were only too willing to spell those out explicitly.[67]

In Hampton Roads, for example, the statistics were deceiving. The unemployment rate in February 1991 was only 4.2 percent, but this overlooked the 12,000 to 15,000 people rotated out of the military each year. More than this, it failed to reflect the gendered advantages of the available labor supply. "Some 45,000 to 50,000 spouses create a huge reservoir of part-time and seasonal labor." Thinking in terms of dependent wives eager to supplement their husband's meager military incomes, *Virginia Business* championed the Hampton Roads area. More than this, Hampton Roads attracted workers from northeastern North Carolina. According to one employer, these mobile North Carolinians carpooled to the area by the thousands in search of employment. In addition, traditional labor statistics failed to capture the vast number of underemployed people who would work for rock-bottom wages. To illustrate this cheery prospect, Mary Helen Frederick recounted the experience of Omni Products, another New Jersey company on the hunt for lower operating costs. The company was concerned about reports of low unemployment and high wage rates in the Richmond area. Here, the Metropolitan Economic Development Council stepped in to test the labor-pool waters and dispel Omni's concerns. Advertising for low-skill jobs starting at $5.50 an hour, the council was bombarded by more than 1,300 applications. That was enough to convince Omni that Richmond was the right place to relocate.[68]

This was not simply a case of business prospects and trade experts collaborating on investment strategy. Here was a case of municipal government celebrating the economic vulnerability of its citizens. The state government, as will become clear in a later chapter, also played an active role in recruiting business and in financing the shift toward lean production. In the case of Stanley Hardware, state financial support for 168 hours of quality management training at John Tyler Community College sealed the company's decision to move to Richmond rather than Kansas City. The additional incentive was that Richmond's workers would be non-union. Stanley executives eventually shuttered that plant as well, all part of a massive assault on corporate costs in its desperate struggle to contest cheap Asian imports.[69] As companies moved toward lean production, the state assisted the process through training that harmonized with company objectives.

The Quality First program at Central Virginia Community College demonstrated the influence of the New Economy agenda in higher education. Community colleges have always had a technical and vocational focus. Yet the Quality First program was unique, not only because it was jointly sponsored by business and municipal government working through the Region 2000 initiative, but because the program itself embodied the principles of one of the key proponents of kaizen, or continuous improvement.

The program began when municipal and education leaders canvassed business for a "wish list" of training programs. According to Roger Beeker, director of the Center for Business, Industry, and Government, quality training was at the top of the list. The Quality First program reflected both the ideological assumptions of neoliberalism and the lean-production strategy of business in the 1990s. As Belinda Anderson reported, "The college describes Quality First as a means of emphasizing the relationship of quality to customer satisfaction and competitiveness in an increasingly global economy."[70] Municipal governments, community colleges, local elites, and state government officials were gearing public resources to meet the demands set by allegedly implacable economic forces.

Managers and machine operators would adopt the team format as they cooperated in resolving irksome production problems. More than this, participants in Quality First would imbibe the philosophy of kaizen guru W. Edwards Deming, who crafted his message while working as a consultant for Japanese business following World War II. When Ford Motor Company started losing its business to Japanese manufacturers, it endorsed Deming's techniques, which include the elimination of goals and quotas, the disintegration of departmental distinctions, vigilant commitment to efficiency, and such ambiguous objectives as "constancy of purpose." Reduced to its central tenet, Deming's philosophy insisted on constant modifications that stretched workers and company resources to the maximum. Managers and line workers were sent on sixteen-week courses to absorb the "philosophy" of continuous improvement. Some experienced the equivalent of a religious conversion to the doctrine of cost reduction through time-saving modifications. Despite the rhetoric, Quality First's methods were undeniably concrete. "This team is studying how to measure setup, idle and production time," workshop leader Bob Staples claimed. Injunctions to cooperation, relationship building, and quality aside, the key was to be able to chart and graph cost reductions. Bill Johnson of Vitramon in Roanoke outlined the objectives underlying the seemingly innocuous jargon: "To make good use of the Quality First program, you have to send people with a quantifiable program, and not just a general notion of improving communications or morale."[71] Quality was a decidedly quantitative concept.

Of course, *Virginia Business* could produce some evidence to suggest that workers actually embraced the changes. Dave Wood, a tool and die worker at the non-union Stanley Hardware, found the system less boring than the old routine: "I get to do something a little different every day."[72] Wood also claimed that the "total employee involvement" gave workers "more freedom" while also utilizing their ideas. And, according to Leigh Anne Larance, workers at the unionized Volvo-GM plant in Dublin, a town in the highly industrialized New River Valley, workers "embraced" the Total Quality Management techniques. According to the vice president of the United Auto Workers local, "You get good work out of happy people."[73]

Virginia workers may not have rejected the new techniques out of hand. Some probably did thrive in a work environment that seemed to value their input and utilize their skills. Yet a note of skepticism is warranted for several reasons. First, when *Virginia Business* conducted its brief interviews, they did so as partisans of business and of Total Quality Management. It is quite likely that employees refrained from criticizing a system that they were expected to adopt. Rhetoric of teamwork aside, it would have been highly unlikely to hear a dissenting voice from a worker who depended on a job for his or her livelihood. Second, the sporadic comments of a few allegedly "happy" workers offer little in the way of a thorough investigation of the impact of the new management philosophy. What it does suggest is the ability of company representatives and a cooperative media to present an image of compliant, flexible workers in rural Virginia.

Moreover, the workers and companies that were surveyed tended to be very favorable to the changes initially, but grew increasingly resistant as the implications of this intrusive management system became clear. Following massive layoffs at DuPont's Spruance Fibers Plant in Chesterfield County, the company began introducing classes to "broaden the scope of their jobs." The union resisted, sensing that this was a strategy to stretch out the production process by loading the responsibilities of downsized workers onto the remaining labor force. Despite the fact that the union had filed grievances over retraining and reorganization, the company moved ahead with its plans. As one company official explained, machinists would make repairs that had previously been the responsibility of mechanics.[74]

The Teamsters eventually went out on strike in 1993 to challenge the imposition of TQM. Company management justified plans to streamline the operation by claiming that the changes were necessary to increase company competitiveness. The Teamsters saw it as an effort to undermine union control on the shop floor. David L. Whitley, a leader in the AlliedSignal strike, commented on the implications of the Total Quality Management movement for labor: "Quality was never a problem with the local union. . . . The people understand quality. It was when management didn't take the time to have the union be part of it" that friction increased. Richmond labor mediator Don Doherty believed that TQM could be beneficial, "but it looks like these other programs . . . were management-instituted to work to the advantage of management. So TQM gets damned by faint praise." According to Doherty, "workers start asking tough questions such as, 'If we're going to give you all these ideas to do something better, [shouldn't] we get something better?'" The union at DuPont's Spruance plant in Chesterfield reacted similarly to the company's "Gemini Project," a campaign to reduce the company's workforce and alter its production systems. To the union, the employee reductions were not the result of downsizing but outsourcing and contracting out. The plan to eliminate 160 additional jobs following the company's dismissal of 9,000 employees since 1991 seemed indistinguishable from the workplace control that the company sought through "benchmarking" and Total Quality Management.[75]

Again, there's little doubt that individual workers adapted themselves to quality management while some even embraced it. After all, TQM held out the promise of active participation in the production process. It promised relief from the drudgery of unskilled, repetitive labor and the opportunity to utilize one's experiences and skills in a creative fashion. Some employees adjusted to company expectations or simply followed union directions in accepting it. Probably for many, the implications of Total Quality Management were not clear at all. They were obscured by rhetoric about worker empowerment and stimulating work environments.

Regardless of their subjective response, the promise of employee participation in decision making meant the reality of heightened managerial supervision. Increased productivity rarely translated into increased wages or benefits. Even where employers were genuinely interested in reducing the stress associated with Fordist production and creating a healthier, vibrant, and potentially rewarding work environment, they adopted the new management techniques in order to maximize production. The central objective was to reduce costs, speed up the work process, and increase competitiveness. If employee happiness ran counter to this objective, it was employee happiness that suffered, not company profitability. As Virginia Commonwealth University business professor Eugene Hunt observed about teamwork, another key technique in the corporate reengineering strategy, it was a means to an end. Employee satisfaction might be a by-product of teamwork, but "happiness isn't what counts for a company," as journalist Mary Beausoleil explained after interviewing Hunt. "Efficiency and effectiveness are what count."[76] Sharing the proceeds of increased productivity through higher wages, better benefits, and additional job security counted even less.

There is also a body of evidence suggesting the negative consequences of these reforms for workers in the 1990s. The most important challenge to the assertions of Total Quality Management proponents came from a team of sociologists who studied the application of lean production at CAMI, a joint General Motors and Suzuki venture in Ingersoll, Ontario. Conducting qualitative research featuring open-ended questionnaires and interviews with management as well as workers, these investigators went beyond company propaganda to discover how workers had responded to kaizen, quality circles, teams, production recalibration, and job rotation.

The responses were not entirely negative. The overwhelming majority of workers genuinely enjoyed the job-rotation feature of quality improvement, citing its tendency to diminish job boredom and reduce the strain associated with some of the more physically onerous jobs. Yet workers and the company endorsed job rotation for different reasons. As James Rinehart, Christopher Huxley, and David Robertson noted, "While CAMI views rotation as a way to increase its flexibility, the workforce uses rotation not only to relieve monotony but also to regulate work and to restrict managerial flexibility." Lacking the kind of job classifications associated with traditional automobile factories, these workers used job rotation as an "informal shop floor work rule." No less important, those workers with comparatively more challenging jobs vigorously resisted job rotation, while those performing the repetitive, mind-numbing tasks of the assembly line coveted the skilled and less easily interchangeable jobs. Despite the reengineering rhetoric, job rotation did not increase worker autonomy, control over the production process, or the acquisition of additional skills.[77]

While companies championed the virtues of teamwork, researchers found them little more than updated methods of managerial control. Proponents of assembly-line teams claimed that they democratized the workplace, increased worker autonomy, and galvanized employees behind the objective of efficient production. Yet teamwork in the 1990s operated under the constraints of lean production. Managerial supervision increased and employees were expected to sacrifice break times and others moments of "non-value-added labor." In addition, the Just-In-Time delivery system and the steady acceleration of the production process precluded workers from gaining additional leverage under the team system. Far from promoting worker autonomy, the teams were designed to use peer pressure to increase production. Instead of building a sense of employee independence, the team concept was intended to erode shop-floor cohesion. At the same time, it would direct collective energies to the service of company objectives. This program included pressure against absentee workers, the solicitation of information on alleged shirkers, and the levying of sanctions against noncompliant team members. Workers would supervise and scrutinize each other. The underlying idea was to create teams in which hired hands competed against each other to fulfil the objectives of lean production.[78]

Just as in the case of job rotation, workers imposed their own meaning on teamwork. They used them in ways that challenged the human resource agenda. As Rinehart and his associates reported, most workers liked the social dimension of teamwork—getting to know other people, mutual assistance, and defending each other's interests. But they increasingly objected to how teams were used to discourage people from leaving the assembly line when injured or sick. The theory held that as companies reduced the workforce and intensified the manufacturing process, teams would direct their grievances against "slacking" team members, draconian team leaders, and sick or disabled workers. Yet, as Rinehart, Huxley, and Robertson found out, the teams did not transmit the company philosophy as effectively as it had hoped. "Teams were not carriers of an enterprise consciousness; the negative consequences of peer pressure increasingly were recognized; and only a minority of workers we talked to reported constant pressures from co-workers." Instead of welding the employee to the company, the teams became instruments for opposing some of the more egregious forms of unilateral management control.[79]

Rinehart subjected kaizen and the quality circle programs to the same scrutiny. While human resource activists claimed that kaizen offered workers an opportunity to contribute meaningfully to the production process, the authors of *Just Another Car Factory* suggest otherwise. They postulated that it was designed to limit employee resistance to company objectives, extract their input to reduce costs, and encourage them to identify with the company's competitive agenda. The survey responses seemed to suggest that employees saw it the same way. While workers had always sought ways to make the production process more efficient, they objected to a formalized system in which they were expected to make suggestions that would accelerate the production process and undermine job security. When workers made suggestions for improvement that promised to reduce costs, they met a warm response. Proposals for change that benefited workers at the expense of the increased-production–reduced-cost agenda were uniformly rejected. Workers at CAMI as well at other "transplant" auto manufacturing operations discovered that kaizen represented a form of "super-Taylorism" that did little to empower or liberate employees. As Rinehart and the others concluded, "While workers are encouraged to improve operations, the parameters of kaizen are defined by the criterion of cost-reduction, not safer, easier, or more interesting jobs, and the disposition of suggestions—other than the most trivial ones—is in the hands of management. . . . Over time workers evinced greater skepticism of kaizen."[80] The researchers noted that participation in quality circle and teamwork diminished over time while managerial supervision increased. Unless we are prepared to believe that southern manufacturing workers represented a docile exception to this trend of resistance to quality management, these conclusions can be reasonably extrapolated to the men and women who filled the ranks of Virginia's globalizing industries in the 1990s.

Yet the experience of manufacturing workers in the early 1990s does not capture the full spectrum of insecurity in the New Economy. At the same time that northern Virginia's boosters were proclaiming it the next Austin, Texas, or Silicon Valley, working-class people were struggling to stay out of poverty. Committed to "destroy the welfare system as we know it," Lieutenant Governor Donald Beyer and his state commission on poverty nevertheless identified the persistence of economic hardship amid the glitter of high-tech northern Virginia.[81] As many as 62,000 people out of a population of more than 750,000—8.3 percent—fell below the poverty line. Additionally disturbing was the realization that almost half of these—25,000—were young people between the ages of 18 and 35. J. Glynne Loope, assistant director of the University of Virginia's Center for Public Service, also noted a connection between poverty and insufficient education. This theme of inadequate education, the failure of higher education to adjust to the demands of the New Economy, and the paucity of skilled technical workers in the state pervaded the period. As one pro-business southern think tank explained, "When teachers are out of touch with market realities, students, businesses, and the entire community suffer from lower productivity, which can lead to job loss and business relocation or closing."[82]

The call for investment in training and education was matched by others demanding lower taxes. Beyer's commission was dedicated to eliminating welfare and generating "good jobs at decent wages."[83] Yet advocating "adult education and job training" while denouncing "welfare" exposed the limitations of the market-oriented ethos that coalesced in the 1990s. To attract business, municipal and state governments had to maintain Virginia's traditional advantage—its low taxes. This "pro-business" environment had little to offer young people, many of whom were black and Hispanic. While boosters, pundits, and high-tech champions crowed about job growth, few cared to dwell on the source of greatest expansion—the service industry. Incomes grew in the area and unemployment steadily declined as Northern Virginia's bustling high-tech sector churned out service-sector jobs that offered little security. Temporary positions, contract work, and part-time jobs proliferated. Business services—including everything from office supplies to printing, telemarketing, and temporary agencies—grew at an annual rate of 7.4 percent between 1990 and 1997 and 10.4 percent in 1998.[84]

Virginia and the high-tech pockets of the South created a two-tiered economy. On one tier, poor, minority, and usually female employees cleaned the offices, ironed the shirts, answered the phones, and took out the garbage for those on the other tier, the technological innovators in Tysons Corner. Even so, higher-salaried service workers shared with their downscale counterparts the same tenuous hold on economic security. Stock options and flexible hours could not reduce the insecurity once downsizing became a constant form of discipline in the white-collar world.

Economic insecurity was no abstraction; it stemmed from forces that were altering American business in the twentieth century as well as from conditions indigenous to the South. Virginia elites marketed the state's social conservatism to businesses searching for relief from high overhead and allegedly unproductive, multicultural workforces. If this was an old game, Virginia's business and political leaders gave it a remarkable facelift. They transformed anti-labor policies into modernizing strategies for economic growth. Virginia was branding itself as a pro-business, anti-labor, high-tech wonderland, a place where the legacy of racial subordination and autocratic politics was all but forgotten. The implications came into sharp focus in the wake of the recession and the corporate restructuring frenzy of the 1990s.

CHAPTER 3

After the Deluge

Office Workers and the Era of Uncertainty in Virginia

The dominant reality for office workers from Richmond to Roanoke was insecurity. The possibility of being laid off or simply eliminated as a result of corporate restructuring burrowed deeply into the subconscious of Virginia's workers in the new Gilded Age. It created an atmosphere of profound social anxiety, one that was no less intense because it happened in Virginia. There was nothing peculiarly southern about the economic forces that were transforming career-minded people into temporary, part-time, and contract workers. What happened to middle managers, secretaries, salespeople, and manufacturing supervisors in Virginia happened to those in Michigan, Ohio, and New York. The economic uncertainties of the new era bound the regions together in a collective experience of reduced hopes, limited expectations, and persistent fears.

Yet the recession of 1990/1991 generated a depth of anguish in Virginia that set it apart from its southern counterparts. According to a Georgia State study, Virginia suffered the "longest and steepest" recession of all among the twelve southeastern states. It lost 20,000 construction jobs and 4,000 financial-sector jobs in 1992, with another 4,000 expected to be lost in the latter part of the following year.[1] In 1991 alone, at the height of the recession, the Virginia economy lost more than 70,000 jobs.[2] Virginia had become a showcase for the technological hyperbole of the New Economy. It highlighted the managerial experiments that aimed at minimizing cost and maximizing flexibility. Yet the recession, corporate downsizing, and the mood of uncertainty only accelerated forces that had been at work since the 1970s.

No less than manufacturing workers, white-collar office workers struggled to hold on to the New Deal social contract. If collective bargaining welded workers to the state, the prospect of a stable relationship with a corporate employer cemented white-collar workers to American industry. Both understood that those relationships were the product an activist government that sought to balance the interests of capital and labor in promoting economic growth. It was the sense of reciprocity that eroded ineluctably in the 1990s. It was the social contract, the set of reciprocal obligations grounded in a sense of fair play and sustained by American prosperity, which disintegrated in the 1990s.[3]

It declined not because of some inevitable economic law, but because of corporate restructuring. Economists Barry Bluestone and Bennett Harrison explain that at the root of downsizing was "the abrogation of the social contract that labor, management, and government had slowly but surely constructed in the course of nearly fifty years of union struggle, collective bargaining, and government regulation." The central theme in each of the management strategies used to streamline the corporation was the reduction of labor costs.[4] Virginia's experience was one chapter in a protracted thinning out of the nation's workforce. Citing Bureau of Labor Statistics data for the period from 1984 to 2004, journalist Louis Uchitelle reported that a full 30 million Americans had been separated unwillingly from their jobs during that time. That nearly incomprehensible number did not account for those compelled to take early retirement or to endure a "disguised layoff." According to Uchitelle, by the late 1990s, eliminating workers had become the standard practice, replacing an earlier era's normative experience of job security.[5] For the administrative assistants, data processors, mail-room clerks, and middle managers in Virginia, the defining experience of the era was the struggle to compensate for the collapse of the social contract. The loss of job security dampened the enthusiasm they might have derived from the technological cornucopia and stock market hysteria of the period. The struggle was to operate in a world where marketplace competition permeated almost every phase of their public lives. As much as the South pioneered the ideology of market dominance and the practices that defined the New Economy, the destabilizing experience of downsizing tied them to the predicament facing workers throughout the United States.

The recession of 1990/1991 profoundly affected the lives of working Americans. It continued to influence their attitudes toward corporate capitalism throughout the decade. It was the product of several forces, including the federal bailout of failed savings and loan banks, the excessive speculation and inevitable correction in real estate and financial markets, the escalation of oil prices during the Persian Gulf War, and the loss of consumer confidence. Together, they jettisoned the heady optimism of the 1980s and plunged more than 7 percent of working Americans and 6.4 percent of working Virginians into unemployment. Those figures failed to include thousands of Americans who simply stopped looking for work and dropped off the official radar.[6] In Virginia, where the recession set in later than most other states, defense-spending reductions and the fear of further cuts eroded consumer confidence and extended the downturn.[7] The bloated commercial real estate market fell precipitously. Manufacturing also declined, losing some 20,000 jobs in 1991 alone. But Richmond's mainstays, including banks, utilities, and government employment, also felt the pinch of economic contraction. Corporate consolidations and restructuring permanently eliminated thousands of jobs. Out-of-state companies purchased Sovran and Dominion, two of Virginia's leading banks, while other banks drastically trimmed their workforces in the wake of failed real estate deals.[8]

A snapshot of the recession provides a better sense of its human impact. In November 1992, Richmond's DuPont eliminated 600 positions, while Reynolds Metals pink-slipped between 700 and 800 workers. Tobacco giant Philip Morris also slashed its workforce, while Ames Department Stores moved ahead with its plans to shut down five area stores and lay off 300 people. In December of that year, IBM, General Motors, BFGoodrich, Norshipco, C&P Telephone, and Dominion Bankshares Corporation publicized layoffs that would take effect the following year.[9] In the case of Dominion Bankshares, its reductions cost the struggling city of Roanoke approximately 2,100 jobs, with another 200 slated for elimination in 1993.[10]

Strolling through the recession-traumatized city of Roanoke on a Tuesday afternoon, reporter John Levin assessed the damage. Surveying five financial institutions in the city, he discovered that between 33 and 80 percent of the tellers' positions were active but between 50 and 66 of the desks of mid-level banking officials vacant. "Dust gathered, no work was in progress; at some banks, even the telephones had been disconnected. They represent jobs that have been eliminated."[11] The character of the recession was also evident in the bleak and empty offices that confronted Levin: "Empty desks are a symbol of the most startling differences between earlier recessions and the most recent downturn. This time the job cuts hit the higher-pay, white-collar positions that have a larger and more direct impact on consumer buying power." When the recovery set in, companies in Richmond, Roanoke, and elsewhere began hiring temporary, easily expendable workers. Increasingly, these employees were considered "costs" to be managed, setting the tone for the uncertainty and contingency that would dominate the 1990s.[12]

The message of lower costs through temporary and disposable labor made remarkable headway in Virginia in the 1990s. *Virginia Business*, the bellwether of business attitudes in Virginia, championed temporary workers as the solution for businesses struggling to manage the business cycle. "Driven by industry's incessant quest to control expenses," wrote Jane Gerring, "temporary employment is changing the nature of the American work force." The principal appeal for temporary workers was cost: "Temps tend to be cheaper than core employees because they normally don't receive fringe benefits and companies can let them go without incurring expensive severance obligations." AccuTech of Chester, the Regency Bank in Richmond, and the law firm of LeClair, Ryan, Joynes, Epps, and Framme were among several Virginia companies turning to temporaries as a solution to reducing costs. Hospitals had become the largest users of temporary work, which was particularly poignant since health care was being touted as one of the key growth industries for Virginia in the New Economy. The connection between the growth of the service economy and the expansion of temporary, lower-paying jobs was clear. Gerring also identified the connection between corporate realignment and the explosion in the use of temporary workers: "A wave of corporate restructuring released thousands of experienced managers and professionals into the job market. Many have resorted to temporary work to pay the bills." A bloated labor market and desperate workers translated into savings for cost-conscious companies.[13]

Hiring temporary workers gave companies a chance to "screen" prospective full-time employees, but the practice militated against the expansion of a permanent workforce. A 2001 Urban Institute study for the Department of Health and Human Services found that the majority of temporary jobs did not develop into full-time positions. In Washington during the period of the study, only 42 percent of temporary workers developed into full-time employees. Using survey evidence from the 1990s that focused on low-skilled workers in temporary employment, the study concluded that a mere 5 percent of companies reported employing temporary workers for longer than a year. On the other hand, an Upjohn survey suggested that 43 percent of companies using temporary work and 36 percent of companies hiring "on-call" workers claimed that they often, occasionally, or sometimes moved temporaries into full-time position. The majority, however, did not, and this was particularly the case for low-income and low-skilled laborers.[14]

Considering that temporary workers earned less, drew fewer benefits, and enjoyed considerably less occupational mobility than full-time workers, its appeal was strictly limited. Yet for *Virginia Business* and the companies that eagerly dipped into the expanding pool of reserve labor, temporary workers exemplified the "extraordinary flexibility of its work force." In fact, it was one of the country's "great competitive advantages in the global economy." The elasticity of the labor force—this ability for companies to shed employees quickly—was allowing companies to lower operating costs and respond to changing market dynamics.[15] For companies, the labor glut following the recession offered a golden opportunity. Newly flexible, they would be able to compete on the global stage.

If the voice of business in Virginia neglected the workers' perspective, the *Richmond Times-Dispatch* at least hinted at it. Commenting on the opportunities in temporary work, Deborah E. Shapiro of Richmond's Manpower, Inc., recommended that "If your ego can take a beating and you can be open to this kind of thing, it might be better for you in the future."[16] Wilma Burke, a peripatetic history teacher and wife of a multiply-displaced employee in the semiconductor industry, shed light on the fragile nature of temporary work. "There is no loyalty to the employee when you're a contract employee. There is none. They tell you on Friday today's your last day. And you're done."[17] Shapiro may have been exceedingly optimistic about the chances for career mobility as a temporary. Even so, she identified the core of the problem for the American worker in the 1990s: the loss of dignity and self-worth, a by-product of the collapse of self-determination in the era of insecurity.

The recession accelerated the labor market upheaval of the 1980s, when corporations adopted downsizing as their key strategy for declining rates of profit. The wave of corporate restructuring followed an era of economic dynamism rivaled only by the decade that followed. Yet, the mergers and acquisition craze, the stock market euphoria that saw buyers trading in overvalued "junk bonds," and the real estate speculation that paralleled to the excesses of the 1920s masked the structural transformations in the economy. In the post-war period of industrial expansion, the size of the company, the power of collective bargaining, and a protected domestic market determined the prevailing wage rates. A social wage underwritten by New Deal regulatory practices guaranteed workers a decent income. Large companies such as IBM paid more than smaller companies in the same field. Profits were distributed far more equitably throughout the corporate hierarchy than they would be in the late twentieth century.[18]

While collective bargaining and a corporate commitment to a stable labor force explained the rising wage levels, the unwillingness of companies to enter into profit-depleting price competition explained the comparatively higher costs. This was not the classical economy working at its ruthless best, relentlessly pushing down price levels and wage rates. This was a case of unions, federal assistance to business development, social investment, government regulation, and an implicit social contract operating to maintain a high standard of living for American workers. Instead of relentless competition, oligopolies dominated the market. They established rules of competition that secured profit margins and employee security. If unions suffered the neutralizing consequences of having traded away control over the production process, they gained a modicum of stability that benefited non-unionized workers as well.[19]

This stability began to erode dramatically in the 1970s. The OPEC oil crisis and the subsequent inflation spiral exacerbated the productivity problems that American companies suffered in the 1960s. The deregulation of several key sectors of the economy, including transportation in the 1970s and telecommunications in the 1980s, added to the profit squeeze. The liberalization of trade laws and the exposure of American companies to global competition intensified it. Since they could not simply impose higher prices, and since the cost of raw materials was increasing from international demand, and since credit had become more expensive as a result of increasing interest rates in the 1970s, companies faced a limited range of choices for maintaining profitability. Facing increased competition and aging plant, American corporations failed to invest in new products or innovative technologies. Rather than designing new and more efficient product lines, manufacturers from automobile to electronic appliances turned to business mergers. At the same time, they sought government relief from regulation and taxation. The final component of the strategy to restore profitability was to "zap labor," as Richard Nixon's assistant secretary of labor put it. That meant relocating businesses offshore. It also called for the importing of components from foreign manufacturers, the elimination of labor unions and the obstruction of union organization, the substitution of part-time and contract workers for more expensive full-time employees, and the shifting of the cost of health care and benefits to the workers themselves. In general, it meant that corporations would aggressively shift the burden of risk from themselves to their workers. The strategies were in place well before the end of the 1980s.[20]

However, the diminishing profitability continued, stimulating the furious downsizing of the early 1990s. The manic leveraged buyouts in the 1980s led to the dismissal of managers, the elimination of inefficient divisions and product lines, and the allocation of profits to shareholders rather than employees. It also created the model for the downsizing deluge of the 1990s. Companies fearful of being subjected to the same slash-and-burn takeovers moved quickly to restructure their operations.[21]

No less important was the advent of computer technologies that eliminated jobs and contributed to company profitability. In an increasingly deregulated environment, companies sought out cost-cutting measures. The introduction of computer systems requiring a modicum of skills placed downward pressure on low-skilled, less educated workers. The result was the aggravation of the income disparity between the workers and the corporate hierarchy.[22]

The proliferation of office computers drastically reduced the demand for administrative and mid-level managerial staff. Increasingly, middle-class office workers were subjected to the same large-scale firings that manufacturing workers had endured since the late 1970s.[23] As companies replaced secretaries and supervisors with voice-mail systems, word-processing and fax machines, and electronic databases storing information once held in file folders and card catalogues, their profitability increased. Fewer people were doing more work, and company costs were declining.

Yet productivity was not necessarily increasing. Economist William Baumol suggested that downsizing did not add appreciably to a company's competitiveness or increase output per worker. What they discovered was corporate America's "dirty little secret": that companies were increasing profitability by simply spending less on wages.[24] Spending less on labor and aggressively introducing computer technology into streamlined office operations, the companies that survived the recession enhanced their revenues and drove up share prices. Resilient companies were now catering to a shareholding constituency that replaced labor as the countervailing power to management. Looking at the manufacturing sector, economist Robert Brenner challenges the point. Productivity increased, he argues, between 1979 and 1996, but it did so at considerable cost to American workers. While manufacturing output and investment declined, labor productivity increased through downsizing and lean production. As Brenner explains, productivity increases "resulted as much from the removal from operation of outdated and inefficient plant and equipment—along with the workers who had manned it—as from the putting into play of state-of-the-art plant and equipment, and also as much from unmeasured increases in labor input achieved through the intensification of work as from actual gains in efficiency."[25] Companies recovered from the shock of recession through massive restructuring and a renewed dedication to competitiveness. The job-generating industries were now those requiring the greatest technical aptitude, and those positions were decidedly fewer and more elusive for people in the downsizing deluge of the 1990s.[26]

If progressive economists offered differing opinions on productivity in the era of the New Economy, they agreed that the drive for corporate profitability was not simply a matter of new technology achieving efficiency. The elimination of old machinery or antiquated filing systems also meant the elimination of jobs. The restoration of productivity—or profitability, as Baumol would have it—meant the intensification of labor as workers logged longer and longer hours in an environment of staggering uncertainty. What was clear was that fundamental changes were overtaking American business and altering the working landscape for most average people.

By the 1990s, the conventional corporate wisdom held that restoring competitiveness absolutely required restructuring. Airlines, computer manufacturers, banks and financial institutions, oil companies, insurance providers, and defense contractors were eliminating jobs by the thousands. Unlike in the recent past, when companies hired back workers that had only recently been idled, most of these cuts became permanent. Economist Christine Chmura of the Crestar Bank in Richmond noted that "Rather than a company saying it's temporarily laying off 10,000 people for two months, they've been closing the factory and laying them of permanently."[27] Wout J. Kymmell, president of a professional search firm for computer specialists, corroborated Chmura's prognosis. "We see no immediate cause for celebration," he told the *Richmond Times-Dispatch* in 1991. "Corporate America will remain cognizant of costs for some time, and their current restructuring and downsizing will instill permanent changes within their environment."[28] Speaking only about the next year, but anticipating the employment trend of the decade, Kymmell expected large companies to hire only for specific projects and primarily to accommodate new technology. Real job growth would be in the small start-up firms, the companies that captured the headlines in the heady days of the technology boom. Yet these entrepreneurial wonders could only absorb a small percentage of the American workforce. Rather than a temporary correction to an overheated economy, Virginians were finding out that the economic ground was shifting under their feet. A combination of defense reductions, manufacturing streamlining, and mergers in the banking industry had precipitated 14,000 layoffs between January and September 1993. In the urban and industrialized Richmond-Petersburg area, approximately 2,800 people had lost their jobs during the same period. Even more ominous was a U.S. Department of

Labor study which reported that almost 8 out of every 10 people who lost their jobs during the recession would not get them back.[29]

Businesses eliminated jobs, but they also consolidated operations. They liquidated unprofitable divisions, collapsed managerial strata, and imposed lean production techniques that intensified the workload. The contracting out of functions that had previously been performed by the company, such as accounting, maintenance, data processing, and public relations, figured prominently in the corporate competitive strategy. Outsourcing was already in wide circulation in the early 1990s. It described not only the transfer of jobs to low-skilled, low-paying labor markets overseas, but also to non-unionized companies in the United States. The virtual corporation seemed imminent, one in which powerful decision-makers hired a few talented technophiles and contracted the physical work out to non-unionized, part-time, working-class drones.[30] As journalist Steve Pearlstein pointed out, the "common theme running through all these big corporate restructurings is the intense competitive pressures these companies are coming under, often after years of fat profit margins and more gentlemanly business rivalry."[31] The competitive corporation would be erected on the pillars of outsourcing, privatization, flexible work, and uncompromising cost reduction.

For the South, the recession aggravated the deterioration of its manufacturing sector, the hope for those who had escaped cotton tenancy and debt peonage. The 1980s had already witnessed the precipitous decline of the textile, tobacco, and apparel industries. While the region gained 6.6 million jobs that decade, only 68,500 were in the high-paying, relatively secure manufacturing sector. Even though southern manufacturing wage rates fell well below national standards, they provided a quality of life that fast-food restaurants, warehouse outlets, shopping malls, and hotels could not. Virginia was something of an exception here, adding valuable jobs in the construction industry to keep apace with the expanding suburbs and relatively mixed economy. Yet even in construction, workers experienced dramatic contraction, losing 18 percent of the total southern workforce. For the region at large, the percentage of workers in manufacturing fell from 27.5 percent in 1969 to 18 percent in 1989. Increasingly, low-paying, non-skilled jobs in the expanding service industry occupied the vacuum that the declining manufacturing sector created. The overwhelming majority of jobs generated in the service industry offered no benefits, minimum wages, and temporary employment. While southern employers shifted to contingent and less expensive labor, southern workers adjusted to lives of underemployment and indebtedness.[32]

This was a new phase in the saga of southern globalization, the same that brought European rice and cotton planters to the alluvial plains of the Carolinas in the eighteenth century and textile manufacturers to the piedmont region after the Civil War. It was not, however, the automatic result of forces beyond the control of American business and political leaders, north or south of the Mason-Dixon line. Corporate downsizing and reengineering was largely a homegrown phenomenon. They were an expression of the market-oriented movement that flourished in the South. The search for inexpensive labor, minimal taxes, and a compliant labor force would also compel manufacturers to look beyond the Sunbelt South to the maquiladoras of Mexico and the sweatshops of Central America. Before this trend spiked, the South once again provided the magnet for cost-cutting manufacturers and low-wage retailers. In 1990, the South led the nation in the number of part-time employees in search of full-time work. Consistent with southern tradition, African Americans crowded into the lowest-paying and least-secure jobs. In 1988, blacks constituted 19.5 percent of the regional workforce, but occupied 68.9 percent of the marginal service and blue-collar jobs in the South. The recession, corporate downsizing, the expansion of the service industry, and the intensification of the production process spelled a tenuous existence for southern workers.[33]

The recession was unique not only because of the unprecedented structural changes it set in motion, but also because of those it hit the hardest: white-collar employees in middle management. "It's a white collar recession," claimed Patricia Haynes of the Commonwealth Personnel Services. "Anything from high level office support right down to high-level management."[34] Middle managers constituted only 8 percent of the national workforce in 1990, but they comprised 16 percent of those dismissed during the recession that year.[35] As John Levin of the *Roanoke Times* suggested, "Empty desks are a symbol of the most startling differences between earlier recessions and the most recent downturn. This time the job cuts hit the higher-pay, white-collar positions that have a larger and more direct impact on consumer buying power."[36] While most retained their positions, few were spared the resulting insecurity.

Job elimination cut a wide swath in the commonwealth. Administrators, supervisors, quality control technicians, and sales managers found themselves vulnerable. The recession bit into the ranks of the corporate stalwarts, those who benefited most from the social contract. These were southerners who expected to move up within the organization and retire from it with a generous pension. Seemingly impervious to economic downturns in the past, this group—largely white, male, and over forty—was now disposable. The corporate rank and file in Virginia was no exception to this rule, which suggests the national scope of the recession and the downsizing cascade. It also suggests the irrelevance of southern exceptionalism. Southern workers might have been attractive to foreign investors in search of a pliable labor force—in May of 1993, the *Wall Street Journal* reported that "German managers have found the laid-back Southern workers more malleable than some of the aggressive, unionized people up North"[37]—but office managers in Richmond and Fairfax were as expendable as floor supervisors in Cleveland and New York. As George Kegley reported for the *Roanoke Times* in 1991, downsizing was running like a scythe through the ranks of middle management. At the Dominion and Signet Banks, at Crestar, Norfolk Southern Corporation, Gardner-Denver Mining and Construction, Service America, and Shenandoah Life Insurance, career managers were finding themselves being escorted out the door. Marjorie Skidmore of the Virginia Employment Commission observed that the "widget makers" were staying put while the supervisors were being eliminated through early retirement and dismissal. Career change seemed disruptive since few had the skills in demand by the New Economy. Yet pundits such as Robert Madigan, a Virginia Tech management professor, justified the developments by appealing to the inflexible laws of business competition. Clinging to the status quo was retrograde, a failure of nerve in an economy demanding toughness and sacrifice. The human losses were the inevitable detritus of an economy shedding its Paleolithic shell.[38] But the human face of disillusionment and economic hardship were all too evident. Their stories became part of the tapestry of American consciousness in the early part of the decade.

Anthony Payne, a second vice president who had spent twenty years at Shenandoah Life Insurance in Roanoke, was one of these. At sixty-two and nearing retirement, Payne was emblematic of the middle-class white workers facing career extinction and downward mobility in the New Economy. Shenandoah Life's decision to reduce costs through downsizing sent Payne tumbling from his position as vice president in charge of general agency operations into the growing fold of part-time contingent workers. First, however, he spent several months unemployed. Ironically, Payne landed a job teaching management at Virginia Western Community College, albeit for a drastically reduced paycheck.[39]

Payne, of course, was not alone. Michael Ludden of CSX Realty joined him in September 1991. The thirty-five-year-old native of Richmond, recent father, and new owner of a house in Henrico County found himself on the receiving end of a dismissal notice and was still unemployed in December. Several job interviews and a desperate willingness to accept a pay cut had still yielded nothing but disappointment. Probably conscious that his interview with the *Richmond Times-Dispatch* represented an opportunity to market himself, Ludden remained relentlessly upbeat. But so too did most of the newspaper reports, particularly the pro-business *Times-Dispatch*. "Though many are disheartened at first," the paper enthusiastically reported, "they quickly realize that through the years they have gained insights into the business world—insights that will serve them well."[40] The implication was that corporate layoffs were a necessary adjustment to irrevocable market developments; downsized workers had better accept that reality or perish. Like media almost automatically did throughout the decade, the *Times-Dispatch* invoked the authority of an expert. Richard J. Chagnon, a leading executive with Right Associates, a career-management consulting firm, pointed to global competition, minority hirings, and a reengineered workplace as the source of corporate downsizing. But Chagnon's advice illuminated contradictions at work in modern American industry. On the one hand, employees were expected to accept these structural changes and adapt. They were encouraged to believe that they could still exercise independent choice in this ruthless environment. Chagnon advised them to identify what was "important to them personally and professionally." Workers were finding out that the two goals were incompatible. Surely most workers would have preferred long-term stability and decent salaries. Now, they were being asked to accept contingency, to embrace "flexible" schedules, and celebrate managerial supervision. Simultaneously, they were required to endorse the corporate ideology of global competitiveness as the highest social value.[41]

The experience of Virginians in the throes of downsizing illustrated the shallowness of the hyperbole about the New Economy. According to business pundits, the middle class had been transformed into computer aficionados and maverick entrepreneurs willing to embrace the bumps and bruises of an unfettered marketplace. Yet few enjoyed real wage gains, let alone stock market profits. Even fewer held what an earlier generation of white, middle-class Americans had almost taken for granted: job security. By 1998, Virginians were no longer suffering the aftershocks of the recession; they were losing their jobs in what had become the permanent discipline of downsizing, an integral feature of a deregulated, globalizing capitalism. In 1995, for example, 14,203 workers lost their jobs between the second and fourth quarter (the numbers are incomplete for the year.) The numbers dipped the following year, but not by much. That year, 12,759 workers were separated from their jobs, a trend which continued for the rest of the decade. In 1997, 14,276 workers found themselves on the street. In 1998, that number climbed to 15,505, and positively skyrocketed the following year to 24,266. By the first year of the new millennium, the proverbial height of the New Economy era, Virginia workers were still losing their jobs in droves. That year, as the stock market soared and as the dot-com hysteria hit the stratosphere, 14,488 Virginia workers received a pink slip. The following year was worse, of course, as companies dismissed 18,803 employees in wake of recession. According to Bureau of Labor Statistics, then, more than 100,000 workers lost their jobs between 1996 and 2001 alone. Those were the best years of the New Economy 1990s.[42]

By 1998, of course, the majority of workers were not losing their jobs and the economy was certainly not in trauma as it had been in 1991. Yet most Americans lived under the cloud of economic uncertainty, job insecurity, and corporate unilateralism. Competitive techno-capitalism seemed to hold sway over competing systems of belief. The idea of social responsibility increasingly seemed a quaint notion. If in the years following the Second World War American business implicitly organized itself around the labor theory of value, ascribing merit to the work that skilled employees performed, in the 1990s, it reengineered itself around the idea that technology and managerial experts had a monopoly on value creation. By adjusting business strategies to the demands of seemingly arbitrary and inscrutable marketplace, they would maximize efficiency and stave off the perils of global competition. In this new economic dispensation, businesses were never certain that they had become competitive enough.

Yet as businesses sought discipline through downsizing, they inadvertently attacked the central pillar of twentieth-century American character: work. Rather than defining themselves by consumption and leisure, Americans had continued to forge their identities through work. For all of the post-industrial anguish of the 1990s, Americans still considered their careers and their work the central, defining feature of their lives. It was the foundation of their identities, and the wellspring of their self-worth. Severance packages, health benefits, and change management aside, Americans struggled to hold on to this core of meaning even while family cohesion, ethnic identity, and regional distinctiveness slipped away. Downsizing did more than challenge people's livelihoods: it threatened their sense of purpose and self-esteem. It threatened the fragile conviction that they lived in a democratic society where the principles of fair play, honest work, responsibility, and mutuality with one's co-workers prevailed. In a time of profound political cynicism, the world of middle-class work, with its rituals of group cohesion and opportunities for individual advancement, echoed the fundamental values of American society in the post–New Deal era. With all of its petty tyrannies and overtones of mass conformity, corporate life offered a stable ground of meaning and individual control for middling Americans.

It was this orderly framework that crumbled in the 1990s. Muriel Hayes was emblematic of the struggle of American workers to understand the fundamental shift in the economic cosmos. A college graduate and an employee of Reynolds Metals in Richmond for eighteen years, Hayes was dismissed in 1997 when the company initiated a restructuring program aimed at increasing industry-wide competitiveness. She earned a stable, $40,000-a-year salary and worked assiduously in an environment that was often stressful. Her work was the basis of her identity. "It was very interesting, very challenging," something which she "loved" and something to which she committed herself strongly. When the company added her name to the list of the six hundred employees that would be eliminated to reduce labor costs, her structure of meaning collapsed. Her experience mirrored that of thousands of American workers in the 1990s: "They called me into the office and told me I had to leave right then. All I could do was try to remember to breathe. . . . They got the stuff from my desk. A girl from down the hall helped me carry my things to my car and I never came back." The draconian dismissal became a familiar ritual in corporate America's downsizing pogrom. The callous ejections dramatically exposed the exploitive tendencies underneath the façade of corporate civility. For Muriel Hayes, it was devastating: "That job was the only stable thing in my life. It was like the maypole—everything wrapped around it. Everything operated because it was tied to that pole."[43]

Job displacement had ramifications beyond wages. Journalist Bob Rayner noted that the loss of workplace friendships, daily customs, and the satisfaction derived from productive labor undermined Hayes's self-worth. Steve Jayne, who lost his job when North Carolina's First Union Corp acquired Signet Bank, echoed Hayes's experience. When Jayne discovered that his son had written "Dad used to work for Signet Bank. He doesn't have a job anymore," for a fifth-grade assignment, he felt a powerful sense of lost dignity.[44] What exacerbated that loss for Muriel Hayes was the inability to get answers for her dismissal: "I think it was political. . . . It seems like no matter what you've accomplished, it means nothing."[45] Hayes's observation is important: downsizing was part of a shifting political economy that favored corporate prerogatives and the ethic of market individualism over social accountability. The commodification of labor was no cliché for the workers who endured the downsizing deluge of the 1990s.

While Hayes felt "empty," seeking solace in her church, Jack Grace, an accountant who lost his seventeen-year job at Reynolds, felt a profound loss of pride. "Not having a job," he reported in the gendered language of masculine breadwinning, "feels like they took a little bit of your manhood away." For hundreds of thousands of middle-aged white-collar workers, the shock of having to sell themselves on the labor market was distressing. What became clear in the era of free-wheeling stock market deals was that workers were not immune to the logic of the marketplace. Of course, they never had been, but the relative security of the New Deal order, with its systems of collective bargaining, corporate welfare, tariff protection, industry regulation, and American economic preeminence had shielded white, middle-class Americans from unrestricted competition. As Grace observed, "One of the hardest things was going to an interview, feeling like you got the job and then you didn't. The rejection part was tough." Despite painful periods of psychological distress, most downsized workers did find employment. For Grace, it was an improvement: a salary increase and additional responsibility. For Hayes, it meant a 20 percent drop in salary. Both reflected the labor-market pattern of the late twentieth century, which favored professionals with highly specialized skills and punished workers who lacked technological expertise. What both shared was a grinding sense of instability. As career consultant Philip Casesa explained, "People feel like they've lost control."[46]

The loss of control and the painful blow to personal dignity that downsizing inflicted was no more evident than in the experience of fifty-year-old Eddie Hurt, a salesperson who lost his $45,000-a-year job in 1997. A year and a half later, Hurt was still unemployed. "It's having nowhere to go that's depressing. . . . it's getting up and having no purpose." For Hurt, the rhetoric of retraining and flexibility offered little solace. He was struggling to find a job that would even approximate his old position, but in 1998 all he could find were jobs paying a third of his previous salary. While younger employees were taking stock options in high-tech, reengineered corporations, Hurt was struggling against lost self-esteem. His family bore the brunt of his despair. As his wife Lynn commented, "If someone would just say, 'I believe in you. You have a lot of knowledge that I need.' It would be such a boost to him. He hasn't had those words of encouragement in such a long time except from us . . . and we get worn down with it." Both had been unemployed in 1997, and when Lynn Hurt found work, it was a job paying a paltry $16,000 a year. The wired, NASDAQ-watching world of the New Economy meant little to white-collar workers like Lynn and Eddie Hurt.[47]

Hurt's experience exemplified the changing economic and social tenor of the 1990s. Using only Hurt's own recollections, it is difficult not to recall Arthur Miller's hapless Willie Loman, a character who encapsulated another generation's loss of individualism to corporate hierarchy. As Hurt explained, "I like working with people and providing a one-on-one service. I solved problems, did sales, dealt with everyone from top management down to the lowest level of employee. I was a one-on-one person." Yet Hurt's personable, low-pressure style seemed obsolete in the new competitive environment. Transforming itself from a not-for-profit mutual insurance company into a profit-driven corporation, Hurt's company began to privilege "bottom line" people over "service" people. Of course, from the company's perspective, the change was in the interest of efficiency and service. What was clear was that Hurt did not fit the profile of the technologically savvy team-player with his eye on increasing company revenues. As journalist Robin Farmer observed, "He believes businesses would rather hire someone half his age—someone with computer skills—and pay half the salary he would command. Hurt still values the ability to interact with the economy." Like Jack Grace, the shock of rejection in a competitive labor market was as distressing as losing one's job. The Darwinian character of the economy seemed inscrutable to people like Hurt. In April 1997, he began talking to a small insurance company that seemed interested in his skills and experience. They provided him literature on the company's marketing strategies and business plans and asked for Hurt's input. Expecting a job offer, Hurt waited through the summer, only to find out in September that the company was not prepared to hire in his area. For Lynn Hurt, the experience was crushing: "You can go through that so many times and then you don't have the courage and stamina to go back and do it again. . . . So I think something inside of you just gives up." Strained family relations, diminishing resources, drastically lowered expectations, and paralyzing disillusionment were no less a part of southern life in the late twentieth century than they were defining features of the national experience.

Eddie Hurt was not representative of all of Virginia's workers, but his experience reflected the hardships of 1.9 million long-tenured workers who lost their jobs in the 1997–1998 period. Nevertheless, this represented an improvement over 1995–1996, when 2.2 million employees were displaced by mergers and downsizing, and 1993–1994, when 2.4 million found themselves on the unemployment line. Those workers who lost their jobs in 1997–1998 tended to find work more quickly than their predecessors from the early 1990s. By 2000, 78 percent had been reemployed. That applied to 84 percent of workers aged 25 to 54. Yet these sunny statistics need to be balanced against other disturbing developments, those which correspond more closely to Eddie Hurt's reality. Of those people who had lost their jobs in 1998, almost 17 percent were unemployed or simply not looking for work any longer. For workers over 55, 40 percent had left the labor force altogether. While 61 percent of workers downsized in the 1997–1998 period reported earning as much in 2000 as they had in the three years earlier, 24 percent of those who found new jobs earned a full 20 percent less. Moreover, 90 percent of the people whose jobs evaporated in the 1997–1998 period had been working at full-time positions. By 2000, only 67 percent of these were working full-time jobs. As for the rest, 6 percent occupied part-time jobs, 5 percent belonged to the ambiguous ranks of the self-employed, while 21 percent were unemployed or absent from the workforce. Perhaps most tellingly for the Eddie Hurts of America, people in the age group from 45 to 64 were the only ones to suffer a median weekly earnings loss. The statistics suggesting that displaced workers suffered almost no loss in median weekly earnings need to be balanced against the evidence that for workers who stayed employed during the entire period, their earning moved up an average of 10 percent, an increase which unemployed workers did not share.[48]

Despite the dislocations of the early 1990s, the job market did expand in the second half of the decade. The majority of the downsized did find work and incomes did gradually increase, particularly for those with professional and technological expertise. By December 1999, the end of a nine-year growth period, the low-inflation economy had generated more than 16.5 million jobs. Yet the job growth had been concentrated in the higher-paying professional and technical sector as well as in the low-wage, low-skill service sector. Job growth in the mid-range, where Eddie Hurt and Muriel Hayes found themselves, stagnated. More than this, the dynamic job growth in both sectors did not result in a significant increase in earnings. Employment and wages in the middle range, where America's middle class struggled to hold onto their status and security, showed no significant change.[49] The polarization of employment and wages was part of a larger polarization of class and wealth. As the Center on Budget and Policy Priorities and the Economic Policy Institute reported in 2000, the earnings of the poorest one-fifth of Americans increased less than 1 percent in the gilded decade of the 1990s. In the same period, the income of the wealthiest fifth of American families grew by a remarkable 15 percent.[50]

Hurt's experience reflected the powerful forces that divided Americans along lines of socioeconomic class, divisions that the conservative rhetoric of the previous twenty-five years denied and which the high-tech hyperbole of the 1990s only obscured. While Hurt and others interpreted their failures in terms of personal loss, and while job consultants advised displaced workers to retool rather than dwell on the past, the ground under their feet was shifting. It was opening up gaps that pulled middle-class workers into the ranks of the temporarily employed, the underemployed, and the chronically insecure. Clinging desperately to their middle-class status, these workers were involuntarily expanding the ranks of the tenuously employed office proletariat. Technology boosters and New Economy champions paid little attention to the declining morale among middle-class workers.

Employees feared economic insecurity, but they also lamented the loss of what some described as "community" in the workplace. For the employees of Signet's consumer-loan unit, the loss was more than financial. The dismantling of that department destroyed the employee cohesion that had bound them together for years. Having worked together for over ten years and shared personal triumphs as well as workplace challenges, the fifteen-member group was despondent at the company's decisions. Through communal meals, shared celebrations, and workplace cooperation, they forged a sense of collective identity that is usually only attributed to blue-collar factory workers. As Steve Jayne recalled, "We were like brothers and sisters, it was that close. You didn't have to have people calling in sick because they needed a day off. . . . It was a very open environment. There was no back-stabbing. If there was a problem, it was dealt with openly. The bottom line was, you enjoyed coming to work." This was not the rapacious and self-interested world of corporate lore. Echoing the thinking of his co-workers who lamented the dissolution of the Signet "community," Jayne remembered that "Everybody got along. We were kind of in our own world; we had a job to get done and everybody chipped in and got it done, no matter what." Jayne and the others had organized themselves around values that benefited the company but did not simply reflect its prerogatives. Employee cooperation was built on joint interests, shared grievances, and collective experiences. Drawn together by the threads of shared responsibilities, Signet's employees established a cooperative milieu that fostered productivity. In the unlikely world of photocopiers and cubicles, they forged an egalitarian ethos that challenged the stereotype of ruthless corporate individualism. As Annette Lane, one of Jayne's co-workers, noted, she did not expect to replicate the communal experience she had enjoyed at Signet. "I don't foresee that ever happening again in my lifetime, and that's really sad. It's an interesting statement about what's happening to our society." The dismantling of the consumer-loan department did more than terminate jobs; it eroded the communal ethos at the center of the working lives of its employees.[51]

The disintegration of communities within the corporate structures of America paralleled the loss of stability that blue-collar workers experienced as a result of downsizing. When Elena Morales, a Cuban American woman, lost her job at the Singer Sewing Machine Company in New Jersey in the 1980s as part of a company-wide restructuring initiative, she felt adrift. "A whole way of life, an entire social contract, has been destroyed," observed historian Katherine S. Newman. "The loyalty that bound her family . . . to the firm has been replaced by a fragile, wary, instrumental work relationship." The patterns of worker-management cohesion that lasted despite labor actions evaporated in this new, pragmatic work environment. Unlike the white-collar workers in Virginia's office towers, Elena did not hold herself individually responsible for the loss of her job. The individualistic ethic of achievement applied more to middle-class Americans than to working-class Americans, who were more than willing to lay the blame on irresponsible companies. Even so, both groups mourned the loss of communities that had made work meaningful.[52]

Of course, companies were sensitive to the public relations fallout of massive layoffs. In an effort to cushion the blow and position themselves as responsible institutions, several companies set up job search agencies for recently dismissed employees. Signet Bank of Richmond, for example, funneled $250,000 into "transition centers" for pink-slipped workers in Baltimore, Washington, and Richmond. With telephones, computers, faxes, training seminar, and job-search counseling, the company sought to minimize employee discontent. Yet many corporate executives defended downsizing as a historical inevitability. They sought to invest it with normative value. As journalist Chip Jones jauntily put it, "Global competition, re-engineering, productivity—these have become the management mantras at Richmond-area corporations that control thousands of careers and a sizable chunk of the area economy."[53] H. Nathaniel Taylor, senior vice president at Signet Bank in Richmond, confirmed the sentiment. He described the process as "right sizing" and "rolling restructuring," emphasizing that it had become a constant in American corporate life. "Rolling restructuring is more or less a normal part of business management rather than a single event." If some companies thought they could get away with one fell swoop, Taylor believed, they were misguided. "This is done on an ongoing basis. American business needs to pay attention to cost structures. We eliminate positions, not people."[54]

But it was the people, not the positions, which had to live with the consequences of being terminated during a staggering recession. White-collar Virginians were losing their jobs at a time when companies were eager to hire low-paid, disposable workers. Having drawn reasonable salaries between $35,000 and $60,000, these workers were now told that they would have "a rough time" if they were "inflexible regarding salary and relocation."[55] Despite the uplifting stories about people using their unemployment to launch into bold new ventures, the reality was generally bleak. For those lacking the capital to start their own businesses, burdened by debt, or too distressed to risk what little they had left, the "opportunity" presented by a layoff was hollow indeed.[56]

Although business executives justified the radical restructuring as a non-negotiable response to the recession, there is some evidence to suggest that they considered it a convenient pretext for reducing company costs. Mary Houska of Hollins College suggested that "we started out thinking it was going to hit industries affected by international competition, companies that would scale down in the blue-collar area. But it's gone beyond that. All types of companies have taken the opportunity to decide they don't need this particular person or this function."[57] Houska's comments are interesting for two reasons. First, she identified the strategic significance that the rhetoric of globalization would play in rationalizing downsizing. At the same time, she underscores the pragmatism that influenced the decisions of at least some companies to shed workers. Even companies shielded from foreign competition would use downsizing and outsourcing to reduce costs.

There is good reason to believe that the globalization rhetoric was designed in part for domestic consumption. Economist Doug Henwood suggests that since the 1970s, "80% of us work in services—and a quarter of those in government—which is largely exempt from international competition." Globalization, Henwood argues, had little to do with Reagan's decision to fire the air traffic controllers, or Clinton's decision to endorse welfare reform, or the rising cost of tuition at public universities. Instead of globalization, Henwood argues that Wall Street's insistence on higher returns from corporate stocks was at the center of corporate restructuring.[58] If Henwood underestimates the domestic repercussions of losses in the manufacturing sector, which is certainly exposed to international trade, he underlines the political benefits that business derived from the leviathan of globalization. Journalist John Levin noted it in 1992. Surveying Roanoke's devastated economic landscape then, Levin submitted that "Either for financial necessity or simply the desire to boost profits, the recession was seen by many corporations as a handy way to slim the ranks of some of their best-paid workers."[59] Historian Frances Fox Piven makes a similar point. "While international competition has in fact devastated particular industries, for most working people globalization matters more as a rhetorical trope to frighten workers than as a direct cause of their deteriorating condition." Less vulnerable to international competition than corporate leaders would admit, the United States was also better able to protect its workers from ruthless competition than political elites would allow.[60]

In the early 1990s, though, the globalization mantra held ideological sway. Hugh D. Keogh, director of the Department of Economic Development, confirmed it. "You get more and more companies these days who admit publicly that it's not so much the recession that's causing these layoffs. The recession provides an opportunity to lay them off because people almost expect them to occur." Unlike Houska, a labor economist who might have been expected to be skeptical about massive layoffs, Keogh, representing a state agency that placed the interests of business first in a trickle-down schematic, applauded the changes. "Really the time has come for massive restructuring in American corporations. . . . to be competitive they have to be leaner. They have to reduce in some cases thousands of employees to be competitive." Astonishingly, Keogh believed that the recession provided a "helpful background to those kinds of layoff announcements." One wonders how "helpful" Anthony Payne and Michael Ludden found the recession.[61]

The recession and the corporate layoffs did more than put people out of work; they shifted the balance of power in favor of business. They created a cultural climate in which corporate decisions carried the air of incontrovertible truth. In the short run, this meant a labor market that favored newly streamlined companies. Rationalized and "right-sized," they became as unsentimental about dismissing employees as Hugh D. Keogh. It was a buyer's market, according to Bruce Potter of the *Times-Dispatch*. The causes were now a familiar refrain among journalists—corporate downsizing, changing marketplace, fiscal austerity at the level of state governments—but the consequences were only beginning to become clear. In Richmond, the public utilities, the banks, and the state government—the foundations of that city's economy—were in a virtual hiring freeze in 1992. For downsized workers of Virginia, the health care field, data processing, high-level computer programming, and entry-level positions ranging from housekeeping to custodial work offered the few signs of hope in a stalled economy.[62]

The shifting balance of power and the unapologetic ethos of business dominance were evident, then, in two important ways. The first was the rise of a human resource–oriented discourse of flexibility and retraining. The second was the persistent struggle of downsized workers to understand their experience in a world of diminished expectations. While businesses implemented the new management philosophy of contingency, employees continued to feel the aftershocks of the recession. At least in the public record, most accepted the new economic realities and followed the rubric of adapting to change.

Notes of discontent surfaced, however, and not only from the unemployed. In some cases, journalists editorialized on the vicissitudes of the New Economy and questioned the reigning economic dogmas. Beyond the glossy magazines announcing the triumph of a technologically driven, lean economy, there was another reality. Invisible to the investors following the stock market quotes at the bottom of the screen on MSNBC, unemployed middle-class workers sought to reconcile their ideals of individual accomplishment and American decline.

The clarion call of career consultants was for retraining. The New Economy required flexibility, not only in manufacturing, as we discovered in the previous chapter, but also in the cubicles of corporate America. It required technological skills of the kind that only specialized training could provide. The economic realities of the 1990s also dictated a willingness to accept change and uncertainty. Commentators eschewed political intervention. They denigrated union organization, dismissed demands for corporate accountability, and ignored calls for corporate executives to share the pain of downsizing. Instead, they offered dire warnings about the need for retraining.

According to Chip Jones of the *Richmond Times-Dispatch*, a "retraining revolution" was under way; those who failed to join its ranks would be swept away with the old order. If readers were "feeling comfortable" about their jobs, they were advised to consider Carol Jones's story, a student nurse at St. Mary's Hospital in Henrico County. After graduating from high school, Jones began working at Thalhimers department store. There, she moved from sales clerk to senior buyer of women's wear, never expecting to have another job in her working life. But workers in fields such as retail and manufacturing were confronting the "cold, hard focus of corporate America on 'downsizing,' 'restructuring,' and other means of cutting costs and boosting profitability. . . . The lean, mean economy has given a new urgency to a topic that used to rest on the back burners of economic development conferences."[63] Community colleges and municipal "transition" centers did a booming business in retraining. For the most part, this amounted to rudimentary computer instruction. Advocates expected that retraining would gear downsized workers for employment in the fast-paced world of information technology.

Yet retraining was part of the larger movement to reengineer the business environment for maximum efficiency. Just as southern industry provided the training ground for Total Quality Management, southern businesses became laboratories of lean office production. It mirrored the Just-In-Time and Total Quality Management initiatives that swept through American manufacturing in the late 1980s. The New Economy may very well have generated a "decentralized, skill-intensive" workplace, but reengineering accelerated the decline of worker autonomy through computer automation, standardization, managerial supervision, and quantitative productivity measuring.[64] The managerial revolution that Thomas H. Davenport championed in *Process Innovation: Reengineering Work through Information Technology* (1993) and which Michael Hammer and James Champy popularized in *Reengineering the Corporation* (1993) perpetuated the business practices that Frederick Winslow Taylor advocated in the early twentieth century. The scientific management project of rationalizing and intensifying the work process, removing inefficient steps, maximizing technology, and increasing supervisory control continued under the rubric of corporate reengineering. The elimination of health and pension insurance, the resistance to union representation in the service sector, and the persistent downward pressure on wages also figured prominently in the reengineering program.[65]

What separated the new managerial program from its Taylorite predecessors was the advent of computer technology. Personal computers and office networks, equipped with work-monitoring and labor-eliminating software, promised unprecedented levels of workplace productivity, control, and standardization. It gave rise to what Paul David described as the "techno-economic regime," which undermined the value of the workers' cumulative skill and experience. It also deprived them of control over the production process. Journalist Simon Head described it this way in his analysis of the computerized jungle: "There is the manner in which skill substitution and skill debilitation are taking place, with much of the workforce finding itself the passive tool of elite management and reengineering teams with virtually unlimited powers." More than this, computer business systems imposed on white-collar workers a level of supervisory control that had previously been the unique predicament of factory workers. More than organizational techniques, computer automation became the key factor in accelerating the proletarianization of white-collar workers in the 1990s.[66]

All that glittered in retraining, however, was not gold in employment during the unsteady days of the early recovery. Extolling the virtues of retraining, Chip Jones argued that "Sometimes, it involves training, other times, retraining. Whatever you call it, it leads to employment." As an example, he cited Ethyl Corporation, which planned to construct a $70 million additives research facility in Richmond. Anticipating jobs, J. Sargeant Reynolds Community College sent a group to the company's St. Louis plant to identify the skills that local residents would need for the new positions. Yet Ethyl had frankly admitted that "most of the jobs" will be filled from St. Louis.[67] What proponents of retraining often overlooked was that the New Economy's high-paying technical jobs required a level of proficiency that was out of reach for most downsized workers. University-educated engineers and programmers, not former sales reps trained in Microsoft Office, would command the highest salaries and greatest mobility in the information technology sector.

Moreover, the jobs were simply not there. All of the retraining initiatives and joint ventures between the private sector and higher education could not compensate for the general job contraction. Retraining was only adding to an already saturated marketplace of educated, skilled, white-collar workers chasing after too few decent jobs in the New Economy era. Writing in the new century, journalist Louis Uchitelle discovered that "the demand for jobs is considerably greater than the supply—at least 5 million greater than the supply, according to a study by Tim Bartik, a senior economist at the W. E. Upjohn Institute for Employment Research, and the existing supply of jobs is not what the reigning theory says it is." Virginia's mainstream newspapers would run dozens of articles complaining about unfilled jobs in the high-tech sector. Invariably, the conclusion they reached was that technological training was not supplying the expanding demand. Yet the abundance of unfilled jobs were often low-paying, contract positions requiring little expertise and offering few prospects of advancement. Instead of job creation, state and federal governments since the era of Jimmy Carter had channeled national resources into job retraining. Rather than job-generating social investment, they opted for the panacea of technical upgrading in the hope that skilled workers would command higher salaries and control their futures. Examining the problem in the early years of the twenty-first century, economist Jared Bernstein discovered that retraining did not alleviate the distress that outsourcing caused for skilled, white-collar workers in fields such as computer programming, radiology, and accounting. "The reason businesses move jobs overseas is the pay differential," Bernstein noted, "not the lack of Americans with such skills." The rhetoric of retraining only obscured the more fundamental changes at work in the American labor market.[68]

While companies eliminated positions and introduced labor-saving technology, workers at the lower end of the corporate hierarchy retrained for low-paying contingent jobs. A *Monthly Labor Review* study pointed out in 1991 that involuntary part-time employment constituted the largest share of contingent workers, a percentage that was growing "because more employers view them as a means to cut labor costs." In 1989, one-fifth of American employees worked part time, amounting to approximately 20 million people. A full 32 percent of these were found in the growing service sector, where 24 percent worked part time. Overall, 13.5 percent of part-time American workers wanted full-time jobs in 1989. Yet, as economist Chris Tilly pointed out, companies were moving toward cost-reducing, flexible employment and away from employee stability. Cost cutting had won out over reciprocal obligations. What made this particularly relevant to Virginia was the connection between technology and part-time work. Automation was transforming the retail and sales world, but it was also changing the way in which companies from financial services to food processing organized work. As Tilly noted, the insurance industry had moved quickly toward part-time employment in clerical areas such as claims processing. This was precisely where technology accelerated the use of contingent labor:

> The computerization of claims processing has facilitated the transition to a part-time work force in insurance—both because automation reduces the skill and training time required for claims processing jobs and because productivity when working on a video display terminal falls off after 4 or 5 hours of work. Thus, as in retail, technological change has speeded the spread of part-time employment.[69]

For some, information technology offered career advancement and power. For countless others, it meant additional de-skilling, reduced independence, and an intensified work routine under the closer scrutiny of cost-minded managers. For all, it meant living under the shadow of global competitiveness.

It was a remarkably amorphous but threatening reality that could be used to justify almost anything from dismissals to demands for overtime. The failure to participate in the company's mission suggested something more than maverick thinking; it indicated a failure to live up to the inflexible demands of the New Economy. According to business commentator Chip Jones, the stakes were internationally high. "For the United States to compete with Japan, Germany and other industrialized nations . . . a new kind of worker is needed: One who can read complex manuals, operate computers, work in teams and, generally speaking, remain flexible." Workers would have to adjust to the new managerial philosophy. Work protections and job control would have to give way to "adaptability" and "motivation and goal-setting."[70]

According to its proponents, retraining was a panacea in the global economy. In April 1994, the *Richmond Times-Dispatch* ran a story from the General News Service that encapsulated the ideological assumptions behind retraining. Recognizing that a new era of instability and downward mobility had begun, author Gene Marlowe encouraged Americans to embrace it. Marlowe introduces Bart Dominus, who left a job at Citicorp for a life of adventure on the uncertain seas of American corporate life. "Dominus is among a growing number of workers who have learned to thrive on the insecurity and change that is coming to characterize the job scene in this country." Dominus had already made the adjustment that American workers would be forced to make in the future. Again, the culprit was the unstoppable tide of corporate restructuring. Like H. Nathaniel Taylor, economist Audrey Freeman considered downsizing a permanent feature of American corporate life. For job consultant Maureen Clark, this meant that workers would have to adopt "a whole new way of thinking," nothing short of a "knock on the noggin—that's the kind of awakening it takes." Again and again, champions of flexible work in the New Economy likened it to a new "paradigm," a new way of looking at the world. Employees would have to relinquish their old habits and accept contingency.[71]

For all of the fanfare surrounding corporate teamwork, employees were expected to see themselves as atomistic units in a constantly shifting cosmos. If anything, corporate downsizing eroded the illusion of teamwork that twenty years of management consulting had tried to instill. *Richmond Times-Dispatch* writer Mary Beausoleil noted the pernicious consequences of large-scale layoffs. "Downsizing tends to work against team-building because it doesn't promote loyalty to the organization—one of the requirements for effective teams."[72] The idea of career was obsolete, "continuous learning," a must. Employees could not defend their positions; they would have to multitask.[73] Of course, by performing multiple tasks, employees participated in the process that increased their insecurity, since they never could gain a monopoly of expertise over a given job.

The essential requirement of the flexibility doctrine was the acceptance of computer technology. The message was simple: do not resist change. Quoting a management consultant, Gene Marlowe warned, "you show any resistance to technology or computers, and you can expect to be out on your butt." Career consultant Norman Feingold agreed: "Someone who is not flexible is not going to make it."[74] It was a mode of consciousness demanded of all workers in the modern economy, in Richmond no less than Seattle. Employees had to accept corporate objectives as the highest social good. They had to surrender control over their knowledge, skills, and much of their personal lives to the company. Companies had extracted obedience in the past, of course; what made this different was the increasingly unilateral character of the exchange.

In Virginia as in Massachusetts, rootlessness became the precondition for success in the New Economy. "As much as anything, people have got to get it out of their heads that they're going to be able to work someplace for a long time—or until they retire," claimed management consultant Maureen Clark. "Just as corporations reinvent themselves to stay competitive, so must individuals," asserted Jackie Greaner, CEO of EnterChange. Business was moving into a "new career model of constant reinvention, and that requires motivation." Clark and others queried the source for this motivation, since, according to her, "people are not motivated." Job uncertainty would provide the motive to propel this process forward. Gene Marlowe noted that "Thousands of telephone workers are expected to lose their jobs as automation of that industry continues. So, in some of the facilities operated by US West and AT&T, joint union-company programs are offered to employees to prepare them for the brave new world they may face."[75] The Aldous Huxley allusion aside, workers were being prepared for a world that generations of Americans would not have recognized.

American workers now had to abandon the idea of careers of reciprocally beneficial contracts and embrace a world mediated strictly by self-interest. If employees found themselves downsized, it was incumbent upon them to retrain. Companies were simply responding to market dynamics and irrevocable economic realities; employees would have to adjust. Yet pundits moved from advising American workers to embrace the reengineering agenda to blaming them for holding back innovation and competitiveness. Training rather than economic policy and corporate accountability would resolve the dilemma of American corporate decay.

While management consultants championed the new streamlined economy, working Virginians questioned an economic order bent on commodifying its workers. As the general economic climate seemed to improve after 1994, these voices were fewer and farther between. Critics were also unlikely to voice their opinions in newspapers and journals which employers just might read. Moreover, the business ethos itself discouraged criticism, not simply because corporate disloyalty is rarely rewarded, but because it reinforced the idea that questioning inevitable changes was simply absurd. Despite these obstacles, some opposed the New Economy. More than likely, they spoke for many others crowded into the nation's cubicles and corridors.

Van Costen of Chesapeake, Virginia, was probably speaking for many Americans when he responded to an article in the *Virginian-Pilot* titled "Is Capitalism Killing the Russians?" Titled "Global Capitalism Victimizes Many," his letter to the editor insisted that capitalism put corporate profits before the interests of average people. There was nothing terribly insightful about this observation, but Costen linked the "inhuman quest for corporate profits" to corporate downsizing, a process that threw people "out onto the streets. They, in turn, compel the remaining workforce to speed up production under the threat of future layoffs. People rendered unemployed in this process (if they can find employment) usually resort to lower-paying, part-time or temporary work to make ends meet." As the workforce atrophied, Costen argued, corporate revenues and CEO salaries increased. Official unemployment rates failed to capture the suffering of the homeless and impoverished, but also the temporary and part-time employees "with no health-care benefits and those whose unemployment benefits have run out." Probably few Virginians would have joined Costen in his denunciation of the IMF and the World Bank, or paid much attention to his attack on American companies operating sweatshops in the Third World. But for those who found themselves on the receiving end of a pink slip during the recession and those subjected to the rigors of retraining, his jeremiad rang true.[76]

So too did an editorial that appeared in 1995 that drove at the core of social insecurity in Virginia. After the obligatory nod to the supposed productivity benefits of corporate restructuring, the editors recited the litany of consequences it visited upon American workers: "Jobs are being transferred overseas. Out-sourcing replaces in-house help. Part-time work without benefits replaces full-time work. Poorly paid unskilled work replaces well-paid." Companies were doing no less than asking workers to "reengineer themselves out the door." Automation may be necessary, and global competition might be unavoidable, but the corporate environment was becoming increasingly hostile to the "humane use of human beings." The corporate agenda of efficiency through persistent downsizing and outsourcing was eroding trust. It was undermining the welfare of American families and the grasp of many families on middle-class status. Yet, as income distribution became increasingly polarized, managers were rewarded for treating workers "as just another commodity. Fire 10,000 and Wall Street applauds. The same management consultants who invented corporate re-invention now warn that more businesses talk the talk than walk the walk when it comes to giving workers a share in the profits their skills produce." Remarkably for conservative Virginia, the editors worried that class polarization threatened to "turn American democracy into banana-republic oligarchy." What the editors of the *Virginian-Pilot* questioned was one of the central dogmas of the 1990s: the idea that market relations should determine social value. Relations between employers and workers were not simply economic relationships. Instead, they were "part of a social contract that creates a stable society or undermines it."[77]

Journalist William Greider suggests that businesses did indeed have a distinctive place in the New Deal order. "Major corporations used to be part of the liberal social contract. They were the institutional partners that distributed health insurance, pensions, labor guarantees and other progressive benefits to workers and communities." Since the 1980s, though, business treated their workers as adversaries who drained away their profits. Reducing wages, pensions, and benefits as well as depriving employees of decent working conditions was part of a strategy to increase profitability. They also made the underconsumption argument that the Great Depression proved: workers without salaries are consumers without disposable income, a situation that is never good for business.[78]

While the *Richmond Times-Dispatch* usually ran stories justifying business practices or advising Virginians on how to manage them, they, too, periodically subverted the downsizing script. In 1992, at the height of the recession, the paper ran a story on the failures of the trickle-down economic theory that had provided the intellectual foundation for the Reagan and Bush era. As author John Cunniff recounted the theory, "If business was profitable, it was argued, it would invest in new plants and equipment, create jobs and enable workers to obtain better wages, benefits and in general a better level of existence." Yet the decline in real wages for the working and lower middle-class continued unabated in the 1970s and 1980s. The Los Angeles riots, which broke out after four police officers were acquitted of assaulting Rodney King, seemed to exemplify the consequences of a society polarized by wealth and power. Massive corporate layoffs and restructuring also challenged the efficacy of the trickle-down theory. Companies were apprehensive about any new hires. Despite the evidence of an economic recovery, the downsizing continued.[79]

In October 1995, for example, corporations laid off 41,000 workers with announcements for additional layoffs to follow. Even while the economy recovered, corporations such as AT&T announced job cuts that would affect up to 78,000 employees, while IBM put 1,200 employees on notice that they would be out of work. From January to October, according to a Chicago job placement firm, companies announced 343,000 layoffs. More disconcerting, Morgan Stanley and Company reported that by the end of 1995, 2.5 million jobs would have been lost since March 1991, the official end of the recession. The investment firm made an additionally distressing observation: employment had increased by only 8 percent during the latest recovery, a shocking contrast to the 14 percent job-creation rate during four previous recessions. This left 6.5 million jobs unrealized. A stalling economy and the impact of additional mergers were to blame. So too were the now-familiar culprits of aggressive cost cutting and profit enhancement through restructuring, outsourcing, and deregulation.[80] With this background, Cunniff and the readers of the *Times-Dispatch* had good reason to question the merit of supply-side thinking. Like the Keynesian economists of the Roosevelt years, Cunniff advocated investment at the base, in infrastructure, in companies that created jobs and invested locally. As other analysts began to realize, company profits were increasing not because the workforce had been magically transformed into an efficient "lean machine," but because the human costs had been radically reduced.[81]

The national economy did rebound from the 1995 regression, job growth at the upper and lower echelons did continue for the rest of the decade, and Virginians, like most Americans, did make real income gains in the last few years of the decade. The general indicators, however, did not capture the persistent mood of despair that underlay the glitter and hyperbole of the high-tech 1990s. Corporate restructuring, job uncertainty, and ephemeral wage gains were part of the story. So too were the psychological consequences of work in an aggressively competitive work environment where skilled autonomy and reciprocal obligations had evaporated. Despite the claims of Sunbelt exceptionalism, these realities persisted for Virginians and southerners.[82]

That reality was painfully evident for Margaret Braddy of Richmond. Nearing the end of a maternity leave in 1993, Braddy's boss asked to bring her newborn daughter to meet her at the Richmond airport. They hugged at the gate, sat down together, and as the employer juggled Braddy's baby in one arm, she handed her a manila envelope containing her dismissal papers with the other. Roche Diagnostics of New Jersey was restructuring, and Braddy, a technical representative in Richmond, was deemed an unnecessary cost. She rebounded from the loss within a few months, finding work with one of Roche's competitors. In 1996, two weeks before Christmas, she received a phone call notifying her of termination—the competitor had introduced a restructuring regime that once again made her redundant. It was Braddy's misfortune, but certainly not hers alone, wrote journalist Mollie Gore, to be caught in the wheels of "the new workplace, where the bottom line rules and companies cut jobs even in the good times. Try telling Braddy how great the economy is." Even though the economy in the Richmond area had generated some 40,000 jobs since 1993, termination through downsizing continued to be the fate of legions of Virginians. Despite the governor's announcement of "rosy employment statistics," her story illuminated the social forces that pummeled Virginians in the 1990s.[83]

The volatility at the center of the economy was equally evident to Bill Currie. A Vietnam veteran with a degree in business administration and twenty-eight years of experience, Currie found himself on the street when Nabisco went through one of its many rounds of downsizing in October 1997. As Currie complained in a letter to the *Times-Dispatch*, "Yes, the economy is great, tell that to the people like me who are looking for employment because of dumbsizing." Business proponents had sound reason to claim that this was part of the larger structural shift from a goods-manufacturing to a knowledge-producing economy. The manufacturing and financial services industries had lost, with tobacco manufacturer Philip Morris leading the pack by a total reduction of 2,500 jobs since 1993. But pundits claimed that growth in the information sector, particularly semiconductor manufacturing, as well as business services and health care would compensate for the losses. Some evidence suggested they were right. The semiconductor manufacturer had hired 800 workers and was planning to add 1,500 in 1999. Motorola, the shining hope for high-tech expansion in the Richmond area, was planning to build a manufacturing center that promised 5,000 new jobs. Yet the Motorola plant never materialized, a victim of the downturn in the semiconductor business. White Oaks, on the other hand, hired workers at $30,000 to $35,000 a year, which might have been attractive to community-college-educated Virginians but a considerable salary loss for people like Currie. Yet the calculations of who would hire and in what field were probably less important than the conditions under which people worked in the New Economy. As career consultant Philip Casesa noted, "Companies are acting as if 'the deal I have with you is . . . I'll keep you for as long as I need you and when I don't need you anymore, I'll shake hands with you and send you off.'" As journalist Mollie Gore understood, "Employers don't look at employees so much anymore as career long investments."[84]

It was the sense of floating in a constantly shifting universe of empty promises and half-truths that dramatically undermined confidence in the American Dream in the 1990s. More than this, American workers found themselves deprived of an idiom for expressing their discontent. Since business efficiency, market competitiveness, and consumer therapy had become the dominant social values, workers were routinely counseled to think positively, examine their own deficiencies, and let go of the past. Opposing corporate downsizing was not simply unfashionable, but wrongheaded and retrograde. With the collapse of social democracy as an ideological worldview, workers lost a critical perspective for expressing their disillusionment. Business imperatives dominated, not only in the workplace but in the realm of ideas and culture. Expected to espouse the platitudes of managerial reengineering, American workers legitimized a political economy that compromised the livelihoods of many.

As late as 1998, this grinding sense of insecurity was foremost in the minds of people who responded to the *Richmond Times-Dispatch*'s series on "Coping with Change" in the New Economy. As the editors pointed out, the idea of doing a story on job insecurity at a time when the economy was in full gear and allegedly churning out scores of high-tech positions seemed suspect. Yet the readers' response underlined the mirage of opportunity at the center of the New Economy. One respondent whose husband had lost a job in the downsizing blitzkrieg urged readers to understand the personal repercussions of unemployment. She also wanted them to confront the financial calculations that underlay corporate rhetoric. "People need to see the reality which we are facing. . . . The reality is that it was done to put money in [the company CEO's] pockets as well as the stockholders. . . . [My husband] lived for that company and served it with the greatest dedication. He also died because of it." Echoing these sentiments, another writer revealed that when her fifty-year-old husband lost his job, he took a lower-paying position, only to move to a series of other equally unattractive appointments. After this experience, "His spirit was broken." One reader pointed to the psychic damage that job loss inflicted at a time of intensified competition. "I'm now over 60 years old, and I find it so difficult to 'sell myself,' since I feel like all of my confidence is gone." Another highlighted the discrepancy between official claims about prosperity and persistent economic insecurity: "There are a lot of people who are still recovering from losing their jobs and taking any job just to survive. . . . No mention is ever made of that point." While many respondents emphasized the personal trauma of downsizing, at least one highlighted the class tensions that boiled underneath the surface of career "transitions": "I believe what we are seeing, if not corrected, may very well lead to the next civil war."[85]

Not all readers were as cynical as these. Some considered the termination of employment an opportunity to try out a new career option, leave behind an unfulfilling job, or spend additional time with families strained by the demands of corporate work. Others emphasized the importance of adjusting to changes and utilizing the resources available to find work that was meaningful. Considering the individualistic ideology that dominated American society in the New Economy era, these responses should not be surprising, although they should raise some suspicions. More than likely, workers invoked the ethic of competitive individualism out of a sense that any other response was socially illegitimate. Others may have emphasized the sunny side of downsizing as a psychological defense against the trauma of job loss. Regardless of how Virginia's workers responded to downsizing, few could escape the economic dislocations of the late twentieth century. Whether they strapped themselves in for a rough ride in the era of economic turbulence or descended into desperate self-loathing, Virginians shared the experience of living through a period when marketplace relations determined social and individual worth. It was anything but liberating.

More than this, fundamental class realignments were at work in the 1990s, pulling suburban southerners into the ranks of the tenuously employed and excessively indebted. The prerogatives of corporate competitiveness shredded the entitlements that many middle-class Virginians had come to expect. Downsized executives, administrative assistants, accountants, and sales clerks found themselves on the economic periphery, dispensable rather than valued and rewarded. Corporate life had never been as entirely secure as some remembered, but the experience of disposability challenged the key myths of American class mobility and business success. Downsizing challenged the ethic of individual self-reliance, one which urban southerners cherished as much as their northern counterparts. Class privilege really was fragile, they discovered; corporations really do operate according to the imperatives of profit and loss, and workers, no matter how qualified, really can be dismissed despite claims about the rewards of hard work. In the 1990s, white-collar employees found themselves adrift in a world where class positions were amorphous at best. The verities of social mobility through education, company loyalty, and dedicated service dissipated as the solidities of industrial America melted into the air of corporate reengineering.

As the editors of the *Times-Dispatch* poignantly noted, the responses expressed "a sense of anger and frustration, but also of perseverance and pride, of belief in the overall system but disdain for a process that sacrifices loyal, intelligent, hard-working employees to make a large profit larger and enhance executive bonuses."[86] Oddly enough, at a time when the wizards of the Internet and the prophets of e-commerce were proclaiming victory for the free market entrepreneur, class discontent was on the rise.

It was fueled by the sense that, for many average Americans, southerners included, opportunity had evaporated. This was not a return to traditional southern poverty or the inevitable result of colonial economic development. It was a moment when southerners joined other average Americans in the common experience of economic fragility. "Individual Americans who are neither economists nor statisticians do not focus on the economy's overall rate of growth," observed journalist Edward Luttwak, but "on the security of their own jobs." An unpredictable economic system, exposed to the gale winds of international competition, left businesses and jobs in jeopardy. Technological advancements meant to increase productivity had increased profitability at considerable human cost. The skyrocketing stock prices had little to do with antiseptic "reengineering"; Wall Street rewarded companies that relentlessly eliminated jobs. That explained why businesses that had recovered profitability were "not adding white-collar or middle-management positions; why businesses whose revenues and profits are stable are eliminating quite a few of those positions; and why businesses in decline are drastically reducing both white collar and management positions." The human costs of a deregulated, hypercompetitive economic order were difficult to measure, but that did not make them any less real. Challenging the Social Darwinian doctrines of the 1990s, Luttwak observed that "it is intuitively obvious that social losses must outweigh economic gains in many cases."[87]

More than debates over historical symbols, cultural pluralism, and moral decay, those "social costs" dominated the lives of working Virginians. The realities governing the experience of textile workers in Martinsville and office workers in Richmond could not be reduced to southern distinctiveness. In an era of fundamental economic change, southern exceptionalism disappeared.

While office workers turned to retraining, at least some working-class Virginians looked to labor unions for protection against corporate streamlining. Virginia had never been hospitable to unions, but the 1980s and the 1990s would test the assertion that the Old Commonwealth had freed itself from the scourge of workers demanding economic democracy.

CHAPTER 4

Wealth against Commonwealth

Southern Labor in the Era of Market Dominance

The misfortunes of organized labor have become such a prominent theme in the history of American workers that the optimism of labor organizers on the cusp of the 1990s comes as bit of a surprise. After more than a decade of concessionary bargaining, dramatic and unsuccessful showdowns between militant unions and resolute corporations, and daunting examples of government hostility toward organized labor—most notably President Reagan's unilateral dismissal of striking air traffic controllers—labor was hardly in a position for a comeback. But the 1989 Pittston Strike in Virginia, which saw coal miners engage in a successful but often violent strike to restore health benefits for retired workers and prevent subcontracting, signaled a resurgence in labor activism. It offered an example of working-class cohesion that emboldened workers and startled corporations.[1]

Propelled by the defiance of Pittston's miners, labor organizers set out with a new degree of determination. They focused on organizing the region's proliferating automobile and foreign-owned manufacturing establishments. What they failed to understand was that the Pittston strike was an anomaly. In a period when corporate interests were adjusting to the demands of an international economy, only a few unions had the solidarity to win on the picket line. For the most part, labor unions struggled on their own, politically isolated and lacking support from a broader public that increasingly imagined itself as consumers rather than active citizens. Considering the explosive growth of the service sector, organizing its employees was critical.

Even so, the last decade of the twentieth century was critical for organized labor. In this decade, labor unions began to capture some of the cross-class, biracial, democratic character that had distinguished its most important achievements. Virginia and the South were at the junction of this struggle to redefine the labor movement in democratic and movement-oriented terms. As private interests promoted a political atmosphere hospitable to market fundamentalism, the South became a model for anti-unionism. The South defined the "right to work" philosophy that was gaining national credibility in the late twentieth century. In the South, the movement for collective action ground against the ideology of self-interest and anti-government individualism.

While Virginia's labor unions failed to generate widespread support, they fostered a debate that redefined the cultural and political terrain in the United States. In conjunction with anti-NAFTA activists, they fashioned a set of ideas that challenged the ideal of corporate competitiveness as the highest social value and the only rational principle of public governance. Failing to restrain the downsizing deluge, they succeeded in generating public awareness of the erosion of democracy and social responsibility in the New Economy age. For the first significant time since the general strikes of 1946, workers began to foster a language of democratic activism and self-determination that challenged the dominance of the marketplace in public life. They did so at precisely the time when the unfettered free market was gaining unprecedented dominion over American workers.

Southern organized labor had always lagged behind its northern counterpart, but in the anti-union atmosphere of the 1980s, its plight was even worse. The collapse of the manufacturing industry, which had been a mainstay of the southern economy since the 1930s, the surge in the use of temporary workers, the expansion of the non-unionized service sector, and an orchestrated corporate anti-union campaign all contributed to organized labor's woes. The recession of 1982 generated widespread anxiety among American workers about simply holding onto a job. Coupled with the rising militancy of corporations determined to reduce costs through mergers and restructuring, American workers had little leverage against free market evangelists and anti-union crusaders, particularly considering that one had landed in the White House. The number of strikes launched in the 1980s was less than half the number that took place the previous decade. In those, almost a third of companies involved hired replacement workers, something which was almost unheard of before President Reagan's destruction of PATCO. More than this, organized labor engaged in seemingly interminable concessionary bargaining, accepting clawbacks, reduced benefits, slashed wages, and management-imposed Total Quality Management schemes that undermined the autonomy and security of manufacturing employees.[2]

Corporate anti-union campaigns and the closing of dozens of textile mills throughout the region left southern labor critically wounded. Between 1984 and 1988, union membership in the region declined by 12 percent. By 1990, a mere 14 percent of southern workers held a union card, compared to 19 percent throughout the rest of the nation. Across a longer historical plane, things looked even worse. Between 1955 and 1994, a time when the American labor force grew exponentially, union density declined from 33 percent to 15.5 percent. Virginia registered the dismal state of unionism in both the region and the nation: by 1995, its membership stood at a paltry 8.7 percent. Despite the exalted claim that anti-unionism had fostered southern economic growth, it was those states with the least union representation that suffered the lowest wage rates.[3]

In Virginia, organized labor rarely exercised political influence, serving instead as the state's "favorite political whipping boy"[4] in the post-war era. Governor Bill Tuck won the favor of Virginia's middle class when he intervened to prevent a Virginia Electric and Power Company strike. He followed it up by endorsing a right-to-work law made possible by the Taft-Hartley Act of 1947. The law prohibited the closed shop, meaning that employees could not be compelled to contribute union dues to a local even when they benefited from the union's contract. The right-to-work law inhibited union organizing and compromised union finances by compelling locals to bargain on behalf of noncontributing, anti-union employees.

Although union organizers succeeded in the tobacco industry of Richmond, the minefields of southwestern Virginia, and in the shipyards of Norfolk during the New Deal era, anti-unionism flourished. It was fueled in large part by McCarthyism and the anti-communist crusade against organized labor. In 1949, Senator Harry F. Byrd Sr. capitalized on anti-union animosity by portraying gubernatorial candidate Francis Pickens Miller as the "CIO-supported candidate." Organized labor enjoyed only brief political ascendancy when the AFL-CIO participated in a liberal coalition that elected Mills Godwin to the governor's office in 1965, followed by pro-labor governors Linwood Holton in 1969 and Lieutenant Governor Henry Howell in 1971. By the 1980s, however, conservative Democrats like Chuck Robb had decided to abandon organized labor for corporate interests and suburban voters.[5] Although Governor Douglas Wilder successfully courted the AFL-CIO, he did little to repay their support. Instead, he vigilantly upheld the state's right-to-work law, ignored union appeal for support against irresponsible employers, slashed state spending during a recession, and courted international businesses determined to take advantage of Virginia's depressed labor market.[6]

Following the dramatic strike at Pittston, unionism was anything but moribund in the region. In a piece titled "Nissan Is Not the Norm," the progressive *Southern Exposure* highlighted the revitalization of southern labor. While 2,300 workers at the Nissan plant in Smyrna voted overwhelmingly against UAW representation in 1989, 1,340 workers at the Freightliner truck plant in Mt. Holly, North Carolina, endorsed the UAW. While the national media trumpeted the Nissan defeat, they ignored the Freightliner victory, a breakthrough that challenged "stereotypes about organized labor in the South."[7] The greatest symbolic victory came at the Firestone Mill in Gastonia, formerly the Loray textile mill, the site of a mythic struggle for union representation in 1929 that led to the deaths of two police officers and one striker. The Gastonia Strike of 1929 had pitted communist organizers and workers radicalized by the stretch-out and declining wages against intransigent owners. Images of communist revolutionaries stirring up allegedly peaceful millhands turned middle-class Gastonians against the strike. In reality, party activists organized an already militant and rebellious group of millhands who had proven on more than one occasion that they were willing to engage in spontaneous, disruptive, but largely ineffective walkouts. It also ensured that the court cases for the alleged murder of the two police officers and the killing of union balladeer Ella May Wiggins became legal travesties. Even more, the failure to organize the Loray Mills cast a pall over union activity that even the General Strike of 1934—in which Gastonia workers eagerly participated—could not lift. Despite company threats to close the shop and despite the failure of organizing efforts in 1987, the United Rubber Workers won an election in 1988 that overturned the myth of working-class indifference to unionism in Gastonia.[8] And despite the membership slide of the 1990s, Virginia unions won almost half of their organizing campaigns in the 1980s. Between 1984 and 1990, AFL-CIO membership climbed by 15 percent to 115,000 members. Despite the hemorrhaging of union membership through the decline of railroads and mining, Virginia's organized labor remained stable.[9] But that was before the recession of 1990/1991.

Workers in the South increasingly faced the prospect that the industries offering the highest-paying jobs and the best prospects for unionization would disappear. The South's low wages, abundant resources, and official anti-unionism had been responsible for drawing northern and foreign investment since the late nineteenth century. That trend accelerated dramatically during the Second World War when the federal government spent millions on defense contracts in the region. Subsequent defense spending and the flourishing of the federal highway system launched the South on a path of industrialization that New Southerners like Henry Grady and the cotton mill boosters could only dream of. Yet foreign manufacturers continued to be drawn to the region for its pro-business climate. In following the charm of cheap workers and low taxes, foreign firms perpetuated the low-wage economy that domestic investors had cultivated for years. As two economic geographers explained, "By turning the region's long-standing dependence on low wages into an asset, the states of the U.S. South have created a business climate that emphasizes deregulation, low social overhead charges, and lax environmental and business standards."[10] Even so, defense spending and foreign investment benefited the region and the rural South in particular. Federal investment in the South increased wage rates and living conditions well beyond what sharecropping and tenancy could ever offer.

In the late twentieth century, the South figured prominently in private enterprise's escalating search for shelter from the costs of social regulation. It made the region one of the principal targets for globalization in the era of transatlantic slavery but also in the twentieth century, as northern corporations fled the bargaining power and social costs of operating in the North.[11] With the decline of the textile industry and the shift toward service industries paying decidedly lower wages than manufacturers, the region's working class found itself on the losing end of the New Economy, which privileged skilled employees over the South's poorly educated and technically uninitiated rural dwellers. While the percentage of white-collar jobs grew in the 1980s and 1990s, many of these positions were filled by highly qualified transplants from the Midwest and the North. Between 1975 and 1994, skilled and partially skilled blue-collar jobs declined from 40.3 percent to 28.2 percent of the total. At the same time, the least-appealing jobs—the largest portion of which were unskilled service-sector positions—increased from 16.7 percent to 19 percent of the total workforce.[12]

The racial stratification of the southern working class remained depressingly consistent. In 1994, almost 30 percent of white men occupied the highest-paying category of white-collar positions, including the managerial and professional strata. On the other side of the spectrum, more than 40 percent of African American men occupied service and manual labor positions, while a mere 8 percent of black men sat behind desks in southern offices. The concentration of African American women in the category of working poor and their negligible upward mobility was even more conspicuous. In 1994, most black women worked in service, pink-collar, and manual-labor positions. That year, 50.8 percent of black women toiled in these positions, a stunningly slight change from 1975, when 51.4 percent of working black women filled service and laboring positions.[13]

These figures tell a larger story of growing economic insecurity and downward mobility in the region. As the authors point out, "Job losses for black and white men in the South have been most strongly felt in blue-collar skilled crafts and semi-skilled operative positions, which accounted for 46.7 percent of the male workforce in 1975 and now only accounts for 37.7 percent of men's work, a 19.3 percent loss."[14] The loss of comparatively high-paying manufacturing jobs in a region where low-wage service-sector positions were becoming the norm for the working class made labor organizing all that more urgent.

In Virginia, this meant organizing the grocery stores in the Hampton Roads–Tidewater area, an economically stagnant region hit hard by military cutbacks in the early 1990s. In April 1990, Local 400 of the United Food and Commercial Workers Union—the second largest in the AFL-CIO after the Teamsters—initiated a campaign to organize 7,000 workers at the Farm Fresh, Be-Lo, and Gene Walters's Marketplace grocery chains in Hampton Roads. UFCW had already tried to break this anti-union stronghold in 1986, but to no avail. As economist Gilbert Yochum of Old Dominion University observed in the *Newport News Daily Press*, the paucity of manufacturing in the region explained the dearth of unionism, since unions traditionally followed large-scale industry. Yochum also ominously suggested that union drives are most effective when they target an entire industry rather than a particular company; in 1990, that is precisely what the UFCW would do.[15]

For the UFCW, a union with 1.4 million members and a virtual monopoly in the Washington area, the Hampton Roads stores seemed a natural extension of their sphere of influence. Yet the campaign was motivated as much by fear as by hope, considering that Super Fresh, with twenty-three stores, was the only unionized grocery chain in the region. Of the UFCW's 43,000 members, only 2,000 worked in Hampton Roads. Even more forbidding was the prospect of organizing where UFCW once had a considerable foothold. In the 1980s, the Safeway and Big Star chains operated some fifty stores in the region, all of which UFCW had organized. By 1990, Safeway had whittled their investments down to one store, while Big Star had disappeared, both allegedly driven out of the Tidewater area by the high cost of labor.[16] As these unionized chains retreated, the non-union Farm Fresh and North Carolina–based Food Lion advanced, opening in excess of one hundred stores and absorbing some 60 percent of the grocery market in Hampton Roads. The Gene Walters's Marketplace and Be-Lo were also non-unionized, meaning that when UFCW launched its campaign, 75 percent of the supermarkets in the area were non-unionized.[17] The *Roanoke*

Times captured what was at stake for the union: "A multibillion-dollar business that dwarfs the non-union Tidewater chains, Food Lion could have the muscle to drive down wages and prices, pushing out both the union and the other chains."[18]

For UFCW and organized labor in the South, eastern Virginia represented the future of American work. It seemed to be a perfect manifestation of the low-wage service economy that absorbed so many nonskilled workers. Yet the struggle over the quality of employment in the grocery industry was equally important for what it said about American society. In an era when Americans imagined themselves principally as consumers rather than as citizens, when the marketplace enjoyed an apotheosis that rivaled popular culture icons, and when corporate executives championed competitiveness as a moral virtue, the lowest prices and the widest selection seemed to define American progress. Advertising and marketing schemes reinforced the idea that shoppers could expect "low" prices and high quality, a dubious combination in any market but even more suspect in an area of depressed wages. The Be-Lo struggle highlighted not only the travail of labor in the anti-union 1990s but also the conflict between market values and the legitimate desire for at least a minimum of workplace dignity.

Under the leadership of Thomas R. McNutt, the outspoken president of Local 400, the union launched a $100,000 campaign to organize the grocery store workers, many of whom earned $4.00 an hour, just twenty cents above the minimum wage.[19] In the course of an emotional year-and-a-half-long campaign, the UFCW would spend $1.5 million.

With so much at stake, and conscious that the campaign was part of a larger movement to restore the democratic ideals of the Great Society, the UFCW called on the Reverend Jesse Jackson to kick-start the campaign. A symbol of liberal idealism and the biracial working-class movement of the 1960s, Jackson promised to build a bridge between black and white workers in the era of corporate downsizing. Jackson brought more than star power to Norfolk. It was the intellectual and moral thread spun by Martin Luther King, Walter P. Reuther, Bayard Rustin, and Robert F. Kennedy to bind American society to something more than profit maximization. It approximated the egalitarian ideals that stirred American reformers from the Populist era to the civil rights movement. Appearing at the Center Theater in Norfolk along with 300 UFCW supporters and a small but energetic crowd, Jackson called on them to "rise together. We are one people. This is our country." For Jackson and the UFCW, the issues went to the core of the southern political economy. Since the era of New South boosterism, the region had predicated its economic growth on low wages, external investment, extractive and rudimentary manufacturing, and labor policies favorable to business. In the midst of textile mill closures, the resurgence of the region as an anti-union haven for northern business, and the rumblings of recession, Jackson encapsulated the dominant issue for average people.[20]

Jackson advocated a program of racial cooperation and economic democracy that reflected the interests of all working people: "The challenge of the New South is justice at the work place. We must move from the battleground of racial hatred to the economic common ground and from there to an ethical higher ground."[21] At a time when the political left championed cultural and racial differences, Jackson and some unionists promoted racial egalitarianism and class unity, the theme of labor progressives in the heyday of reform. Invoking what would become one of the central tenets of progressives in the last decade of the twentieth century, he called for a "living wage." He also appealed for health care for the millions of uninsured workers who served as a constant reminder of the limitations of New Deal reform.

In Norfolk, at the beginning of an obscure union drive, he directly challenged the individualistic, neo-Darwinian code that dominated the United States in the late twentieth century. He asked the most obvious question of modern labor relations: "If work won't get you of out poverty, what will?"[22] The two-time Democratic presidential hopeful rejected the neoconservative argument that any job was better than none, regardless of the wage. "It's not enough to have a job. In slavery everybody has a job."[23] Local 400's Thomas McNutt situated the campaign to organize the supermarkets in the context of economic developments that dominated the national landscape in the 1980s: "I think people here are fed up. Every time there is a merger or a leveraged buyout, these people lose money. . . . Workers see their wages and benefits cut, while management and the stockholders divide huge profits."[24] More than this, Jesse Jackson drew the connection between the economic despair of working-class Americans and the ideological values lodged at the highest levels of power: "The government has induced poverty, and placed the burden on the backs of poor people." Accusing then-president George Bush of equivocation on taxes, he castigated Virginia's right-to-work law, arguing that the Old Dominion and its southern counterparts used the measures to attract companies hunting for low wages.[25] Disentangling exploitive labor practices from the thicket of free market rhetoric, Jackson made the case that political elites had advanced private corporate interests at the expense of the working majority.

For the supermarket management, the central issue was not justice in the workplace but survival in an intensely competitive industry. Michael Julian, president of Farm Fresh, cast the struggle in terms of the tension between consumer and worker demands. "My responsibility as chief executive of this company is to find a way to satisfy the needs of our customers and at the same time satisfy the need of our employees."[26] In a business in which low prices had become the dominant axiom and where small chains competed against expansionist supermarket giants, profit margins were distressingly meager. Citing a 1988–89 Food Marketing Institute study, the *Newport News Daily Press* explained that most grocery stores earned $1.41 on each $100 of net sales, with 15 percent of company expenditures dedicated to employee wages and benefits.[27] Julian claimed that wages would rise when productivity increased or when the company acquired the equipment to increase employee efficiency.

In effect, what Julian and the other supermarkets endorsed was the retail version of manufacturing's "management by stress." Through longer hours, unpaid labor, fewer benefits, intensified supervision, the looming threat of dismissal, and replacement through automation, Virginia's supermarkets, like its manufacturers, would wring additional profit from labor. More than this, the supermarket's predicament reflected the willingness of business to compete over wages and benefits, jeopardizing the livelihoods of low-income southerners in the process. As economist Michael Zweig pointed out in *The Working Class Majority*, competition can promote productivity and the efficient utilization of resources, but it does not necessarily achieve these results or improve the lives of working people. Limiting competition—in effect, removing wages from competition—was the solution in the post–World War II era. At that time, industrial unions like the UAW compelled the leading companies in an industry to provide equitable remuneration for all workers. Standard agreements in mining, automobiles, rubber, steel, clothing, and trucking stabilized wages and protected profits. This system of industry-wide negotiating disintegrated in the late 1970s, when Chrysler convinced the United Auto Workers to accept wage and workplace concessions in order to save what the company claimed were 200,000 threatened jobs. The era of concessionary bargaining had begun. General Motors and Ford—both of which were profitable at the time—used the Chrysler precedent to demand concessions from their workers as well. When Congress endorsed the deregulation of the airline and trucking industries, shredding the industry standards that had protected customers as well as employees, companies engaged in ruthless competition that put pressure on unions to yield ground on job security and wages. Nonunionized companies flourished in the new competitive environment. The Teamsters' saw their industry-wide agreement disintegrate as companies insisted on negotiating on a one-to-one basis with the union. Zweig argues that the "easier it is for management to respond to competitive pressure in destructive ways, the less likely it is to take the more difficult path of technical innovation or quality improvements."[28] Facing market pressures and the burden of managing health care costs that the federal government would not assume, supermarkets brought wages, benefits, and the jobs themselves into full competitive play.

The ramifications of the service industry's commitment to low wages and limited job security were clear to many of the workers in the Hampton Roads area. Concealing the identity of a worker "too afraid to let her name be used in a newspaper," the *Virginian-Pilot* humanized the campaign by including the perspectives of the workers themselves. The paper recorded the grievances of a thirty-five-year-old single mother making her living as a part-time checkout clerk at a Farm Fresh store in Norfolk. On an average week, she earned $150, or $7,200 a year, almost half of which she spent on rent for a one-bedroom apartment. Lacking health insurance and spending most of her income on basic necessities, the anonymous Farm Fresh employee faced an unpredictable future. Angry at her predicament, the checkout clerk hoped that the organizing campaign would deliver a union to the Farm Fresh employees. "Nobody should have to try to live on what they pay. . . . A union could change that."[29] When UFCW organizers Chad Young and Lynn Colbert visited a supermarket delicatessen employee at home, they found that she earned $3.80 an hour and worked part time. They also found someone ready for union representation. Making $100 a week and lacking health care coverage, the female employee "hope[d] they [would] get a union in here. . . . They need something."[30] Evey Brake, a twenty-eight-year-old seafood wrapper at a Farm Fresh store in Newport News, echoed these sentiments. "We need higher wages. . . . I really like working for Farm Fresh and I like the people I work with, but I don't see a future in it." Earning $4.15 an hour while supporting three children, Brake belonged to the working poor that staffed the service sector of the modern South.[31]

It was in response to grievances from workers like Evey Brake that Local 400 launched the 1990 organization drive. When a former Food Lion employee initiated a lawsuit against the store's profit-sharing program, Local 400 began receiving inquiries from dozens of grocery workers in the area expressing an interest in unionization. The union added its support to the lawsuit, alleging that Food Lion dismissed employees before they could collect on their profit-sharing increment. Employee discontent at Food Lion convinced the union to try once again to organize the more vulnerable Farm Fresh. Union organizer William Freund observed that the renewed campaign generated immediate interest. "The more we asked questions, the more we found people being used."[32]

Convinced that the time was right for a union push, UFCW 400 sent fifty organizers, including Thomas McNutt, into the Hampton Roads area. They simultaneously launched a media campaign featuring billboard, radio, and television advertisements. Organizers approached workers on their lunch breaks to promote union representation, only to find many too anxious to discuss the drive in proximity to managers and supervisors. As organizer Juanita Fridley explained, "If you're a worker and management wants to get rid of you, they scheme something up. The workers are frightened of management. They're frightened of us. They're afraid of losing their jobs."[33]

Not all Tidewater grocery store employees yearned for a union, and local newspapers were at pains to highlight the other side of the story. Kathy Bright, a backup scanning coordinator working full-time at a Farm Fresh store in Chesapeake, shared management's antipathy to the union. According to the business reporter assigned to the story, Bright was pleased that the company recognized her talents and had given her a chance for upward mobility. "To me, a supermarket is no place for a union. Why should I go to a union and let a union talk for me when I've got a mouth and I can talk for myself?" Bright's individualism—perhaps even her southern independent streak—was noble, if naive. Considering the capacity of companies to dismiss or simply ignore employees when their expectations exceeded the company's willingness to comply, Bright's confidence in her ability to negotiate on her own was misplaced. She also failed to acknowledge that the resilient independence she cherished so much played directly into the company's strategy of divide and conquer. But Bright wasn't alone. Laura Brickhouse, a fifty-seven-year-old floral delivery person for Farm Fresh, told the *Virginian-Pilot* that she simply ignored the organizers. "I've worked for a lot of companies, but as far as I'm concerned, Farm Fresh is one of the best. I don't think the union could give us more than what Farm Fresh has done."[34] According to Letha Gaythan, a thirty-year-old woman in charge of a Farm Fresh bakery in Virginia Beach, the union was a nuisance, a sentiment which she believed her employees shared. Earning $425 a week and looking forward to a $4,000 bonus, Gaythan was certain that Farm Fresh was a better employer than the unionized Super Fresh where she had once worked. "You always hear hype about how unions can get you so much money. . . . They didn't do nothing for me."[35] Clearly, not every Farm Fresh employee groaned under the weight of capitalist oppression.

Yet each of the pro-management employees interviewed was themselves in a quasi-management position, enjoying higher wages than other front-line workers and at least a modicum of independence on the job. Delivering flowers and running a bakery were not the same as logging hours behind a cash register or stocking shelves under close company scrutiny. At the same time, not every employee understood the vulnerability of other workers or themselves when companies decided to downsize, merge, or shift work to another facility. In addition, Gaythan expressed the persistent southern suspicion of so-called outside agitators, a sentiment which regional business actively cultivated.[36] Gaythan's comments are revealing: to her, the organizers were "professionals" with "New Jersey or Massachusetts plates on their cars."[37] While Gaythan recapitulated age-old resentments of non-southern unionists—a theme that pervaded the Gastonia strike as much as the General Strike of 1934—she also pointed to one of the weaknesses in the union's strategy: its inability to develop solid leadership from within the ranks of company employees. When the UFCW came to town, Hampton Roads' grocery employees were once again faced with organizers who were at least unfamiliar and at most threatening, particularly since two unionized chains had recently fled the area rather than pay a union rent. Conditioned by the media's generally negative appraisal of unions and cynical about union promises of improved wages, some workers dismissed them as an unwanted intrusion.

Yet the company's anti-union tactics and its determination to make labor more "flexible" were fully evident in the weeks leading up to the election. Even before Jesse Jackson arrived in Norfolk, the UFCW filed grievances with the National Labor Relations Board, citing Farm Fresh and Bonnie Be-Lo with unlawful surveillance as well as intimidation and threats against workers and union organizers. In reporting the charges, the *Daily News* typically sought comments from Farm Fresh executives, but not from union officials. Linking the grievances to Jackson's appearance, the paper implied that they were part of a publicity stunt that included the antics of America's best-known civil rights preacher.[38] Closely observing the operation at Farm Fresh and meeting with its staff, the union documented what it believed were unfair labor practices. As union organizers reported to the *Daily Press*, employees were forced to work more than forty hours without overtime pay, to work "off the clock," and to continue working through break times without additional pay. Company officials dismissed the charges, but they also provided insight into prevailing attitudes about unionism in the South and in the United States at the time. According to Farm Fresh CEO Michael Julian, "The union mentality does not fit Farm Fresh Inc."[39] And what was the "union mentality"? Presumably, what Julian invoked was the well-worn stereotype of the self-serving, time-clock-watching union member oblivious to productivity and more than willing to fleece the company. But this rhetoric stood in stark contrast to the ideals and behavior of the unionists themselves. In meeting with grocery store employees, organizers asked them about their experiences, identified their grievances, and legitimized their perspective. They offered the hope of democratic representation in a workplace defined by arbitrary authority.

Of course, one shouldn't romanticize a union drive or overlook its pragmatic features. Organizers were interested in signing people up; to do so, they had to sell the organization, and the union hierarchy benefited from additional dues as much as members from the bargaining power that unions provided. They launched organizing drives to benefit unions hammered by attrition. At the same time, they endured company intimidation, worker suspicion, hostile communities, and the likely prospect of failure to promote the idea that working southerners should have some control over their economic destiny and a measure of dignity in the work they performed. While the 1990s turned into the decade of the sales pitch for stocks, bonds, mutual funds, and company loyalty programs, UFCW organizers fanned out across Hampton Roads to remind workers of a tradition of American economic democracy and of their rights as productive citizens. Instead of top-down managerial manipulation through paternalistic metaphors, the UFCW tried to redress the inequalities of power at the center of the service industry in the South. This challenge to the ideology of consumerism over citizenship, of unearned returns on investment over the value of production, and of buyer entitlement over workers' rights stands at the center of why the labor movement mattered in the post-Reagan era. It also put the union and sympathetic workers on a collision course with the companies.

The companies stepped up their anti-union campaign in the months prior to the March 1991 election at Be-Lo. The *Roanoke Times* reported that Farm Fresh CEO Michael Julian had written to employees asserting that unionization "could lead to loss of benefits and to strikes, union dues, assessments and employment of replacement workers who would put striking Farm Fresh workers permanently out of their jobs." In language reminiscent of countless efforts to stigmatize northern labor and civil rights activists,

Julian appealed to his "Farm Fresh family" not to allow "the outsiders to divide us."[40] According to union officials, Be-Lo—which, as the weakest link in the chain, had become the focus of the union election drive—fired forty workers for union activism and for wearing union badges and T-shirts. By the time that employees voted on union representation, the National Labor Relations Board had determined that there was sufficient evidence to warrant an investigation. The board also lodged a complaint against Harrell and Harrell, Inc., the owner of a number of Be-Lo stores in Hampton Roads.[41]

The Be-Lo campaign raised and dashed the hopes of organized labor in Virginia. Despite the yearlong campaign, the massive expenditure of resources, and the optimism of union supporters (lawyer Carey Butsavage believed on the day of the election that "it looks real good. . . . I think our people are solid. . . . It's going to be a great victory for us"),[42] the election at thirty Hampton Roads Be-Lo stores went against the union, 377 to 220.

Or so it seemed. Immediately following the disappointing results, UFCW lodged a protest with the National Labor Relations Board, claiming that company intimidation voided the election results. "This kind of situation is usually the kind of situation where the NLRB will issue a bargaining order," Thomas McNutt believed. "There's no question we'll get a rerun."[43] Company officials didn't see it that way. According to Be-Lo lawyer Stanley G. Barr, the election tally suggested that the employees were "a smart bunch of people. . . . They understand the company is doing the best it can for them. We think this is an expression of confidence in the company."[44] But the allegations of wrongful dismissals for union activity wouldn't go away. Michael Salazar, a former assistant manager, told the *Virginian-Pilot* that one week before the election, "They fired a bunch of people," including himself, for supporting the union drive.[45] McNutt was even more indignant with the *Richmond Times-Dispatch*. "Given the level of intimidation, harassment, and threats that the work force has been subjected to, it's amazing that there were as many pro-union votes as there were."[46] The drive for unionization generated a spark of hope for people battered by military and corporate downsizing, the recession, and the frustrations of underemployment. As Rob Crawford, a Be-Lo night stock clerk and union supporter, explained after learning of the election results, "People here are tired of getting a raw deal. . . . They want a better life."[47] That sentiment would soon be shared by the workers and activists who joined the anti-NAFTA campaign.

For McNutt and the union, delivering on the promises of a better life meant escalating the pressure on Be-Lo through a full-scale boycott. In this effort, they tapped into a reservoir of resentment toward what some believed were discriminatory company practices. By April 1991, the union had mobilized pickets against the store and was calling on residents to boycott Be-Lo. Local church leaders lent assistance to the campaign, which eventually picketed ten of the thirty stores in the area. The Reverend Rudolph Smith of the Bethany Baptist Church in Chesapeake played a key role. He organized churchgoers to protest what he claimed was the supermarket's practice of selling out-of-date and poor-quality food to its inner-city, largely African American customers. He and other religious leaders established the Ministers and Concerned Citizens of Tidewater. They also contended that the store routinely charged its inner-city customers more than its suburban patrons. Activists held a rally at the Norfolk Downtown Plaza Be-Lo, distributed thousands of leaflets at local churches, and volunteered vehicles to transport customers to other stores. Stanley Barr acknowledged that the boycott was hurting the company. Thomas McNutt fully expected that to happen: "The purpose of a boycott is economic pressure. . . . If that results in the fact that they can no longer operate, they know the consequences."[48] The problem was that the boycott also negatively affected Be-Lo workers, some of whom presumably may have been sympathetic to the union. "They're trying to destroy our jobs," one anonymous employee asserted, "that's the way I see it."[49] The divisions were clearly evident in the parking lots of Be-Lo supermarkets, where management, workers, unionists, and customers exchanged heated invective.[50]

The boycott suggested both the strengths and weaknesses of organized labor in the South and the United States in the late twentieth century. On the one hand, here was evidence that unions could forge alliances with the wider public and other social organizations to challenge corporate power. Church leaders, African Americans, newly militant workers, and at least some sympathetic citizens joined the UFCW in protesting corporate practices that seemed at the least unfair. Here was a challenge to the public perception that organized labor was yet another "interest group" concerned primarily with protecting or extending its own bailiwick. As Be-Lo attorney Stanley G. Barr inadvertently conceded, the boycott went well beyond "informing" the public. "They're talking about working conditions, conditions in the stores, pricing policies, the quality of food and sexual harassment," albeit using what Barr described as "vulgarity, threats, and intimidation."[51] And this took place in the public forum, not behind closed doors, where unions throughout much of the post-war period had bargained away worker autonomy and union democracy in the interest of cost-of-living increases.

Yet despite the effort to address a broad range of issues and to use the public forum to contest corporate dominance, the boycott held little hope of generating widespread sympathy. The focus on one company—what industry analyst Jeff Metzger described as "one of the more vulnerable players in the market"[52]—and the fact that the boycott took place *after* the election, however contested the results, limited its effectiveness. Instead of a public campaign aimed at mobilizing grocery store workers to sign a union card or directly challenging the election results, the union found itself entangled in an exchange of accusations about company practices that proved difficult to document.[53] A widespread campaign that targeted the most powerful supermarkets—particularly Food Lion—stood the chance of generating the kind of momentum that might have carried over to the other retail chains. As it was, the boycott pressured a company that was on the decline and would, by 2001, file for bankruptcy.[54] Despite the dilution of UFCW's message, the boycott challenged the dubious election results in a highly public and dramatic fashion. It also suggested the possibilities for a broad-based, community-wide mobilization of working-class people.

But if the UFCW benefited from a margin of public sympathy, Be-Lo benefited from the legal system's historical alignment against labor. In June 1991, the company secured five court injunctions preventing picketing in the parking lots of five Be-Lo stores in Hampton Roads. In an unusual reversal of fortune, a National Labor Relations Board decision permitting union picketing at a Makro grocery store in Ohio set the precedent for board rulings to supersede state court injunctions. Realizing that it had lost this battle, Be-Lo acquiesced to the picketers, who returned to the Hampton Roads stores in December. Meanwhile, the company set its sights on reversing the order in the Sixth Circuit Court of Appeals. At the same time, the union prepared to challenge the election results of March 21, 1991. Despite the alliance with local ministers and activists against Be-Lo's higher downtown prices and out-of-date merchandise, it was the contested election that provided the main impetus behind union picketing. As Thomas McNutt noted, "What would cause us to pull the (picket) lines down would be for the company to allow the employees to exercise their (unionization) rights free from coercion."[55] The struggle moved into the legal domain and out of the parking lots of Hampton Roads. When it did so, it followed the pattern of litigation that had become dominant in the Reagan era.

The appeal to the National Labor Relations Board vindicated the UFCW's claim that the company had flagrantly transgressed labor law. Citing "numerous and serious" labor law violations,[56] the board upheld administrative law judge Martin J. Linsky's decision to compel the company to bargain with the UFCW. In effect, the board invoked the most punitive measure at its disposal—a mandatory bargaining order under the provisions of *NLRB v. Gissel Packing Co.* (1969)—to remedy multiple labor law infractions. These ranged from the unlawful intimidation and dismissal of unionist employees to the dissemination of mock "pink slips" designed to convince workers that voting for the union would mean voting for the termination of their jobs. The board also cited the company for discriminating against the union by using its no solicitation policy to prevent union picketing but not to prevent incense merchants and Girl Scouts from plying their wares. As the board members somberly observed, the majority of these violations occurred in the weeks prior to the election. "During this same period, the Respondent unlawfully . . . interrogated employees regarding the Union, created the impression of surveillance, and disparately enforced its work rules against the Union to prohibit union apparel, union buttons, and conversations about the Union." Finally, as the election loomed, the company moved beyond threats and "actually discharged six union adherents because of their support for the Union."[57] Cumulatively, Be-Lo's anti-union campaign amounted to a series of "'hallmark' violations" and the "most flagrant of unfair labor practices" involving the "management from top to bottom."[58] Clearly, the company's coordinated anti-union campaign had more to do with the failure of UFCW's organizing drive than the union's strategic miscalculations.

The decision exposed the political and economic factors arrayed against labor unions in the late twentieth century. Most importantly, though, it vindicated the union's claim that it had indeed represented a majority of workers at the time of the election. Supporting Judge Linsky's contention that a majority of the 756 employees eligible to vote had signed cards authorizing UFCW Local 400 to bargain on their behalf even without an election, the board endorsed a *Gissel* order, requiring the company to negotiate with the union and rejecting the company's call for a new election. The board took this unusual step because of the company's egregiously anti-union practices. In this case, the NLRB clearly went against the conservative judicial grain of the post-Reagan era by rejecting the company's argument that high employee turnover mitigated the effects of its unfair labor practices. Invoking a Fifth Circuit Court opinion—"'Practices may live on in the lore of the shop and continue to repress employee sentiment long after most, or even all, original participants have departed'"—the board departed from pro-business legalism and acknowledged workplace realities. The board conceded that, despite laws designed to protect employee rights, and despite the era's rhetoric of worker empowerment and managerial sensitivity, companies could still create workplaces permeated by intimidation, fear, and expectations of employee subordination.[59] Since more than 250 still remained from the 1991 campaign, the memory of employer intimidation and anti-union hostility persisted. The company's prohibition on union picketing and its dismissal of an additional four pro-union employees confirmed that little had changed.[60]

The report and Judge Linsky's opinion shed light on the anti-union strategies that became standard fare in the South in the 1980s. As industrial relations expert Kate Bronfenbrenner reported, companies threatened to shut down their operations in a full 60 percent of union elections between 1993 and 1995. According to Bronfenbrenner, the North American Free Trade Agreement accelerated this practice. Almost 12 percent of employers who threatened to close actually followed through on their threats by shutting down operations in whole or in part. This was triple the rate of company transfers that took place in the 1980s, suggesting that "where employers can credibly threaten to shut down or move their operations in response to union activity, they do so in large numbers."[61] Moreover, in union certification campaigns where companies threatened to close a plant, unions won at a rate of 33 percent, considerably below the 40 percent rate where such threats did not occur.[62]

The tactic was part of a larger campaign of union intimidation that had become an integral feature of the New Economy in the South. In Virginia, officials at the Tultex plant in Martinsville required employees to view a videotape featuring abandoned textile plants in New Jersey where the Amalgamated Clothing and Textile Workers Union—the same union trying to organize the Tultex plant—had succeeded. By the 1980s, companies operating in the South would regularly hire anti-union consultants and law firms to advise them on how to crush organization drives. One of the key elements of the corporate anti-union campaign was the anti-union film. Workers could be compelled to view such a film under the provisions of the Taft-Hartley Act of 1947, which gave employers the right to make a unilateral case to employees considering unionization. Former anti-union-film producer Bob Powers explained that the films carried intimations of plant closings, lost jobs, and images of the union as "an outside force invading the privacy of the plant and the community."[63] As Powers notes, anti-union consultants had been active in Virginia in the 1990s: "I remember elections at Hanes, a subsidiary of Sara Lee, at their plants in Galax, Virginia[,] and Sparta, North Carolina. The preliminary vote was running more than 80 percent against the company. We went in with these shows and turned it *totally* around in six weeks."[64] Historian Timothy Minchin notes that the "South was at the forefront of corporate efforts to take on organized labor in the 1980s." Propelled by the fact that the region was a magnet for companies seeking low wages and no unions, Charlotte, North Carolina, and Greenville, South Carolina, became staging grounds for anti-union consultants. Union deterrence became a highly profitable business in the South, as some seven thousand management consultants advised businesses on everything from how to make workers identify with the company to how to portray unions as agents of "violence, suffering, and community division."[65]

Of course, the organizing drive at Be-Lo preceded NAFTA, but the company's anti-union strategy anticipated those adopted at Tultex, Hanes, J. P. Stevens, and other southern businesses. The principal objective in each campaign was to generate fear and uncertainty about union representation. For Be-Lo, this included dismissals and threats of dismissal for union support. It also included letters from the manager, Manual Sanders, suggesting that unionization would lead to economic ruin. According to administrative law judge Martin Linsky, the company "strategy was to instill in its employees the false and unsupported fear that the Union caused the demise, not only of Virginia grocery competitors, but of union companies in other industries." In other words, a union vote at Be-Lo would be a vote for unemployment.[66]

Even so, Linsky ruled that Section 8(c) of the National Labor Relations Act, which recognized the right of employers to challenge union campaigns under the First Amendment, protected the employers' anti-union messages. The board upheld the judge's decision but castigated the next arrow in Be-Lo's anti-union campaign. Weeks before the election, the company sent its employees a pink slip that carried the statement: "you may want to take another look at what the UNITED FOOD AND COMMERCIAL WORKERS UNION got for their former dues payers in this area—A PINK SLIP." The management attached a pink-hued letter on phony Big Star, Safeway, and Colonial Stores letterhead with the following text: "Dear Unionized Employees, I regret to inform you that because we have lost our ability to compete in this extremely competitive market, we shall be forced to close this store and put you out of work."[67] While the judge allowed the pink slip, the board did not, since the pink slip seemed to imply that voting for the union would result in reprisals against employees.[68] For the National Labor Relations Board, this was the "type of severe and pervasive coercion that has lingering effects and is not readily dispelled by the passage of time."[69] Paying restitution to employees fired for union activity would not be enough; the company would be compelled to bargain with the UFCW. For union attorney Carey Butsavage, this would rectify the election fiasco: "At one point, we had more than 400 authorization cards saying, 'Yes, we want to have union representation.' . . . In a two-month period, they were able to scare about 180 of those workers."[70]

Yet the fail-safe corporate strategy for thwarting union gains was litigation, and this strategy worked. On review of the case in 1997, the United States Court of Appeals for the Fourth Circuit overturned much of the NLRB decision. The court rejected the board and the union's contention that the January list of eligible voters was the authoritative list. The court also rejected their claim that the company's "revised" list, reflecting discharged and newly hired employees, was invalid. With the revised list, Be-Lo was clearly the winner of the March 21 election. The court also accepted the company's contention that employees had signed several authorization cards under the false pretense that they were strictly meant to facilitate an election, not union representation. Moreover, the court threw out the board's conclusion that the pink slip violated section 8(a)(1) of the National Labor Relations Act. In the court's opinion, the pink slip, like company executive Manual Sanders's letters, were protected, since an employer—and here the court quoted Judge Linsky—has the "right to 'make a prediction as to the precise effects he believes unionization will have on his company'" and to speculate "'as to demonstrably probable consequences beyond his control.'"[71]

In addition, the court also reversed the board's conclusions about the circumstances under which five Be-Lo employees were dismissed or not re-called. Citing earlier decisions, it asserted that "the mere fact that an employee—even a union activist—[is] discharged during a union campaign, standing alone, will not support a discriminatory finding if there is a 'supportable cause' for the discharge."[72] Most significantly, the court overturned the compulsory *Gissel* bargaining order, concluding that the company's conduct had not undermined the union's allegedly majority status. It also believed that the passage of time and staff turnover had dissipated the negative repercussions of the company's transgressions. Quite simply, the Court of Appeals did not consider Be-Lo's behavior to be particularly reprehensible. Based on this reasoning, the majority saw no reason not to hold a new election.

But that was the majority opinion, not the only opinion, and in Judge Samuel J. Ervin III's dissent, we discover how contentious this case really was. In a blistering rebuttal to the majority decision, Judge Ervin proclaimed that "If the facts of this case cannot sustain a bargaining order, then almost none will. Substantial evidence plainly supports the Board's findings of nearly 80 violations, many of them so-called 'hallmark' violations, the vast majority of them unbriefed by Be-Lo and not even discussed by the majority here."[73] Ervin's dissent is interesting for several reasons, one of which is his objection to the court's presumption in challenging the board's assessment of the credibility of witnesses. In essence, the board credited the employees and organizers who appeared before it over the company's witnesses. According to Ervin, the court overstepped its jurisdiction when it superseded their informed judgment: "Throughout its opinion the majority simply ignores this well-established standard of review and engages in its own *de novo* review of the evidence, substituting its own judgment for that of the Board at almost every turn. The majority thus refuses to acknowledge that this court sits only as an appellate court of limited jurisdiction whose powers to review Board proceedings . . . have been greatly circumscribed by Congress."[74] Ervin was making an important point about jurisdiction. At the same time, he was suggesting that the courts had become the adversaries of the National Labor Relations Board and the champions of business dominance. The judge pointed out that the board possessed "broad discretion to choose an appropriate remedy" [i.e., the compulsory bargaining order], and that the court was obligated to enforce the board's decision unless there was evidence that it had used its authority to impose a result contrary to the National Labor Relations Act.[75] If the board was the place where labor could expect a sympathetic hearing from experts with at least some insight into American workplace realities, the courts frequently provided the forum for business to undo the damage.

Returning to the majority decision of Judges J. Michael Luttig and Claude M. Hilton, we find clues about the difficulties that unions faced when litigation became the principal avenue of resolving labor disputes. Calling into question the board's evidence for "imposing" a collective bargaining order, the court dismissed the board's conclusion that the company's misconduct was "widespread and far-reaching." Instead, it asserted that there was no evidence that company behavior undermined a union majority prior to the election. Specifically, what the court dismissed was the NLRB's claim that Be-Lo committed "hallmark" violations. Instead, it acerbically concluded that the *Gissel* bargaining order decision was "due in no small part to the

Board's increasing practice of characterizing even relatively minor unfair labor practices as 'hallmark.'"[76] Indignantly, the court observed that the board's willingness to invoke the compulsory bargaining clause flew in the face of its "repeated warnings, and similar warnings from our sister circuits" to substantiate the reasons for such a decision.[77]

Yet this was precisely what Judge Ervin challenged, and it was at the very core of the union's case against the company: the willingness to consider intimidation, dismissals, and threats of store closings as minor labor infractions. As Ervin argued, "In its refusal to enforce the Board's bargaining order, the majority has focused on the forest of the Board's remedy but ignored most of the trees that make that remedy appropriate in this case. The Board found nearly 80 violations of the NLRA. *Be-Lo contested only a handful of those violations before us, however, and the majority concentrates its energies on only that handful*" (emphasis added)."[78] Ervin believed that the violations which the court did consider had to be examined in the context of countless other infractions which the company did not even contest but which created a "backdrop of a company hell-bent on preventing unionization at nearly any cost."[79] Ervin was driving at the pattern of antidemocratic practices that flourished in the workplace under the aegis of a legal framework designed to protect workers but almost uniformly applied in the interest of business.

Judge Ervin's critique shines light on the legal wilderness that southern workers found themselves in during the late twentieth century. First, Ervin challenged the majority's assertion that the notorious "pink slip" message was protected by Section 8(c) of the NLRA. This section allows employers to present their views on unionization and to predict its impact on the company provided they do not threaten reprisals and that they present concrete evidence to support their claims. According to Ervin, Be-Lo never came close to fulfilling these requirements. "Furthermore," Ervin added, "a reasonable mind could conclude that, given the substantial number of times that Be-Lo did, in fact, directly threaten store closure and job loss, this was nothing but a thinly-veiled threat of retaliation." Instead of acknowledging the board's expertise in determining whether or not the company used coercive language, the court ignored it. Instead, it drafted an opinion that acknowledged the right of companies to intimidate employees at will.[80] Second, the judge excoriated the company's attempt to discredit forty-three union authorization cards on the grounds that organizers had claimed they would only be used for an election, not representation. Quoting the administrative law judge, who had ascribed unqualified credibility to the union organizers and dismissed Be-Lo's witnesses, Ervin skewered the majority decision:

> Not only don't I believe [Be-Lo's forty-three] witnesses . . . but I'm convinced that the fact that these otherwise intelligent, decent people would have come into a court room and testify as they did is evidence that the unfair labor practices of Be-Lo have not been dissipated by the passage of time and that a fair rerun election is not possible in this case. Many of these employees, I conclude, were so terrified about their job security and staying on Be-Lo's good side that they were ready, willing, and able to help Be-Lo's case by saying that union organizers said things to them in soliciting them to sign authorization cards that were not said.

Tabulating Be-Lo's train of labor law abuses, from intimidating union supporters to obstructing legal picketing, Ervin utterly repudiated the majority opinion: "There ought to be really little question that the Board properly issued a bargaining order in this case. Indeed, because so many of the violations are hallmark violations, being, on the whole, 'outrageous' and 'pervasive,' the bargaining order was warranted even without a showing of majority support for the union."[81] For Ervin, the cumulative and lasting effect of the company's campaign of employee coercion justified the imposition of a bargaining order. The majority's "rhetoric and hyperbole" would not convince him otherwise.[82]

What do these legal interlocutions tell us about organized labor in Virginia and the South in the New Economy era? The legal arena was precisely where contested certification elections, strikes, and collective agreements ended up. Unlike the New Deal era, when organizers took direct action to resolve labor disputes, sometimes through sit-down strikes and occasionally through disruptive wildcat strikes, the post-Taft-Hartley era constrained labor activism within a web of legal restrictions that dampened activism and augmented the power of the courts. In the era of corporate-led globalization, business restructuring, and government minimalism, the courts became a key element in the anti-union southern front. Tying up contested elections in protracted administrative hearings and appeals inevitably drained union resources. It also whittled away employee support for organization. It meant that companies did not have to face the consequences of employee dismissals for some time. When they did, the penalties were so negligible that it was usually in their interests to pay them, having already reaped the benefits of intimidating and discharging troublesome workers. As Kate Bronfenbrenner succinctly explained,

> the penalties for illegal plant-closing threats and other labor law violations are extremely limited. If employers fire union activists, the worst penalty they face is reinstatement and back pay for the dismissed workers, with no possibility of punitive damages. If employers refuse to negotiate, they merely receive another order telling them to bargain in good faith.[83]

A Human Rights Watch study focusing on the predicament of American labor concurred: "Many employers have come to view remedies like back pay for workers fired because of union activity as a routine cost of doing business, well worth it to get rid of organizing leaders and derail workers' organizing efforts. As a result, a culture of near-impunity has taken shape in much of U.S. labor law and practice."[84] Since companies were only expected to remunerate workers for the period during which the discharged worker was actually unemployed, the penalties were nominal at best.

Considering the courts' willingness to repeal bargaining orders on the grounds of high employee turnover and the passage of time, the corporate strategy of litigation was a sound investment. On this point, the NLRB and the courts were clearly at odds. Attorney Gil A. Abramson, who, oddly enough, worked as a business consultant on "union avoidance," observed that "For years the Board was reluctant to consider these factors because it felt that . . . [it would] . . . allow employers who commit unfair labor practices to benefit from unavoidable delays inherent in the system. The courts, in contrast, are almost unanimous in their requirement that these factors be considered when deciding whether or not to enforce a *Gissel* order."[85] In the Be-Lo case, a full six years elapsed between the election and the Supreme Court decision, during which two-thirds of the original employees left the company. Judge Ervin was aware of how businesses could use this employee turnover and passage-of-time clause to their benefit. Without evidence that turnover was a result of "normal attrition," the court was justified in "speculating, contrary to the majority's presumptions here, that [citing *So-Lo Foods* 985] 'the significant turnover is attributable to management maneuvering from a Company intent on dissipating a pro-union group of employees.'"[86] Knowing the courts' predilection for overturning bargaining orders suspended by litigation, companies could use the time to dilute their pro-union workforce. In effect, companies could depend on the "passage of time" and employee attrition to mitigate labor law violations. Unions would then have to think twice about expending resources on trying to organize a business that had proven its determination to resist unionization.

And yet the burdens that the legal system placed on organizing workers extended beyond the courts, back to the workplace, into the election process itself. Here is where southern workers lost the effort to unionize again and again, on a playing field that was inherently unequal. Since the Taft-Hartley Act gave employers the right to promulgate their anti-union case, they had free rein to use techniques ranging from compulsory, captive-audience meetings to one-on-one meetings with employees. Historian David Brody explains that the Taft-Hartley Act transformed the election campaign into a "platform" for "coercing workers." This was something that Robert Wagner, the author of the National Labor Relations Act, clearly understood. As Brody notes, Wagner knew that "employers should be neutral during representation campaigns because anything they said was inherently coercive (and because they had no more legitimate interest when workers organized than did workers when employers organized)."[87] Through the Taft-Hartley Act, a measure which southern conservatives enthusiastically endorsed, business-led anti-union campaigns gained the legitimacy of "free speech."

Giving companies the chance to inflict their case on people who depended on the employer for a job subverted the right of association—the right to form a union of their own choosing—which the NLRA protected. It did so not because anti-unionism was illegitimate, but because companies were in the unique position to compel their workers to abide by their views. As Lance Compa of Human Rights Watch concluded, "Underlying all this employer opposition to workers' organizing is the raw power of the employment relationship—the power to assign work, to pay a wage, to impose discipline, and ultimately to dismiss the worker. Workers hear employers' views with this power in mind."[88] Southern companies used the rhetoric of freedom as effectively as southern political elites to obscure the inequalities in the region's political and economic life.

The fact that American workers had to rely on acrimonious elections to achieve representation reflected the judicial bias in favor of ownership. David Brody reminds us that the NLRB election was not originally mandatory. As the bill provided, the board "could use 'any other suitable method'—underscoring that the process was in service to the self-organization of workers" rather than in the service of companies trying to badger workers into submission. Under Section 9(a), employers were obligated to bargain with an organization "designated or selected" by the membership, meaning that elections were not the only method of achieving representation.[89] In other words, card-checks were originally as valid as elections in determining union status.

Against the grain of the right to associate which had been at the center of the NLRA, congressional conservatives inserted liberty of contract and the individualistic "right to work" in the Taft-Hartley Act. According to Brody, the courts were left to "fashion a case law based on the Taft-Hartley revisions squaring the workers' right of free choice with employer 'free speech' and property rights. What gives this case law its astounding prejudicial bent is the presumption, subterranean but ever-present, that workers' rights count for less than employers' rights."[90] Be-Lo's right to deluge its employees with anti-union propaganda, to threaten the loss of jobs consequent to unionization, to discharge employees on the flimsiest of pretexts during the election campaign, and to dismiss authorization cards as evidence of union support exceeded the workers' rights to protest the election. It also exceeded their right to an election free of coercion.

The imbalance between labor and business was painfully evident in the South of the late twentieth century. By the early 1990s, the "right-to-work" clause had been enshrined as a corollary of the right of free speech. It became the first principle of generating a "business friendly" environment. In Virginia, political scientist Thomas Morris observed in 1990, the right-to-work law "remains a litmus test issue . . . a political commentary on the status of organized labor within the state."[91] Any claim that organizers and company owners met on a level playing field during certification campaigns was an illusion.

Be-Lo's coordinated campaign against the UFCW—ranging from captive-audience dinner meetings to anti-union videotapes and mock pink slips—reflected a pattern of anti-union hostility meted out during organizing campaigns. After another unsuccessful organizing campaign in Hampton Roads, the UFCW filed charges with the National Labor Relations Board alleging that Camellia Food Stores discharged several employees sympathetic to the union while intimidating and interrogating others.[92] At DuPont in Martinsville, where workers were considering union membership in 1994, the management screened a film and gave speeches portraying the United Mine Workers as violent thugs who would fine employees for attending church rather than a Sunday union meeting. More than this, the UMW claimed that the company threatened to close the plant if the union won. The union alleged that the company assigned managers to function as observers during the union election. According to union representatives, DuPont went "too far" in promoting a company union which eventually won out against the miners.[93]

These were charges, of course, not complaints, which can only follow an NLRB investigation. According to Walter Grant, president and chief executive officer of Camellia, union charges in the weeks before an election were "common. It's standard procedure."[94] But if filing grievances had become routine, it reflected either the predictability of company efforts to undermine worker rights during election campaigns or the frustration of labor unions in confronting a consistently uneven playing field. Two days after the failed campaign, UFCW president Thomas R. McNutt claimed that "Their scare tactics, threats and intimidation made a farce of what is supposed to be the most basic right we enjoy: democratic elections."[95] The acrimonious atmosphere that suffused almost every organizing drive reflected the profound divisions that afflicted the workplace in the New Economy South. It illustrated the profound intolerance of business leaders and judicial authorities for anything resembling collective action. Despite the rhetoric of employee-management parity and shop-floor empowerment, the gulf between decision-makers and employees with little control over their work and less over their future widened in the last decade of the century.

The intensity of union organizing drives reflected this reality. Unionists fought not simply to organize underpaid clerks at a Be-Lo in Norfolk, but to bolster a system of protection that was crumbling under the weight of free market fundamentalism. At the same time, service-sector industries struggled against diminishing margins, rising costs, and intensifying competition to stay above water. With the advent of superchains like Food Lion and then Wal-Mart, the competitive struggle reached a crescendo, catapulting several into bankruptcy and others in mergers, solidifying the trend toward the concentration of economic power in the late twentieth century.[96]

Public policy and the prevailing ideological winds supported the coercive practices that regularly obstructed union drives. As Sandra D. Bowen, director of government affairs for the Virginia Chamber of Commerce noted in 1991, "I can think of no issue in which the business community and organized labor were on opposite sides, in which the business community did not win."[97] In Virginia, as political scientist Larry Sabato warmly pointed out, even supposedly liberal governors mouthed platitudes about labor while promoting an agenda favorable to business. Governors Chuck Robb, Gerald Baliles, and Douglas Wilder ran on programs "to provide centrist business-oriented government with a human face. The emphasis [is] on business. Not *labor*. But a government that was business orientated."[98] Reporting on the resurgence of unions shortly after the Be-Lo campaign, the *Richmond Times-Dispatch* cheerily asked, "What is it about unions that could drive a company to break the law rather than accept them?" In the nomenclature of the period and with the conviction of Virginia tradition, Keith Cheatham of the Virginia Chamber of Commerce insisted that "unionizing decreases the flexibility a company has to run its business" and that "it drives up their [companies'] cost of production." In a matter-of-fact, advice-column tone, it suggested that "the best way to protect themselves from union organizing efforts is not to wait for an election to begin and then fight, but rather to keep their employees happy enough that they will feel they don't need a union."[99] For journalist Michael Buettner and no doubt many of his readers, companies had to be "protected" from the threat of unions. Operating on the assumption that democratic representation in the workplace could be circumvented by pay raises and incentives, he advised companies to make employees "happy." As for the suggestion that public employees be permitted to organize, Cheatham had this to say: "we know that's not going to happen."[100]

The alignment of southern political forces against labor unions was no more evident than during the debate over national legislation to prohibit the use of replacement workers. Conservatives wheeled out tried-and-true anti-union myths that conveniently suited the needs of the New Economy as well. At the same time, the debate gave progressives an opportunity to articulate a revitalized notion of democratic citizenship. This development was unexpected and surprising, considering that marketplace freedom and entrepreneurialism had become the highest social ideals in late-twentieth-century America. It was additionally important, since the greatest achievement that business could claim in this era was ideological primacy. As labor journalist David Moberg explains, the "tyranny of the marketplace" was almost uncontested in the new Gilded Age, as Americans paid homage to the unfettered marketplace as "the most efficient and . . . just means of making all decisions." Government was expected to be hypersensitive to market demands while corporate downsizing was tolerated as the inevitable result of beneficent market forces. Yet the "celebration of the market deliberately conceal[ed] the power relationships behind what seem to be simple exchanges of money for goods and services."[101] It was these power relationships that labor unionists in Virginia addressed.

The bill to prohibit companies from hiring replacement workers promised to restore some of the balance between capital and labor. Following

President Reagan's liquidation of PATCO in 1981, employers sought out a strategy for eliminating striking union employees and found it in the 1938 Supreme Court *Mackay Radio* case. This decision allowed companies to operate by hiring "permanent replacement workers" rather than conceding to striking employees. Technically, the decision provided that strikers would only be replaced, not terminated, and the company was obligated to activate them as soon as new jobs developed. In a period of corporate restructuring, however, positions disappeared permanently, leaving replacement workers with jobs and striking workers on the street.[102]

The rediscovery of the *Mackay* decision in the 1980s gave employers a new weapon in breaking strikes, and they used it aggressively. A depressing litany of companies hiring permanent replacement workers soon emerged, including Continental Airlines in 1984, BASF and Hormel in 1985, Eastern Air Lines and Pittston Coal in 1989, Caterpillar in 1992, and Bridgestone/Firestone as well as the Detroit newspapers in 1995. In congressional representative William Clay's estimation, companies replaced approximately 300,000 striking employees during the 1980s.[103] Historian Philip Yale Nicholson described the situation in the late twentieth century this way: labor no longer had the protection of law behind its decision to strike, which left "contemporary workers and their unions [to engage] in collective bargaining with their employers in an atmosphere of coercion and fear."[104]

Passed in the House in 1993, the bill to prohibit replacement workers floundered in the Senate when conservatives threatened a filibuster. President Bill Clinton gave lukewarm support to the measure to make amends with organized labor following the North American Free Trade Agreement debacle.[105] While Washington liberals offered tacit support, Virginia conservatives came out strongly against the measure.

Their opposition justified many of the key practices that damaged working-class Americans. The striker bill was "bad for business," claimed the *Virginian-Pilot,* since it challenged the drift of economic practice toward corporate unilateralism. Endorsing trucking deregulation which forced the Teamsters to "settle for what they could get" while celebrating the "globalization of world trade" as a "law of economic gravity" which "Big Labor" could not possibly defy, the paper condemned the bill as "the pushbutton strike bill," a phrase it lifted from the anti-labor National Right to Work Committee. Instead of protecting workers' jobs by exercising the only mechanism at their disposal to counter the demands of business, the bill would give workers "lifetime tenure." More than this—and here again the paper engaged in pernicious myth-making—the "industries they work for would become hostage to union demands." Assuming that unions were indifferent to the need to ensure productivity, ignoring contractual conditions that gave companies the authority to dismiss incompetent workers, and overlooking the fact that the bill would only begin to restrain the power of companies over their employees, the paper insisted that "globalization," not calculations of corporate advantage, lay behind opposition to the bill. The ideology of competitive global capitalism was no more evident than in the paper's belief that the bill would send jobs "overseas at a record rate as employers sought to escape the new law." Whatever the objective economic circumstances were—the rise of the service industry, the nontransferability of most American working-class jobs—the editor was content to condemn the measure using the rhetoric of globalization. Moreover, the paper recapitulated the idea that the prerogatives of business—employers escaping the new law—trumped the interests of working people, let alone the law itself.[106]

But it was the *Richmond Times-Dispatch* that once again encapsulated the issues for its business-first readership. The bill's "mischief lay in altering the balance between labor and management," an assertion that never came close to squaring with the reality which workers faced. In a region where intimidation, unlawful discharges, misinformation, surveillance, and threats of plant closings had become the norm, the suggestion that labor and management met on a level playing field was at best disingenuous. More than this, according to the *Times-Dispatch*, it would violate the "strict neutrality" which government should exercise in management-labor disputes.[107]

What the editors overlooked was that the state had whittled away at labor solidarity, the very premise of union organization, since the 1960s. Citing one example, the 1972 *Granite* decision, historian Nelson Lichtenstein pointed out that the courts conceded the right of employees to abrogate their union membership during a strike and cross the picket lines without suffering any procedural retribution from the union. Ironically, it was liberal judges who carried these decisions. The cumulative effect of that decision was to alter "the meaning of union solidarity into a coercive set of legal/administrative pressures that merely trampled on the work rights of the individual ex-unionist."[108] With the idea of democratic labor collectivism invalidated by atomistic individualism, and with unions facing countless restrictions on their ability to protest grievances or challenge managerial decisions, the assertion that capital and labor were equal competitors was vacuous. Moreover, government officials, the courts, and the media had promoted the imbalance.[109]

If the editors were erroneous about the dynamics of labor-management relations, they at least understood that the bill threatened certain vested interests in Virginia. Claiming that "Virginia had a huge stake in the Senate debate," and that Senator John Warner would stand "solid" against "Big Labor's special interests" and "lackeys," the paper also indicated who might stand to lose the most—the defenders of the state's right-to-work "tradition." According to the *Times-Dispatch*, the law not only "protect[ed] the interest of workers who choose not to join unions" but also "contribute[d] to the state's economic health."[110] Contrary to the editors' claims, the paper itself later reported that states with right-to-work laws suffered lower average earnings—$24,600 yearly—than those that did not endorse the law. In non-right-to-work states, average pay ran at approximately $29,100 annually.[111] While the high-tech economy flourished in northern Virginia, the economy of western Virginia had "stalled during the nation's greatest economic boom," burdened by declining labor-intensive, low-wage industries.[112] And as the *Virginian-Pilot* reported for the Hampton Roads area, per capita income for the region fell 11 percent below the national average, meaning that people living there earned less than Americans performing the same job elsewhere in the country. Compounding this distress was the rising cost of living, which included a 12 percent hike on housing prices between 1991 and 1995.[113]

Certainly, some Virginians benefited enormously in the 1990s. Businesses gained the most, and there is little doubt that its gains were unevenly distributed in Virginia. Moreover, as Old Dominion economist Gilbert Yochum explained in 1990, deregulation and the decline of the unions only accelerated the income disparity. "Without protection from unions," this Virginia analyst concluded, "their wages today are not even remotely close to what they once were."[114] Indifferent to the growing concentration of corporate wealth and the neutralization of working people as a countervailing force in American society, the *Richmond-Times* was left to rail against the illusion of "Big Labor."

But working-class Virginians raised their own defense of the bill, in the process offering a critique of the radical free market agenda of the 1990s. It is important to see this defense of the striker bill on a continuum of public challenges to the hypercompetitive ethos of the era. Working people articulated this challenge during the Be-Lo campaign as well as during the striker bill debate and on throughout the rest of the decade. Together with the *Times-Dispatch*'s virulent anti-unionism, this labor-oriented challenge demonstrated how contested the political economy really was in the South.

By surveying the public debate that preceded and followed the striker bill, we see the common themes of a working-class perspective come into focus. We do not find a coherent analysis of class relations, corporate interest, and the racial dimension of poverty and powerlessness. What we do find, though, is a set of convictions that would propel a reconsideration of the governing ideals of the New Economy era.

When G. D. Lewis wrote to the *Virginian-Pilot* questioning Jesse Jackson's motives and suggesting that unions compelled their members to go on strike, he provoked an impassioned response from union supporters.[115] Not surprisingly, Thomas R. McNutt weighed in passionately. He challenged Lewis's insinuations by pointing to Jackson's record of support for working people struggling to manage on minimum wage and no health insurance. But McNutt also challenged some of the deeply ingrained anti-union myths which the *Times-Dispatch* and countless other Virginians imbibed. Unionization does not precipitate bankruptcy, McNutt explained, since "20 million union members" understood that their "employers have to make money if the workers themselves are to make money." He reminded Lewis and like-minded Virginians that unionized workers earned more in wages and fringe benefits than their non-card-signing counterparts. But more importantly, he cast Jackson's trip and the union's mission in the language of American egalitarianism. While opponents of organized labor trumpeted the supremacy of the competition imperative, McNutt invoked the common verities of "fair pay" and "decent treatment on the job." These were rights, not entitlements. In reminding readers that they were protected by federal law, McNutt challenged the states' rights tradition that lived on in Virginia under the guise of right to work.[116]

Others joined McNutt in presenting an oppositional view of labor unions in Virginia. Jeffrey Hufton of Ironworkers Local Union 79 reminded Lewis of the disparities between unionized and non-unionized workers. For the grocery store workers of Hampton Roads, these statistics must have been particularly revealing. According to the Department of Labor, unionized retail workers in 1990 earned $381 as a weekly median while non-unionized employees pulled in considerably less—$270 a week.[117] For Hufton, the union "ensured a better standard of living" through health insurance and pension plans. Virginia's unionists were reviving the redistributionist arguments that had been so compelling in the 1950s, the height of American unionism, but which had fallen into disfavor in the years of supply-side economics. Quite simply, they argued that well-paid unionized workers translated into healthy local economies and social investment through tax revenues.[118] Like McNutt, he emphasized the moral legitimacy of unions, arguing that "their sole reason for existence is to make life a little better for people who have to work for a living." For Hufton, and probably many average people in Norfolk, Virginia, it was incomprehensible how "someone would have a problem with an institution that helps people fight for fair pay and health insurance."[119] If Hufton underlined the material impulses behind unionism, the very premises on which conservatives would attack them, he identified the moral and political underpinnings that gave them legitimacy.

Rosa P. White of Norfolk also responded, challenging the cliché that unions had outlived their usefulness. Adopting a historical perspective, she confronted the assertion that unions were narrow-minded interest groups that offered little to American society: "Let me remind him that many benefits we take for granted may not have been won except for the long hard fight by organized labor—such things as Workmen's Compensation, unemployment compensation, Social Security, public education, health care, child care, equal opportunity, safety standards, retirement benefits and other important programs."[120] In White's estimation, labor unions became the vehicles of the progressive agenda that flourished at the center of American life in the years before the Cold War. For all of their democratic failings, labor unions since the New Deal era had promoted an agenda of liberal social reform that produced tangible benefits for working people. White refuted Lewis's assertion that unions "force members to strike," countering instead that the decision to withhold labor depends on a majority decision, a democratic exercise. Instead of the conspiratorial racket that Lewis imagined, unions offered workers an instrument of self-representation: "Workers perform the work in the workplace and, through a union, they have a voice in their workplace." The benefits were material but also psychological and political. It was through union membership that White achieved "good wages, good working conditions, and a voice in my workplace—a chance to live with dignity." While many unions perpetuated gender discrimination as actively as their corporate counterparts in the years after the Second World War, at least some provided women an opportunity for self-expression and advancement. Equally important, they offered women a bulwark against economic exploitation, something which few women in the office towers of America could expect. As White explained, "I joined the union with great pride and became an active member. . . . Being a good union woman has been most rewarding to me. I am now retired and enjoy retirement benefits my union helped make possible. I still support my union because the union was always there for me."[121] For White, McNutt, and Hufton, unionism fostered bonds of mutuality that insulated workers from the atomistic relations of the marketplace. It alerted them to grievous power imbalances that still pervaded the American workplace, despite stock options and the team concept.

While some workers emphasized the benefits and rights that came from unionism, others addressed the critical question of unions in the globalizing South: do they make business uncompetitive? Bernard F. Hopkins, president of the Greater Tidewater Central Labor Council of Virginia, took the question head-on. He pointed out that monopolies, not callous unions, force prices up on consumer goods. In effect, he returned to the Progressive Era argument that monopolies deter competition and punish consumers. "I can point to dozens of stores of all sorts in Hampton Roads that charge outrageous prices, and not one of them has unionized workers." If Hopkins overlooked the struggle between supermarket giants like Food Lion and small retail chains like Be-Lo, he identified the growing problem of concentrated corporate wealth in American life. Challenging the myth of the lazy worker, he argued that union members were good for business. "The fact is, studies have shown that unionized employers tend to be more productive than non-union. Businesses operate more efficiently. There's less turnover, because the workers are happy." By taking wages out of competition, the ownership achieved workplace stability—"Managers can spend their time running their business instead of trying to train an ever-changing work force." Strikes, Hopkins added, are also a last resort, something which usually does not happen, since "99 out of every 100 labor contracts are settled without a strike."[122]

The question of the impact of unions on business productivity was highly contentious, and Hopkins could not resolve it in a letter to the editor. For that matter, he and most others could not address the key question for business: did unions promote company *profitability*? Labor historian David Brody suggests that while "union workers may be more efficient than nonunion workers, there is no question that unionized firms are less profitable than nonunion firms. The gains in labor productivity do not counterbalance the union wage premium. In effect, unions redistribute the earnings of the firm to the advantage of their members."[123] If Hopkins and other labor leaders were reluctant to address this reality—to challenge the assumption that business profitability should be the only measure of social value—he cast doubt on the prevailing assumption that unions equaled employee indolence.

Registering the growing debate over the impact of globalization on the South, some addressed the larger economic dynamic. Again, Thomas R. McNutt of the UFCW responded first, attacking the May 15 *Virginian-Pilot* editorial that denounced the bill as "Bad for Business." Commenting on the historical anti-union bias of southern media—"Your editorial . . . is what working people have come to expect from the Virginian-Pilot"—McNutt turned the tables on the editors who ridiculed the bill for ignoring the demands of global competition: "The major industrialized nations of the world that we compete against reject striker replacements and have far stronger trade-union representation than we do." Much of the blame rested on the shoulders of American media: "Such hostile treatment of unions is socially unacceptable in Japan and Germany and most other countries, but our press embraces the most anti-labor management in the world." International standards aside, the right to strike was a function of democratic citizenship. Like Jeffrey Hufton, McNutt defended the right to strike as a matter of federal law. But like Rosa White, he argued that legal unionism was not simply a matter of self-interest or brokerage state politics. Legal unions had translated into social benefits: "Unions have been a positive force in this country by negotiating wages and benefits that helped build a strong middle class. With unfair labor laws weakening unions"—a point which Virginia economist Gilbert Yochum made in 1990—"that middle class is in decline." This decline tracked the disintegration of the New Deal state in the trickle-down 1980s: "One fifth of our jobs pay below the poverty line. During the Reagan-Bush administrations, when union-busting became a national pastime, real wages of American workers declined by 20 percent." Protecting the right to strike was a matter of social welfare, but at its root it was a question of law and democratic citizenship: "Respect for the law is the cornerstone of our democracy. So put yourself in the shoes of today's worker who, under current law, cannot be fired for striking but can be permanently replaced."[124] The right to strike was intimately tied to the right to join a union, and both were jeopardized by a media and business alliance against working people.

Echoing the emphasis on the law and fundamental rights, Bruce Wooldridge of Norfolk untangled the rhetoric of the "level playing field." Wooldridge wrote to the *Virginian-Pilot* in response to an article by Republican senator Lauch Faircloth of North Carolina, which concluded that the bill, sponsored by liberal Democratic senators Howard Metzenbaum and Edward Kennedy, would be "pure economic poison."[125] Instead of a sinister maneuver to gain advantage over a helpless company, the "right to strike is their legal, protected right, guaranteed by federal law." The right to strike, Woodridge argued, "without fear of reprisal is fundamental in a democratic society." But the "scales are overwhelmingly tipped in favor of management" when the law allows it to dismiss workers on strike. Under these circumstances, "Workers' rights and dignity and genuine collective bargaining suffer." The bill prohibiting replacement workers had nothing to do with the right-to-work law, a distinction which opponents failed to make in order to generate public suspicion. What Faircloth meant to do in threatening to filibuster the measure was to "assure that the dignity of all workers' right to strike without being permanently replaced is denied and that the scales of labor management relationship must *stay* tipped in favor of management" (emphasis added).[126]

The right to strike was a matter of law and rights, but these rights ran headlong into the prerogatives of ownership. The courts and legislators had privileged these rights since the Taft-Hartley Act and assertively promoted them again in the Reagan era. Despite Senator Metzenbaum's effort to generate support for a measure to "give back to workers economic leverage to make collective bargaining work," the political atmosphere was simply too hostile to any legal remedies for the failing fortunes of organized labor. A product of business self-interest as well as deeply felt anxiety about international economic change, the ideology of global competitiveness ensured that the bill never became law. The argument that the "legislation would force American companies to send jobs abroad," as the *Richmond Times-Dispatch* described it, was compelling in its simplicity. It was additionally persuasive because the memories of corporate downsizing remained very much alive in places like Virginia.[127] In an era when NAFTA became law, any other outcome was unlikely.

The bill collapsed but the oppositional perspective continued, kept alive in large part by Virginia conservatives' continuing fear of organized labor. These fears were fueled in part by labor's very real successes, most importantly in the landmark UPS Strike of 1997. The Virginia-based National Right to Work Committee, which advocated a national right-to-work law and the vigorous enforcement of comparable state laws, fanned the flames of anti-unionism throughout the rest of the decade. On the verge of the new millennium, Virginians were still engaged in a debate over organized labor. It reflected deeper uncertainties about a society geared so acutely to the dictates of the marketplace, one in which the language of social responsibility sounded quaint, if not pernicious.

For Virginians, the lightning rod continued to be the right-to-work law.

When Stefan Gleason of the National Right to Work Committee published an article titled "Big Labor's Week of Propaganda" in the *Roanoke Times* in 1999, he elicited a response from working Virginians that challenged some of the most cherished axioms of the New Economy ideology. Arthur R. Poskocil, a teacher from the Blue Ridge area, confronted the duplicity of Right to Work's democratic assertions. While Gleason described the law as a protection of individual freedom against union strong-arming, Poskocil appealed to the "well known truth." As he put it, the "so-called right-to-work laws invariably advance the interests of employers at the expense of their workers. Wherever such laws hold sway, as in Virginia, workers toil for lower wages and weaker benefits than do their counterparts in more labor-friendly states." The right-to-work laws damaged organized labor because they eroded solidarity, the collective strength that grew from freedom of association. The law allowed "free riders" to acquire union-won wage and benefit gains without paying membership dues. This, of course, was the intention behind the Taft-Hartley Act—to divide workers in union shops and undermine their financial capacity to go on strike. It also helped produce a geographical stronghold of union opposition that profoundly influenced the direction of American capitalism in the late twentieth century. Business-oriented Republicans joined southern conservative Democrats in promoting right-to-work laws in the region, crystallizing the region's status as a safe haven for anti-unionism. With the Taft-Hartley Act, the "geography" of American unrestricted capitalism tilted decidedly toward the South.[128]

According to Poskocil, the committee represented corporate interests, not the needs of discontented workers. "If it is workers' rights that he truly cares about, I urge him to abandon his wrongheaded and outrageously inflammatory assault on unionism (does he not know the brutish and bloody history of labor exploitation in pre-union America?) and turn his organization's efforts toward support and defense of countless working Americans who are unjustly and often illegally retaliated against by their employers for their lawful support of union activity." Like Rosa White and others, Poskocil appealed to a history of labor's struggle for recognition in an effort to counter the mythology that underlay contemporary animosity to organized labor. As for "criminal" behavior, he pointed to J. P. Stevens's notorious anti-unionism. It was a company "which has been repeatedly admonished and fined for illegally and brutally repressing lawful union organizing in its factories." Poskocil was right: the labor movement was protected by national laws, but in the late twentieth century, businesses had no compelling reason to obey them.[129]

But it was Phillip Hawks, an inspector at a Volvo assembly plant in Dublin, Virginia, who encapsulated the democratic principles of organized labor in the 1990s. After the punishing years of the early decade, unions did rebound, aided in part by the ascendance of John Sweeney to the presidency of the national AFL-CIO. With Sweeney came a renewed campaign to expand the ranks of organized labor and "give America a raise." The successful UPS strike gave the movement a renewed sense of purpose and momentum, which the AFL-CIO sustained through a week-long series of rallies, demonstrations, town hall meetings, and presentations. By the time that Hawks and Poskocil commented in the pages of the *Roanoke Times*, a new idiom of grassroots democratic activism had emerged. It provided advocates a set of terms for interpreting social change. Unabashedly, Hawks spoke in the language of neopopulism, identifying at once the rural origins of the southern working class and the communal tradition it fostered:

> I am an old country boy from Carroll County who barely made it through the old Hillsville High School in the early 1960s. . . . So I am speaking in the language of a blue-collar worker for the past 35 years. I was a one-year member of a United Auto Workers local in Niagara Falls, N.Y. and a 21-year member of the UAW Local 2069 in Dublin.

Challenging Stefan Gleason's assertions that workers are forced to join unions, that union leaders have abandoned average people, and that the week of protests was a "week of propaganda," Hawks argued that demonstrations were designed to "focus on workers' struggles for their freedom to choose unions and against anti-worker tactics employers used to block workers' voices." Contesting Gleason's belief that most Virginians had little interest in labor organizations, he postulated that average people continued to see them as a vehicle for achieving a higher standard of living and greater control over their work. Here, Hawks moved beyond the idiom of "workers' voices" and "freedom" and invoked a language of collective protest reminiscent of the labor movement of the New Deal era:

> By standing together, people can have a stronger voice in their workplace. We all need to bear in mind, workers of America everywhere, white- and blue-collar, what President John F. Kennedy had to say in a speech in October 1960. . . . "Those who would destroy or further limit the rights of organized labor—those who would cripple collective bargaining or prevent organization of the unorganized—do a disservice to the course of democracy." Employees represented by free and

> democratic trade unions of their own choosing participate actively in determining their wages, hours, and working conditions.

Assessing the material benefits of union membership, Hawks challenged the stereotype of the cynical labor racket:

> Our labor unions are not narrow, self-seeking groups. . . . Through collective bargaining and grievance procedures, they have brought justice and democracy to the shop floor. But their work goes beyond their own jobs, and even beyond our borders. Our unions have fought for aid to education, better housing, development of our natural resources and saving family-size farms. They have spoken not for narrow self-interest, but for the public interest and for the people.[130]

While champions of the New Economy promoted a marketplace free of government interference, some Virginia workers revitalized the New Deal vision of organized labor as an agent of democratic reform.

In revitalizing the idiom of grassroots reform—"the public interest" and "the people" versus "narrow self-interest," "justice and democracy" versus profit maximization, "free and democratic trade unions" rather than top-heavy bureaucratic organizations—Hawks and others discovered a way to regenerate the institutions that had been so central to American social reform.

Local college teacher Eileen Huey highlighted the anti-democratic treatment of unions in Virginia by turning to the Constitution and the state's exalted past. The state's Right to Work Act did more than disrupt the ability of unions to raise revenues; it violated workers' freedom. Real "individual rights require a voice in the marketplace for all sectors of the economy, not just owners." Freedom was denied to working Virginians so long as they did not have the right to association, free speech, and collective bargaining. "How ironic that the spawning ground for Patrick Henry and Thomas Jefferson, the foremost champions of rights for the common man, evolved into the state government most repressive of workers' rights." Like Rosa White, Huey appealed for a historical perspective on organized labor. Only that way could Virginians escape the grip of a seemingly timeless, anti-democratic ideology that had stood in the way of black equality as well as workers' rights in the Old Dominion. It was the labor movement that "produced the family living wage, retirement security, health insurance, the 40-hour week, the two-week vacation, sick pay, overtime, worker's compensation, unemployment insurance, prohibition against child labor and safety in the workplace." In Virginia, though, benefits and protections were being relegated to an allegedly uncompetitive past. Permitting children to work at age fourteen and allowing worker's compensation levels to decline to the lowest in the country, the commonwealth had proven itself indifferent to the needs of working people.[131]

The issue at stake was the decline of working-class stability and the social contract in modern America. Using the more palatable American notion of the "middle class," Huey called for the abolition of the Right to Work Act to stave off its decline. She drew an ominous portrait of class polarization in the Old Dominion. Social order would require "a repressive government" to control the "80 percent" who had suffered from the dilution of labor laws in the state. What is astonishing is that, in the middle of the panglossian New Economy, the *Virginian-Pilot* published an article warning of class conflict. Albeit written by an academic versed in the history of social movements, the piece resonated with a democratic idiom that had all but disappeared from public life. Virginia's workers were not simply disadvantaged consumers but "second class citizens"; the failure to redress unfair labor laws was not simply a matter of pluralistic balancing but fundamental American principles; the union movement was not an interest group but the protector of hard-won rights and freedoms for average people. There was more to be lost through the mistreatment of workers than productivity. A "stable, self-sufficient, and prosperous middle class" was essential to guarantee "the great American experiment in democratic government." She called on workers to reject the rhetoric of those who benefited from laws that denied them their freedoms. It was mendacious to claim that "Virginia could not compete in the global economy without its repressive labor laws." If Virginia participated in the global market like others states, "it should not need its workers to be second-class citizens in order to be competitive."[132] This was not a matter of southern regional traditions or paternalism. For Huey, Virginia's workers had built the democratic tradition that defined the nation.

In trying to unlock the grip of anti-unionism on the South, Huey, Hawks, and the others invoked the language of the progressive movement that regenerated civic democracy in the early twentieth century. Unconsciously, they began invoking the language of industrial democracy that had been so fundamental to the labor movement of that time. They challenged the assertions of unalloyed prosperity in the age of market supremacy and stock market hysteria. What was unclear was whether that could translate into a political movement.

CHAPTER 5

Trading in Southern Futures

NAFTA and Virginia

No issue symbolized the promise of the New Economy more than the North American Free Trade Agreement. It captured the imagination of those who placed their trust in the marketplace as the vehicle of social progress and material improvement. For corporate leaders and centrist politicians, it represented the apotheosis of free market social engineering. By embracing market deregulation, the reduction of trade barriers, the mobility of capital, and the termination of heavy manufacturing as the leading force of American economic growth, NAFTA would restore American competitiveness. Through revitalized competitiveness, America would enjoy a new dispensation of prosperity. It was the centerpiece of the neoliberal project for reinventing American society along the lines of economic flexibility, the equivalent of the nineteenth century's Open Door policy and colonial expansionism.

Yet because the proposed trade deal encapsulated the promise of freedom from New Deal–era social regulation, it focused the minds of people whose security depended on those arrangements. Organized labor, environmental groups, citizens' organizations, and fair trade intellectuals weighed in on the debate. They brought to the fore the issues of democratic governance and class conflict that had been erased from American political discourse in the late twentieth century. The South had been the historical locus of economic colonialism in the United States and a region that stood to lose considerably from economic integration with low-wage Mexico. It figured prominently in the debate, and Virginia played a critical role in solidifying the deal. The purpose of the discussion here is not to rehearse the NAFTA debate but to focus on how Virginians made sense of it in the context of their world, one dominated by corporate restructuring and economic uncertainty. It was a time in which the free market, personal investment, and unimpeded entrepreneurialism seemed to offer more than hollow promises.

The struggle over NAFTA forced southern workers to confront the implications of the ideology of individualistic, market-oriented freedom. The doctrine sounded remarkably like Jacksonian independence, but it offered little defense against concentrated economic power and transnational private interests. On the front line of the NAFTA debate, southern labor leaders, citizens, and sympathetic journalists forged a set of ideas that rejuvenated the collectivist, egalitarian ideals of the progressive tradition. Together with organized labor, they challenged the assertion that market dynamics and concentrated private interests should dominate American life. That they did so at precisely the same time that southerners were assailing New Deal liberalism makes it additionally important.

By focusing so intensively on international trade, however, opponents tended to overlook the domestic sources of social decline and economic dislocation. The focus also distracted organized labor from the critical task of organizing service workers, recent immigrants, Latino and African American women, and countless other Americans caught in the service-economy vortex. Even so, it gave southerners a chance to reconnect economic and political questions, to challenge the conventional assumption that domestic economic arrangements are the product of natural forces rather than political decisions.[1] The debate gave southern liberals a national forum to address the declining fortunes of southern workers. It briefly lent legitimacy to the claim that the interests of working people mattered, even in the era of microchips and semiconductors.

Although the Mexican government first proposed the idea of economic integration for North America, the plan evolved out of the drive to create a more open-market economy which accelerated in the 1970s. In the years of stagflation, rising oil prices, anti-regulatory corporate sentiments, and growing demand for access to foreign markets, the clamor for international trade increased. Through the Tokyo Round of GATT negotiations in 1979, American decision-makers successfully placed nontariff barriers to trade—including domestic social policies and production regulations—on the table. In the process, they advanced the idea that market dominance should become the global standard.[2] While the Office of the Trade Representative in the White House pressed countries to repeal protectionist practices, the president sought authority to negotiate "fast-track" trade deals that proscribed additional amendments once the proposal had been submitted to Congress.

A domestic constituency also coalesced around trade liberalization. The coalition sustained momentum for greater market integration throughout the last two decades of the twentieth century. Composed of leading Republicans and Democrats, major media outlets, and liberal internationalist advocacy groups, it also included American companies increasingly committed to world trade. "As American firms have become more dependent on foreign markets and foreign suppliers—and this is especially true in the more 'high-tech' areas of the economy—they have become more active and vocal in opposing any policy choices that might harm the larger global trading systems."[3] Proponents of trade liberalization worked to expand markets overseas and reduce domestic resistance to foreign imports. Government advocates of free trade also fostered international institutions that would promote trade liberalization while insulating decision-making from the influence of domestic opponents. Through GATT and later the WTO, free trade administrators would promote market integration beyond the reach of domestic defenders of trade restrictions.[4] At its most basic, the NAFTA agreement represented an extension of the project to insert the United States into a global trading system keyed to the interests of unrestricted capitalism.

While the rhetoric of ineluctable globalization gave market integration an air of common sense, the intense corporate and political support it gained gave it an air of urgent necessity. The fight over the proposed agreement—which would gradually eliminate tariffs between the United States and Mexico over a fifteen-year period—began in earnest before the treaty was drafted in 1991. In this prologue to the NAFTA debate, the president sought renewal of fast-track authority to negotiate the deal. Congress granted the extension, but only after vigorous opposition from organized labor and environmental groups who pressured House Democrats to extract concessions from the administration. In return for the authority to negotiate a deal that could not be substantially revised once it was submitted to Congress, the Democrats gained a number of assurances. First, they were guaranteed that negotiations would address workers' rights in Mexico. In addition, they were offered remuneration for lost jobs in the United States and guarantees of environmental safeguards.[5]

The contest over fast track mobilized business leaders as well as labor and environmentalists. When the AFL-CIO circulated a video in Washington depicting deplorable working conditions in Mexico and warnings against job loss in the United States, business executives fanned out across Capitol Hill to counter the message. "Armed with figures on every state's major exports, export growth, and exports markets," reported the *Washington Post*, "they argue that the free trade deal means more jobs, greater wealth and cheaper products on both sides of the border."[6] Both the Bush and Clinton administrations would enjoy overwhelming support from American business for NAFTA. What emerged was a coalition of government and business elites committed to policies of neoliberal economic development in the United States and beyond.[7]

By the time that the agreement was submitted to Congress, the business campaign for free trade had become a highly coordinated and massively funded affair. The influential Business Roundtable lined up behind NAFTA. So too did USA*NAFTA, a corporate lobbying group representing Fortune 500 interests, which organized leading employers from each state to persuade legislators to do the right thing. The group spent millions on an advertising campaign to convince congressional representatives to vote for the deal.[8] Citing an Institute for Policy Studies' report on USA*NAFTA, Virginia unionist Gerald Meadows claimed that of 32 "state captains"—corporations in charge of leading the pro-NAFTA movement in each state—29 had plants in Mexico. Several, including AT&T, General Electric, and General Motors, had played a decisive role in shifting approximately 180,000 jobs from the United States to Mexico between 1981 and 1992.[9] After a statistical examination of the corporate leaders in the pro-NAFTA campaign, political scientists Michael Dreiling concluded that class interests motivated and directed their actions. "It is widely acknowledged that politically unified corporations represent a threat to the operation of democratic institutions," Dreiling observed. Corporate convergence on NAFTA was no mere matter of organizational affinity or fortuitous events. A class consensus galvanized state captain corporations.[10]

Pointing to President Carlos Salinas's effort to liberalize Mexico's economy and exorcise the ghost of its undemocratic past, pundits claimed that NAFTA would sustain the momentum. The editors of the *Richmond Times-Dispatch* proclaimed that "if NAFTA fails, we will see a reversion to protectionism in Mexico, not to mention less stability in the political order." "Stability" became a code word in the 1990s for free market capitalism. Even the former Soviet Union could be considered "stable" despite its massive unemployment and the disintegration of social services since it had adopted free market reforms. According to Virginia Citizens for a Sound Economy, the NAFTA agreement would only accelerate the rate of exports to Mexico, which had grown from $41 million to $158 million since 1987. The group said nothing about the projected losses once Mexico became a tariff-free magnet for low-wage jobs. This, however, was the point: the promise of growth itself eclipsed considerations of democratic representation or the disruptive consequences of expert-brokered deals. In fact, all that the Citizens for a Sound Economy could offer were dire warnings about the loss of new jobs that would allegedly be created once NAFTA was in place. "Since NAFTA would lower trade barriers much more rapidly than in the past, many more than the 9000 jobs mentioned above are at stake. Perhaps another 5000 or even 8000. No one knows for sure."[11]

Indeed, NAFTA curiously replicated the risk and allure of the stock market. Proponents speculated in employment futures while exposing existing jobs to the caprices of the marketplace. For the editors of the *Times-Dispatch* and for the proponents of a society that exalted atomistic individualism over social bonds, those objections were invalid. According to them, a vote for NAFTA "would mean not only more jobs but more personal freedom and consumer choice."[12] In its implicit attack on labor regulations ("personal freedom") and its celebration of consumer choice over democratic participation, the *Times-Dispatch* exemplified the uninhibited market enthusiasm of the 1990s. The assumptions that underlay the drive to redesign the workplace in favor of managerial prerogatives and global competitiveness permeated the defense of the NAFTA agreement.

The Richmond paper was not alone in trumpeting the free market virtues of the NAFTA agreement. Rather than the "rhetorical flourishes" of John F. Kennedy's Alliance for Progress or Franklin D. Roosevelt's Good Neighbor Policy, noted the *Roanoke Times*, the trade agreement provided "pragmatic opening wedge that could lead Mexico and others from a state-based economic system that has produced poverty and tyranny to a market-based system that might produce prosperity and freedom." Here again was the axiom of the 1990s, the equation between democracy and free markets. The central assumption was that environmental restrictions, business regulations, labor protections, and tax-supported programs violated freedom and denied prosperity. What else could the paper's editors have meant when they blamed Mexico and Brazil's poverty on their failure to endorse "the proven pragmatism of free markets"? A history of colonial exploitation, agricultural feudalism, and economic dependency stood for little in comparison to the detrimental effects of "political utopianism."[13]

Of course, the principal consideration for NAFTA advocates was the benefit to Americans. The *Roanoke Times* claimed that this would come in the form of 450 million "potential customers in Central and South America." Admittedly, the paper demurred, those customers had little buying power at the time, but the alchemy of the free market and its invisible hand would invariably solve that problem: "But the history of free trade, from its inception in 19th century Britain, is one of an expanding pie that feeds all comers.

That is, the wealth of nations is not finite, but capable of almost infinite expansion by free men operating in free markets."[14] Adam Smith—or William Graham Sumner—could not have put it better. What the editor overlooked in his historical reverie was the role of abysmally low wages and deplorable working conditions in the success of free trade. In addition, the relentless search for new markets and favorable conditions for manufacturing had taken on global dimensions. The American South would look comparatively less attractive to companies engaged in the high stakes of low-cost production. What he also overlooked was that the comparative advantage of production in America—high-tech resources, capital reserves, manufacturing, and research capabilities—were themselves mobile and transferable. Now, one nation's facility with research and development could easily become another's should the shipping costs and labor rates be favorable.

Above all, the *Roanoke Times*, like the *Times-Dispatch*, was most concerned about lost opportunities. America's loss would be Japan's gain, which would prevent the two from "going forward as partners in free trade that could be a liberating force throughout the hemisphere."[15] The editors had a point in arguing that relatively low tariffs on Mexican products shipped to the United States had not provided the kind of insulation that unions might have expected. Theoretically, eliminating them would not trigger a manufacturing stampede for the Mexican border. Yet as economist Harley Shaiken observed in a contemporaneous *Washington Post* article, the biggest threat was to wages, not relocation. Since Mexican workers had reached comparable productivity with their American counterparts but earned one-eighth the wage, the impact on wages in the United States would be devastating. As author Steven Pearlstein explained, the removal of even a few firms south of the Rio Grande would "send a powerful competitive message to every owner and worker in the industry to hold down wages." For Shaiken, this leveling effect would span out well beyond the manufacturing sector, reducing wages and impoverishing American workers across the board.[16]

By November 1993, Virginia's opinion-makers had come onboard with NAFTA. In the economically depressed port of Hampton Roads, the agreement suggested prosperity, as congressional representatives and media looked forward to increased shipping volume from reduced tariffs.[17] With unbridled optimism, local media saw the agreement as an extension of America's civilizing and liberalizing mission. The *Newport News Daily Press* proclaimed that "Free trade benefits the United States. Yes, some pain is involved for some industries, but they should not be protected against competition at a cost that must be borne ultimately by American consumers." Proponents of NAFTA echoed marketing gurus and advertising executives in imagining Americans primarily as consumers, not producers. Moreover, according to the *Daily Press*, "Rejection of NAFTA is a rejection of what's best about the American tradition: the desire for growth, for competition, for a better, broader world."[18] Driven by a Darwinian fear that globalization would leave the United States behind, one *Daily Press* editor claimed that the agreement "represents an optimistic vision for the future. To reject it is to try to hold on to the past. Nations that do that get passed by."[19] In this struggle for survival, the "past" was a burden. The era of regulated trade was but an earlier stage in the inexorable process of global capitalist evolution.

What motivated the bargaining and its enthusiastic endorsement, then, was fear, not hope. To many champions of market dominance, it seemed as if a global economic march of nations was leaving the United States behind, a protectionist relic in a world of rising Asian tigers and chauvinistic European trading blocs. In one of the *Times-Dispatch*'s more dispassionate treatments of the contentious agreement, journalist Gene Marlowe highlighted the driving impulses behind NAFTA. For business, the principal motive was anxiety about a listless economic recovery following the recession of 1990/1991. "With the economy in low gear," Marlowe bluntly explained, "business needs new markets and Mexico is the nation's most promising prospect. NAFTA will allow many U.S. industries into Mexico for the first time, and it gives us a competitive advantage against the Japanese and Europeans, who will continue to pay Mexico's high tariffs." Although Marlowe avoided the equally compelling motive of reduced production costs and lowered wages in the United States, he hit upon the theme of uncertainty in an era of shaky profits and global capital mobility. Interestingly, Marlowe also underlined how southern labor history informed union opposition to the free trade deal. Acknowledging that hundreds of jobs lost to Mexican competition in the previous decade had come from the ranks of organized labor, Marlowe observed that "Trade unionists fear a repeat of what happened when the South industrialized, taking jobs from the North. AFL-CIO president Lane Kirkland says unions 'know from bitter experience' what will happen when a 'super Sun Belt' offering corporations poorly paid labor with restricted rights opens in Mexico."[20]

Following the national current, Virginia's media defined the debate as a contest between pragmatic advocates of economic growth and narrow-minded economic crackpots.[21] The invidious comparison echoed the representation of William Jennings Bryan the Populist Party election of 1896, the decisive moment in the Gilded Age contest between progressive forces and consolidated business interests. In an effort to deflect the grassroots Populist movement, which aimed at restraining corporate power and increasing democratic control over the economy, leading businesses portrayed Republican William McKinley as the standard-bearer of "sound money" and the Boy Orator as a dangerous idealist.

In the conflict over NAFTA, business and government elites once again wheeled out the rhetoric of Sound Economic Policy to invalidate NAFTA's opponents. Maximum market integration became legitimate and sensible; discussions of the rights of workers, the integrity of the environment, and the dangers of unrestricted competition were portrayed as antagonistic to American national interests and ideals. Along with national media, the *Virginian-Pilot* dismissed NAFTA opponent Ross Perot as a treaty "gadfly" who was simply "wrong about the treaty's deleterious effects."[22] In rhetorical guilt-by-association, the *Roanoke Times* suggested that organized labor was the American equivalent of Mexican strong-arm caudillos: "The AFL-CIO and Ross Perot are the main forces opposing NAFTA. The first is somewhat like the old Institutional Revolutionary Party that has ruled Mexico since 1929, specializing in liberal rhetoric and illiberal policies." As for Perot, the paper tarred him with the brush of homegrown demagoguery and political opportunism: "Perot, who spoke warmly of the agreement before the presidential bug bit in earnest, is looking for anything populist to keep his kite flying. We might take note of the millions that he (and the U.S. government) have [*sic*] poured into developing a Perot-operated free-trade zone in Texas designed to serve the Mexican market."[23] The populists had once again become dangerous dreamers.

Virginia's leading opinion-maker mirrored the national media's attempt to portray NAFTA opponents as irrational zealots. The *Richmond Times-Dispatch* described union critics as "angry labor leaders" threatening "ill-will" while repeating the president's accusation that organized labor had resorted to "roughshod, muscle-bound tactics," reinforcing the stereotype of thuggish labor racketeers.[24] Positioning NAFTA as a question of progress versus stagnation, the *Newport News Daily Press* called on its readers to "embrace the future," since rejecting the deal represented a futile effort to "hold onto the past. Nations that do that get passed by."[25] Even following Congress's endorsement of NAFTA, Virginia's media continued to castigate free trade opponents. Asserting that "trade liberalization is always right," the *Richmond Times-Dispatch* ominously concluded that defeat of NAFTA would have initiated a descent into "isolationism, xenophobia, obstructionism, reaction, and protection." Merely opposing the measure, let alone raising objections based on social considerations, was tantamount to obstructionism. It was an opinion quite consistent with the belief that unmitigated market competition was normative and necessary, the governing assumption of the period. More than this, "Organized labor has been revealed in all its scarecrow impotence. The twit Perot is down." The opposition had cobbled together an alliance between "the hard right," "the populists," and "Big Labor" in order to "promote a protectionism woefully out of place in a world with ever more global interests."[26] Organized labor was "Big Labor," the mainstream media's standard rhetorical device for denigrating labor unions. Yet it hardly accorded with the reality of a shrinking labor movement on the defensive against consolidated corporate interests.

NAFTA proponents argued that global market forces were inexorable and that movements for international justice or labor standards would only impede progress. Virginia media subscribed to the neoliberal equation of free markets and democracy, but it was nevertheless attentive to the political expediency that underlay negotiations. Quite simply, the administration engaged in an orgy of pork barreling to guide NAFTA to safety. "Simultaneously, while Clinton has driven down the Pecos populist's popularity, he has placed more of his own political future in the Republicans' hands."[27] Long before the administration capitulated to welfare reform and terminated its fight for national health care, it signaled its absorption of the free market business agenda that had been at the center of Republican policy since the 1970s. While Virginia Republicans endorsed the campaign to dismantle New Deal social policies, they had no reason to challenge the central tenet of President Clinton's economic policy.

The *Richmond Times-Dispatch* matched the national media's effort to utilize the past in defense of trade expansion. The issue was one of "leadership," which fell to the United States when it cast aside the isolationism of the 1920s. In the paper's estimation, the Smoot-Hawley Tariff, with its defensive protectionism in the midst of the Great Depression, only exacerbated the international crisis and drove Europe toward fascism. Yet the paper's historical memory was selective in recounting the decline into autarky and fascism. The impact of the billions of dollars in reparations imposed on Germany and the American insistence on Allied debt repayment were never mentioned. Considering the frequency with which NAFTA proponents invoked the Smoot-Hawley example as a warning against the perils of protective tariffs, it is worthwhile considering countervailing viewpoints from the debate, which soon focused on the proposed Central American

Free Trade Agreement. William R. Hawkins, a researcher with the U.S. Business and Industry Council, an organization that represents small businesses and opposes unfettered globalization, put the matter of misusing the Smoot-Hawley Tariff this way:

> The myth that the Smoot-Hawley Tariff "caused" the Great Depression is nonsense. The act was signed in June 1930 to go into effect in 1931. The stock market had already crashed in October 1929. What made the depression so "great" in scale was the collapse of the banking and financial system. By the end of 1931, over 1,300 banks had failed, wiping out the life savings of millions and most of the nation's money supply. That is why the key reforms enacted to prevent future depressions focused on providing deposit insurance and on insulating banks from the stock market. . . . Trade played only a small role in the American economy at the time, and changes in tariff rates had nothing to do with the economic downturn. Indeed, the U.S. continued to run a trade surplus after the passage of Smoot-Hawley, as it had done before.[28]

The paper compounded the dubious historical parallel by arguing that the United States discovered the benefits of free trade in the post-war period, when it engaged in "trade among equals" to the mutual benefit of Europe and America.[29] Of course, Mexico and most of Latin America were not the equals of the United States in the early 1990s. This low-wage, economically underdeveloped region could not become the market dynamo which NAFTA advocates claimed. Furthermore, as the paper noted, Europe benefited from the Marshall Plan and returned the favor by purchasing American goods. NAFTA, however, offered no massive social investment in Mexico. If anything, NAFTA flowed from the same kind of thinking which prompted the IMF to insist on a structural adjustment program. In that unilateral scheme, Mexico would privatize its public sector, fix its currency in order to favor continued imports, and drastically reduce social programs. As analyst Kim Moody put it, under the provisions of the IMF settlement to salvage Mexico's troubled economy, the country had become "the sort of free-market Third World country that U.S. capital could learn to love. . . . Its economy was largely privatized, deregulated and structurally adjusted by the most rigorous IMF standards." This prepared Mexico for the role it would play as an unregulated, low-wage, free market haven for American enterprise. The NAFTA agreement would powerfully advance this agenda.[30]

Virginia's political and business elite followed the national pattern by mobilizing behind the NAFTA agreement. Former governor Gerald Baliles weighed in on the debate by raising the prospect of European trading partners punishing the United States for protectionism and stalling the movement toward a global trading system. American "competitiveness" was at stake, and a debate that operated on "emotion" rather than "reason" or depended on "fiction" rather than "facts" would jeopardize the country's economic future.[31]

In post–Cold War America, the national interest would reflect major corporate interests and the caprices of the international marketplace. Strengthening American infrastructure or spending on social priorities such as education, health care, and job creation were increasingly subordinated to the requirements of international competitiveness. Empowered by the savings that flowed from cheap imports and retrained for the demands of a high-tech economy, Americans would relinquish their attachment to the regulatory state and relish the opportunities of unrestricted global capitalism.

The belief in the inevitability of global integration was abundantly evident in the remarks of economist David Orr, who championed free trade at a breakfast forum for 150 of First Union National Bank of Virginia's corporate clients. Pointing to capitalism's constant dilemma—the search for "more people to sell things to"—Orr claimed that NAFTA symbolized "whether we look to the future or futilely try to protect the past. No country has ever been able to do it." By keying in on telecommunications and information technology, the United States could capitalize on change. Orr conceded that jobs would be lost, but that would be the result of technological change, not inexpensive imports. Even more to the point, as the *Roanoke Times* reported, "That's neither good nor bad, he said, but it is inevitable." Creative destruction—the mantra of corporate engineers—merged with the widespread conviction that maximum capital mobility defined freedom in the new era. With this kind of rhetoric, NAFTA proponents sidelined alternative paths to economic stability. At the same time, they invalidated the notion that national economic policy was subject to majority will.[32]

Despite the administration's supplementary agreements on labor and environmental issues, passage of the bill was anything but certain. In fact, by August 1993, a solid majority of Americans had rejected the agreement, fearing it would diminish national sovereignty and generate job losses. In addition, House Democrats seemed poised to reject the measure.[33] The administration responded by launching a determined effort to persuade individual Democrats to endorse the deal and to shore up Republican support.

What transpired was "the most massive mobilization of pro–free trade forces since 1940."[34] The campaign included television advertising, press conferences, vice-presidential appearances on popular television talk shows, and appeals to corporate interests such as the one that took place in Richmond in early November. Considering that Virginia had been ravaged by textile plant closings and manufacturing losses, the state's workers were acutely sensitive to the threat of additional job erosion. In a last-minute drive to generate "grassroots support" among corporate sponsors, the president dispatched Deputy Secretary Roger Altman to Richmond to address a Fortune 500 forum. Altman understood that the corporate mobilization campaign would have to overcome the objections of the anti-NAFTA popular majority: "Congressman after congressman have [*sic*] said that they're hearing great volumes from the opposition but very little from supporters. . . . This will be a very close vote. . . . It is winnable, but if we win, it will be by one vote."[35] It's difficult not to conclude that the corporate "grassroots" campaign was designed to overwhelm an actual grassroots sentiment against the treaty.

Considering prevailing business opinion about NAFTA opposition, Altman's position was not a surprise. According to Marvin L. Mann, chief executive of Lexmark International in Kentucky, a company which President Clinton visited in his full-court press for NAFTA, "The issue is one of ignorance. . . . Working people don't know what this is about."[36] Tom Brock, vice president of GE Systems in Salem, Virginia, shared Mann's opinion. The AFL-CIO had engaged in "rabble-rousing" and "emotional pleas" to convince Americans to reject an agreement that would "benefit American workers."[37] Brock and Mann echoed Gerald Baliles's belief, one that was shared by the mainstream media: NAFTA opposition was fueled by emotion rather than a sober understanding of economic realities.

Galvanized by the fear that union meddling would squander trade opportunities, corporate executives swung into action. The corporate campaign resembled the pressure tactics that southern business deployed in union election drives. Charles A. Hayes, president of Guilford Mills in Greensboro, North Carolina, set up an information hotline for employees concerned about the treaty. The information was anything but impartial. Within three weeks, Hayes had persuaded 3,000 employees to write to their congressional representatives on behalf of the treaty.[38] While Hayes disseminated "information," Tom Brock sent pro-NAFTA letters to some 1,200 non-unionized GE employees and availed himself of media in the interest of advancing the NAFTA cause.[39]

While corporate executives led the charge for open borders in the name of export opportunities, some Virginia academics gave it intellectual credibility. George Grayson, professor of government at George Mason, captured the relationship between NAFTA and the world historical moment that followed the end of the Cold War: "Remarkable changes have swept the world in recent years. In just a short time, we have seen the Berlin Wall collapse, Germany reunified, the Soviet Union dismantled, and democracy installed in countries throughout the world. Freedom, political and economic, continues to replace oppression as the world embraces a free-market global economy."[40] If company executives were magnetized by the prospect of reduced manufacturing costs and a hidden Mexican middle class, academics were often swept up in the conviction that NAFTA would advance Henry Luce's dream of an American Century. Freedom meant unlimited choice in the great bazaar of international commerce, yet this version of freedom neglected the fundamental imbalance at the core of American society. Rather than an equal exchange between rational maximizers, Americans confronted a social arena in which private corporate interests dominated the terms of employment. At the same time, they molded public policy and set the nation's economic priorities. In an era when advertising campaigns pervaded almost every crack and crevice of public life and when corporate consolidation in media and telecommunications drastically reduced the public space for dissenting opinion, it was wishful thinking to imagine that liberated consumers could limit business influence. Consumer opinion might matter in marketing strategies and product lines, but citizens could do little to challenge the framework in which companies operated. Freedom was the ability to choose among products, not to limit the influence of business in public life.[41]

The administration's strategy for salvaging NAFTA depended not only on corporate support but also on convincing reluctant congressional representatives to endorse the deal. Here, Virginia and indeed the South played a key role. With the concentration of manufacturing in the Petersburg-Hopewell area and the textile industry in southwest Virginia, representatives had to think carefully about an agreement that threatened that sector. Republicans generally supported the agreement. Apparently persuaded by AT&T and Reynolds Metals—both of which were in his Richmond district—Republican Thomas Bliley endorsed the agreement. Bliley believed that "we're going to wind up manufacturing more goods for export than we will lose through import."[42] Democrats were less certain. Torn between the president's market triumphalism and their traditional ties to organized labor and African Americans, they struggled with the agreement. The prospect of job flight in the early years of an economic recovery gave every representative pause for thought.

Fearing that an open floodgate to Mexico would mean further downward mobility for African Americans in Norfolk, congressional representative Robert Scott of Newport News joined the Black Caucus in rejecting the agreement. After visiting Mexico and dispelling the myths about budding middle-class consumers, Democrat Leslie Byrne of Annanport also rejected the agreement. "It's very hard to sell television sets to people who don't have electricity, or washing machines to people who don't have running water." Presumably having visited the maquiladora manufacturing regions, Byrne concluded that Americans were deceiving themselves if they believed that the agreement would respect labor and environmental standards. Byrne and Scott both eventually voted against the agreement. Democrat Rick Boucher also struggled with the prospect of jeopardizing some 9,000 textile jobs in the Ninth District of southwest Virginia. Despite a direct appeal from President Clinton, Boucher held out and voted against the treaty.[43]

These votes certainly mattered in early November, when the agreement seemed in peril, but none of these representatives were power brokers. As a member of the House Ways and Means Committee and leader of the congressional "Textile Caucus," Representative Lewis F. Payne certainly was, and the administration went after him aggressively. Payne's support was additionally important because he represented the Fifth District, an area that included Martinsville and Danville. Symbols of the New South, these were places where thousands of southerners still drew their livelihood from textile manufacturing. The assumption was that Payne could exert influence over southern Democrats representing comparable textile- and apparel-producing districts throughout the middle South.[44]

With this in mind, the president deployed Commerce Secretary Ron Brown to bring Payne onside. Brown was no doubt persuasive, but the administration made things more interesting for Payne by promising to locate a "manufacturing technology center" in Martinsville in exchange for his vote. The day after Payne announced his support for NAFTA, he met with Clinton and Vice President Al Gore at the White House. According to the *Richmond Times-Dispatch*, Payne suggested that "it would be very helpful to get an indication the administration 'was looking favorably at [the center request].'"[45] Almost immediately, he received a letter from the president expressing his confidence that Martinsville would be a serious contender for the manufacturing center. As a measure of the importance of Payne's vote, Trade Representative Mickey Kantor announced it. When the letter arrived, Payne had the pleasure of informing the people of Martinsville.[46]

Payne did more than cast his vote for NAFTA; he also used his position on the House Ways and Means Committee to modify NAFTA-enabling legislation to provide for "rules of origin." This clause, Payne believed, would ensure that only textiles and apparels using material from North America would be considered duty-free when imported to the United States. An exercise in optimism—or cynical political maneuvering—it would do little to stem the tide of imports from Asian countries producing at lower costs than Mexico.[47]

The Lewis Payne episode exemplified Clinton's modus operandi. The president ran, dined, and golfed with as many as a hundred legislators in an effort to win support for NAFTA.[48] According to Representative Gene Green of Texas, bridges and highways were on the menu for legislators willing to cast a vote for the trade deal. Facing the most immediate threat from Mexican labor and low-cost imported food items, southerners were in a unique position to leverage the president for concessions. Representatives from Florida concerned about citrus and sugar imports, representatives from Oklahoma anxious about Canadian subsidies on wheat and peanuts, and representatives from Texas simply worried about job loss won promises for everything from cargo planes to reduced airline taxes, from money for worker retraining to a North American Development Bank.[49] As for Payne, he announced that he would try to convince fellow southern congressmen to vote for the deal.[50]

The responses to Payne's decision exposed the class divisions exacerbated by the NAFTA debate. The *Richmond Times-Dispatch* took the opportunity to recapitulate the free trade dogma that prevailed in Washington. As the paper put it in an editorial, "Free trade benefits all parties. The greatest economic success occurs during periods of free trade; global protectionism encourages stagnant economies. . . . His constituents have reason to be proud."[51] According to Dean Goad, president of the International Brotherhood of DuPont Workers, the agreement tacitly approved "slave labor." Hyperbole aside, Goad was convinced that Payne's decision privileged corporations over working people: "I guess it gets down to who you represent. . . . Do you represent the average John Doe on the street or do you represent corporate executives? That's who stands to gain."[52] While NAFTA solidified the relationship between business and centrist Democrats, it also brought southern Democrats and Republican economic conservatives together.

More than the repudiation of welfare or the endorsement of GATT, the NAFTA agreement signaled the assent of southerners to the Washington Consensus. Just as southern Democrats had rejected New Deal social reforms while embracing Rooseveltian largesse for the South, southern Democrats increasingly found that they could abandon social protections and still win votes. Endorsing trade deals that seemingly fostered the New Economy, Democrats gained credibility as economic realists. Yet when the Republicans forged a narrative of decline in which the Democrats figured prominently, they had little response. Southern Republicans would offer American working-class voters a story of decline *and* opportunity, one in which ruthless individualism and government minimalism supposedly shielded them from the worst that globalization had to offer.

NAFTA opponents did not craft a comprehensive answer to these social problems. In fact, their focus on international trade tended, as mentioned earlier, to obscure the domestic sources of working-class decline. Moreover, critics *did* occasionally decline into xenophobic, chauvinistic rhetoric, positing a zero-sum game in which American losses were Mexican gains. In this uglier side of anti-NAFTA activism, jobs were "shipped" to Mexico, where abjectly impoverished workers eagerly awaited. As one NAFTA opponent callously put it, "NAFTA is a Mexican truck driver in your rearview mirror. That's what it is." Tom Tewell, a member of the anti-NAFTA United We Stand group, captured the America First thinking that often crept into the rhetoric of workers frightened by the prospect of job loss. NAFTA would "take jobs away from the American people middle-aged and older. Once Americans have good jobs, clothing on their backs, food in their bellies, and roofs over their heads, then let's go out and help the world."[53] While Tewell isolated the problems facing American workers in an era of corporate restructuring, his comments suggested the strain of intolerance that accompanied at least some anti-treaty activism. Furthermore, the habit of presenting Mexican workers as a threat undermined what American workers needed most: cooperation with their Latin American counterparts. As Kim Moody suggested, "the tendency of AFL-CIO literature and spokespersons as well as others in organized labor to dismiss Mexican workers as victimized cheap labor who act as a disincentive to American technological innovation is a serious miscalculation. It is also insulting."[54]

Although at times anti-NAFTA activism slipped into narrow-minded chauvinism, it could also be principled and attentive to the larger forces at work in the campaign. The objections they raised against a trade deal that seemed to benefit corporate multinationals over working citizens exposed the power imbalances at the center of American life that intensified despite the proliferation of shopping malls, mutual fund investments, and gated communities. While the rhetoric of free market individualism, southern cultural distinctiveness, and religious fundamentalism obscured the persistence of class divisions and racial inequities in the modern South, the economic restructuring of the late twentieth century sharpened and widened them.

Treaty advocates routinely accused opponents of sensationalism, but Virginia's anti-NAFTA forces were at least as proficient at using data to raise reasonable doubt about the agreement. The AFL-CIO took the lead by challenging the "fast-track" authority which the Bush administration sought to negotiate the agreement. Daniel LeBlanc, a feisty northern transplant who would lead Virginia's AFL-CIO throughout the 1990s, pointed to the evidence indicating that free trade meant the evasion of labor and environmental standards. Invoking statistics from the General Accounting Office, LeBlanc noted that 78 percent of the twenty-eight manufacturers that had relocated from Los Angeles to Mexico did so to circumvent Environmental Protection Agency standards controlling the use of paint and solvents. More than this, American companies that used the special maquiladora trade zones along the Mexican border produced for the American market while paying workers slightly above the Mexican minimum wage of 50 cents an hour. To LeBlanc, it seemed, the trade agreement had less to do with market access than low-cost, unregulated production. LeBlanc and Gerald Meadows of the Roanoke Valley United Central Labor Council had only to look as far as AT&T. In 1991, it shifted its Fairlawn manufacturing establishment from New River Valley to Matamoros, Mexico, terminating employment for the 900 people who had remained after the company downsized from 2,500 in the 1980s. In Virginia, workers had earned $8.56 an hour plus benefits; in Mexico, they were paid approximately $1 an hour. For Meadows, conceding fast-track authority for a treaty that opened the United States to competition from Mexico meant unemployment. At the same time, it would give companies additional leverage in wrenching concessions from labor during contract negotiations. For LeBlanc, the administration's insistence on retraining for workers displaced by NAFTA was quixotic. With little evidence of job creation for displaced manufacturing workers—and with the prospect that most would end up in poorly paid service positions—the loss of high-paying manufacturing only strengthened the pattern of declining wages and waning union strength.[55]

This argument resonated with Larry Eanes, a General Electric employee in Salem and a member of the International Union of Electrical Workers. Challenging the administration's key argument in favor of the agreement—that Americans should abandon low-wage work to developing nations in exchange for technologically advanced, high-paying positions—Eanes observed that "We build high-tech stuff, but the way they got it broken down, everything is compartmentalized. . . . There's no job here that a Mexican cannot do."[56] Eanes anticipated a pattern that would come into sharp focus in the next century: the outsourcing of high-paying as well as low-end jobs. Through the division of labor as well as the offshoring of jobs to eminently qualified and educated workers in other nations, companies could avoid the American labor premium.[57]

When President Clinton intensified the ratification campaign by castigating labor unions, LeBlanc retaliated by arguing for fair rather than free trade. He cited studies from the Economic Policy Institute and Skidmore College projecting some 490,000 lost jobs as a result of the agreement. These kinds of numbers may have been rhetorically effective earlier, but as the debate wore on, they entered into the nebulous world of statistical overkill. They became as much a matter of economic conjecture as the proponents' claims of job growth and unheralded prosperity. More compelling was LeBlanc's evidence of past practice. "Across the board, from food-processing firms such as Green Giant and Birdseye to auto-parts makers, such as Trico; from electronics manufacturers such as Zenith to hospital-equipment houses such as Johnson & Johnson, companies have moved to Mexico to take advantage of poverty-level wages—Mexican workers earn as little as $1 an hour with lax environmental enforcement and the general lack of concern about child labor, health and safety and other work standards." LeBlanc also went after the oft-cited claim that Americans benefited heavily from trade with Mexico. A trade deficit of some $4 billion a year suggested that American workers had already lost jobs to low-wage competitors.[58]

The centerpiece of LeBlanc's rejoinder, however, was a challenge to the assertion that the displacement of American jobs was necessary for success in the global economy. Echoing the national AFL-CIO, LeBlanc argued that the labor movement endorsed trade, but not at the expense of workers in all three countries. "The American labor movement does not believe that our nation wants to promote poverty and pollution in other countries so that multi-nationals can make a profit."[59] While LeBlanc may have underestimated the nation's tolerance for "poverty and pollution" elsewhere, he articulated the abiding working-class fear that free trade agreements would further jeopardize their tenuous security. He reminded readers that this agreement was drafted at a time of real wage decline for American workers.[60] With unsubstantiated claims about generalized prosperity and plenty of evidence that American companies saw the treaty as safe passage to a low-wage El Dorado, working people had good reason to be concerned. Instead of a shift in public priorities, NAFTA seemed an extension of the Reaganite program to dismantle labor protections and make private enterprise the primary arbiter of national economic policy.

Others challenged the assertion that Mexican and American trade had grown in the recent past and that NAFTA would sustain this development. Tom Cadorette of Norfolk challenged former governor Gerald Baliles's contention that American exports to Mexico had climbed from $14 billion in 1986 to $40 billion in 1991. Instead of exporting items manufactured in the United States to consumers in Mexico, American companies were shipping supplies and machinery to Mexico for assembly there and reshipment to the United States. According to Cadorette, some $15.5 billion of Baliles's figure was spent on American factories and machinery in Mexico.[61] Turning again to the recent historical record, Cadorette questioned the former governor's assertion that NAFTA would be a job engine. NAFTA was built on an earlier free trade agreement between the United States and Canada. Since the ratification of that deal in 1988, the neighbor to the north had bled some 475,000 manufacturing jobs to the marginally lower-wage United States.[62]

Declaring his allegiance to Ross Perot, NAFTA's leading opponent, David A. Whitt of Bristol also reminded readers of the Canadian example. "In 1989 Canada signed a free-trade pact with the United States and lost 25 percent of its manufacturing jobs. In just three years!" According to Whitt, the losses would be astronomical for the United States, since it would enter into an agreement with a country where wages averaged $1 or $2 a day.[63] While Baliles and Virginia's free trade champions projected employment gains based on mathematical modeling and the wisdom of mainstream economists, Virginia's NAFTA opponents invoked historical evidence. For opponents, NAFTA represented another installment on a larger plan to eliminate the protections that limited the concentration of economic power. Roger Ethier, international trade chairman of United We Stand America and Alexandria resident, exclaimed that business and government "elitists . . . who have been out of touch during the last decade with grass-roots America, will have completed a process they started 20 years ago. They will have given away our manufacturing industries and the wealth that they represent, as well as having displaced millions of our workers and virtually destroyed our large middle-class tax base."[64] While fear of lost opportunities and intensifying international competition motivated NAFTA's defenders, anxieties cultivated by years of wage decline and de-industrialization propelled its opponents.

NAFTA opponents in Virginia separated themselves from the rhetoric of the New Economy by framing their objections in the language of democratic self-determination. They were not content to make their case solely on the grounds of business efficiency, the supposedly neutral economic standard that carried enormous ideological weight in the 1990s. For labor organizers, environmentalists, educators, and average citizens concerned about the implications of the trade deal, NAFTA seemed to symbolize the loss of democratic accountability at the center of American public life. E. Alfred Picardi argued that NAFTA would accelerate the loss of jobs that had already undermined the tax base that provided a decent health care system, family stability, and a favorable trade balance. But Picardi also criticized the unrepresentative process that produced the deal: "NAFTA was negotiated in secret with participation primarily from global corporations that stand to benefit from it. NAFTA-dispute tribunals will meet in secret and have no provision for appeals or citizen participation. The wage difference between foreign and American production does not benefit the American consumer and satisfies only the greed of the global corporations."[65] In criticizing the undemocratic character of NAFTA negotiations, Picardi challenged the influence of private financial interests over public policy. Writing to the *Virginian-Pilot* in Norfolk—an area hit hard by the recession and afflicted by high unemployment—John McAllister expanded on Picardi's sentiments: "Most opponents of NAFTA favor an agreement that will allow expandable trade, harmonize labor and environmental standards, and include a link to democratization and human rights. But NAFTA as it now stands makes no effort to raise standards, and it completely ignores democracy and human rights. If it passes, any chance of labor-market reform in Mexico is buried." As critics of the World Trade Organization would soon point out, multilateral trade deals that imagined private enterprise as the engine of social progress diminished national political control. Endorsing NAFTA would "be one step toward enforceable trade rules throughout the hemisphere based on a low-wage competitiveness strategy and explicit deregulatory pressures that supersede national and local policies."[66] In the NAFTA episode, southern legislators took a prominent role in advancing the idea that a deregulated marketplace should determine social policy.

According to some critics, "free" trade really obscured the power imbalances at work in the deal. Dick Austin, a farmer and teacher at the Appalachian Ministries Educational Resource Center, observed that conditions in Mexico made a mockery of "free" trade between the two countries. "The major reason NAFTA is not real free trade is that Mexico is not a free country. One party has ruled for 80 years by rigging elections. Unions are controlled by the government, which holds down wages to attract foreign investment. Laws that confer worker rights and environmental protections are routinely subverted by the government itself." Virginia progressives were beginning to draw connections between the exploitation of Mexican workers and the corporate practices that dominated in the United States in the latter part of the twentieth century. If globalization meant market expansion for business executives, it meant class alliances and a greater sensitivity to the subordination of nonwhite workers for others. Southerners familiar with the pattern of northern economic colonization were acutely aware of how this story was playing out south of the American border. As Austin understood, companies with limited accountability to the American electorate were being permitted to design trade agreements that militated against the interests of workers in both countries: "NAFTA will surely enrich many large, international corporations willing to exploit production opportunities regardless of national or community needs. These corporations, through their economic might and political influence, are tightening their grip on the political processes in this country. NAFTA will promote their interests at the expense of democracy, labor and the environment."[67] Able to connect the fortunes of American and Mexican workers and identify a pattern of unilateral decision-making, anti-NAFTA activists sounded the theme of democratic responsibility that would be critical to social reform in the latter part of the decade.

This theme of corporate ascendancy and democratic collapse galvanized a coalition of activists. Anti-sweatshop activists, proponents of environmental control and protection, advocates of fair trade, and defenders of the rights of workers in America converged on this notion of democratic action and accountability. It served as a diagnosis of what was wrong with America and as a general template for change. Local networks of cooperative exchange, anti-branding initiatives, living-wage campaigns, and calls for citizen pressure on corporations offered the hope of regenerating a moribund public sphere. Against the grain of rhetoric about employee empowerment and the democracy of the marketplace, these activists fostered an alternative narrative of the period.[68] In this reading of the new age of global integration, private interests justified critical social decisions by invoking the doctrines of global competitiveness. While some of these decisions were benign, others precipitated job loss, the decline of entire communities, the polarization of wealth in an affluent society, the disintegration of social security, exposure to the caprices of an ungovernable international marketplace, and the despoliation of a fragile environment.

The NAFTA controversy generated more than studied debate; it also galvanized people into action in a way that corporate downsizing could not. After years of quiescence, Americans challenged the business ethos that underlay the campaign for deregulation, anti-unionism, and unrestricted free trade. If the dramatic Pittston Strike in 1989 excited labor about the possibilities of turning back the tide of concessionary bargaining, the NAFTA struggle convinced working southerners that the issues they confronted were not isolated grievances. Global consciousness was indeed dawning for average Virginians, but what this meant was a deeper understanding of how their fortunes were tied to the decisions of multinational businesses and to the economies of peripheral countries. It did not mean cheery optimism about the benefits of an integrated global free market or a broader worldview. The trade agreement precipitated rallies and mass meetings that foreshadowed the labor and environmentalist alliance that would challenge the policies of the World Trade Organization and the International Monetary Fund.

In Roanoke, an area blighted by the decline of the textile industry, labor unions held a joint rally to "inform the community of the 'harsh realities' of the plan." The protest was part of a national AFL-CIO program of rallies on behalf of fair trade.[69] In Virginia Beach, a branch of Perot's United We Stand America held a rally shortly before Congress voted on the agreement. Carrying placards reading "No Slave Wages, No to NAFTA" and "NAFTA—That Giant Sucking Sound," the group of 24 protestors tried to convince Representative Owen Pickett to vote against the deal. In the end, 4 out of 11 of Virginia's representatives voted against the treaty.[70] And in the southeastern corner of the state close to the North Carolina border, 200 textile workers at Narricot Industries protested against an agreement which they believed would only accelerate the loss of manufacturing jobs in their area. In this effort, they had the support of the company, whose vice president claimed that "NAFTA will create a permanent underclass of unemployed Americans who currently do unskilled, semiskilled and technical jobs for

American manufacturing firms." In addition to rallying in protest, workers sent some 700 letters to congressional representatives in both states appealing to them to reject the agreement.[71]

Even before the height of the NAFTA debate, working-class Virginians had started to look at plant closings, layoffs, and trade agreements that favored capital mobility through the lens of working-class discontent. In a piece on the misfortunes of working Virginians, the *Roanoke Times* told the story of Karen Beard, an employee at American Safety Razor in Augusta County who started organizing fellow employees to register to vote. When congressional and later vice-presidential candidate John Edwards toured the plant, Beard challenged him to justify the Mexican free trade agreement. "Our jobs are leaving. . . . Every time I take a vacation, a machine is missing when I come back. Over Christmas, four machines were gone. That's 12 people." A meeting to nominate a mayoral candidate for the city drew an unusually high turnout from "blue-collar voters, many of them union members—and their families." According to Jeff Weeks, educational director for IUE Local 173, economic stagnation and continued layoffs were politicizing workers. As the paper described, Beard was struggling with "the more permanent structural changes in the American economy." The dramatic loss of manufacturing jobs convinced Beard that business interests were "trying to create a service economy," a development that would fall lightly on professionals but would translate into minimum-wage jobs for the working class. The division between the proponents of market liberalization and the workers who saw their livelihoods disintegrating was becoming increasingly conspicuous. For Republican congressional candidate Bob Goodlatte, manufacturing jobs would invariably disappear as the United States opened its borders to Mexican trade. The answer was to retrain displaced workers for "high-wage, high-tech jobs." What Goodlatte—and most Democratic legislators—offered workers like Karen Beard was the standard refrain of the era: success through rugged competition. "The economy is on the move again and we'll give businesses incentive to expand." The emphasis was on business priorities, not the immediate realities of working-class decline. "There'll be jobs for every American who wants to work and I'm confident American workers can compete."[72] Confident in the possibilities, resigned to the unavoidable losses, Virginia's political leadership only intensified the sense of powerlessness that working-class southerners confronted in the early 1990s. Far from allaying these sentiments, the NAFTA campaign deepened their discontent, fueling a powerful challenge to the story of southern sunbelts and American microchip success.

This, of course, was not the only way of looking at the era of the New Economy. Nor, for that matter, did it take into account the real productivity gains and relative material wealth that many Americans enjoyed in the 1990s. Nor, for that matter, did all Virginians oppose NAFTA. To take but one example, one resident of Newport News applauded the NAFTA agreement. Attacking the union position in the debates, the reader of the *Daily Press* asserted that "when the European Community finally gets its feet on the ground, who is to say it will not slam shut the door to American imports. . . . It is also conceivable that South America, China and Asia could go the same way, closing many doors at once. Manufacturers are going to have to be very fast on their feet indeed to keep from being ground to powder. It's already a different world out there."[73] Although we do not have extensive evidence from Virginia, we do know that, according to a Mason-Dixon poll from early October 1993, 40 percent of Virginians endorsed NAFTA, 30 percent opposed it, while a full 30 percent were undecided.[74] Closer to the vote in Congress, national public opinion seemed almost evenly matched. According to a Harris poll conducted in November 1993, Americans opposed the agreement by a slim majority. Interestingly, once the agreement was ratified, the public anxiety seemed to decline. When polled again in December, 50 percent of Americans endorsed the measure, while 40.5 percent objected.[75] It is worth keeping in mind, however, that the way in which media framed the debate probably influenced the popular response. As political scientist Mark Rupert observed, Americans were willing to change their opinion based upon whether or not the agreement was presented as a source of job creation or an agent of job loss. Since media and mainstream economists defined the agreement in terms of economic growth rather than democratic representation, NAFTA opponents had considerably less leverage to influence public opinion.[76]

In castigating the assertion that majority opposition to NAFTA was evidence of public ignorance, one Virginian probably spoke for many. The agreement may be intellectually plausible, Robert Terry of Bedford suggested, but Virginians had grown skeptical of the motives and promises of NAFTA's defenders:

> Your polls show most of us are opposed to the North American Free Trade Agreement. You then presume we must be misinformed. We don't understand. The unions, the Jesse Jacksons and the Ross Perots have misled us. Not so. We can reason and we know what's wrong with NAFTA. We think the concepts are wonderful, but we just don't

> trust the sellers and the signers. If supporters of NAFTA want to convince us, tell us what safeguards are built in for now. Tell us how the signers and enforcers would suffer personally if they fail to enact and enforce strong environmental laws, good minimum wage laws, workman's safety and health-care requirements, and fair laws governing access to local markets.[77]

Criticizing media's suggestion that opponents were unenlightened rubes who failed to understand complex trade matters, Terry also took NAFTA proponents to task for advancing an agreement that violated democratic norms. The standard for Terry and working southerners was not business efficiency but the egalitarian social practices that evolved out of the New Deal and the Great Society.

Beyond the ambiguities of media slant, NAFTA opponents offered a challenge to the tenets of marketplace triumphalism that dominated the era. They questioned the notion that government regulation was inherently antagonistic to economic growth and American freedom. NAFTA opponents offered a reasoned consideration of recent history and a rational analysis of the economic forces that conditioned American life. Democratic, grassroots activism was emerging throughout the United States, not only in Seattle and traditional liberal enclaves throughout the Northeast. While Richmond and Norfolk were drawn into the network of a New Economy, they also harbored thinkers, activists, organizers, and citizens who questioned the direction of national life as much as their counterparts in California and Washington. Yet because it was the anti-union South, the region that fostered the modern conservative movement, that critique was additionally important.

Writing three years after the ratification of the trade agreement, Gerald Meadows of the International Union of Electrical Workers captured its larger significance: "Perhaps the greatest tragedy of NAFTA is its impact on democracy. NAFTA threatens democracy by substituting the 'market' as the principle by which economic activity will be organized. It does this by prohibiting governments from developing new public-sector productive activities and effectively limiting the power of governments to regulate private businesses."[78] In 2000, with perspective on the treaty from the growing resistance to the WTO's free market program, Karl E. Balliet of Bedford challenged the rhetoric of freedom that underlay the globalization project. Taking on a Cato Institute report, Balliet rejected the assertion that America would "lose" if "anti-trade activists" were permitted to "win their war against economic liberty and expansion." Rejecting the simple dichotomy of trade versus anti-trade and freedom versus protectionism that neoliberal advocates had constructed, Balliet argued that the conflict over the NAFTA-WTO project was about power, not exports. Seattle protestors were not "anti-trade," Balliet argued, but opposed to the "dictatorial, undemocratic, big-business controlled nature of the organization [WTO]. What 'economic liberty' really means here is the liberty for large corporations to do whatever they choose. But what 'economic liberty' do laid-off textile workers have?"[79] In 1993, the debate over NAFTA frequently degenerated into a statistical shouting match, one that lost sight of the "social perspective" that journalist Edward Luttwak advocated. By the end of the decade, Balliet and others were challenging the business alliance's monopoly on the language of freedom. They were challenging the idea that stock quotes and inflation rates could substitute for economic democracy.

What Meadows and Balliet criticized is what journalist Thomas Frank later described as "market populism," the reigning consensus of the 1990s. In this version of populism, the marketplace was the most efficient, humane, and democratic vehicle for promoting social welfare. This was the essence of the New Economy, Frank believed, the "assurance that no matter what happens or who wins in November, a strong labor movement and an interventionist government will not be returning," which has "made possible the unprecedented upward transfer of wealth that we saw in the Clinton years, that has permitted the bull market without end, and that has made the world safe for billionaires." Cast in the idiom of hip, entrepreneurial iconoclasm, the new market populism provided the ideological cover for the disintegration of the social responsibility state. It also justified the cultural authority that business leaders and their political allies exercised in the waning years of the twentieth century.[80]

The NAFTA treaty exacerbated a general sense of frustration about social decline. It convinced many working- and middle-class Americans that they had lost control over the economic and social forces that shaped their lives. Because the debate over NAFTA was so public, acrimonious, and inseparable from the hyperbole about globalization, it focused the attention of average people in a way that strikes and plant closings simply could not. Negotiated by a Republican but championed by a Democratic administration, this treaty brought into sharp focus the drift toward a centrist, supply-side consensus.

At the same time, the NAFTA debate gave Americans a chance to focus on an enemy without. For corporations and business-minded legislators, this was competitive foreign enterprise; for American workers, environmentalists, and many citizens, this was the specter of cheap Mexican labor. In some ways, the debate repeated the Populists' tendency to focus on the "moneyed interests," a rather amorphous threat that originated in powerful urban centers and at the hands of scheming financiers. Yet the Populists were not misguided about the dangers of corporate consolidation or the decline of democratic government in the Gilded Age. Neither were their 1990s successors. In challenging the free market dogmas that dominated American public discourse, anti-NAFTA activists restored categories of democratic thought that had declined sharply in the years following the civil rights movement. By formulating alternatives to unrestricted free trade, by identifying the corporate imperatives behind the ratification campaign, and by critiquing the undemocratic decisions that produced the treaty and which the treaty institutionalized, anti-NAFTA critics challenged the market dominance that political economist Karl Polanyi had once critiqued. This was particularly important in the South, since it was here that economic individualism and anti-federal-government animosity flourished most intensely, creating an ideological compound that threatened working-class Americans well beyond the region.

But did NAFTA work? Working from an establishment angle, government economists publishing in the *Journal of Economic Perspectives* believed that "The mainstream forecasts during the NAFTA debate were basically correct: NAFTA has had relatively small positive effects on Mexico." Furthermore, trade benefits "necessarily involve shifting resources across sectors, which in turn will involve adjustment costs, especially for labor." For the most part, they concluded, job dislocations had been minimal—the authors estimate that only 299,000 positions were lost as a result of trade between Mexico and the United States between 1990 and 1997—and had been compensated by economic expansion. In addition, the authors warned that the implications of trade liberalization could not be measured in terms of aggregate trade balance. Eliminating "distortions" (tariffs and domestic subsidies) may influence bilateral trade balances, but national aggregate trade balances are determined "primarily in asset markets." Job loss, they argue, are not the main issue; the performance of the money markets and the gains accrued from less expensive imports are more important.[81]

Labor-oriented critics were much less sanguine about the deal. Writing for the Economic Policy Institute in 2003, Robert E. Scott expressed no reservations about discussing the connection between the NAFTA and the U.S. trade deficit. According to Scott, 879,280 American jobs were destroyed as a result of NAFTA. Of these, 78 percent, or 686,700 manufacturing jobs, vanished as a result of the agreement. "Increases in U.S. exports tend to create jobs in this country, but increases in imports tend to reduce jobs because the imports displace goods that otherwise would have been made in the United States by domestic workers." By emphasizing exports over imports, NAFTA proponents obscured the deleterious impact of the agreement on both the trade balance and American jobs. Instead of a dramatic increase in the export of consumer goods, as NAFTA proponents promised, the preponderance of exports to Mexico were (as earlier critics noted) component parts for assembly and shipment to the United States. While domestic exports increased some 95 percent to Mexico and 41 percent to Canada after the agreement, a 195 percent growth in imports from Mexico and 61.1 percent from Canada more than canceled out the gains.[82]

Scott's statistics on job loss for each state are particularly intriguing. Using Bureau of Labor Statistics and Census Bureau data, he concluded that each state lost manufacturing employment as a result of the agreement. The greatest impact—considered a net loss of more than 20,000 jobs—was on northern and midwestern states, with Tennessee, Georgia, North Carolina, Texas, and Florida suffering the most in the South. Virginia, by comparison, suffered a net loss of 17,016 jobs as a result of the agreement. As Scott admitted, the job drain had to be seen in relation to the overall economy, which continued to generate jobs throughout the late 1990s. Even so, "the promise of new jobs was the principal justification for NAFTA."[83] Promoters claimed that these new positions would balance the environmental decline and economic uncertainty. Quite simply, the return on the investment in NAFTA did not meet the promises of its proponents or compensate for the impact on working people. More than jobs lost or won, the agreement "contributed to rising income inequality, suppressed real wages for production workers, weakened workers' collective bargaining powers and ability to organize unions, and reduced fringe benefits."[84] In addition, defenders of the agreement failed to acknowledge the jobs that were lost were in the manufacturing sector. More often than not, what replaced them were positions in the low-wage, insecure service sector.

The question of whether or not trade agreements have been the principal force in depressing wages and eliminating American jobs is, of course, highly contentious.[85] Decidedly less ambiguous is the extent to which NAFTA and its proponents promoted the agreement as part of a larger assault on social Keynesianism at home. Republicans and conservative Democrats converged on the common ground of trade liberalization at the expense of security for working people. Writing at the end of the decade, economic geographers Amy Glasmeier and Robin Leichenko highlighted the contrast between southern conservative rhetoric and southern economic reality.

> The region's contemporary political complexion also includes strong advocacy for a smaller, less interventionist government—just at the time when the region's protectionist shackles are coming off. . . . The contradiction between the contemporary political rhetoric calling for less government and the region's long-standing dependence on huge infusions of resources from the federal government may precipitate a new crisis in the U.S. South, one not easily resolved when free-market rhetoric faces free-market reality.[86]

The South's traditional low-tax, labor-intensive strategy of industrial development would ultimately devastate the South, Glasmeier and Leichenko argued, as trade regulations that once protected the region's workers were dismantled. Yet the key issue behind the NAFTA debate was not the abstract benefit of free trade but what journalist Thomas B. Edsall described as "the extension of wage erosion from working-class and blue-collar men into the white-collar, well-educated middle class." The popularity of Pat Buchanan and Ross Perot, both opponents of NAFTA, had everything to do with "a new economic ground that linked blue-collar 'losers,' whose wages have been falling for decades, with the white-collar men who had been 'winners' until roughly 1987–1989."[87] Low-wage workers would suffer the most from trade liberalization, but white-collar workers would also face the growing threat of outsourcing. They had already seen what corporate downsizing could do to their sense of security.

For all of their disparagement of Perot and Buchanan, the Republicans learned a critical lesson: populist appeals worked. The Republicans absorbed the populist trope from Perot, used it to justify further deregulation of the economy, and successfully deployed it against their political opponents. This is why the Republicans did as well as they did in 1994: they turned the anti-government, populist rhetoric against their erstwhile NAFTA allies. Endorsing NAFTA, the Republicans also fabricated an ideological defense against its most destructive implications. The enemy was not free trade, Mexican workers, American corporations, or foreign bond traders. It was the Democrats and their special interests, which supposedly prevented working people from realizing the full potential of a "free" market. While liberals such as Labor Secretary Robert Reich spoke of "symbolic analysts" achieving technocratic victory in the new age, conservative Republicans spoke the language of freedom. That rhetorical trope worked not only because of the disintegration of the Soviet Union but because southern proponents of NAFTA defined what that victory meant: freedom for investment, freedom from government regulation, freedom of economic opportunity. Even if the rhetoric grossly distorted the realities of trade liberalization, it harmonized with the movement to dismantle government social programs, a project that bore the Democratic stamp and which had fallen hopelessly out of favor. Freedom was the centerpiece, and the Republicans used it both to promote neoliberalism while simultaneously discrediting their political opponents.

United by a common experience of economic insecurity, workers in the manufacturing sector, unionized employees, and white-collar workers began to share the same social terrain. In advancing an agenda of market primacy, NAFTA's proponents in the South joined the wider effort to diminish citizen participation in the public sphere. At least in 1993, Anne S. Evans of Norfolk seemed to have captured the overarching significance of the agreement. When the dust settled after the NAFTA debate, it was clear that "The working people lost."[88]

CHAPTER 6

Virginia Is for Business

Selling the Commonwealth in the Competition Era

While a resurgent labor movement made news in a state where unions were supposedly moribund, it was business that dominated the political and social landscape of the 1990s. Although Virginia and the South paralleled the national mood, the business agenda was intensely concentrated in the region. If anything, the unfettered free market doctrine made its comeback in this region, albeit under the aegis of the new era of global integration. Despite the attention paid to Silicon Valley as the symbol of New Economy bravado, the South offered the most fertile terrain for the idea that an unrestricted free market offered the solution to American decline. What emerged in Virginia was not simply a haven for technological wizardry but an ideology of market fundamentalism in which corporate giveaways figured prominently. The spirit of the age flourished in the boardrooms, the law offices, and the Senate chambers of the commonwealth. In this vision, technological innovation was inextricable from the dismantling of the welfare state, the reduction of taxes, the suppression of labor unions, and the creation of a favorable "business climate." Virginia aggressively advanced this ideology, one that fused political conservatism to a zealous commitment to economic growth through corporate incentives.

While the Republicans may have laid claim to being on the cutting edge of the new political economy, this ideology enjoyed bipartisan support. Democrats and Republicans rallied around it, struggling to outbid each other in their commitment to the contradictory objectives of fiscal responsibility and new jobs. It allowed each public champion to sound pragmatically forward-looking and simultaneously antagonistic to Great Society liberalism. While this worldview was on display in everything from trade missions to China to exhortations on educational reengineering, it was particularly evident in the campaign for corporate relocation, euphemistically known as economic development.

What is important to note is that the strategy of attracting high-tech, "knowledge industry" firms seemed to make perfect sense at the time. Manufacturing was on the decline, the South had historically suffered from an educational deficit, and the region's economy was generally overreliant on low-skilled jobs. This was in no small part the South's inheritance from an earlier period of extractive, export-oriented industrial underdevelopment.[1] It also seemed to most analysts that the path to a prosperous future was paved with microchips and lighted by fiber-optic cable.

Equally important, Virginia's political leaders were genuinely committed to generating new jobs. They too lived in the shadow of corporate downsizing, the recession of 1990/1991, and the apparently ubiquitous threat of global competition. Yet in pursuing a political agenda that made corporate privilege the first principle of economic growth, the state's elected leaders played a pivotal role in legitimizing the argument that corporate interests trumped all others. In advancing the low-tax, pro-business agenda that claimed the mantle of common sense in this era of diminished expectations, political elites promoted the idea that what was good for GM—or Motorola, in this case—was good for America. Business success became the sine qua non of social progress; its values became the standard for measuring social values. It was not a huge leap to conclude that those who had divined the mysteries of the hypercompetitive marketplace should then define social policy. Figures documenting high-tech economic growth substituted for a careful consideration of the social consequences of unlimited business expansion. In this atmosphere of anxiety, business influence over social policy went largely unquestioned.

The obsessive focus on attracting high-tech investment and corporate relocations obscured the devastating losses suffered in the manufacturing sector. New technology-sector growth often failed to compensate, either in terms of economic security or working conditions, for the positions lost to NAFTA or global competition.[2] Corporate giveaways—the practice of offering financial incentives, tax abatements, and infrastructure expenditures to prospective business clients—also came at the expense of investment in public services. Drastic tax reductions only exacerbated this pain. Promises of new jobs did not always materialize. When they did, they failed to compensate for the loss of tax revenue to public needs ranging from education to road construction. Even so, the greatest legacy of the economic development blitz of the 1990s was the notion that corporate-led globalization precluded any other strategy of economic growth. Together with business executives, government leaders solidified the idea that policies which protected the rights of workers, increased investment in the social infrastructure, or regenerated a withering public sphere were the relics of a discredited "tax and spend" liberalism.

Offering incentives for businesses to relocate was nothing new in the southern experience. In the 1870s, states provided bonds to railroads in an early campaign for northern investment. Wracked by the Civil War and the economic dislocations attendant on the end of slavery, the region was economically destitute. Municipal boosters, journalists, and business entrepreneurs championed industrialization as a path out of poverty. By the 1920s, the South had developed a distinctive pattern of industrial development. By fostering industries that did not require skilled labor, borrowing technology and expertise from the North, focusing on competition through price rather than quality, and minimizing costs that ended up preventing economic diversification, the South did in fact industrialize.[3]

By the following decade, the strategy no longer looked sustainable. International competition and the beginning of the long decline of textiles signaled the need for a strategic change. The threat of a large-scale exodus from the agricultural revolution wrought by the New Deal together with the expansion of southern infrastructure convinced regional elites to adopt a new tactic. They would champion public power and highways while using the state government as a central agency for industrial development. Public infrastructure, tax subsidies, capital allocations, and cash payments would be used to draw external investors to the region.[4] Mississippi pioneered the innovation through its "Balance Agriculture with Industry" program. Southern state legislatures continued to use the technique effectively into the 1960s.

It was in the Reagan era, however, that southern boosters realized the greatest benefits of dangling tax incentives in front of corporations seeking escape from the Rustbelt. For example, the Southwest Virginia Economic Development Commission commissioned a study on what it would take to rejuvenate the depopulating towns of the New River Valley. Not surprisingly, the commission considered taxes, access to markets, wage levels, the availability of labor, and the "business climate" critical to attracting new business. So too, however, were "attitudes" and "labor conditions." In the southwest, development officials noted the "independent" spirit of people in the mountainous region, which experts hoped to use in mitigating the region's reputation for pro-unionism. Commission members were eager to point out that, in addition to having "entrepreneurial" proclivities, the workers of the southwest were in fact less supportive of unions than events at Pittston would suggest. The key for development experts was to find "comprehensive data" to "counter the commonly held belief that locating a business in Southwest Virginia meant dealing with confrontational labor relations." By the mid-1980s, development experts were busily crafting an image of Virginia's workers as resistant to unionism, desperate for work, and reliably docile.[5]

Economic development strategies accelerated in the 1990s as recession and corporate downsizing convinced business-minded leaders that incentives were the only way to attract revenue and jobs.[6] Virginia was certainly not the first to jump on the economic development bandwagon. In Tennessee state officials offered $20 million to General Motors for "employee training," no strings attached.[7] Governor Lamar Alexander also played a key role in ushering Nissan into an 850-acre site at Smyrna. Traveling to Japan to meet with company executives, Alexander made the case that Tennessee offered a superior work climate in comparison to Kentucky, its nearest competitor, since Tennessee had a right-to-work law.[8] The corporate welfare bonanza—which included tax deductions as well as investment in utilities, low-interest loans, free enterprise zones, economic development offices, assistance for training, foreign trade missions, subsidies for research and development, and an implicit anti-union policy—dominated southern economic policy in the 1980s. The automakers benefited the most. South Carolina gave BMW $100,000 for each job it created at an assembly plant in Spartanburg. Kentucky mimicked the practice, offering Toyota $150 million in 1998 but paying out only $50,000 for each job since the plant employed 3,000 workers. Tennessee became experts in the field of corporate giveaways, offering $70 million to General Motors to assist in establishing its Saturn plant there. Alabama exceeded them all, providing $250 million in direct subsidies to Mercedes to lock down the deal on the company's promise of 1,500 jobs for the state. But the incentive program under the "Mercedes Law" was available to other companies as well. All told, 86 companies took advantage of it. Additionally, the state agreed to pay more than $28 million in training workers for Mercedes and recent transplant Boeing, more than it spends on elementary and secondary students.[9] The jobs that Tennessee won with its Saturn plant cost the state $23,000 each. Alabama's 1,500 new jobs at the Mercedes sport-utility-vehicle plant wound up costing the state $167,000 apiece.[10]

Of course, the shift to automobile manufacturing represented a considerable improvement over the low-wage, nondurable-goods manufacturing that dominated the South since the late nineteenth century. Attracted by the region's historical commitment to business friendliness, textile, apparel, tobacco, chemical, and lumber-processing companies flocked to the region. The influx only accelerated following the Second World War. Locating in the South, these companies reinforced the region's largely unskilled, poorly educated, and racially divided southern labor force.[11]

The prospect of drawing comparatively higher-paying manufacturing jobs to the South in the form of auto assembly plants excited regional dreams of yet another avenue of industrial prosperity. In addition to Mercedes, BMW, and Nissan, Hyundai also established a manufacturing site in the South. Each plant was fiercely anti-union.[12] Despite the relocation of auto parts manufacturing plants to the region, wage rates remained low while poverty levels remained distressingly high: with a 72 percent increase in auto parts manufacturing in North Carolina between 1975 and 1980, which brought the total number of auto industry jobs in the state up to 22,000, the average wages for workers in North Carolina's factories in 1980 was only $5.46 an hour. Considering that the national average was $7.31, southern workers were still paying the regional differential that continued despite New Deal efforts to nationalize wage rates. In median family income for 1979, North Carolina ranked forty-fourth in the nation. Anti-unionism and the preponderance of textile manufacturing in the state sustained the tradition of a poorly paid, underskilled southern workforce into the 1980s.[13]

It was a sense of the failed promises of the Sun Belt that generated visions of high-tech deliverance for the South. These dreams were fueled by recession and the larger climate of national economic stagnation. Governor James B. Hunt of North Carolina took the lead, traveling to Silicon Valley to solicit Intel and Hewlett-Packard while garnering legislative support for a $24 million microelectronics center in the Research Triangle area of Raleigh-Durham. During Hunt's administration, Northern Telecom established a $20 million digital switching facility near Raleigh and General Electric committed to a $55 million microelectronics research center in the area. Between 1979 and 1981, seven electronics plants located in the area, bringing the promise of some 5000 jobs to the state.[14]

Virginia was not far behind. While its manufacturing economy still relied heavily on tobacco, chemicals, and textiles, its political leaders understood the need to modernize. Designed as a nexus for private enterprise, government, and academe for promoting the burgeoning sector, the Center for Innovative Technology materialized in 1984 with a $30 million cash infusion from the state government. Located in Fairfax and Loudoun Counties, the center became a magnet for further high-tech development and a symbol of Virginia's investment in the New Economy. Like its North Carolina counterpart, the center reflected the New Economy conviction that university research should foster economic development and advance private enterprise. The University of Virginia, Virginia Commonwealth, the University of Richmond, Virginia Tech, and James Madison would establish links with the center, solidifying the relationship between the private and public sector. North Carolina and Tennessee, through its Technological Foundation, had already made dramatic headway in this area. If the precedent had been established as early as the Progressive Era, it flourished in a period when Americans embraced the ethic of market supremacy.[15]

The recession of 1990/1991 and a wave of corporate restructuring convinced Virginia's leaders that aggressive incentives could revitalize the local economy. Having dismissed Keynesian solutions to economic downturns and the idea that a maldistribution of wealth might be at core of the crisis, state leaders were left only with supply-side solutions. Attracting high-tech business that depended on a trained and limited workforce now seemed more compelling a solution than support for the troubled manufacturing sector. Initially, high-tech recruitment was only part of a larger strategy to attract business. In fact, even when it became the central focus of economic development strategy, Virginia's boosters were more than willing to cast the incentives net wider than microchip manufacturers. When the sense of desperation intensified, Virginia's strategists portrayed almost every business deal as an installment on the state's information economy program. Every new branch plant became additional evidence of the state's commitment to the New Economy. However low-tech and traditional the state economy continued to be, boosters heralded the advancement of technical innovation whenever a new firm set up shop. For Virginia's boosters, it was a seamless part of the campaign to make Virginia "globally competitive."

The state promulgated its newfound faith in business subsidies in 1991. That year, United Airlines went trolling for a new maintenance facility. Secretary of Economic Development Larry Framme and Governor Douglas Wilder assembled a package of subsidies that amounted to $200 million over twenty years. Despite the unprecedented offer, United found friendlier skies in Indianapolis, where state authorities outbid Virginia for the lucrative investment. Even so, Virginia believed that the lesson was clear: offer more incentives and they will come. And not all initiatives came from the state level. In Christiansburg, a town in Virginia's economically depressed southwestern region, municipal officials offered water and sewer lines while county leaders chipped in low-interest loans to try to land a Blue Cross–Blue Shield subsidiary. Despite the exorbitant commitments, it was not

Christiansburg but Charleston, South Carolina, that won the bid, through a combination of low-interest loans and grants worth $3 million. For Don Moore, executive director of the Montgomery Regional Economic Development Commission, the failed bids illustrated the need for a "deal-closing fund." At a time when many states were questioning whether the bidding wars had already reached the heights of fiscal and political profligacy, development officials began to champion a war chest to seal the deal.[16]

Despite the United bid, corporate recruitment was never high on Governor Douglas Wilder's priority list. Constrained by the impending recession, Wilder called for fiscal restraint in the form of a freeze on tax increases, drastic reductions to state services, and a budget reserve in the event of an economic downturn.[17] The first African American ever elected to a governor's seat won the praise of fiscal conservatives by rationalizing environmental permits to benefit corporations. Anti-tax crusaders were elated when Wilder announced reduced spending on social programs and government administration. Yet development enthusiasts balked at Wilder's elimination of the state's advertising budget in 1990. Pro-growth champions at *Virginia Business* faulted Wilder for allegedly arriving a half hour late for a meeting with the pharmaceutical company Hoffmann–La Roche. In the magazine's estimation, the governor's tardiness had cost the state the $500 million project.[18]

More odious to the development critics was Wilder's interest in promoting trade with sub-Saharan African nations. Portraying his trade missions to the beleaguered region as an exercise in political puffery, *Virginia Business* dismissed the governor as a development dilettante. Having lost companies such as Bristol Compressors to North Carolina's "$18 million package of road improvements and other benefits," the governor squandered opportunities at a time when every deal mattered. Yet growth-at-any-cost pundits overlooked the contradiction at the core of their ideology. While they applauded Wilder's fiscal conservatism in a recessionary time, they castigated his failure to give away millions to companies in search of sweetheart deals. When Cathleen Magennis, Wilder's economic development secretary, expressed reservations about the giveaway program, *Virginia Business* swatted her away. Magennis argued that the incentive program "extracts from our existing tax base the fund which should rightly be spent, or 'reinvested,' for the taxpayers' benefit." According to *Virginia Business*, she was emblematic of the "sporadic top-level interest" which made for "unhappy campers in economic development."[19]

What this verbal jousting really exemplified was the ideological contest over the character of economic growth. Magennis and presumably Wilder as well were convinced that corporate giveaways threatened the social infrastructure and did not promise the economic returns that proponents imagined. Even as they accommodated the fiscal conservatism of centrist Democrats and Republicans, they were wary of the notion that tax relief for private enterprise would produce enduring economic recovery. In essence, they rejected the business-first ideology championed by *Virginia Business.* Inadvertently, they challenged the perspective ascendant in the national Republican Party, and espoused by George Allen, Virginia's hope for conservative revolution.

Swept into office on a wave of antipathy for the Wilder budget cuts and held aloft on the current of Republican anti-government rhetoric that won Congress in 1994, George Allen proclaimed a new day for economic development. "There is no more important role for the governor of Virginia than to bring jobs and economic opportunity to our citizens," he claimed during the 1993 campaign. "Under my watch, Virginia will not be 'out-hustled' when a company is looking for a new home. . . . Corporate executives will never be kept waiting or made to feel as though their business is not important to Virginia."[20] If Wilder had been insufficiently solicitous of business, Allen would correct the mistake. He set a tone that suggested that business had the answers for the commonwealth. More than this, he positioned himself as a CEO in a multinational operation, ready to sell Virginia to private interests.

If the administration's commitment to the social safety net was ambiguous, its corporate strategy was crystal clear. It would offer a series of "baseline incentives" geared to the magnitude of the operation. Job training, roads, water supply, and sewers would be available, but so too would direct cash contributions, tax abatements, buildings, land, and additional training provisions. The key for the Allen government was to target twenty-first-century industries, including microchip processors, telecommunications companies, and biotechnology firms. No less resonant of the free market fundamentalism that prevailed, Allen would promote what *Virginia Business* described as "a more active role . . . in economic development." The idea was not simply to market Virginia for business, but to offer suitable financial incentives for relocation. The Allen administration would preserve a pro-business climate, actively recruit companies to relocate from other states, and invite private industry and public sector agents to frame public economic policy through "host committees." Together, private and public agents would "pave the way for outside investors." Eventually, the Virginia

Economic Development Partnership, dominated by business executives, played a key role in marketing the state, a frank admission that public policy should be set by private corporate interests.[21] Allen would expand the free market but would use taxpayer resources to do it. It was a curious reminder of how the Gilded Age model had become the norm in American economic life.[22]

Galvanizing Allen's determination to sell Virginia was more than his own ideological faith in the free market. He was also prompted by high-profile studies from the Chamber of Commerce and the National Association of State Development Agencies. Led by Robert Skunda and Hugh D. Keogh, two prominent figures in the business development inner circle, the report celebrated the typical leading indicators of the state's pro-business ethos. Topping the list were its "well-enforced right to work law," its "pro-business climate toward major policy issues," its access to major northeastern urban centers, its "equitable" (low) tax structure, and the "quality and availability of labor at affordable wage rates."[23] In comparison with other state "competitors," such as Kentucky, North Carolina, and Maryland, the analysts concluded that Virginia was particularly impressive in the tax field, having preserved its image as a "low tax state" through the legislature's "continuous support of pro-business legislation designed to maintain a competitive tax climate."[24] Yet judging by the responses of no more than twenty-five entrepreneurs, business executives, and economic development professionals to questions posed during phone interviews, all was not well in Virginia's business climate.

Under "impediments to competitiveness," interviewees suggested that Virginia would miss out on opportunities because of its unwillingness to "adapt to a changing economic world." In the nomenclature of the go-go 1990s, "adapting" became a code phrase for anything ranging from longer hours at the same pay to the elimination of pension plans. Interviewees were specific: the state lacked a "long-term plan" and a "state-wide vision" supported by business and citizens. It featured a "cumbersome, slow environmental permitting process." While defending public spending on public education, they expressed a "widespread belief that Virginia is not competitive with other states in recruitment/retention and expansion incentives." This meant promoting development incentives to facilitate business expansion. It also included "one-stop shopping" for companies in search of environmental permits, public and private cooperation in marketing the state, and a renewed determination to protect the right-to-work law in Virginia. Evidently, organized labor's efforts to overhaul the Taft-Hartley Act and regenerate through determined work action had gained the attention of business elites.[25] The Governor's Opportunity Fund—a stash for closing promising deals established during the Wilder administration—had to be expanded. In addition, military establishments had to be converted to civilian use and education programs had to be geared primarily to workplace demands to "meet the specific needs of Virginia's employers."[26]

The most glaring weakness, according to Chamber officials and development entrepreneurs, was Virginia's relatively low level of direct financial incentives. "Subsidized financing assistance is among the fastest growing among forms of incentive programs nationally, and is currently under review for possible expansion by most of the states in this region." The less-than-subtle conclusion was that Virginia could only beat its aggressive neighbors to the South by getting into the game of direct financial assistance to prospective business transplants.[27] This was the message promulgated at the Virginia Economic Summit in April 1993, where three hundred business and government leaders met to reinforce the foregone conclusions of the Chamber of Commerce report.

The Allen administration would take its lead from this report and its direction from people like Keogh and Skunda. It was convinced that economic expansion through massive corporate giveaways, the stifling of organized labor, the reduction of welfare and unemployment insurance, and cuts to the education budget could be reconciled with a philosophy of growth and innovation. Yet this was the constant challenge for Republicans: how to synthesize the demand for education and social investment with corporate and personal income tax reductions? In some ways, 1960s liberalism seemed to provide the answer: guns and butter—or in this case, microchips and tax breaks—would be purchased through growth itself. Public sector downsizing would be more than offset by the revenue generated by new investment, or at least so Allen and his followers believed.[28]

The governor's commitment to economic growth was part of a larger ideological program unveiled more completely in his State of the Commonwealth address of 1995. Flushed with the 1994 Republican electoral victories, which gave the party control over Congress and the impetus for a wide-ranging attack on the New Deal, Allen imagined Virginia in the vanguard of a national conservative movement. Legislators had to struggle with two competing visions of government. "Will our state continue down the path of big government [Allen seemed to overlook the sizable reductions and fiscal austerity imposed by his predecessor], increased spending and taxes, deepening dependency and declining values? Or will we make government smaller and more focused on core governmental duties—allowing you to keep more of your hard-earned money?" The new governor was determined to "reduce the size and reach of government," "make state government more efficient," cut taxes by up to $2.1 billion, and slash the state budget by reducing funding for programs the poor, the disabled, and the mentally ill. At the same time, he wheeled out the tough-on-crime agenda that had proven so effective for Republicans in the 1990s. He called for an end to parole for violent criminals, millions to build two major prisons to house the unregenerate, and legislation easing restrictions on the carrying of a concealed weapon. The same budget also demanded major revisions to the welfare program. This would promote "opportunity and independence" while striking at the misguided idea that "it is somehow compassionate for government to do for people what they are capable of doing for themselves. Before big government made us dependent on its largesse," Allen argued, private institutions had met these needs. Just as private institutions offered the solution for an economy allegedly in the stranglehold of government regulation, so too did private arrangements offer the solution to welfare dependency.[29]

When Allen turned to economic development, though, he found considerable room for "big government largesse" through business incentives. Virginia would excel in the struggle for jobs by "re-focusing our economic development resources and [use] them in partnership with the private sector, by unshackling free enterprise and insisting on regulatory policies based on sound science." What Allen presented was a prescription for social realignment through free market engineering. Environmental restrictions and corporate regulations would diminish. Simultaneously, state government would dwindle and financial incentives to high-tech corporations would increase. Personal income taxes would decline, but so too would "regressive taxes" on "small businesses." Economic development was designed to generate jobs in an era fully mindful of the uncertainties at the core of the international economy, but it would do so by restoring the marketplace to the dominant position it enjoyed before the Great Depression. As Gary Kendall, a Charlottesville labor and environmental lawyer, put it, "Virginia is being sold to the highest bidder. . . . We're telling business, 'Come to Virginia; we'll let you have your way.' The theory is we have cheap taxes, cheap labor, and no government interference, employers will come. We're becoming the Mexico of the U.S."[30]

This was southern republicanism merging with neoliberalism to create a potent ideological compound. This intellectual alchemy included family values—"Our hope for the future lies in strong families"—an unflinching belief in the unfettered free market, and law-and-order toughness. It was a dogma uniquely suited for a time of fear, not hope. It was defensive to be sure, but it also reflected the belief that in a time of uncertainty the old verities of authority and control had to be restored. For all of the New Economy rhetoric about boundless opportunities, the ideological atmosphere was suffused with the belief that America was in decline—and liberalism was largely responsible. This "radical conservatism," as Robert Reich described it, increasingly defined what it meant to support global competitiveness and sound fiscal policies. It fit neatly into a worldview that insisted on rugged individualism for southern workers and the poor while extending generous assistance to corporations more than willing to play state governments off against each other.[31]

> Allen's rhetoric was powerful, backed up by the conservative world historical moment that seemed to be manifesting at the national level. His logic, however, was questionable. Absent from Allen's doctrine was the realization that a low-tax environment—a fact which the Chamber of Commerce and Allen's own development specialists admitted—prevailed in the state. In fact, Virginia ranked 46th in terms of income tax rates, 48th in corporate taxes, and had the lowest sales tax in the nation.[32]

That reality raised the possibility that tax cuts were designed almost as much to reward corporate supporters as to advance an uninhibited marketplace.

The governor's rhetorical assault ran headlong into legislative opposition. The Democrats and a handful of Republicans soundly rejected his plan, which called for $2.1 billion in tax reductions, large reductions to local governments, restrictions on sex education, draconian controls on welfare, parental involvement in adolescent abortion, and the creation of semiprivate charter schools. According to Democratic critics still clinging to a majority, the governor's tax plan would have saved the "average family" no more than $33 a year. That was a sum which one legislator insisted was not enough to "sell out the future of Virginia."[33] Democratic senator Richard L. Saslaw criticized the budget proposal for transferring the tax burden from businesses to homeowners. It was middle-class homeowners, not corporate executives, who would pay for the business incentives in the form of higher property taxes. Democratic senator Richard Holland argued that the governor's plan would hurt local governments. The revenue shortfall would put unmanageable pressure on social services, a loss for which a proposed state reimbursement would never compensate.[34] House Finance Committee chairman Richard Cranwell of Roanoke County brought the implications of the budget into sharp relief during a joint public hearing in January 1995. When Bill Bolling, Republican chairman of the Hanover County Board of Supervisors defended the budget, Cranwell retaliated, "You would be willing, then, to cut $52 million from education to get $33 a year?"[35] As another Democratic representative exclaimed, "I didn't hear any support for the income tax proposals from my people at all at the expense of millions of dollars to public education, mental health. I think people just felt those programs are far too important."[36]

The defeat at the hands of a Democratic Assembly convinced Allen to redouble his efforts at economic development, at least until he had a Republican majority. Rather than concentrate so intensively on budget reductions, he would court business. But the governor's effort to persuade Disney to construct a Civil War–themed amusement park close to the site of the Bull Run Battlefield raised the ire of a coalition of opponents. Historians, preservationists, environmentalists, and local residents vigorously objected to the plan, fearful that it would trivialize the historic site, produce traffic gridlock, and foster yet another colony of strip malls. The park project, which the governor and the assembly promised to support through a $163 million donation, illustrated the bipartisan privatization impulse of the 1990s. The promise of jobs and additional tax revenues easily persuaded legislators to sign on to the deal, despite the threat it posed to the integrity of the battlefield. Historical representation would suffer as well, since Disney planned to package and sell a version of the conflict that was palatable to customers in search of entertainment. Yet quite apart from historical memory, the $650 million project encapsulated the Faustian bargains that economic developers struck in the era of high-stakes corporate recruiting. After Disney withdrew its proposal—a decision that reflected the power of citizen mobilization against corporate encroachment—the *Times-Dispatch* discovered that the governor had failed to disclose the final cost of the deal. Virginians were shocked to learn that the incentive package for the park was projected to go well beyond $163 million. More damaging to the economic development case, which had been predicated on Disney's promise to create jobs, was the Department of Tourism's revelation that the average salary for most positions would have been $8,528, not the $20,000 that the company had claimed.[37]

While state developers responded to the lingering fears of economic stagnation left behind by the recession of 1990/1991, they pursued policies that often contradicted their ambition for job creation. Devoting resources to corporate incentives meant draining resources from retraining and education for higher-paying positions. It deprived local communities of tax revenues for infrastructure development, something which the low-tax South desperately needed. This pattern of chasing after corporations with lavish subsidies often failed to translate into high-paying, skill-intensive jobs. It also meant investing in companies that failed to make a lasting commitment to the states that landed them. As relatively high-wage, unionized manufacturing jobs slipped away as a result of NAFTA and corporate relocation, southern state governments raced to replace them. Yet the jobs they created often failed to compensate for the ones they had lost, a reality that became painfully evident in the economic slowdown at the beginning of the new century. Perhaps more importantly, it illustrated the extent to which critical decisions about economic policy were determined by political elites operating in conjunction with cost-conscious corporations. Together, they followed a model of market preeminence that left little room for social investment.

Yet the social implications were not the lead story in the mid-1990s. In what would become a familiar refrain if not a resounding cheer heard throughout Virginia's business-friendly media, the *Richmond Times-Dispatch* endorsed the Chamber of Commerce report calling for increased business incentives. "Virginia traditionally has relied on its natural assets, such as its location and work force, to attract businesses and industry, the study found. But while competing states upgrade their marketing efforts and add incentives, those assets may not be enough." Like the Allen administration, the paper considered business incentives a natural evolution from the state's "traditional assets," which included "its pro-business government, affordable labor and right-to-work laws."[38] Surveying Assembly opinion, the *Times-Dispatch* also concluded that the Motorola deal was "a winner" and that the state incentive program enjoyed "broad support."[39] Other newspapers echoed the boosterism of the *Times-Dispatch*. They cast economic development strategies in the narrative of Virginia's campaign to become what George Allen described as "the Silicon Dominion." For the *Newport News Daily Press*, the state's successful recruitment of three major high-tech manufacturers and the appearance of a *U.S. News and World Report* titled "The Silicon Dominion: Yes, Virginia, You're on Your Way to Becoming a High Tech Powerhouse" suggested that a new technological dispensation was dawning.[40] Similarly, Norfolk's *Virginian-Pilot* ran a breathlessly enthusiastic story about Virginia's arrival in the big leagues of microchip production. For its part, the *Roanoke Times* endorsed extravagant economic development expenditures with a story about B. B. Thomason, who went from earning $4.75 an hour to $8.30 an hour when the state gave the New Jersey–based Hanover Direct $2 million to relocate in Roanoke County.[41]

Like Virginia's mainstream media, political elites saw economic development as a function of marketing the state. For them, the marketplace was sovereign and Virginians were obligated to sell the state. Robert Skunda, Allen's secretary of commerce and trade, explained that "Selling the state is fundamentally no different than selling a product. . . . You've got to have that personal touch." For Lieutenant Governor Donald Beyer, jobs required governments to be "fast and friendly" to their customers, currying favor with small businesses through tax policies that kept their operating costs down. And even though the state's 6 percent corporate tax rate made it one of the lowest in the country—something which even *Virginia Business* admitted—leaders like Skunda and Beyer championed business tax reduction as the essential ingredient of job creation and economic growth.[42]

While few would have faulted efforts to promote small business, Virginia's workers might have wondered about the interests served by a friendly business climate. For many, Skunda's warning that an inhospitable business environment would make Virginia "ripe for being a cherry picked by other states" probably conjured up a mixture of fear and frustration.[43] Preserving a friendly business climate meant protecting the region's traditional assets—low taxes and anti-labor policies—together with the new policy of using public money to court private business.

The poorest of Virginians had already experienced that fear and frustration. Their fortunes had steadily declined relative to the richest fifth of the state's inhabitants, reported Kathryn Larin and Elizabeth McNichol of the Center on Budget and Policy Priorities, A Washington-based economic think tank. The latter group's incomes exceeded their less-fortunate counterparts by a factor of 11 in 1998, the height of the decade's boom. The Center on Budget and Policy Priorities identified a widening wage and class disparity not only in the nation but also in Virginia. Over the course of the previous two business cycles the average earnings of the middle fifth of Virginia citizens declined by 5 percent, while the worst off saw their incomes fall by 11 percent. Pointing to the increasingly familiar culprits—an eroding manufacturing sector leading an increasing number of Americans into low-wage jobs; the expansion of the stock market to the benefit of the wealthy; technological changes in the workplace benefiting educated employees and adversely affecting less-skilled workers; and the steady decline of trade unions—the paper identified several paths toward resolving the disparity. At a time when corporate tax abatement had become economic development dogma, Larin and McNichol advocated tax relief for the poorest of the commonwealth's families. "Virginia currently taxes a larger share of the income of poorer families than of high-income families," Larin and McNichol noted. Families earning as little as $8,200 a year—which put them considerably beneath the poverty line—paid income tax. Out of a budget surplus that had accumulated from economic growth, the analysts advocated a tax cut or a tax credit for Virginia's working poor.[44] To his credit, Allen had called for exactly this kind of tax relief in his otherwise supply-side budget.

In addition, the center's analysts called for an increase in the minimum wage, at least to the level it had been at in 1978. And while the *Virginian-Pilot* encapsulated the state's increasingly conservative consensus by claiming that "No one seriously suggests raiding corporate revenue, coddling organized labor, enriching injured workers or unleashing the dogs of environmental regulation,"[45] analysts across the Potomac pointed to the glaring inadequacy of the state's unemployment insurance program, which failed to provide coverage for 80 percent of the state's idled workers because of eligibility rules. They also called on the state to humanize its welfare policy to the benefit of those suffering eroding incomes from low-wage jobs. Rather than helping the most vulnerable, state leaders had reduced assistance by 52 percent between 1975 and 1996.[46]

Yet according to Governor Allen, these were precisely the "folks" who "keep saying if they're not making $100,000 a year as a bank president, it's unfair. . . . But people have to start at the bottom and work their way up."[47] The same ethic of individual striving did not apply to corporations that, according to Secretary of Labor Robert Reich, engaged in "zero-sum games in which jobs are simply moved from one place to another and there is not a net improvement in job growth or in the quality of jobs."[48] What Virginia had engaged in was a high-risk game of corporate recruitment that pitted it against neighboring southern states equally desperate to gain jobs but equally uncertain about the escalating costs of subsidizing growth.

In the mid-1990s, though, the game seemed to be working in Virginia's favor, and Governor George Allen led the charge for incentives. After a failed bid for a steel mill that promised as many as 500 manufacturing jobs paying approximately $30 an hour—a bid that eventually went to South Carolina—Allen and Skunda landed Motorola, Inc., which planned to build a $3 billion semiconductor assembly plant near Richmond.[49] Promising to create 5,000 jobs in Virginia over ten years, the company was rewarded with a $60 million performance grant. In addition, it pocketed a $4.6 million tax credit, the state's commitment to invest $16 million in an engineering school at VCU, and $5 million in community college training programs.[50] According to the *Virginian-Pilot*, Motorola decided on Richmond because of its "low-cost turf" and its abundance of "untapped, but qualified, workers," suggesting that low labor costs were more decisive than lavish incentives.[51] But Motorola won a remarkable set of cost concessions, offering in return not only jobs but the promise that northern Virginia would finally become a dominant force in the high-tech economy.

The Motorola deal sparked a flurry of high-profile, lucrative investment deals. Using the deal-closing Governor's Economic Opportunity Fund and Governor Allen's claim that Virginia was "open for business again," Skunda, Economic Development director Wayne Sterling, and the governor himself sealed what seemed to be the deal of the century. They negotiated a joint venture between Toshiba and IBM for a $1.2 billion microchip plant in Manassas. With claims of generating 4,000 jobs in ten years, IBM/Toshiba, later known as Dominion Semiconductor, won a $38.4 million performance grant. It also secured tax credits and state commitments to education amounting to a total of $48.2 million.[52] Likewise, Motorola and Siemens entered into an agreement to build the White Oak semiconductor plant in return for $15 million of state money.[53] In September of that year, the state and the city of Hampton also closed a deal with Gateway 2000, another of the era's symbols of entrepreneurial and technological dynamism. State-authorized corporate income tax credits, $1,000 job grants, $1 million from the Governor's Economic Opportunity Fund, and infrastructure upgrades from the city locked down what promised to be a $20 million project employing upwards of 1,000 people. In the celebration over yet another recruiting coup, residents probably overlooked the fact that the company only expected to hire 250 people in 1996 and would pay annual salaries of approximately $18,000, anything but the equivalent of the high-paying manufacturing jobs that were disappearing from Virginia. Not to worry, the *Newport News Daily Press* counseled readers: the real benefit of acquiring Gateway would be in the inevitable "spinoff" effect.[54] Citizens might also have overlooked another important feature of the Motorola and Toshiba

IBM deals: both represented the state's use of direct cash payments, euphemistically known as "performance grants," to induce corporate investment.[55]

According to *Industry Week*, these investment gems represented the state's effort to pursue a targeted developing strategy. Aimed at recruiting electronics, biotechnology, and telecommunications companies to the Old Dominion, it would solidify the state's status as a high-tech haven. It was also a strategy that made at least some effort to extract concrete commitments from prospective investors. Companies were "expected to live up to their investment and job promises" by operating for at least five years and fulfilling their job-creating projections to receive manufacturing grants.[56] Of course, that did not preclude the application of other types of incentives, including infrastructure expenditures, tax credits, and land grants, which were not time sensitive. Nor did it guarantee that companies would stay put after they had received such extravagant grants.

Yet the development program grew aggressively. Despite the state's interest in recruiting high-tech firms to Virginia, it was more than willing to spend on low-tech companies that offered some hope of job creation as well as political rewards for the governor's office. But as during the Wilder administration, it wasn't simply the state that enticed companies to locate in Virginia. In fact, the Governor's Opportunity Fund was designed to support incentives offered by local governments. Local governments would end up spending considerable sums to attract investment. In 1994, Pulaski County paid out $3 million and committed to $150,000 of road improvements to persuade Volvo Truck Corporation not to relocate to North Carolina. The state initially contributed an additional $5 million, but the incentives package eventually ballooned to $30 million, an unprecedented sum considering that the company was expanding its operation, not relocating.[57]

Not surprisingly, Volvo stayed, pumping an additional $200 million into its operation and eventually exceeding its target of an additional 200 jobs by more than 500. While the local paper justified the deal by pointing out that starting employees earned $14.50 an hour, it failed to mention that the Volvo plant was unionized.[58] And while local and state authorities may have convinced themselves that state incentives kept businesses in place, Ralph Nader was not so sure. Speaking at Virginia Tech in 1998, he suggested that companies as formidable as Volvo do not make relocation decisions based on government incentives. Instead, they understand that "it's a seller's market," one in which labor costs and access to markets was critical. Companies, in effect, were claiming that incentives were critical while basing their decisions on market factors. Incentives were not so important after all, but they did represent a drain on public funds.[59]

Although development officials imagined themselves building a "Silicon Dominion," they sold the state on its traditional pro-business virtues. Despite the rhetoric about high-tech training and the state's surfeit of "knowledge workers," this is what drew companies to the Old Dominion. As the *Richmond Times-Dispatch* noted, northern and foreign manufacturing firms found Virginia appealing because it was the most northerly right-to-work state.[60]

This was precisely how the governor sold the state in foreign trade missions. When the executive of a major German manufacturing interest asked Allen what Virginia had to "offer," the governor responded that the state was "pro-business." He reassured the German prospect that tax and regulatory policies reflected business priorities that the state featured a right-to-work law, and that he was determined to "make sure that Virginia is a good place for business." Allen also mentioned the ports, the roads, the airports, and the geography, but first and foremost he made it clear that in Virginia, business could set its own agenda.[61] The prospect of lower operating costs attracted new business to the state in the 1990s, not the idea of paying high wages to low-tech Virginians.

The New River Valley region of Virginia was emblematic of the economic development game. Hampton Roads, Richmond, the Roanoke Valley, and other areas also marshaled their resources to provide matching incentives for new business. Even before the Allen administration's drive for business subsidies, the *Roanoke Times* sniffed the air of desperation that permeated economic development campaigns:

> They [economic developers] talk about how hard you work. They tout your "quality of life," citing the school systems, comparatively low tax rates, the mountains, the cultural attractions. Using your tax money and funding from businesses, they publish brochures full of pristine pictures and bar charts intended to make the case for doing business in and around the Roanoke Valley.

Detailing the slick marketing schemes designed to sell a region to prospective investors, the paper also offered insight into the forces behind the development campaigns:

> Increasingly, development specialists across the country—and Western Virginia's are no exception—are chasing fewer prospects even as the Stakes increase. Recession and its twin, "downsizing," make the quest for new jobs and tax revenue more important than ever, prompting localities to offer deals they wouldn't have considered two years ago.[62]

While the *Virginian-Pilot* conceded that "Virginia had little choice" but to offer incentives, since other states did as well, it at least acknowledged that some experts had misgivings. State bidding wars often took place without consideration for the costs that new companies imposed through street improvements, schools, and utility demands. In the frenzy to buy corporate investment, states often ended up subsidizing low-paying, unskilled jobs. At the same time, corporate giveaways encouraged in-state businesses to jump into the incentives game by threatening to pull out if they didn't receive comparable tax breaks. In general, however, media coverage was favorable. The overriding preoccupation was with creating the right "business climate." As David M. Poole of the *Virginian-Pilot* noted, the idea of creating 9,000 semiconductor jobs silenced those who might otherwise have been critical of the Motorola and Toshiba deals.[63]

Like the drive for corporate restructuring, economic development was motivated in large part by fear that the region would be left behind in the global rush toward economic integration. Virginia joined other states in grappling with anxieties about job flight, declining corporate profitability, and American industrial decay. Just as white-collar workers suffered persistent uncertainty about their future amidst media hype about stock market windfalls, economic strategists championed the New Economy while anguishing over their own region's ability to compete.

Yet mixed up in uncertainties about global competitiveness were ideological assumptions that clouded as much as clarified the issues. The bedrock belief in the primacy of capital and the expendability of labor, in the indispensable need for retraining and retooling for the New Economy, in the inevitability of high-tech jobs to replace lost manufacturing positions, and in the wisdom of tax abatements and business subsidies obscured the social costs of development. Preoccupied by the dangers of organized labor and convinced of the self-regulating character of the marketplace, lawmakers failed to look critically at the agenda they pursued. Policymakers and corporate elites exalted unfettered market competition even while capital flight and job degradation challenged the tenets of market fundamentalism. Most Virginians were unwilling to examine the ideological assumptions underlying economic development.

As the decade wore on, however, some began to question the economic and social merits of business subsidies. Virginia media started paying attention when state legislators expressed alarm at the massive expenditure on the Volvo expansion deal in the New River Valley. It began to dawn on legislators that the program was operating without constraints. Realizing that the incentives were flowing without sufficient strings attached, Allen struck a task force to study the problem.[64]

Under the leadership of Robert Vaughn, the General Assembly's subcommittee on appropriations for economic development recommended that incentives should only assist companies paying "above-average wages." The committee also insisted that subsidies should be directed at infrastructure improvements and worker training. It also called for the termination of incentives if companies reneged on the agreement. Of course, the Economic Development Department claimed that this was precisely how the Allen government operated. "It sounds like Mr. Vaughn is reading our script very well," claimed Morgan Stewart, the department's spokesperson. "He seems to be pretty much on target with our philosophy and the way we act, especially with Motorola and IBM and Toshiba and just about every other company."[65] Most importantly, the subcommittee study revealed just how unaccountable the incentives program really was. "Right now," Vaughan claimed, "these deals are cut and there is no legislative involvement" before the incentives proposal came before the Assembly.[66]

Yet even though media coverage of incentives was generally positive before the report, the *Roanoke Times* ran a story that implicitly challenged Stewart's assertion that economic development translated into high-paying jobs. Of the sixteen state-subsidized investment projects that the paper examined, six planned to pay employees less than $8.65 an hour. That was the hourly rate that workers would have to be paid in order to generate the income taxes needed to equal—according to a model developed in Oregon—the amount that the state spent on each taxpayer for essential services.[67] Of course, what this meant was that even if companies benefiting from generous subsidies paid workers $8.65 an hour, they would still only earn approximately $18,000 a year. That was hardly a high-wage job and almost certainly nothing close to Virginia's average annual salary of $45,000.

Five companies simply would not disclose the starting hourly wages of new employees. One of these claimed that pay would be "in the teens" and another asserted that pay would be "competitive for the area." One company, which received more than $290,000 in incentives, claimed that hourly wages would be "more than $10." Another, which received a land discount totaling $125,000, asserted that wages would be between $8 and $12 an hour. If Richmond and northern Virginia benefited from lucrative investment deals that at least held out the possibility of decent salaries, if not the promise of permanence, the rest of the state had to accept considerably less. For them, economic development meant expensive incentives packages that offered jobs providing little hope of recovering the kind of security that accompanied an earlier generation's manufacturing jobs.[68]

The skepticism about economic development mounted as legislators and businesspeople critiqued a deal that gave $45 million in incentives to a Texas steel recycler. When Chaparral announced that it would establish a $400 million plant in economically stagnant Petersburg which would provide 400 jobs to local residents, state leaders were jubilant. Virginia's own scrap dealers were considerably less so. Their vocal discontent eventually compelled the Assembly to investigate the deal and solicit a report from a group of Virginia Tech economists on the wisdom of economic development. In this case, scrap metal recyclers expressed the common concern that state officials used tax dollars to attract new companies and give them unfair cost advantages over in-state businesses. The specifics of the scrap recycling controversy are less important than the way that state officials justified economic development. According to John B. Sternlicht, director of community relations for the Virginia Economic Development Partnership, the state was not responsible for protecting in-state companies. "I don't think the free market system is about that," Sternlicht claimed. "I don't think our duty is to protect the profitability of anybody from competition. . . . Our duty is to create a higher standard of living for Virginians, which I think we have done." Like the governor, Skunda, and the architects of economic development in Virginia, Sternlicht selectively applied the principles of free market economics. Some corporations deserved subsidies while others did not.[69]

The criteria for choosing which companies should be privileged in this conservative version of Keynesianism were ambiguous. Political advantage, however, seemed to be an unspoken rule for allocating resources. According to Robert C. Turner, political scientist and economic development scholar, the calculation of political benefit is critical to explaining the gubernatorial obsession with "smokestack chasing." Surveying the proliferating literature on the economic consequences of economic development, Turner concludes that the evidence pointed toward the "economic inefficiency" and "detrimental side effects" of business incentives. "The recognized problem with these incentives are threefold," according to Turner. "First, they are typically too small to affect firms' site selection decisions. Second, certain incentives, like tax abatements, erode a community's tax base, undermining its ability to provide critical public goods. Third, these incentives can lead to detrimental competition among the states that produces no economic benefit for the nation as a whole." Then why was Virginia preoccupied with attracting investment through incentives, considering the known risks? According to Turner, the "conventional wisdom" tells governors that job growth and firm relocation translates into political rewards. The relocation of firms also has a statistically significant impact on per capita income for a given region, at least in the short term.[70]

Yet Turner also found that improving the level of education in a given locality exponentially improved income levels and employment. Spending on education was more effective in raising income levels than money spent on business relocation. While corporate recruitment might lead to county-level income growth, so too could education and local business assistance. The central issue was whether or not these strategies would be as politically beneficial. Paradoxically, he found that incentives might add jobs but not reduce unemployment, particularly not in time for reelection. No less intriguing, Turner also found no evidence to corroborate the claim that smokestack-chasing was politically beneficial. Although governors labored under the assumption that business relocations meant votes from local beneficiaries, the evidence supported no such conclusion. Instead, he hypothesized that political benefits were probably a function of generally good economic times, which seemed to cancel out the governor's exertions on behalf of job creation. Still, "while governors may realize that incentives for firms may be poor economic policy, they seem to believe that they satisfy their political need to do something to address voters' concerns."[71] What makes this study additionally relevant is that Turner used Virginia during the Allen administration as one of his seven case studies.

Examining tax policies and highlighting the Motorola and IBM/Toshiba deals, David Brunori, public policy professor and tax expert at George Washington University, came to similarly skeptical conclusions. In the short term, tax incentives deprived states of revenue in the expectation that the company would eventually produce more through retail sales, rising property values, and income. Yet economic developers based their decisions on conjecture. No study supported the notion that mammoth giveaways made for sound tax policy. Brunori was at a loss to substantiate claims that targeted tax incentives produced new revenue for state governments. If anything, the huge tax breaks and infrastructure expenditures represented a cost that compounded state budget deficits. Tax deals that benefited large corporations while adding burdens to local services such as schools and roads ended up costing local homeowners more. Targeted tax incentives deprived states of desperately needed revenue, but they also violated the principle of equity, a postulate that Brunori offered using the authority of none other than Adam Smith. "In the end, targeted tax incentives create a much more regressive system of taxation by foisting the financing of government services on those least able to do so." They also discriminated against businesses that lacked the size and allure of companies like Motorola. Insufficiently accountable to the states that lured them, companies often took large incentives but failed to follow through on their commitments or even maintain their investment. That sinking sense of broken promises would strike home in Virginia by the end of the decade. Like Turner, Brunori found no evidence that tax incentives actually worked. Instead, "nearly every econometric study of the subject concludes that state and local taxes do not necessarily attract business, create jobs, or enhance economic performance." He was left to conclude that "political expediency" more than economic planning lay behind the incentives program.[72]

The point is not simply to highlight the political calculations that underlay the development strategy but to underline the competitive ethos that dominated southern life. For Skunda and Sternlicht, South Carolina, Maryland, and even New Jersey were competitors, even enemies, requiring diligent intelligence and formidable opposition.

The economic development task force mobilized aggressively when it learned that "New Jersey is undertaking a concerted effort to target Virginia." The Virginia Department of Economic Development quickly generated "talking points" for the governor to challenge New Jersey governor Christine Todd Whitman's efforts to reverse the tide of business relocations to the Old Dominion. Whitman was incensed that Virginia had engaged in an aggressive marketing campaign targeted at New Jersey, one which included advertising in *Fortune*, *Forbes*, and other trade magazines. Campaigning for other states' companies also included direct mail to businesses in Texas, California, Michigan, and New Jersey. The Virginia Department of Economic Development was responsible for "generating leads" which "project managers" would then cultivate through meetings with company executives. The premise of the advertising campaign was the increasingly well-worn mantra that in a "competitive global market companies must make the most of their capital by being located in a state that provides a low cost of doing business, skilled workforce and a tax structure conducive to success." Companies would relocate whether Virginia advertised or not; the state was only helping them along. And New Jersey was an ideal target. According to the department's statistics, Virginia's corporate income taxes were lower, as were its unemployment taxes, workers' compensation insurance, state and local taxes, and labor costs. For companies beset by unions, taxes, and industrial development regulations, Virginia's "assets—a lower cost of doing business; a right-to-work environment; an excellent location; and, an educated workforce"—sounded ideal. In fact, Virginia could count Trenton's "two largest employers—Carter Wallace (300 jobs) and Hill Phoenix (500 jobs)" as its greatest New Jersey acquisitions. Under the subheading "Governor Whitman's Sensitivities," the developers were pleased to report that these companies had been drawn to Virginia by its "low taxes, skilled labor, low cost of living and doing business, [and its] right to work laws."[73]

Here, then, was the southern development strategy updated for use in the global marketplace. The traditional virtues of cheap labor, low taxes, and minimal government regulation were repackaged as the solution for modern business. But Virginia's gain was New Jersey's loss, a fact that never seemed to enter into the frenzied strategizing for growth. The ethic of competition swept these sentimental considerations aside, neutralizing and justifying them in the upbeat, fast-paced, go-go rhetoric of the 1990s.

The central and absolving assumption was that the imperatives of business were unassailable. Even so, the struggle between states over jobs illustrated another poignant reality of the era: business had become rootless and transnational, detached from reciprocal obligations to their communities. As the *Bergen County (N.J.) Record* commented, "A tussle between New Jersey and Virginia for the attention of companies in search of an inexpensive place to do business underscores an economic fact of life: corporate America's declining allegiance to the place long called home."[74] Virginia, of course, was no exception to the rule of competition at any cost. But it defined itself as one of the states most demonstrably committed to the notion that economic growth meant a transfer of capital from one region to another. The marketing campaign, the incentives, and the fawning devotion to business profitability belied any claims about a social contract in the United States.

It also undermined any presumptions about regional unity that organizations such as the Southern Growth Policies Board may have entertained. When the Assembly cut $30 million from the governor's development financing proposals and eliminated $20 million from the Economic Opportunity Fund, Commerce Secretary Robert Skunda retaliated. Quoting Allen's assertion that "we are in a war of competition with other states for new jobs and investment," Skunda claimed that surrounding states "lay in wait for Virginia to weaken its position." In particular, North Carolina and Maryland "will be watching closely over the next several days, hopeful that our General Assembly will stumble—allowing them and other competitors to pillage and plunder Virginia's jobs." Referring to a Greensboro news item in which the governor complained about South Carolina and Virginia winning some thirty major contracts and thousands of jobs at the expense of North Carolina, Skunda urged Virginians not to "unilaterally disarm." He was deeply concerned lest nervous nellies deprive the government of the "arsenal" it needed to win the war of competition.[75]

A *Virginia Business* article covering the rivalry between the two southern neighbors identified the connection between economic development and the competitive ethic that dominated American business in the 1990s. In the paper's estimation, which reflected the attitude of leading economic developers in both states, North Carolina had "lost" Motorola to Virginia, whose "slick, performance-based incentive package" won the day against a state that had "become a little inattentive." Virginia had behaved "like a state hungry for new business." The loss of Motorola, according to former North Carolina economic development director Bob Goforth, was a "a kick in the head." As far as the magazine was concerned, the recession and the military downsizing of the 1990s left the state with little choice but to join the nationwide incentives bonanza. The Old Dominion had to stop North Carolina from "eating our lunch," as Virginia's Economic Development director April Young put it in 1993. Wayne Sterling, the CEO of the Virginia Economic Development Partnership, summed up the worldview of most development technocrats. North Carolina was the "competition." It was Sterling's conviction that his focus should not be on the Tar Heel state but on "the customer—the prospective business."[76]

The governor enthusiastically endorsed this worldview. Discussing a lucrative incentive package that lured a Frito-Lay potato chip factory to Lynchburg in an interview given after he left office, Allen filtered his administration through the prism of business marketing. "I viewed my role as the CEO of a state talking to the CEO of a major corporation, and looking him in the eye . . . I wanted them to rest assured that the government will see to it that our promises are kept."[77] Then working as a corporate relocations specialist for a Richmond law firm, Allen was willing to advise fellow southerners on landing big deals. Addressing the Southern Economic Development Council in Williamsburg in 1998, the governor advised them to emphasize the region's traditional assets: its right-to-work laws, its low cost of living and tax rates, and, in many states, improved educational systems." Interestingly, Allen made no mention of corporate incentives, high-tech infrastructure, Virginia's knowledge workers, and its geographical bounty.[78] Neither had the German corporate executives been fixated on incentives; if anything, tax incentives and business subsidies were simply the cost of doing business. Any dreams of regional coordinated political efforts to resolve the problems of deindustrialization dissolved in the heat of the jobs war. Imagining themselves as CEOs recruiting savvy customers, southern political leaders repudiated the notion that state leadership was anything but good salesmanship.

Economic development officials collected information on Virginia and the other southern states. They assessed their strategies, critiqued their incentive packages, and kept scorecards on business relocations. When the *Washington Post* ran a piece in 1996 describing a "faltering" Virginia economy and a resurgent Maryland, economic development officials went into damage control mode. Advisors wrote memos detailing the alleged inaccuracies of the *Post*'s numbers, assuring themselves that Virginia was still leading in the race to generate jobs. They counseled the governor that the "job growth lull" was temporary, simply the result of "short term layoffs in textiles and some ongoing defense downsizing in Tidewater." They even contemplated whether a letter to the offending reporter might be necessary.[79]

There was nothing unusual about Virginia Power's William Stafford sending Robert Skunda an article from *Business North Carolina* that critiqued that state's development strategy. The article simply confirmed that business experts in both states had been engaged in a high-stakes game that reduced public policy to advertising slogans. "Take Virginia. It's ninth on the list but had a much better year bringing in business. The Tar Heel State announced more new projects—180 to 80. But it got creamed on capital investments [and] Virginia's created more jobs. . . . Georgia and South Carolina have taken their share of projects, but Virginia has been on a tear the last three years. It landed 12 of the Southeast's biggest projects." The lesson was that North Carolina had grown comfortable while Virginia had perfected the full-court press. Since wage levels were rising and unemployment had steadily declined, North Carolina's developers found it increasingly difficult to sell the state on the South's traditional assets, even if they were packaged in the idiom of high-tech global competitiveness. The answer was to "seek high-capital projects that don't need large numbers of employees." This was an admission that widespread job creation was not the only consideration in economic development. North Carolina also had to "do a better job of training its work force," a familiar assumption in an era which believed that the supply of skilled workers would equal the demand from companies that had yet to discover outsourcing.[80]

For Virginia's economic development experts, the *Business North Carolina* article confirmed that the state had, in fact, successfully put the heat on its southern competitor. Southern elites had fully absorbed the competitiveness ethos but incorporated it into a worldview which celebrated the South's traditional business-friendly virtues. From this perspective, social needs had to be strained through the narrow filter of business efficiency, market share, and return on investments. Ironically, one of the greatest accomplishments of the Allen administration according to southwestern Virginians was the location of two major prisons in the region, which produced 860 jobs at a cost of over $400 million. Here was a distressing commentary on the conservatives' enthusiasm for law and order, but it was also an enduring public works project, even if by the end of his administration critics were pointing out that many beds went unoccupied.[81]

Legislative apprehension about the Chaparral deal opened a discussion on economic incentives which the *Virginian-Pilot* briefly sustained during the Jim Gilmore administration. The willingness to consider the limits of corporate welfare may have reflected the looming sense that the good times could not last. As Allen left office, Professor Lawrence L. Schack of Virginia Commonwealth University "graded" the governor on economic development. Paying homage to his role in creating 300,000 jobs and $14 billion in investments, he also cautiously challenged Allen's assertion that he was *the* economic development governor. "While Virginia's economy is today competitive . . . the groundwork for enduring economic development must still be laid." Genuine economic development required more than new jobs and business investment. Offering an opinion that rarely made it into Virginia's mainstream media, Schack suggested that it required "welfare reform to help unemployed people first get job skills and then get jobs, and to provide day care for working mothers so they can continue to hold jobs." Throwing people off of public assistance and into low-wage jobs was not the equivalent of building "human capital" or fostering a "knowledge economy."[82]

Schack also took the governor to task for failing to develop infrastructure and social programs, invest in existing businesses and in highways and ports, or protect the environment. He was equally skeptical about the governor's unwillingness to solicit assistance from Washington or contribute to research and development with the same alacrity that he pursued business relocations. Perhaps most importantly, the VCU academic criticized the governor's reluctance to endorse substantial educational improvement. Relative economic prosperity allowed governors like Allen to claim that they had added appreciably to their state's share of jobs and investment. Yet "it is the rare exception who fulfills the requirements of economic development writ large. The Allen administration was not one of these rare exceptions." A tame criticism, to be sure, but a challenge to the hyperbole about Allen the economic miracle worker, particularly considering the anti-public-spending consensus that prevailed in the South in the 1990s. What Schack's criticism outlined was the disparity between the neoliberal rhetoric about skilled education for the competitive global economy and the reality that trickle-down, government minimalism often precluded such efforts.[83]

The *Washington Post* also took the governor to task for pursuing a "grow-at-all-costs" policy that left the state bereft of sufficient roads and choked by overdevelopment. It quoted developer Til Hazel, an architect of the northern Virginia renaissance, who criticized the governor for spawning the growth without providing the roads and schools to support it. "His record is almost irresponsible in that regard. He has milked the issue of job growth without any recognition of the cost of job growth." The governor fostered the "Motorolas, the AOLs, the WorldComs," but failed to provide the infrastructure to sustain them. Mo Eleithee, a campaign coordinator for Chuck Robb, who opposed Allen for a Senate seat in 2000, echoed Hazel's sentiments. He contended that national economic policies had more to do with Virginia's success than Allen's relentless boosterism. He suggested that the national job growth rate for the decade was 10.9 percent, while Virginia's was 10.4, hardly a stellar performance. In addition, the *Post* suggested that one of highest-profile incentive deals of Allen administration also cost more than the *Richmond Times-Dispatch* had reported in 1995. To land this cooperative venture between two icons of the high-tech industry, the state paid out an incentive package worth $95 million over ten years.[84]

Schack's commentary was not entirely accurate or fair. In the governor's last budget, covering 1998–2000, he reversed course on fiscal austerity by authorizing $40 billion in expenditures and tax cuts. The budget included plans for $275 million in spending on higher education, with $85 million dedicated to raising faculty salaries, the hiring of one thousand new grade school teachers, a tuition freeze at public colleges compensated for by an additional $37.3 million, and an additional $50 million incentives package for universities that met a number of performance indicators, namely graduation rates and retention.[85] This did not exhaust Allen's farewell largesse. He authorized $874 million to pay for the implementation of state-mandated standards, the provision of technical training for teachers, and the delivery of remedial courses for students. The outgoing governor also found $63 million to rehabilitate the polluted Chesapeake Bay and $30 million to provide comprehensive health care for needy children whose parents earned too much to qualify for Medicaid.[86]

Yet there were clear limits to Allen's benevolence. Although the Council called on the governor to dedicate some $62 million to assist financially burdened students, the governor offered nothing. Public employees also continued to suffer from the administration's policy of government downsizing and privatization. Although the Virginia Governmental Employees Association requested a 5 percent raise, Allen offered only 2.25 percent, with additional incentives for an already drastically streamlined and overworked sector. State-mandated standards also did little to address educational challenges facing minority and low-income children. Nor could Virginia's commitment to education simply be assessed in terms of financial support. At a time when media globalization pundits called for a "flexible" workforce, the administration pushed through standardized testing that emphasized the accumulation of data, not analytical reasoning. The Virginia Commission on the Future of Public Education—a bipartisan, state legislative committee—urged the administration to encourage "teaching methods designed to develop skills in critical thinking, problem-solving, and decision-making."[87] Schools would also maintain their accreditation on the basis of whether or not 70 percent of students passed the standardized tests. In this scheme, American history was reduced to reciting the date of the founding of Jamestown and identifying George Washington. Thinking about the multiple motives behind independence, the social upheaval of the American Revolution, and America's early implication in the African slave trade were by comparison unquantifiable. As one teacher described it, "If it's not in the [standards], I think to myself, 'Why bother?' We've been trying to teach students to think, but now we're going back to bare facts."[88] In effect, standardized learning conformed to the information age idea that knowledge was data.

It also reflected the governing assumptions behind the market-driven worldview. Learning ultimately was not a matter of critical thinking, of serious reflection on the political and cultural forces that shaped the world, and the social value of seeing a given issue from different perspectives. It was a matter of absorbing information in order to develop "skills"—in the parlance of the era—for deployment in private enterprise. Of course, education had served this function since the nineteenth century, but in the late twentieth century, alternative models of education had all but lost their legitimacy. Civic virtue, social criticism, active citizenship, democratic participation—each had been subordinated to the task of outfitting students for the "competitive global economy." If the rhetoric of citizenship surfaced, it usually did so as a surrogate of the competition ethos that held axiomatic sway in the 1990s. This was the vision of education that prevailed in Virginia, in no small part because of Allen's program of standardized learning.

Community colleges and universities had to reengineer to supply the New Economy with a steady stream of Knowledge Workers. Emblematic of this kind of thinking were the comments of Jack Davenport, economic development director for Petersburg. "Prepared workers are a key component to business and industry in the Tri-Cities area. As companies increasingly compete in a global economy, employees must be ready to match or exceed skills and production of foreign work forces."[89] Universities would become centers for workplace training and engines of productivity with faculty embracing a new curriculum oriented toward business skills and the ever-present challenge of international competition.[90] Neoconservatives may have rallied around notions of education for moral certainty and liberals around vague assumptions about multiculturalism, but neither challenged the idea that the ultimate justification for education was competition in an unforgiving global marketplace.[91] As states engaged in the incentives endgame, they encouraged their school systems to inculcate children in a Social Darwinian mentality that belied the claim of globalization as agent of international harmony. Education was training for survival in the international jobs war.

Yet educators, New Economy pundits, and political leaders from both parties vastly oversold the capacity of the high-tech sector to absorb reengineered university graduates. One of the central claims that Virginia's high-tech industry leaders made at the height of the boom was that there were simply not enough qualified workers to fill the demand for programmers and analysts in the Silicon Dominion. "In Northern Virginia, high-tech companies report 18,000 job vacancies representing $500 million in lost wages for the region's economy. Their recruiters are scouring the country for workers."[92] The alleged skills deficit and tight labor market became the entering wedge for demanding access to foreign workers. It would also provide the justification for outsourcing a larger and larger percentage of high-tech jobs. In September 1998, Virginia's technology elites claimed that 30,000 technology jobs went unfilled because of a lack of qualified candidates. Where education could not fill the gap, recruiting immigrant workers through H-1B visas would. These visas provided 3- to 6-year permits for specialized high-tech foreign workers. In 1997 and 1998, American companies reached the 65,000 limit. The Senate and the House jumped into action to assist American business. They drafted legislation to raise the quota to 115,000 by 2000. Kathleen Ferris of American Management Systems in Fairfax claimed that this was all for the best. "It is in our best interest as a country to fill these jobs [otherwise] businesses go under. We are going to buy, build, and borrow whatever resources we need," Ferris claimed, even at the expense of American workers. With an internal training facility that cost $16,000 for each new employee, the 8,000-employee company was eager to lift the limit on H-1B visas. For Joe Freeman, federal-state special assistant to Governor Jim Gilmore, "the international marketplace" and capital's demand for "the best talent" meant that the "benefits clearly outweigh the negatives on this one."[93]

Economists attuned to the disintegration of America's manufacturing sector and the implications of outsourcing disagreed. In 2000, Alan Tonelson reported that the H-1B program had become a racket for exploiting foreign workers and discriminating against American job seekers. According to a Labor Department study from 1996, the program had not protected American workers as legislators had expected and it did not respect the "prevailing wage." In fact, the study suggested that 74.6 percent of workers recruited under the auspices of H-1B "worked for employers who did not adequately document the specified wage." The pattern of regulatory evasion that the study detected threatened moreover to drive the "prevailing wage" down.[94]

Perhaps more striking was Tonelson's conclusion that the high-tech employee deficit was an illusion. The absence of significantly increased salaries—despite claims to the contrary—seemed to confirm this. Citing a Department of Commerce report from 2000, Tonelson observed that the median weekly earnings for computer scientists, computer engineers, and computer systems analysts increased by 17.5 percent, only a few points ahead of the 15.4 percent inflation rate and simply on par with the earnings increases for all occupations between 1992 and 1998. Interestingly, he also cited a 1999 *Washington Post* study which found that high-tech workers in the Washington, D.C., area were already on the slide. Programmer/analysts and web programmers saw their wages decline while systems engineers, network analysts, and client server developers found their wages stagnating. The inability of 6.1 percent of computer science PhDs to find jobs—a rate that exceeded the jobless rate for American workers—and 17 percent unemployment among computer programmers over the age of 50 added weight to the claim that employee shortages were misleading at best. Rather than having exhausted the supply of qualified workers, high-tech companies "just do not want to hire even experienced techies who have families that prevent them from working 100-hour weeks, or who might require more expensive health insurance coverage than 23-year-olds or foreigners. Thanks to their Washington lobbyists and a compliant Congress, they don't have to." Besides, Tonelson suggested, if so many jobs had gone unfilled for so long—for example, John Fain of Virginia Beach claimed that he had searched in vain for 20 years and published 1,040 newspaper ads to fill positions at his Metro Information Services—then it was evident that employers "have decided that making do with what they have is better than taking the measures usually taken by companies truly desperate for workers—offering much fatter paychecks."[95]

While southwestern Virginia and other parts of the state bled manufacturing jobs, the Allen administration, with the enthusiastic support of most Democrats, desperately sought to import jobs that often paid less and offered little security. Replacing textile workers was never the highest item on the agenda; instead, the administration devoted the greatest energy to landing knowledge jobs for northern Virginia. More than this, Allen, Gilmore, and legislators from both parties subscribed to the dubious proposition that Virginia's businesses were starved of employees and had little choice but to import computer experts from abroad. What was sold as a temporary expedient quickly became a permanent feature of the renewed struggle to manage international competition. Along with industry leaders and technology pundits, Virginia's leaders subscribed to the notion that education would save American workers from the maw of competition. Committed to business preeminence, they believed that training would equip Virginians to manage the threat of low-wage competition. At the same time, the amulet of training would protect current victims of corporate restructuring. What they failed to realize was how few would win in this game.

Most Virginians and indeed Americans were destined for the service industry, the real growth sector. Here, wages were uneven at best and job security was notoriously fragile.[96] In 1995, for example, the service industry was responsible for 48.9 percent of new jobs in the state. According to the *Roanoke Times,* more than 30,000 of the 47,300 new jobs in this sector were of the high-wage variety. This was a dubious claim, considering that the *Virginian-Pilot* reported no more than two years later that only half of the 60,000 jobs created in the state paid an average of $46,403. The rest paid in the neighborhood of $25,624—these jobs were anything but high paying, professional, or technologically specialized.[97] In fact, as the *Roanoke Times* reported, the "second largest increase in the state was in the trade sector, where 31,800 were added."[98]

What this meant was that the retail industry was growing dramatically, adding jobs to the economic development balance sheet that promised little in the way of security. The future that the economic developers and the academic boosters mapped out diverged widely from the one outlined by national economic forecasters. Citing a Bureau of Labor Statistics study, economist Doug Henwood suggested that some of the fastest-growing jobs between 2000 and 2010 would be combined food preparation and serving workers, customer-service representatives, registered nurses, retail salespersons, computer support specialists, cashiers, and office clerks. These were only seven of the top thirty, very few of which sounded even remotely high-tech or high-paying, but which cumulatively composed nearly one-third of the workforce in the early twenty-first century. They also represented 46 percent of the projected growth for the new millennium's first decade. What Henwood detected was labor-market polarization. "Of the top 30 occupations, about 40% of the job growth will be among those in the lowest quarter of the earnings distribution. Another 28% will be in the top-paying quartile, with only 31% in the middle two." Although IT jobs were expected to generate 10 percent of overall job growth during the same time frame, so too were retail salespersons, cashiers, truck drivers, telemarketers, and office clerks, all of whom earned two-thirds less than their high-tech counterparts.[99]

Loosening environmental regulations that supposedly tethered business was also an essential part of the Allen economic development program. The governor's policies in this area reflected his underlying ideological premise: that privatization and limited government control was good for business. Under the leadership of Becky Norton Dunlop, secretary of natural resources and conservative activist, the Allen administration sent the message that environmental protection would be subordinate to economic development. According to the *Roanoke Times*, disenchanted Department of Environmental Quality employees believed that the agency had capitulated to business interests. "The agency's emphasis on economic development has overshadowed its mission to protect Virginia's natural resources and people's health, they say."[100] Under Dunlop and Allen, the agency was to assist business "customers" rather than impede the rush to market. It was a new "paradigm," one that clearly signaled the ascent of market fundamentalism in southern political life. Interviewing Dunlop, the *Roanoke Times* presented her perspective this way: "Unshackling business from excessive environmental rules, trimming budget and staff for optimum efficiency, and turning to the private sector and citizen volunteers to assume personal stewardship of natural resources are essential to the new order." More than this, reduced regulation would mean business success and higher tax revenues for county-level environmental protection efforts.[101]

Under Dunlop, the agency made speedy permit processing its main objective. By 1994, Virginia was faster and less expensive than five other states in reviewing environmental applications.[102] The new, business-friendly agency altered a 1987 regulation that controlled the discharge of TBT (tributyltin), a powerful pesticide used to prevent barnacles from attaching to boat hulls. The decision was made without public consultation. The department suspended cleaning operations at some two thousand sites where leaking underground storage tanks had been detected and insisted only that companies fix sites that posed an imminent threat. The decision represented savings in the millions for tank owners. In 1995, the DEQ also suggested a new regulation that would give the agency greater latitude in determining whether or not water polluters had to be monitored for toxic chemicals. In addition, the department postponed designating five streams in western Virginia as "pristine" for fear that it would inhibit economic development. More than this, Virginia law only allowed the applicant for a water-discharge permit to go to court against the agency. Although the state law regulating air permits was modified to permit judicial procedures or "standing," it was available only to those who could demonstrate that they had an immediate financial interest at stake. The state regulation on standing was the most antagonistic to citizen activism in the entire country. The Allen administration rejected calls to alter the air permit regulations or comply with Environmental Protection Agency orders requiring the change.[103]

Together with budget reductions and the elimination of at least one employee who was a vocal opponent of the new policy, the administration set an environmental tone that reflected the dominant tenets of the free market ideology in the 1990s. Commenting on the governor's decision to concede control of a car dealership regulatory board to none other than car dealers and to reduce its budget, *Southern Exposure* highlighted the central theme that ran through the Allen administration. The car-dealer board was

> [p]art of a broad effort underway in Virginia to let business interests and campaign contributors decide what's best for the state. In effect, Allen has moved to lock average citizens out of the governing process, stacking regulatory boards with representatives of the very industries they are supposed to regulate. His administration has weakened state agencies designed to protect consumers and the environment, making it easier for shady businesses and polluters to operate.[104]

Although Allen and the militant Republican gave these policies a peculiar neo–states' rights twist, the dismantling of environmental regulation reflected the prevailing southern belief that government intervention was inimical to economic growth. The free market would triumph where "excessive" regulations had failed.[105]

While Allen, Skunda, and the regional developers dreamt of prosperity through corporate recruitment, they ignored the character of the social order taking shape around them. It was easy to ignore, considering the eye-popping growth in northern Virginia and the real wealth generated by an economy rebounding from recession. But beyond the innovation centers, the private-public research ventures, and the announcements of yet another software company locating in the Golden Crescent, a decidedly different economy ground along, churning out part-time, contract work, erasing manufacturing jobs, shipping call center jobs overseas while downsizing or contracting out others. Although the governor announced the arrival of semiconductor jobs, his administration did precious little to stop the erosion of the textile industry. It also did little to check the decline of living standards outside of Fairfax, Alexandria, and Hampton Roads, or to ensure that workers had the tools to negotiate massive restructuring. Globally conscious universities and generously funded retraining programs could not mitigate the effects of a New Economy which the Allen administration championed. Neither ecstatic claims about subsidized jobs nor assertions about the need for a highly trained workforce seemed powerful enough to counter unregulated competition. They could not compensate for the suppression of labor unions that offered some hope of redistributing income.

Incentive and trade policies designed to benefit business and inflexible dogmas about the errors of intrusive government closed off opportunities for managing the crisis through meaningful government action. In the South, those forces operated freely, and southern workers felt the full brunt of them. They set the pace for a country that began to share the region's long exposure to the currents of global economic change.

By the time that some of the most glittering economic development promises began to fade, Governor Allen was out of office. As the semiconductor industry declined from overcapacity, Motorola delayed its plans for a massive assembly plant in Goochland. In September 1998, it announced it was suspending construction. According to the *Washington Post*, the announcement was a "vivid case of global economic forces hitting home, of how crippled economies in Asia cost the Richmond area thousands of jobs."[106] It also illustrated the vagaries of economic development strategies. Chasing after the New Economy's cutting-edge industries, the state heaped incentive on top of incentive to reel in companies peculiarly vulnerable to market fluctuations. Linking its fortunes to fickle corporations, Virginia became a needy supplicant, willing to adjust to the caprices of businesses that owed little allegiance in return. More than this, the smokestack-chasing policies of Allen and his southern counterparts did not generally attract high-wage, high-skilled jobs. Instead, argues economist Gavin Wright, "these policies have largely attracted firms engaged in relatively unskilled, labor-intensive production. When state manufacturing is ranked by capital-labor ratios or by the share of employment that is skilled, the southern states persistently appear in the lowest percentiles, in the 1990s as in the 1950s."[107] If this was an old southern story, it was one that became painfully new again. In an era of transnational corporate interests, unprecedented capital mobility, and an international labor market that consistently undermined the South's comparative advantage, the illusions of Henry Grady's New South returned.

And Motorola was not the only example of failed development. After a multimillion-dollar incentive package drew the computer manufacturer Gateway to Hampton in 1995, the company began to feel the turbulence of an overheated high-tech sector. It started laying off its 2,100 Hampton employees and selling its assets in February 2001. Over the next two years, the company closed its call center and its assembly site, shifting all of its manufacturing to Asia. It also shut its stores in Newport News and Virginia Beach. All told, Hampton lost $214,000 in taxes, an estimated $35 million that 450 employees generated in the area. When the company failed to meet the job targets it had agreed to under the incentives deal, the city and the state demanded repayment of its $936,000 debt. Protracted and acrimonious negotiations finally produced an agreement which saw the company return eleven acres to the city and pay $353,000, with the city's taxpayers contributing an additional $100,000.[108]

If Virginia's media had been reluctant to criticize economic development policies at the height of the high-tech boom, the collapse of the technology sector and the recession of 2001 added new perspective. After an intensive investigation of the Gateway deal and similar ventures, this is how the *Daily Press* introduced its special series on the topic: "Virginia loses millions of dollars in many of its most hyped economic-development deals when companies fail to live up to job and investment promises and either go bankrupt or refuse to repay subsidies." The newspaper found that inadequate recordkeeping kept the magnitude of the failures away from prying public and legislative eyes. "At least $233 million was given in the five years ending in 2003. Almost half the deals went bad in 1999, one of only three years for which records exist. Even worse, a patchwork system for overseeing incentives makes it hard to get the money back."[109] The failed Gateway venture stood out as a particularly poignant example of the risks of economic development and the primacy of corporate interests in American life.

Perhaps the most symbolic failure came in Dickenson County in southwest Virginia. Hurt by the loss of the coal mining and textile industries, the county was euphoric when Nexus Communications announced that it would open a call center in Clintwood to facilitate its client-customer locating service. The decision was in part a result of Governor Allen's "red carpet" tour, which introduced several business executives to the charms of low-cost production in southwest Virginia.[110] The company hired 188 workers and laid them off not more than three years later as the high-tech industry began to plunge. According to Charlotte Mullins, industrial recruiter for Dickenson County, "It has devastated us and the employees as well. We really looked at Nexus as the ray of hope for attracting technology companies." Reflecting the desperation that blanketed the region as well as the prevailing assumption that technology start-ups offered deliverance, Mullins asserted that "We're still going to go after those companies regardless of what happens. We still have a work force for any company that wants to come here."[111]

And they did. In 2001 Travelocity, an online travel agency, set up a call center in the former Nexus building that employed 275 people. Paying workers $8 an hour, Travelocity promised a modicum of hope for a region that had known 20 percent unemployment while the rest of the state recorded levels around 4 percent. A $250,000 loan from Dickenson County economic development authorities secured the deal. Then, in 2004, the company terminated its Clintwood call center, sending its jobs to India, where, as the *Newport News Daily Press* acerbically noted, "their replacements will earn less than one-quarter" of what Clintwood's employees earned.[112] And yet the Nexus and Travelocity implosions were not enough to cure the region of the call center panacea. Representative Rick Boucher, who had sponsored Showcasing Southwest Virginia tours to attract potential call center companies to the region, announced in the wake of the Travelocity decision that "collaborative tactics" would be necessary to help southwest Virginia respond to the "situation."[113] But it was the "collaborative tactics" of state and local economic developers, elected officials, and corporate interests that put Clintwood's residents in the position of watching yet another fragile opportunity slip out of their grasp. It cost taxpayers money, but it also cost the town's residents a sense of hope, possibility, and dignity. None of these could be quantified by economic developers, but each was at the center of the story of the New Economy in the South.

The company had a perfectly reasonable explanation for the call center closure. "Travelocity's key competitors are already outsourcing most of their customer-service calls, and Travelocity made the decision to be cost-competitive in this area and focus its resources on the growth and development of its business."[114] Nothing illustrated more clearly the realities that had settled on the Sunbelt South. A region of opportunity had become an economic frontier where corporate interests fled to avoid taxes and government regulation and to find workers uncorrupted by expectations of decent wages and working conditions. What they found, of course, were hardworking and intelligent people not a little frightened by the prospect that their livelihood would disappear on the winds of sound business decisions. Others simply left Travelocity, "unable to endure the cranky customers and strict regimen," as the *Daily Press* delicately put it. What they left was a job that gave license to customers to treat their "service representatives" like subordinates and employers to implement the full discipline of management by stress. If the company tried to position the withdrawal in terms of competitive restructuring, local media offered another perspective. "At the heart of off-shoring is the question of what a company owes its workers and its community. It's a topic with particular resonance in Appalachia, where the coal companies once owned everything and the miners had to fight for basic human rights."[115]

Yet in the 1990s, Virginians well beyond the coal fields of the southwest discovered that the rhetoric of business-employee partnership was remarkably shallow. While business influence crested, working Americans were expected to accept the axioms of business competitiveness, cost efficiency, and creative destruction as positive, universal norms. Many did, internalizing their misfortune, blaming themselves, believing that the decisions that corporate executives made would ultimately be for the best. But Virginia's workers could not wait for the long term. They could not patiently anticipate the distant return on investment which pundits claimed would come if they only retrained, educated themselves, retooled for competition, and achieved suitable flexibility for the bumpy ride ahead. Many had no choice, of course, but to accept the disparity between the promise of high-tech deliverance and the reality of declining living standards. As historian David Carlton reminds us, "the progress experienced by large areas of the postwar South has proved to be thin and easily reversed. Even now 'deindustrialization' plagues much of the small-town and rural South, and even such high-tech showpieces as North Carolina's Research Triangle have yet to generate the entrepreneurial vitality of a Silicon Valley."[116] Some southerners refused to accept the era's uncritical celebration of business ascendancy. For them, it was a question of challenging dogmas that failed to deliver.

CHAPTER 7

Dreams of Revolution

Virginia's Conservatives in the 1990s

Corporate incentives were part of a larger movement to make business the principal agent of social policy. Advocates believed that tax breaks, anti-labor policies, and minimal environmental regulation would reverse industrial decline, combat global competition, and restore American responsibility. Free market libertarianism was the central tenet of this worldview, and Virginia became one of its leading purveyors. The Republican Party was the central exponent of this perspective, but by no means was it the only one: the neoliberal agenda which came to dominate American society in the 1990s and which southern business and political elites stridently championed was never a strictly partisan affair. In rejecting the social democratic heritage of the New Deal and adopting a business-first philosophy, the Democrats assisted the Republicans in promoting the market-oriented agenda.

The Republicans in Virginia did not triumph simply because of ideological and organizational bravado. They gained the political advantage in the region because most Democrats capitulated to the agenda of low taxes, law-and-order toughness, fiscal stringency, and laissez faire social policies. The Democrats dominated Virginia in the 1980s, controlling the governor's mansion and the Assembly at a time when the state was voting for Reagan. Led by Governor (and later Senator) Charles Robb, the Democrats banished the image of "tax-and-spend" liberalism from Virginia. The son-in-law of Lyndon B. Johnson and a former Marine, Robb was considered corporate-friendly and suitably anti-labor during his bid for the governor's mansion.[1] He and his successor, Gerald Baliles, continued to fund transportation and education improvements, largely on the strength of increased revenues from economic growth. But they abandoned any progressive initiatives that would have alleviated chronic poverty or significantly redistributed wealth.

The strongest indication of the Democratic repudiation of social democratic reform was their opposition to organized labor. The party turned a cold shoulder to the movement for public employee collective bargaining rights. It also assured business that it had no interest in repealing the venerable right-to-work law. At the same time, the Democrats opposed any meddling in abortion law and paid lip service to African American civil rights. Opposing social democratic reform while engaging in the symbolism of liberal empathy, the Democrats found a winning formula.[2]

The Virginia Democrats had decided to move more rapidly toward centrist, fiscally conservative policies than the national party. They did so in large part to capture the massive influx of white middle-class voters into northern Virginia. The state's population grew by more than 500,000 in the 1980s as out-of-state migrants flooded into the suburbs of northern Virginia and the southeast. Driving up the voter rolls in Fairfax, Loudoun, and Alexandria, these new voters displaced rural Virginia and Richmond as the arbiters of political power. They brought with them an attachment to fiscal conservatism and limited government. They wanted to make money in Fairfax and Loudoun, avoid taxes, and minimize business regulations. Middle class and educated, they repudiated Virginia's racist past. They were social liberals, tolerant of abortion, women's rights, and sexual freedom. By the end of the decade, northern Virginia represented a substantial voting presence in the state. As much as 60 percent of the state's votes were cast in suburban areas such as Fairfax, Prince William, Loudoun, Chesterfield, and Henrico Counties. Almost 30 percent of state voters resided in northern Virginia alone. The suburbs of Virginia had taken the balance of power from the rural areas where the Democratic political machine once held sway.[3]

Suburban voters rejected the moral absolutism of the Christian Right. Instead, they embraced a "libertarian brand of conservatism" based on minimal taxes and pro-business legislation.[4] Like their counterparts in other areas of the country, suburban voters wanted reduced government intervention, except in areas that directly benefited them. They were fiscal conservatives who nevertheless tolerated racial diversity and sexual choice. More than this, they embraced privatized forms of leisure and social interaction that relinquished interest in the public sphere. If northern Virginia's temperate liberals had once endorsed the 1960s ethic of strenuous citizenship and social reform, they abandoned it in the 1980s for tax rates that favored the middle class while still maintaining a minimal social commitment to the urban, nonwhite poor.[5] As political commentator Frank Atkinson explains, "blurring the ideological differences between the parties was the chief prerequisite for Democratic success in the 80s."[6] By positioning themselves as racial progressives and the Republicans as the party of Massive Resistance, they appealed to suburban voters who imagined themselves enlightened on civil rights. By rejecting social reform and distancing themselves from organized labor, Virginia Democrats endorsed the business-first agenda that the Republicans had perfected at the national level. In fact, the same Virginians who kept the Democrats in power at the state level voted for Reagan at the national level. For them, Reagan's hostility to the welfare state and commitment to business profitability over social investment paralleled the Democratic agenda at the state level. With candidates like the pro-labor Walter Mondale and pro-racial-equality Jesse Jackson bidding for nomination, the national Democrats appeared far too liberal for Virginia voters.

The change in the direction of the Democratic Party was clearly evident in the ascendancy of Douglas Wilder to power. An African American who became lieutenant governor in 1985, Wilder symbolized the party's synthesis of social liberalism and the business agenda. When Governor Gerald L. Baliles proposed a half-cent increase in the state sales tax, Wilder was careful to distance himself from it. He invoked the symbolism of racial justice, accusing his Republican opponents of using the term "liberal" as a racial "code word" and adopting the slogan "Let's Make History" to underline the significance of electing an African American to the position of lieutenant governor. Once in office, Wilder proved to be a friend of fiscal conservatism. Low taxes and toughness on crime caught Wilder's attention, not inner-city poverty. Having honed the message of social liberalism and business primacy between 1985 and 1989, Wilder was ideally placed to become the first elected African American governor in American history. After beating Republican Marshall Coleman in a close election, Wilder defined himself as a tough-minded administrator who won the praise of *Financial Magazine* and the *Wall Street Journal* for his reduction of state spending.[7]

Wilder was not without his liberal accomplishments. In the midst of a crushing recession, the newly elected governor was still able to win support for measures that required at least a minimum of government activism. He was able to secure Assembly approval for a child health care program for families that were not eligible for Medicaid, a jobs training program, limits on tuition for in-state college students, and a mortgage assistance for low- and middle-income families. He won approval for a program to subsidize the relocation of low-income residents from public housing to their own residences (although one might argue that this inevitably increased the cost burden for working-class families while eliminating expenses for the state). In his fourth year, Wilder authorized a youth services project that taught trade skills to unemployed, impoverished, or delinquent young adults. In a state that cherished the right to bear arms, Wilder also secured a law prohibiting more than one handgun purchase a month.[8]

Yet it was his fiscal "responsibility," not his limited social reform program, which left the deepest impression. Facing a budget deficit inherited from the previous administration as well as a recession, Wilder chose fiscal management over crisis leadership. Conservative publications and political pundits cheered his fiscal restraint during the recession. Instead of initiating public works or turning to other Keynesian strategies to manage the devastating economic crisis, Wilder balanced the budget. He set aside $200 million as a "rainy-day fund," froze the salaries of state employees, reduced the benefits of the state health insurance program, and approved $1.3 billion worth of cuts from the state budget.[9] Raising taxes was out of the question; the only viable political solution was to limit state spending. Echoing the market ethos of the era, Wilder insisted that "we have to recognize that the role of government is to deliver essential services, not to be the employer of last resort." Wilder endorsed the privatization of highways, railroads, and minimum-security prisons. He rejected the idea that state-owned or -operated hospitals would benefit Virginians. Echoing the principle of market dominance that prevailed in the 1990s, Wilder claimed that there "are many areas where government should look into privatization, because many people usually work more effectively and put in their best efforts when they can make profits through good service."[10]

The governor's ideological arsenal included more than privatization and budget contraction. It also included a plan to remove six hundred families from the New Deal's Aid to Families with Dependent Children. Participants would relinquish their benefits in exchange for a job, a savings of some $36 million to state taxpayers. Saving taxpayers' dollars had triumphed over providing for the most vulnerable or protecting them against an unforgiving labor market. The tough-on-welfare plank was coupled with a tough-on-crime initiative. In this case, however, the crime and anti-labor positions were in complete harmony. Wilder revitalized the inmate work-release program which, according to a sympathetic biographer, would "increase the flexibility of Virginia's correctional system and . . . help inmates become re-acclimated to society before being released."[11] Working inmates in jobs that law-abiding citizens might have occupied could hardly qualify as progressive job creation.

In fact, the Wilder experiment became an example for the Republican Allen administration. Under Jerry W. Kilgore, Allen's secretary of public safety, the state built work centers that would house nonviolent inmates assigned to community construction projects. Putting inmates to work sounded like a perfect solution to rising labor costs. "Having more inmates working lowers capital and operating costs as 75 percent of the work center inmates perform agri-business duties and facility maintenance." The program also harmonized with the era's competition ethos. "As Virginia continues to maximize inmate work programs and minimize administrative and operating costs, we are becoming increasingly recognized as a national model." Public works projects were being completed, impoverished African American prisoners were learning the "benefits of work," and the state was claiming that escalating incarceration rates were not costing the taxpayers.[12] What was happening was that Virginia was becoming a model for revitalizing the convict labor system of the New South. Few policymakers thought to relieve the persistent unemployment of places like Danville, Petersburg, and Martinsville, by hiring their residents at a living wage.[13]

While the governor adopted new programs designed to solidify his reputation as a supply-side executive, he carried forward the Democrats' disdain for organized labor. Thomas R. McNutt, the pugnacious president of the UFCW in Virginia, highlighted the increasingly business-oriented direction of the Virginia Democrats. Relinquishing social reform in favor of a business-first agenda, Virginia's Democrats paralleled the changes in the national party: "The conservative Democratic Leadership Council pointedly excluded the Rev. Jesse Jackson from its recent Cleveland meeting, where Wilder was a featured speaker. Jackson has walked countless picket lines in Virginia, showing his concern for working people who are the core constituency of their party. Wilder, by contrast, is a firm believer in his state's right to work law and rebuffs labor entreaties for his help against unfair employers."[14] At the same time that the governor reduced state services, he courted international business on trade missions that emphasized Virginia's right-to-work law. In a 1991 interview with the Washington-based *Europe* magazine, Wilder claimed that Virginia's "ready work force" made it attractive to European investors. "We are a right-to-work state, which means we are not slowed down by strikes and things of that nature." Added to that virtue was the fact that "we have a very low tax rate—corporate taxes, income taxes, and sales taxes."[15] The Democratic Leadership Council and Governor Wilder had largely reconciled themselves to the Republican's business-first philosophy.

In an era of post-war economic expansion, the Democrats abandoned progressive reform for managerial liberalism, which used the benefits of economic growth to assist disadvantaged groups. When economic decline returned, the Democrats rejected redistributive policies and endorsed fiscal restraint in the interest of capital ownership and management. According to McNutt, the governor and the DLC "turned their backs on the legacy of Franklin D. Roosevelt, who made working people full participants in the American Dream." Critical of Wilder's pragmatism, McNutt astutely assessed the implications of the governor's conspicuous ambitions for the White House. Wilder's program represented "the New Mainstream—less government, fewer services. Like most simple ideas, it ignores reality. In tough times, people need more help from government, not less. Unfortunately, services Virginians desperately need are being sacrificed on the altar of Governor Wilder's national political ambitions."[16] Winning the applause of business journals and conservative pundits, Wilder departed from the tradition of government activism that had defined the Democrats since the New Deal.

Virginia's Democrats had never been that progressive, however. Before the early 1970s, when the Democrats under Lieutenant Governor Henry Howell embraced racial equality, corporate regulation, and support for organized labor, the party had been the stalwarts of Massive Resistance. Under Senator Harry F. Byrd, the Democrats operated a political machine that minimized voting, limited black political participation, and ensured a racially divided working class. In the 1980s, economic growth permitted the Democrats to fund a number of politically appealing social improvements through increased tax revenue. Middle-income African American voters, suburban white voters, and small businesses also found the Democrats a palatable alternative to a Republican party torn by factionalism. Despite the limited depth and duration of Virginia's Democratic liberalism, it represented an alternative to the Republicans, a party that seemed archaically conservative in the post–civil rights era. As economic contraction set in and as the market-oriented philosophy achieved ascendancy, Virginia Democrats changed course. By the late 1980s, the Democratic Party was actively endorsing the low-tax, fiscally conservative, anti-labor position of its adversary.[17]

The party's trajectory was evident to readers of the *Virginian-Pilot* when it interviewed Democratic House majority leader Richard Cranwell. Journalist Margaret Edds wanted to know if Cranwell believed that the success of the Republican Party was the most significant political development in Virginia during the 1990s. Hardly, he replied. The two parties were converging on common ideological terrain. Instead of a Republican monopoly, the delegate from Vinson detected "a greater allegiance to a conservative mind-set. The new folks coming into Virginia have not been able to distinguish Virginia Democrats from national Democrats. We have got to re-establish that we are not a liberal party; we're a moderate centrist party, conservative with taxpayers but fair on social issues." Cranwell and his Virginia colleagues exaggerated the "liberalism" of the national party. It had already defined itself as pro-business, pro–free trade, and antagonistic to the welfare system. What Cranwell meant, presumably, was that Virginia's Democrats still had to distance themselves from a national party that bore the burden of having once championed racial equality, women's independence, and workers' rights. The idea was to provide a more humane version of supply-side social policy.

Cranwell had already made that clear a year earlier while running for reelection. When the *Roanoke Times* asked several candidates to state their positions on economic development and the challenge of living on the minimum wage, he articulated the business-first perspective. "Economic incentives are a fact of life. If Virginia wants to be a player in attracting new industry, it will have to offer incentives." While Cranwell was troubled by the lack of a general policy on state incentives, he endorsed the idea that taxpayers' money should be used to purchase jobs. As for wages, the "key" was better jobs through education, not improving the minimum wage or promoting collective bargaining.[18]

The Democrats made the conservative ascent possible by endorsing some of the central tenets of its philosophy. According to Bill Wood of the Sorensen Institute for Political Leadership, Virginia's Democrats offered only mild opposition to Governor George Allen's conservative program. For Republican successor Jim Gilmore, the "problem" was that "welfare reform, lowering taxes, [and] abolishing parole have all been done."[19] The Democrats under Governor Douglas Wilder inaugurated the welfare reform initiative. It moved ahead after Democratic lieutenant governor Donald Beyer's Commission on Poverty and Welfare Reform advocated a major overhaul of the system. Accompanied by amendments that allowed Governor Allen to claim it as his own, the General Assembly endorsed the Virginia Independence Program in 1994. The governor's plan for prison reform, which would build twenty-seven new prisons, put the incarcerated to work, abolish parole for violent offenders, and impose longer sentences, gained the support of conservative Democrats. In fact, Democratic delegate Glen Croshaw of Virginia Beach became the bill's leading proponent in the Assembly. Despite Allen's aggressive style and his virulent attack on the state's dwindling liberals, he could depend on the support of conservative Democrats to advance his agenda.[20]

By 1995, with the Democrats still in control of the Assembly, progressive legislation had all but vanished from the public agenda. Instead of protecting labor unions, providing for downsized textile workers, or injecting resources into local job creation, skilled trades development, health care, or urban renewal, the Assembly focused on law and order, welfare reform, a partisan struggle over the budget, prisons, concealed weapons, and parental notification for minor's having abortions. The Democrats did sponsor an Omnibus Education Act that provided resources for technology in the classroom, school/community health centers, and dropout prevention. Yet even here they paid homage to the Republicans' "personal responsibility" mantra, which absolved the state from social leadership. This bill would require "parental responsibility for student's behavior," a reflection of how dogmatic the radical individualism ideal had become in the Commonwealth.[21]

Virginia's Democrats had not capitulated completely to the free market agenda. Pushed in large part by the Black Caucus and political pragmatism, they successfully countered the $2.1 billion income tax cut that Allen proposed in his 1995 budget. They were able to prevent the crusading governor from eliminating the Meals on Wheels program or canceling assistance for school dropouts. They compelled the governor to assign $125 million to implement a computer network between Virginia's public schools and state colleges. The Democrats extracted additional money to reduce class sizes in elementary education. Despite the apparently progressive overtures, they did not target educational spending at low-income and predominantly African American areas. They did not advocate massive spending on impoverished areas suffering from white flight or from de-industrialization. Nor did they advocate an end to the right-to-work law or a raise in the minimum wage. While they secured resources for politically popular programs like education, they simultaneously embraced the idea that social inequalities could be resolved by retooling for the New Economy.[22]

More than this, they endorsed a Republican governor's budget that included the elimination of $230 million from social spending. Revised under pressure from the Democrats, the budget would still cut $6.8 million targeted at working people who did not qualify for federal assistance. The Democrats were able to extract $250 million for state colleges and construction projects. Yet the overall spending cuts occurred at a time when state revenues were increasing dramatically. In fact, most of the spending increases would be financed out of revenues from economic growth. This was but two years after a recession that had left thousands of Virginians out of work or desperately retraining for new employment. The cuts would occur at a time when New Economy advocates championed training and education as the path to success in the new economic order. Whether computers in school classrooms would be enough to resolve those relentless social problems was far from certain.[23]

What was clear was that the Democrats were losing their grip on power. By 1999, the Republican takeover of the General Assembly was complete. In part, this reflected the Democrats' inability to offer an identifiable alternative to the Republicans. Commitment to alleviating the sources of poverty, attention to persistent racial inequalities, and devotion to social investment had largely disappeared.[24]

Southern conservatives were galvanized by the conviction that they were opponents of a corrupt status quo. They imagined themselves as revolutionaries, the authentic descendants of America's original freedom fighters. They were reclaiming individual liberty from the hordes of feminists, limousine liberals, homosexuals, and racial minorities pushing their unholy agendas. They believed that they were protecting beleaguered citizens from a grasping federal government that had aggressively undermined their freedom over the past fifty years.

Despite the heat of the culture wars and the prominence of thought patrols on America's university campuses, the cultural left did not dominate the political agenda. If anything, the big political story of the late 1990s was the fusion of economic and cultural conservatism. While grassroots reform organizations critiqued economic globalization and environmental neglect, evangelical Christians mobilized throughout the state against the erosion of what they defined as tradition. For them, the "consensus" was a secular, permissive, libertarian society that had abandoned bedrock Christian values. According to this narrative of social decay, liberal elites and their special interest allies had enshrined moral relativism at the center of American life. They had banished the Christian truths that had supposedly guided the nation's founders. Christian evangelicals imagined themselves as spiritual insurgents in the nation's culture wars, but they subscribed to the very tenets at the core of the nation's cultural consensus. While they lauded traditional values, they embraced the corrosive individualism, consumerism, and free market extremism that was dissolving the bonds of communities across the country.

While the Religious Right never dominated state politics, it nevertheless emerged as a formidable political force in the 1990s. Like the larger national Christian alliance, Virginia's consisted of a variety of local action groups tied together by mailing lists, faxes, meetings, telephone notification systems, and Internet sites. The Christian Coalition was the largest, but it cooperated with smaller groups such as the Concerned Women for America, the Family Foundation, the Old Dominion Association of Church Schools, and myriad other community-based organizations. What they had in common was a degree of political sophistication that surprised critics and defeated liberals. By the time that George Allen ran for governor, Christian conservatives realized that compromise and the forging of a larger conservative coalition was the avenue to influence. Departing from tradition in 1993, Virginia's Christian right leaders endorsed George Allen despite his qualified pro-life stance. Having learned that visceral righteousness did not win elections, Christian conservatives modified their strategy in the interest of electing candidates who met most of their expectations. Allen certainly did, supporting parental consent and waiting periods for abortion and objecting to tax support to perform them.[25]

And their support paid off: Governor Allen richly rewarded the Religious Right for its support. He appointed Anne Kincaid, a prominent pro-life activist and lobbyist for the Family Foundation, to the position of director of constituent services. Allen placed Michael E. Thomas of the Virginia Society for Human Life in charge of his campaign and then made him secretary of administration. Republican evangelical Kay Coles James, who had served as public affairs director for the National Right to Life Association, became secretary of health and human resources, while James's husband, Charles Everett James Jr., was appointed director of personnel and training. Charles James had previously served as director of the Family Foundation and co-chair of the Bush-Quayle Family Coalition.

The most remarkable appointment was Beverly Sgro as state secretary of education. Sgro objected to the Family Life Education program and supported state vouchers for private schools. The administration did more than appoint loyalists of the Religious Right. It also endorsed policies that expressed their interests. Once in office, Allen set up a Blue Ribbon Strike Force to eliminate government regulations and spending, and he put a number of leading religious conservatives in charge. He endorsed a parental notification of abortion bill in 1994 and then vetoed a compromise measure that reduced the age for parental consent. The governor signed a bill that allowed student-led prayer in public schools and supported legislation that would authorize the state Board of Education to fashion guidelines for student prayer. Encouraged by Christian Right activists, the Allen administration also rejected federal education funds through the Goals 2000 program. For evangelical activists, federal funding threatened to impose national educational standards on localities that wanted to use schools to disseminate conservative ideals.[26] Calls for local rather than state regulation of sex education and religious charter schools rounded out the governor's proposals, most of which went down to defeat before a Democratic Assembly.[27]

While religious activism was a critical part of the conservative revitalization in the 1990s, its relationship to the wider political currents are often overlooked. As political scientist Mark Rozell explains, the successive defeats of the 1980s taught Virginia's Religious Right the benefits of coalition building. Rather than harping on the prohibition of abortion, religious activists drew voters' attention to waiting periods for abortions, parental notification, and the fact that taxpayers funded the termination of pregnancies. Most importantly, they identified with anti-tax, pro-business, pro-family, and anti-union factions that repudiated the cultural and political gains of liberalism since the 1960s. Compromising on moderate candidates who showed sensitivity for their issues, the Religious Right played a key role in electing Allen to the governor's office in 1993. It also mobilized to elect John Warner to the Senate (although it had vigorously opposed him in the primaries for failing to endorse an anti-abortion candidate for lieutenant governor) in 1996 and the business conservative Jim Gilmore to the governor's office in 1997. By 1993, Virginia had produced Jerry Falwell's Moral Majority and Pat Robertson's Christian Coalition. It had also built a Republican Party in which Christian conservatives wielded powerful influence. This was the shape of the Republican Party in the South in the late twentieth century. Virginia had been on the cutting edge of the change since the early 1970s.[28] A measure of this faction's growing strength came in 1997, when it elected the Christian arch-conservative Mark Early to the office of attorney general. As state senator, Early had drafted the legislation requiring parental notification of teenage abortions.[29]

Southern Christian conservatives offered a religious sanction for the economic individualism that dominated American life. For them, Christianity was a doctrine of individual redemption and individual moral discipline. It required an individual relationship with a savior that spoke directly to them as individuals. Here was a savior who demanded pure thoughts but little in the way of a social conscience. The battleground of modern secular life demanded individualistic resolve, stoic opposition to sexual and gender ambiguities, and stringent moral accountability. In effect, conservative evangelicals called for a modification of the neoliberal consensus. They wanted to synthesize social conservatism and free market fundamentalism. The irony was that conservatives now joined a movement that had crystallized as a response to the economic crisis of the early 1990s. While conservative evangelicals offered spiritual solace in a period of growing uncertainty, they could not provide the solutions to a South beset by de-industrialization, a weakening social security state, and capital flight.

By fashioning a persuasive account of social decay in state and nation, evangelical Christians increased their prominence in Virginia politics. They did not dominate the Republican agenda; in fact, astute conservatives realized that there was such a thing as too much evangelical support. Virginia's suburban middle-class voters and many of its working-class voters endorsed libertarian conservatism but not a Puritan commonwealth. While Republicans wove a narrative of social decay, the Democrats failed to generate a coherent response to the crisis facing most Virginians. That crisis was rooted in the deterioration of the social security state and in the collapse of economic opportunity. Fueled by an indictment of liberalism as the antithesis of American ideals and the cause of national decline, the Republicans swept the congressional elections of 1994.

While the rhetoric was effective, the results said more about the underlying crisis than about public assent for dismantling the federal government. Commenting on the Republican landslide in the 1994 congressional elections, Ajene Quillin, a youth worker in Lexington, captured its larger significance. The November elections were important not because of the Republicans' legislative proposals but "because of its recognition by the electorate that there is something critically wrong with America."[30] Quillin astutely identified the source of the deepening malaise: "A widespread disgruntlement among a work force working increasingly more hours and feeling less secure," she argued, was the at the center of it. The movement toward low-paying service-sector employment and contract work, the loss of benefits and health care, the relentless corporate downsizing, and the pervasive disenchantment of people working longer hours under conditions of insecurity could not be captured by "balancing the budget." Fiscal responsibility could not resolve this social crisis. In fact, the Republicans' "Contract with America" lost steam when it became clear that the middle class would not tolerate radical cuts to key social programs.

Conservatives met the crisis of the 1990s by imagining a new day of moral order. For the wealthy, opportunity would flourish by eliminating social regulations and reducing taxation. For the working class and poor who did not threaten the established order, a new day of unforgiving competition in the marketplace was in store. For all, however, conservatives promised deliverance from the uncertainties of global integration through individual self-reliance. By recapitulating the myth of rugged individualism in a market-oriented society, the Republicans at least offered Americans a framework for imagining social and economic restoration. In a period of dramatic social uncertainty, the conservative message prevailed. It answered questions which most Democrats and the left were not even asking. Content with the histrionics of cultural politics, middle-class entitlement, and a modified version of the anti-state agenda, American liberalism atrophied. Liberals abandoned the terrain of social and economic policy to the caprices of the marketplace. Having relinquished the New Deal politics of working-class egalitarianism, Democrats had little to offer workers, regardless of their race or ethnicity, in the 1990s. They faced the trauma of economic realignment alone, convinced that individual retraining and workplace flexibility was their only hope.

Conservative Republicans turned to the unfettered marketplace as a model of rugged individualism. They imagined that Jeffersonian freedom was the corrective to the alleged excesses of the New Deal state. From the conservative perspective, the government had become a grasping octopus that thwarted individual ambition and expropriated hard-earned income. In the hands of liberal elites, it became an agent of social dependency and economic inefficiency. Through its bloated social welfare programs, big government allegedly dulled the American habits of industry and self-reliance. Reform meant dismantling state government, reducing social assistance, punishing rather than mollycoddling offenders. It meant encouraging personal "responsibility" and individual "accountability." It also meant unleashing the purifying forces of unfettered market competition. Stereotypical images of African American welfare mothers rose up in the minds of Republicans who eagerly awaited a return to the days of Hoover and Mellon.

Yet Democrats also shared this vision of market preeminence. What separated them was their willingness to live with the social and cultural changes unleashed in the 1960s. Moderate Democrats like Bill Clinton easily reconciled the pluralistic ethos of the 1960s with the market forces that supposedly promised a new era of prosperity. What they left behind was the era's radical hope for a form of democracy that addressed deep-rooted economic inequalities and power imbalances. Leading Democrats championed the stock market surge, the suspension of trade restrictions in favor of American corporations, and aggressive deregulation. Under the Democratic Leadership Council, the party solicited corporate donations and abrogated its commitment to organized labor while enthusiastically endorsing tax cuts. Although southern conservatives recoiled against the alleged moral ambiguity of the liberal left, they did not deviate dramatically from the Democrats' economic perspective. On the fundamentals of economic development, the revision of welfare, the discouragement of labor organizations, the forging of multilateral trade agreements that benefited American businesses, and the privatization of government services and American public life, Allen and conservative Democrats agreed.[31]

While African Americans, Latinos, and organized labor believed that the party should continue to champion egalitarian principles, insiders sought to transform it into a vehicle of the business consensus. Republicans at the state and national level championed market-oriented individualism to reward their business supporters and advance their political fortunes. Yet this ideological vision also appealed to Americans searching for a psychological anchor in a period of economic turmoil.

It had the added benefit of appealing specifically to working-class whites who had been pounded by the rhetoric of black empowerment at the expense of poor whites. Of course, white working-class southerners and Americans *had* experienced downward mobility. This, however, was not the result of affirmative action but de-industrialization. It was not racial entrance quotas but the decline of private sector unions, the loss of decent-paying industrial jobs, and the collapse of social spending programs that hit the white working class the hardest. The exposure of American workers to international competition and the drive to bring organized labor to heel advanced dramatically under Democratic Congresses. Republicans stood poised to take advantage of the disenchantment. In Virginia, the Allen administration tapped into this undercurrent. It fostered a series of initiatives that showcased radical conservatism for the rest of the nation. In this, the South played a critical role as staging ground for the conservative movement.[32]

George Allen left office on a wave of popularity that reflected careful public relations and the good fortune of governing in prosperous times. In the first two years of his administration he sculpted an image of himself as a maverick conservative battling the tax-and-spend Democratic elite. Even though several of the governor's proposals went down to defeat—the most disappointing of which was his call for a massive tax cut—his anti-liberal rhetoric and law-and-order pronouncements won him the favor of an electorate eager for security and resentful of its supposed enemies. It was Allen's minimal-government rhetoric that won him 58 percent of the vote in 1993; delivering on those promises would not require much sacrifice from Allen's supporters. If anything, building prisons, eliminating parole, whittling away at welfare, requiring teenage girls to seek parental consent to terminate a pregnancy, and disciplining schools through "tough" new standards targeted conservative wrath at relatively powerless Virginians. These policies played on public fears of rampant crime, of governments handed over to "special interests," and to the traditionally southern penchant for tax reduction as the solution to declining living standards. A year before the Republican "revolution" of 1994, which saw conservative militants gain ascendancy in Congress, George Allen was perfecting the ideology of the conservative backlash. The elements of this worldview had been in play since the 1970s, when Virginia Republicans made remarkable gains at the state level.

Allen and his conservative allies may have dreamed of economic revitalization and popular empowerment, but they pursued policies that frequently undermined these objectives. They neglected public education, made huge tax concessions to fickle corporations, suppressed labor unions that aimed at improving working-class living standards, and slashed government positions that provided stable employment for thousands. As journalist Thomas Frank described it, the conservative backlash "imagines itself as a foe of the elite, as the voice of the unfairly persecuted, as a righteous protest of the people on history's receiving end." Conservatives may trumpet family values, but once in power they tried to restore "an economic regimen of low wages and lax regulations."[33] Allen played on the image of a conservative revolution against the liberal status quo. Describing his campaign as an "insurgency"[34] and his Democratic opponents as "monarchical elitists," the governor positioned himself as a maverick reformer, an instrument of the people's determination to dismantle an intrusive state. No doubt, the party faithful were pleased but not surprised when, at a state party convention in 1994, Allen encouraged 13,000 Republicans to assist him in kicking the Democrats' "soft teeth down their whiny throats."[35] The ideology was in large part a response to concrete developments, yet militant conservatism was curiously void of any economic analysis. It lacked any appreciation for the power of corporate interests in shaping American life. In celebrating individual initiative and private economic action, conservatives like Allen overlooked the public influence that large-scale interests exercised in modern America. They imagined a world of rugged individuals regenerating

American character through independent work, but they ignored the concentration of economic power and its impact on average people. Conservatives would not acknowledge the insurmountable disadvantages that individuals faced at a time when corporate relocation threatened the extinction of entire communities.

Nevertheless, the rhetorical strategy was remarkably successful. On the eve of his departure from the governor's office, the *Richmond Times-Dispatch* applauded his "beliefs and character." It was his sympathy for the people's "principles" and "values" that explained his success. The paper made much of his cowboy-style bravado. Here was a man of action, not an "effete" intellectual or a pawn of special interests. Despite Allen's abysmal environmental record, here is how reporter Ross Mackenzie recalled the governor's action on that front: "Even in the realm of the environment, one of liberalism's last redoubts, conservative George Allen overcame ingrained Democratic hatred and fear to elevate Virginia's environmental policies to the realm of right reason, and thereby improved the environment's quality and condition."[36] Even though Virginia under the Allen administration generated no more than a 2.5 percent annual increase in jobs, a rate that paralleled the national average, journalists celebrated him as a master of economic development.[37] Tax cuts targeted at reducing unemployment insurance, regulatory reductions designed to free the environment for despoilment, and welfare reforms that channeled poor and largely African American citizens into unskilled, minimum-wage jobs amounted to a "revolution" for journalist Ross Mackenzie, one which left "the people applauding wildly."[38]

Attorney Frank Atkinson, who had served as Allen's legal counsel, best encapsulated Allen's significance for conservatives. Referring to the popular musical *Les Misérables*, Atkinson asserted that the show's "rousing revolutionary chorus well captures the spirit that animated the Allen governorship for the past four years." Against "well-heeled politicians and special interests . . . playing partisan political games and manipulating the system for their own benefit," Allen offered populist leadership that echoed the people's anger. Despite the appeal of conservative individualism in the New Economy era, the consequences of corporate downsizing and multilateral trade agreements mattered very little in this encomium. Instead, the people were angry about "revolving-door prison practices and wasteful welfare programs." When he did address pocketbook issues, he asserted that government taxes rankled individuals and businesses the most. The disintegration of the manufacturing sector and its replacement by low-wage service-sector jobs counted for little; what mattered was to have a government that "reflected their character and values." According to Atkinson, George Allen delivered this in abundance, helping "Virginians reclaim control of their government, and so their destiny, from a stagnant ruling elite and unresponsive bureaucracy."[39]

Political elites like Allen offered a set of symbols and an inflammatory idiom that spoke to the white working class at a critical moment.[40] The Democratic Party did not. While the Republicans served up a witches' brew of ideas about family values, states' rights, and untrammeled individual liberty as the solutions to social decay, the Democrats mouthed the platitudes of neoliberalism. While that might have appealed to internationally minded financiers, it could neither capture the imagination nor quell the fears of average southerners. The Republicans had traditionally benefited from the alignment with business, but in the 1980s, the Democrats joined them. Even liberal Democrats "learned to scorn unions as a special interest, and to champion much of the corporate agenda—balanced budgets, free trade, deregulation, privatization, capital-gains tax cuts, opposition to the minimum wage, even the sort that gave CEO's a multi-million dollar personal incentive to cook the books."[41] Despite the success of the corporate strategy, state Democrats could not forge a set of ideas that addressed working-class anxieties.

The Republicans may not have provided the right answers; their proposals for the withering of the state only compounded the problems that afflicted working-class southerners. What they did provide were *some* answers, and those answers seemed to provide a roadmap for negotiating the treacherous road of global integration. They offered a compelling narrative of decline from an alleged golden era of freedom and tradition. Rejecting the language of class but embracing the rhetoric of populism, they channeled widespread anxiety about America's economic future into a movement to dismantle the welfare state and promote business dominance. They invoked the image of liberal elites presiding over an expansive, intrusive bureaucracy which threatened individual freedom. That trope had debuted well before the 1990s. Yet conservative southerners articulated that message with growing clarity and force in the early 1990s, linking it to the economic crisis that persisted despite the stock market euphoria.[42]

The Republicans were no more adept at countering the decay of the manufacturing sector or the expansion of the low-wage service industry. In fact, many Republicans championed developments that steadily corroded the framework of southern security. The contradiction was lost on most white southerners, working class or white collar. What mattered was that political leaders had provided an ideological lens that explained, however erroneously, the predicament that average people faced. Conservative Republicans defined the political debate and won the support of Americans who lacked an alternative political solution. This crisis of liberalism left African Americans, Hispanic workers, young people, middle-class office workers, and the white working class without a prescription for chronic instability. In the twilight of the Sunbelt South, militant conservatism explained the forces that were transforming the region. However disingenuous or pernicious, conservatives offered a strategy for managing the challenge of economic disruption. The key was individual responsibility in a marketplace that assisted corporate consolidation while disciplining the working class.

Despite the Republicans' success, they could not institutionalize a new worldview. Republican apologists may have liked to believe that Allen's election signaled the triumph of the conservative Contract with America at the state level, but Virginia's voters were less certain.[43] By September 1995, midway through Allen's administration, polls indicated that citizens were ambivalent at best about the governor's conservative agenda. While he championed an end to parole and a get-tough anti-crime message, voters strongly preferred rehabilitation and other forms of restitution over prison sentences. While the governor called environmental regulations an unnecessary infringement on free enterprise, citizens called for vigilant enforcement of environmental laws. Despite the governor's appeal for government downsizing and drastic tax reductions, the majority of voters wanted to preserve state services and had little interest in lower state taxes. A 70 percent majority, however, believed that education should be the government's highest priority. According to the same study, 61 percent of Virginians believed that road construction was imperative, while 28 percent endorsed mass public transit as the solution to the state's transportation woes.[44] Slashing government services and returning power to the states seemed low on the agenda for most citizens.

According to the voters that the *Virginian-Pilot* interviewed in 1995, concrete economic issues mattered more than victory in the culture wars. Meeting with four parents and sixty-two other Virginians across the state, the paper concluded that aspiring leaders had failed to grasp the material issues that troubled them most. With state legislative elections pending, the respondents expressed the common anxiety of the period that education was not matching the rapidly changing economy. Their children would bear the weight of the system's inadequacies while "short-sighted squabbling and quick-fix politics" dominated political debate. As staff writer Warren Fiske explained, the primary sentiment among almost all of the respondents was "making ends meet in today's difficult economy and fears that standards of living will decline for their children." Instead of the optimism characteristic of the young, their adolescent children were plagued by a "growing restlessness and a sense of despair." Martin Ferrier of Giles County seemed to capture the group's nagging sense of decline in a time of apparent prosperity. "Everybody wants industrial growth to have more jobs, we want better education, but we want to keep what we have. We don't want to raise taxes or anything." Obviously, middle-income southerners had no interest in additional taxes, but the state's traditional aversion to taxation was concomitant with the struggles facing its schools. More than this, the state's tax policies *did* hurt average citizens by privileging corporate giveaways at the expense of wage-earners who paid property taxes. At least one respondent grasped the connection between failing social services and relentless tax cuts. "If you get a $100 tax refund from the state, of course that's good and dandy. But what kind of long term impact is that going to have for the future of the state? . . . When there is a tax deduction and at the same time there is an increase of debt, then that's not really good."[45]

More than this, they rejected elite efforts to control the terms of political debate. As the paper noted, "The conversations bore little resemblance to much of the high-volume debate that has dominated Richmond in recent years. The citizens had no interest in discussing perennial hot-button topics such as abortion rights, gun control and school prayer." If anything, the citizens in this sample seemed acutely alert to the economic realities that governed their lives. According to Norfolk business manager Dean Heffelman, "All of these things are nonissues that attract a lot of debate, but they're not the main focus. They're just distractions to get people off what's really going down." Survey participants did not accept the conventional pro-business argument that government should be reduced through aggressive tax cuts. They complained about federal taxes but had no objections to state tax rates. At the same time, the sixty-two interviewees were fully cognizant of the state's abysmal ranking in funds spent on public schools and universities. For these Virginians, spending on prison construction at a time when education required the state's utmost attention was inexplicable. Participants were equally perplexed by Allen's welfare reform program, which covered recipients for two years before requiring them to find a job. As Chesapeake adult educator Adele Whitener noted, "They're saying they're going to put them off welfare in two years. Well fine, but what are they going to do? They're no jobs [*sic*]."[46] While Republicans and many Democrats championed social conservatism and corporate giveaways, citizens from Norfolk to Roanoke seemed to be worried about job security and education. The rhetoric of technological innovation, government "right-sizing," and global competitiveness could not galvanize people who lived and breathed the economic insecurity of the 1990s. And while the rhetoric of radical individualism and government minimalism did launch George Allen into the governor's office, it failed to provide solutions to the social distress that clearly afflicted working and average Virginians, whether they toiled in the office towers of Tysons Corner or the supermarkets of Hampton Roads.

Even so, Allen achieved an enormous amount in his administration. He was able to secure a less-restrictive concealed weapons law, the abolition of parole, parental notification for minors seeking abortions, and welfare reforms that required recipients to find work after ninety days and that deprived them of benefits after two years. The declining welfare roles seemed to indicate success for Allen's program, yet few could document a better standard of living for those who left social assistance. In the field of education, Allen was able to impose stringent standards that emphasized rote learning over critical thinking. Schools categorized as troubled could be taken over by the state.[47]

By legitimizing the idea that the federal government stood in the way of individual freedom, he achieved an ideological victory as well. Quite simply, Allen and his conservative allies validated a neo–states' rights philosophy, one that harmonized perfectly with the agenda of corporate globalization. By obstructing federal assistance to education in 1994, Allen promoted a new brand of federalism antagonistic to the entire idea of government regulation. Interfering with environmental regulations and winning the dubious honor of being the only governor to reject Goals 2000 funds for education (Republicans eventually convinced Allen to accept the money), Allen reinforced his image as a defender of states' rights against a liberal, interventionist federal government.[48]

In grandiose fashion, he also promulgated it at the Republican governors' conference in Williamsburg in 1994. Adopting an affected colonial revolutionary style, he and the other opponents of federal regulation drafted the "Williamsburg Resolve," a manifesto calling for the drastic reduction of federal government authority and the restoration of states' rights. "Today," according to the alarmist decree, "the challenge comes from our own Federal Government—a government that has defied, and that now ignores, virtually every constitutional limit fashioned by the framers to confine its reach and thus guard the freedoms of the people."[49] The Republican landslide that year in Congress signaled a "second revolution," according to Allen, one that would decide the issue of "whether we have control of our state and our destinies." Recently elected governor George Bush of Texas agreed. The states "like to be left alone as much as possible."[50] The gubernatorial activists called for the strict enforcement of the Tenth Amendment. According to Allen, the amendment reserved to the state governments just about every power with the exception of making treaties and coining currency. The idea was to undermine the federal government's ability to regulate environmental standards, corporate practices, women's rights (which Allen disparagingly referred to as a "social cause" which the federal government was using to "ruin" the Virginia Military Institute) and gun ownership laws.[51]

In a conspicuous demonstration of the neo–states' rights agenda, Allen appeared before the Legislative Exchange Council, which held a conference in Richmond on "State Sovereignty: The Next American Revolution." At a conference that championed states' rights in the former capital of the Confederacy, Allen defended freedom against government interference. While conference participants invoked high-minded principles that would have impressed Jefferson Davis, they were clearly interested in more mundane considerations. Holding sessions on "state sovereignty and the free enterprise constitution" and discussing how to limit federal enforcement of environmental regulations, the legislators revealed that, when it came to thinking about state freedom, releasing business from social constraints was not far behind.[52]

The anti-government rhetoric might have been for public consumption, but it defined the southern political economy of the 1990s. Motivated in large part by the desire to minimize government regulations, the "new" federalism legitimized the individualistic market ideology of the era. More importantly, it obstructed precisely what was necessary to manage the challenges of corporate globalization and international competition. Quite simply, that was state and federal cooperation. Even had the federal government been more attentive to the economic losses inflicted by trade liberalization, it would have found southern state governments antagonistic to coordinating a response to industrial collapse.

For all of the law-and-order hyperbole, Allen's popularity on leaving office reflected his decision to abandon the anti-government rhetoric in favor of major spending programs. Virginians supported the government downsizing agenda as long as it applied to politically vulnerable groups and those who had become associated in the public mind with indolent dependency.

Allen's $37 billion, two-year budget aimed at improving the state's education system and upgrading local infrastructure demonstrated the limits of his ideology. Keying in on the U.S. Senate, Allen understood that commitments to increased spending would generate more goodwill among voters than the rhetoric of government minimalism. Well before 1997, Allen had already learned the political virtues of public spending by lavishing millions on new prisons in high-unemployment areas of the state and on recruiting corporate interests to the commonwealth. While animosity toward "special interests" solidified the Republican rank and file, spending coupled with strategic tax cuts attracted a broad cross-section of Virginia's voters. White suburban voters were considerably less conservative than Allen's ideologically motivated advisors may have hoped. While they were happy to endorse a governor who delivered a "tough-on-crime" message, they supported him and eventually elected him to the Senate because he relinquished his commitment to potentially disastrous tax cuts. If anything, he passed these on to his successor, Jim Gilmore.[53]

The promise of tax reductions won Gilmore the governorship and solidified the southern Republican strategy of using taxes to win public office. The Republicans did not invent the strategy, nor was the strategy the exclusive preserve of southerners. The no-tax pledge became a standard feature of Virginia elections in the 1980s. Republican Wyatt Durrett used it against Gerald Baliles in the 1985 contest, and Republican Marshall Coleman wheeled it out again in 1989, only to find Douglas Wilder duplicating the commitment and depriving Coleman of its edge. By the 1990s, tax reductions had replaced tax freezes as the key to success. George Allen happened upon the political benefits of radical tax cuts after learning of New Jersey governor Christine Todd Whitman's success. In a close race for the governor's mansion, Whitman promised a 30 percent reduction in the income tax rate. When Allen learned more about Whitman's strategy at the governor's convention at William and Mary, he returned to Richmond convinced that aggressive tax reductions could solidify the Republican movement.[54] While Virginia citizens recoiled from tax cuts that would obviously affect state services, they were more than willing to vote for those that seemed less imminently threatening.

Deprived by Allen's success of standard conservative issues like tougher sentences for criminals and work requirements for welfare, Gilmore settled on tax relief. While alleviating the tax on food might have been the most beneficial for working people, Gilmore and his advisors settled on repealing the personal property tax on cars. The choice was politically astute:

middle-class suburban voters invariably drove cars and, unlike other taxes that were paid almost imperceptibly, the car tax required voters to write a check. At a time when Allen, many business leaders, and leading Democrats were advocating for investment in education, Gilmore and the Republicans called for a tax repeal. Critics pointed out that delivering the tax cut would have an enormously deleterious impact on the state's budget. Based on assumptions of continued economic prosperity, the plan failed to account for revenue losses from a business downturn. Perhaps most importantly, the car-tax repeal contributed to the belief that government was the enemy of personal and economic liberty.[55]

The significance was not that Virginia suffered a severe budget crisis which impaired its ability to finance key services like higher education (which it did). Rather, it was that a philosophy of government indifference had won out over social responsibility. Endorsing tax cuts, corporate liberation, and toughness on crime, as well as "standards" and "accountability" for schools allegedly neglected by overpaid teachers, the Republicans found a winning formula for the 1990s. Governor Allen outlined his moralistic worldview in an interview with *The American Enterprise* magazine: "We need accountability also in people, and people see a decline in individual responsibility."[56]

The elements of the bipartisan conservative worldview may be familiar, but the origins should be underlined. Conservatism had been on the rise since the 1960s and enjoyed enormous success as a result of the economic crisis of the 1970s. But it was the recession of 1990/1991 and the crisis of globalization that solidified the conservative movement. The 1991 election—in the midst of the recession—was the pivotal moment for Virginia Republicans, as they acquired eight seats for a total of eighteen in the Senate. By 1995—a year in which Virginians were still losing jobs and feeling the aftershocks of the recession—the Republicans matched the Democrats in the Senate. In 1997 they gained control of the Senate.[57] At the national level, Republican senator John Warner and conservative Democrat Chuck Robb prevailed throughout the 1990s until the latter was unseated by George Allen. The conservative movement coalesced around the economic crisis of the 1990s, but it also made the Republicans into the primary vehicle of that movement.

The irony is that while conservatives championed government minimalism, they endorsed aggressive market intervention on behalf of business. Through tax rebates, incentives, and interference against organized labor, activist governments ensured the success of the corporate agenda. Claiming to reduce the "burden" of taxation in a state that ranked forty-sixth out of fifty in tax rates,[58] political leaders deprived the state of the resources it needed to manage the crisis of economic restructuring. Claiming to support education, retraining, and global competitiveness, Virginia's leaders neglected its colleges and universities, the very institutions that offered at least some anchors in the torrent of the New Economy.

Fashioning a coherent narrative that interpreted the social and economic crisis of the late twentieth century, Virginia's Republicans won the majority support. They crafted a political program that expressly favored corporate interests, addressed white working-class discontent, and won the endorsement of social conservatives. Jim Gilmore and Republican congressman Tom Davis raised in excess of $4 million for local campaigns. The national Republicans helped the Gilmore cause by contributing $1.2 million. Companies in the high-tech sector played a decisive role. America Online, Electronic Data Systems, and others that had claimed impartiality earlier in the decade exercised their economic clout by contributing $1.5 million to the campaign, more than two-thirds of which went to the Republicans. The logic was simple, political contributions were a business investment. "Both Gilmore and former governor Allen have been aggressive in establishing a pro-business environment in Virginia," observed journalist Alicia Montgomery. Both had also "been especially welcoming to high-tech. The business community, in turn, understands how to keep its bread buttered."[59]

The business community also seemed pleased by the behavior of a Republican legislature following their long-sought victory in the House of Delegates in 1999. While the legislature increased Virginia's appallingly low unemployment benefits, it gave economic developers generous funds for industrial parks and new enterprise zones. Dale Masten of the Virginia Retail Association encapsulated the legislature's activities: "It really was a very good [legislative] session for business. . . . Virginia . . . really is a business friendly state."[60] The business-friendly environment, however, was not simply the result of Republican dominance or corporate support for the GOP. The Democrats had been cultivating it since the 1980s and continued to do so in the 1990s. The evidence was in the fact that business lobbyists observed no difference in the way that business legislation was managed under a Republican House of Delegates.[61]

Virginia was also at the center of American political life in the 1990s. Its proximity to Washington had always given the state a higher profile than many of its southern counterparts, but with people like conservative superstar Oliver North, the state achieved a special prominence. The Republican insurgency in Virginia preceded the Republicans' capture of Congress in 1994. The state continued to draw attention from Washington analysts trying to glimpse the future, one which was apparently unfolding in the Old Dominion as Republicans solidified their control over the state government. Allen and Gilmore both seemed forerunners of George Bush's "compassionate conservatism." Gilmore's tax cut offered Bush a template for political success at the national level. Both Allen and Gilmore reinvented themselves as market libertarians sympathetic to, but not under the thrall of, the Religious Right.

At the same time, they accommodated their message to the Religious Right. Once elected, they followed through by endorsing measures like the parental notification bill and appointing Christian conservatives to key posts. It was George Allen who perfected this strategy of embracing religious and secular, suburban-dwelling conservatives. Conservative opinion-makers touted George Allen as a presidential possibility. No less importantly, Allen had molded a political agenda of government minimalism, corporate support, anti-federalism, and law-and-order toughness that encapsulated Washington priorities.[62]

The era of two-party competition had arrived as Virginia, like its southern counterparts, relinquished the era of Democratic domination. Yet this was competition between professional organizations that increasingly shared the same basic convictions about the social order. A white working class, believing itself aggrieved by government policies that neglected them to the advantage of minorities, turned to the Republicans. African Americans, still bearing the burden of racial discrimination and additionally weighted down by economic inequalities, looked to the Democrats as their only political hope. As the Republican Party drew away white voters in the 1990s, the Democrats in the South increasingly became the party of African Americans.[63]

Yet continued African American support for the Democratic Party did not mean that the Democrats had earned their votes. Inferring a liberal democratic agenda from continued black support neglects the paucity of alternatives available to minority voters. It ignores the changing character of the Democratic Party and overlooks the anemic liberalism of the party even after the civil rights movement. By the 1990s, the Democrats in the South, much like the DLC, had relinquished progressive reform in favor of a market-oriented, color-blind agenda. Pursuing racial equality had been replaced by insisting on the formalities of equal opportunity. Political scientist Alexander Lamis is skeptical that the Democrats will ever become a black-only party, since the Democrats now appeal to the very constituents who had migrated so aggressively to the Republicans in the early 1990s. Lamis explains that conservative Democrats like Governor James B. Hunt of North Carolina and Senator Zell Miller of Georgia typify the new party: "They are moderate coalition-builders . . . [who] . . . stress fiscal responsibility, support public education, favor welfare reform, and promote efforts to fight crime. They shy away from the unpopular 'tax and spend liberal' label associated with their party's losing presidential nominees of the 1980s. The next generation of Democratic leaders will likely follow the successful moderate course adopted by Hunt, Miller, and others."[64]

A market-oriented, individualistic consensus seemed to have achieved preeminence by the late 1990s. Describing the Virginia political scene in the late 1990s, political scientist Mark J. Rozell observed that while black political activists were trying to ameliorate inequalities in primarily black school districts and promote improved social services, political elites were determined to maintain the status quo: "Despite much change, Virginia remains strongly committed to a view of fiscal conservatism that favors limits on spending programs." The leaders of *both* parties believed that reductions in federal social programs and the concomitant increase of responsibility at the state level did not warrant "big government approaches to solving public problems."[65] The Democratic Party offered only a pale ideological alternative to the Republicans. It certainly was not a party of working-class southerners. The era of party competition, so enthusiastically heralded by the state's insular political commentators, benefited the state's suburban voters. It did little to change the social and economic distribution of power.[66]

We've turned to Edward Luttwak before and should do so again to highlight the political changes that overtook the South and the United States in this period. While identity, religion, and social values were important and should not be dismissed as "mere" cultural issues, they often obscured more fundamental questions of economic power. Looking at the political situation in the early 1990s, Luttwak noted that both parties "take it for granted that globalization has increased and can continue to increase the country's total GNP (true), that it must therefore increase the income of all Americans or at least most of them (false), and that because protectionism is always bad for U.S. consumers (true) it must always be bad for the country (false.) What is missing is anything resembling a social perspective."[67] Railing against taxes, attacking labor unions, ignoring the demand for living wages, and reducing social services were inseparable from the effort to reengineer the South for the global economy. Developing countries adopted the same strategies, usually at the insistence of the IMF or the World Bank, in order to ensure continued investment and trade opportunities. The South was doing the same thing; the rest of America was not far behind. The South of the 1990s did not lack for political competition at the highest levels; what it lacked was "anything resembling a social perspective."

CHAPTER 8

Democratic Vistas in the Old Dominion

Organizing for Change among Working Virginians

Focusing on governors and conservative newspapers obscures the dissident voices that occasionally broke through the din of free market triumphalism. Beyond the political maneuvering in Richmond, some Virginians kept alive the notion that government could play a positive role in resolving complex social problems. That belief was founded on an even more basic assumption: that social and economic injustice existed, one which mainstream media could not accept in the era of the NASDAQ miracle. The Virginia Organizing Project was only one of these groups, but its multi-issue focus made it a particularly prominent fixture on the landscape of progressive reform in Virginia. In an era of atomistic individualism, it was representative of the democratic regeneration emerging in the late twentieth century South.

Motivated by the desire to coordinate reform efforts throughout the state and modeled after similar ventures in Minnesota and Washington, the VOP dedicated itself to "shift[ing] the balance of power in the state." Contrary to the prevailing rhetoric that suggested all Virginians were middle class and indifferent to race, the VOP addressed itself to "low-income and working class people" and to a "multi-racial grassroots constituency." The Virginia Organizing Project echoed the local-action orientation of progressive reform in the 1990s. Dedicated to community mobilization, the group's manifesto featured leftish clichés about "empowerment" and "organizing models" that would "build relationships" and advance the "development process." The idiom of grassroots liberalism had become as banal as the jargon of business reengineering. It offered little sense that decisive action would accompany liberal rhetoric. The organization also operated under the assumption that local leadership would naturally translate into effective political action at the state and national level.[1]

Even so, the Virginia Organizing Project challenged the assumption that racial inequalities had disappeared from America. That may have been the operating assumption of many liberal academics engaged in questions of racial identity and theory, but it was anathema in the public arena. In an era when the discourse on race had reduced the issue to a debate over affirmative action, in a period when African American joblessness and welfare dependency was dismissed as evidence of moral failure, at a time when the *Fresh Prince of Bel-Air*'s glossy vision of middle-class tranquility obscured the drug-besotted hopelessness of inner-city black youth, the VOP's recognition of racial inequality was remarkable. It was countercultural because it admitted that the problem of racial inequality was inextricable from the problem of class and economic power, a perspective that rarely appeared in mainstream media and debates over cultural studies. Despite the progress of the black middle class in the years after the Voting Rights Act, the era's official color-blindness overshadowed the miles yet to be traveled in mitigating the social and economic factors that perpetuated black poverty. The unwillingness to acknowledge the persistent race and class nexus was nowhere more apparent than in Virginia, where Governor George Allen dismissed black activists as yet another liberal interest group.

The VOP restored the question of race to political life in Virginia by insisting that any social reform movement must practice and promote racial diversity. Of course, "diversity" was the less challenging, New Age version of what civil rights champions would have called equality. Despite the loss of an idiom that connected black civil rights and the nation's most venerable ideals, the group made ethnic diversity, gender "inclusion," and tolerance of sexual orientation front and center in its call to arms. Chairperson Anita B. Lawrence announced at the project's founding convention on June 21, 1997, that "Where there are racist programs, practices, and policies, VOP will work to dismantle racism." In words that recalled southern liberals like Lillian Smith, Lawrence declared that she was "committed to being a white anti-racist ally." More than this, the VOP would challenge homophobia and embrace "gay and lesbian brothers and sisters."[2]

The organization issued a challenge to discrimination on a number of fronts. It opposed the mistreatment of the elderly and immigrants, employing the "widest definition of diversity" to solicit the voices of those "who have traditionally been left out." Against the prevailing belief that racial and gender inequalities had been solved and that these categories had become meaningless in an era of unbounded prosperity, Lawrence announced to the 150 people at the Smith Mountain Lake 4-H Center that "We have to learn about our racism, our own sexism, our own homophobia, our own ageism and other oppressive systems and mechanisms in our society today." The language of liberal inclusion was familiar to the progenitors of cultural studies, but the VOP joined it to the problem of economic injustice. As the project's "Statement of Beliefs" contended, a living wage, adequate housing, health care, and a secure retirement were "entitlements" of the commonwealth's citizens. The organization advocated the "elimination of the extremes of wealth and poverty" that had developed despite the microchip revolution. Rather than champion the interests of stockholders or consumers, the VOP represented the "rights of workers, consumers, shareholders, and taxpayers to democratic self-organization."[3] While the outlines of "democratic self-organization" remained ambiguous, the VOP was clearly determined to revive the racial egalitarianism of the Rainbow Coalition and the early New Left in the context of a program that addressed economic injustice.

The group's dedication to racial diversity was manifested in its "Dismantling Racism" workshops. Most of these took place at community churches and colleges. In Lee County, for example, the local VOP chapter generated discussions among "eighteen individuals" who addressed "personal experiences about racism, learn[ed] about white privilege and internalized racist oppression" while exploring "ways in which they can interrupt the cycle of racism in their community." For VOP board member Kathy Rowles, the workshop's diminutive numbers belied its social significance. "Before we started meeting and having workshops, not many people were willing to talk about racism here." Harking back to the tradition of the Highlander Folk School and Septima Clark's citizenship schools, the VOP created an environment in which blacks and whites could discuss the persistent problem of racial inequality away from the dynamics of the workplace. The workshops directly challenged the dominant color-blind dogma of the 1990s. The participants became conduits of information, but they also hoped to become agents of reform by confronting "racism in the schools and in their workplaces." The training led to meetings with public officials and community leaders about the paucity of black teachers in the school system. They highlighted what participants believed was the need for "major curriculum changes to include diversity." With the addition of two prisons to the county, VOP participants expected an increase in the county's African American population. The organization was determined to "make sure that law enforcement officers, health providers and others are prepared to treat every person with dignity and respect."[4] The program may not have offered very much in the way of a coordinated program of reform. By addressing the persistence of racial inequality in a public forum, however, it challenged the assumption that the South had solved the "American dilemma."

Despite its proclivities toward cultural politics, the project's leadership seemed to grasp that democratic reform required more than proclamations about diversity. Despite sometimes muddled thinking about how an egalitarian coalition could achieve political reform, the organization sought more than inclusiveness. It set out to restore active citizenship through small group meetings that cultivated "public relationships." This group would consciously cultivate democratic life in the South.

Organizers were committed to more than "bowling alone"–style theorization. They dispatched activists to engage local residents in conversations about the issues that mattered to them. Middle-class activists and college-affiliated reformers played a prominent role in the group's early leadership. The "public relationships" strategy, however, was expressly designed to incorporate relatively powerless Virginians in the inner circle. More than any state agency or political party, the VOP devoted itself to the needs and interests of African Americans, Hispanics, and women in the state. In effect, the VOP set out to regenerate public consciousness among people who had been encouraged to embrace the individualistic ethic of late-twentieth-century consumerism. Addressing the privatization of American life in the late twentieth century, the organization rejuvenated the notion of the "common good" and social consciousness. It challenged the technologically fueled self-absorption that defined consumerism in the 1990s and militated against social activism. [5]

More than this, the project tried to transform the image of poor and minority Virginians from troublesome dependents, or worse, into politically engaged stakeholders. They were eager to include women, African Americans, and Hispanics in the organizational machinery.[6] While the VOP focused its energies on community-level reforms, it tackled time-honored forms of racial discrimination that afflicted all southern blacks. In a bristling broadside, Eileen Huey—a history professor at Tidewater Community College who had penned a newspaper piece excoriating Virginia's anti-labor practices—condemned the state's discriminatory voting laws. Originally published in a progressive newsletter, it was reprinted in VOP's own newsletter, *Virginia.Organizing*. It offered a penetrating reminder that a Silicon Virginia had not erased the commonwealth's history of racial inequality. Denying voting rights to former convicted criminals meant disfranchising over 40 percent of Virginia's African American population. The practice, which distinguished Virginia and much of the South from the rest of the Union, even deprived blacks who had committed drug-related offenses of their civil rights. In fact, Virginia was one of only twelve states that disfranchised former convicts. According to Huey, the practice deprived some 245,000 Virginians, including 145,000 African Americans, of their voting rights.[7] The law barring former felons from voting violated the Constitution and perpetuated the Jim Crow tradition. More than law-and-order toughness, the proscription on voting denied blacks the right of "self-government."[8]

Huey situated the voting prohibition in the context of a criminal justice system that bore all the signs of racial discrimination. Its "police profiling, targeting of black neighborhoods, unequal prosecution and conviction of minorities, disgraceful exploitation of cheap prison labor and refusal to automatically restore voting and other civil rights after time served" amounted, in Huey's estimation, to a continuation of Jim Crow, a system of institutionalized powerlessness which Martin Luther King had once condemned. The "War on Drugs" had become a convenient strategy for denying blacks their civil rights. Instead of encouraging rehabilitation, the practice stigmatized and punished citizens who had paid their debt to society. Blacks caught using or trafficking in drugs were incarcerated at a disproportionately higher rate than whites. Virginia's legal practices offered compelling evidence that the state was still part of the South and that the most obnoxious of southern traditions had not died.[9] The VOP did more than write about the deprivation of former convicts' rights. In 2002, it lobbied Governor Mark Warner to repudiate the practice. It also encouraged people on the Eastern Shore to write to the governor and appeal for the restoration of felons' rights.[10]

White academics were not the only contributors to *Virginia.Organizing.* In a provocative meditation, journalist Bill Maxwell challenged the moral complacency of "color-blind" modern America. Although a reprint from the *St. Petersburg Times*, the piece encapsulated the VOP's racial ethic. It disrupted the unofficial silence on race that settled over Virginia for most of the 1990s. Silence and denial, Maxwell argued, were the seedlings of racial intolerance. "Many people gain great comfort in pretending racism is a thing of the past, a moot issue, something only the 'civil rights industry' wants to keep in the public eye." For Maxwell as for many other African Americans, racism thrived in a society that consigned it to the past of grainy newsreels and uplifting hymns. For Maxwell, each day "is a fight to maintain individual dignity," an "experiment" in peaceful coexistence with whites. "Each day is a struggle to subdue the desire to strike back with a vengeance."[11] While Maxwell perpetuated the misconception that black voting, equal education, and economic opportunity had been successfully addressed, his commentary reminded readers that institutional remedies had not eliminated racial prejudice. It was the personal experience of "slights and indignities" that escaped the attention of whites but amounted to a "weight often too heavy for me to carry."[12]

That weight manifested itself in a series of encounters that convinced Maxwell that the color line had continued right on through to the twenty-first century. Real estate agents had discouraged him from homes in upscale neighborhoods; a landlord rejected his application for an apartment because he "sounded black," and a store security guard followed him closely lest he pocket "some trinket." The indignities were not always the product of white actions but self-inflicted externalizations of white prejudice. Walking five miles a day just before dawn, Maxwell was careful to cross the street when he encountered a white woman. It was a socialized reaction, a survival technique absorbed from the days of segregation, one that responded to white women's persistent fear of black men.[13]

Despite the indignities, Maxwell believed that change was possible. He was committed to overcoming his own "racial prejudices by cultivat[ing] relationships with white people who care." Racial discrimination could not simply be rooted out by law. Like abolitionists Wendell Phillips and Frederick Douglass, and like the white and black progressives who collaborated in liberal reform groups such as Richmond's own Southern School for Workers in the 1940s, Maxwell understood that personal contact eradicated racism by humanizing those on both sides of the racial divide. "The real key, of course, is getting to know people intimately, being with one another after work and after school. . . . I have a hard time hating people I get to know intimately, people with whom I have dinner and drinks."[14]

It was this social vacuum that undermined southern claims of racial amelioration. After surveying the racial landscape of the South in the 1990s, historian David Goldfield concluded that genuine racial integration remained a distant objective. Despite anecdotal evidence of black and white southerners mingling in social spaces and whites denouncing ugly racist outbursts, the racial archipelago had not changed. "The instances of racial contact that we see all around, in restaurants, businesses, and schools, are for the most part superficial." In Atlanta, a city often exalted as an example of racial harmony, blacks and whites lived in separate districts and carried on separate lives. The description fit Richmond, Petersburg, and several other Virginia cities perfectly. In shopping malls, blacks and whites mixed equitably enough but drew sharp, invisible lines around their churches and homes. Voluntary or not, the separatism was pernicious, since it "reifies racial stereotypes that in turn enforce separateness and inequality." Southerners had apparently forgotten that separate never meant equal.[15]

Black southerners were struggling against more than the accumulated detritus of southern history. Along with blacks throughout the United States, they confronted a political climate permeated by the conviction that the problem of race had been solved in America. Emerging from the reaction against the Great Society, a new racial consensus fell into place during the years of the Reagan and Bush presidencies. According to this dominating view, the civil rights legislation of the 1960s decisively solved the problem of racial inequality. The lingering presence of racial inequality could only be explained by the unwillingness of blacks to maximize the chances provided by civil rights legislation. Additionally, convinced that the United States had become a color-blind society, proponents maintained that affirmative action and programs aimed at overcoming racial inequalities were pernicious. Using the words of Martin Luther King out of context and against his aspirations for economic justice, these "racial realists" claimed that race-oriented policies deny his vision of an egalitarian society.[16]

In the 1990s, conservatives in both of Virginia's major parties endorsed this view. It was perfectly consistent with the libertarian individualism at the core of conservative thought. Individual African Americans chose to live in self-segregated neighborhoods, they maintained; individual African Americans neglected to receive adequate education for high-paying jobs, and individual, unenlightened whites sometimes discriminated against blacks. What the VOP understood was that racial inequalities were historical and deeply entwined with patterns of economic exploitation; they accumulated over time, insinuated their way into the warp and woof of the social order, and worked to the benefit of some groups and to the detriment of others. Associations made from access to business networks, fraternities, union halls, colleges, and corporations paid dividends in the form of racial capital. The immediate liabilities of inadequate health care, inadequate education, and joblessness translated into long-term disadvantages, lost opportunities that continue to accrue over time. The restrictions imposed by discriminatory lending agencies and real estate brokers created legacies of exclusion and disadvantage. While the VOP promoted individual encounters of racial reconciliation, it operated on the conviction that institutions carried the patterns of racial inequality forward. Labor unions, the military, schools, corporations, and the political institutions of American life were implicated in the persistence of racial inequalities.

African Americans, however, were no less susceptible to the radical individualism of the late twentieth century. Assaulted with the message that racial inequality was largely a black problem, that it was something which individual African Americans had to overcome, and something which black militants only exacerbated, many blacks turned to a romanticized past.[17] Frustrated by the limits of racial change and the deterioration of their communities, blacks began to celebrate the era of segregation as a time of community cohesion. Reminiscing about community independence, however, displaced painful but accurate memories of the indecency of Jim Crow. Moreover, suggests David Goldfield, the "focus on group exclusivity and uniqueness hampers integration efforts if difference becomes the sole definition of identity."[18] Blacks and whites both engaged in exercises of historical fabrication that provided comfort while also reinforcing traditional boundaries. For Goldfield, as for many historians, the essential conundrum was the "inability to understand each other's history, find common ground, and respect our differences."[19] Historical consciousness still hung heavily in the late twentieth century. Historical distortions, the kind that diminish the central place of slavery in the Civil War, or the realities of slavery before the war, or the inhumanity of segregation, or the accomplishments of Reconstruction, continued to polarize blacks and whites.

Important as historical memory is to the South, it did not displace the economic divisions that obstructed the achievement of "common ground" in the South. White and black blue-collar workers often continued to see each other as adversaries. For many whites, African Americans were claimants on a welfare state that extended them special privileges. That perspective, however valorized by right-wing pundits and media commentators, was patently erroneous. At a time (2001) when the real median income for black males was 67.5 percent of white males and the real median income of black families was 62 percent of the income accrued by white families, claims about black privileges at the expense of whites were delusional at best.[20] In American political life, however, those delusions mattered. For blacks, white workers continued to draw the benefits of racial entitlement, monopolizing the best-paying skilled and professional positions. Lacking political organizations that registered the grievances of a multiracial working class, one increasingly populated by Hispanic immigrants, the drift continued. Racial animosities grew in a political culture that failed to address the fundamental economic inequalities of the New Economy era. Progressives of the Popular Front era understood what Democrats and the cultural left of the 1990s did not: racial equality had to advance hand in hand with a program of economic democracy.

* * *

The Virginia Organizing Project began to address the need for a multiracial movement focused on social democratic reform. It raised questions that Virginia business leaders and political elites preferred to ignore. Fostering collective possibilities, it sought to alleviate the sense of fragmentation that afflicted American society in the years after the activist 1960s. If atomizing individualism and political ennui had been a recurring theme in post-industrial America, its resurgence in the Reagan era accompanied a dramatic redistribution of wealth and loss of power for working people. If the era of liberal consensus disturbed analysts who feared that mass society would eclipse personal autonomy, the era of corporate downsizing, declining government responsibility, black resegregation, and anti-unionism threatened the complete collapse of progressive alternatives. The 1950s, after all, had John Kenneth Galbraith, C. Wright Mills, and the Montgomery Bus Boycott. The 1990s offered no equivalent prospect of renewed democratic dissent and social reform. When progressive change did seem possible, as when Hillary Clinton championed health care reform that would extend protection to millions of uninsured Americans, it fell under the hatchet of free market orthodoxy and the power of concerted lobbying interests.

At a time when stock market speculation fueled economic growth, the governing axiom was that a rising tide would lift all boats. Fundamental reform was no longer necessary; the marketplace was the engine of social progress and the great equalizer of opportunity. While organized labor struggled to overcome the debilitating losses of the 1980s and environmentalists struggled to convince Americans that their world really was fragile, large-scale reform initiatives atrophied. The Reagan years had already discredited liberal reform. Progressives seemed entirely unable to resist the conservative tide. Welfare reform, prison proliferation, law-and-order militancy, and the liquidation of social investments undermined efforts to expand public health care to millions of uninsured Americans. The increasing polarization of wealth and the impoverishment of African Americans and Hispanics barely registered in the mainstream media.

Mired in debates over cultural identity and post-modernist fantasies of "resistance," the American left offered little in the way of genuine political alternatives. Having abandoned the sphere of electoral politics for the comparatively safe terrain of academics, the New Left used popular culture as a surrogate for significant social reform. "Throughout the English speaking world," sociologist Todd Gitlin explains, "class inequality may have soared, ruthless individualism may have intensified, racial misery may have mounted, unions and social democratic parties may have reached an impasse," but these could all be ignored by the study of popular culture.[21] There, academics could imagine a world of subaltern discourses and anti-hegemonic agency that offered little hope for the difficult project of social reform. It certainly did not address the lives and experiences of average Virginians.

In moving toward the recognition that social reform had to address basic economic disparities, the Virginia Organizing Project raised the prospect of a rejuvenated left. The VOP implicitly understood that social injustice had to be fought on the plane of class inequalities. It seemed to understand that reform depended on a coalition of minorities and working-class whites working toward the restoration of public institutions. In some ways, it was caught between two worlds or two modes of thought, one that celebrated diversity as an end in itself, and one that connected racial and gender equality to the task of economic regeneration. Through local initiatives against corporate abuses and the sponsorship of a tour for the president of the Richmond Federal Reserve Bank of economically depressed Martinsville, the Virginia Organizing Project focused attention on the needs of people who had been left out of the New Economy equation.[22] Blacks, women, and Latinos were also active on its executive and in its local branches. Here was an organization that practiced the kind of racial egalitarianism that Democrats and Republicans claimed was the norm in modern America. Although genuine racial equality was conspicuously absent in public schooling, the corporate hierarchy, and the upper strata of American society, it was a defining feature of the Virginia Organizing Project. The South was not homogeneously conservative in the 1990s. Beneath the surface of New Economy punditry and conservative evangelical revivalism, some southerners were fashioning a political movement that stitched together the categories of class and race severed in the 1990s.

The organization expressed its commitment to a critical investigation of New Economy myths through its regular column "Understanding the Economy." The columns evolved out of workshops conducted under the same rubric in places such as Martinsville. A community in the foothills of the Appalachians, Martinsville was emblematic of the textile-dependent southern town. Between 1998 and 2000 Martinsville lost two of its major textile employers, while a third, Tultex, declared bankruptcy, throwing 1,100 people out of work. In 1999 alone, Martinsville lost 4,000 textile jobs, a stunning rebuke of the claims that Virginians were enjoying the blessings of a new economic order.[23]

The VOP targeted communities like Martinsville in an effort to explain the economic devastation that had generated widespread despair. What the VOP did was take up the almost forgotten effort to discredit the pernicious strain of American individualism that assigned moral failure to victims of economic forces beyond their control. Instead of extolling the virtues of unregulated entrepreneurialism, the VOP newsletter educated its readers on the mechanics of the New Economy. The objective was to demystify an economic system over which technocrats and business pundits claimed an exclusive monopoly of expertise. "Press accounts say the economy is going great guns: low unemployment, low inflation, ample credit, record profits, a soaring stock market. But are these good times producing prosperity and security for average Virginians?" Clearly the answer from Martinsville residents was no, and this was before the traumatic Tultex bankruptcy.[24] By informing their readers, the VOP challenged what Ellen Frank has described as the "obscure and confusing economic arguments about finance" that prevent "discussion or even consideration of policies that might generate a more egalitarian distribution of the economy's output." Instead of generating support for policies that favored tax breaks for stock investors, atrophic monetary practices, and federal debt repayment that undermined social programs,[25] the VOP set out to restore the idea that government action in the economic sphere could benefit average southerners.

It did so by challenging the assumption that the economic rules governing American life were fixed, inflexible, and resistant to modification. The VOP brought into question the motives of policy elites and the interests served by the highest levels of economic power. By informing participants "about major economic trends—from the surge in income inequality to the growing power of financial investors over a broad range of economic decisions," the VOP questioned the basic axioms of American economic life in the late twentieth century. In its first installment, the editors of the VOP's magazine cited the Economic Report of the President to demonstrate the decline of average hourly wages from a high of $13.60 in the 1970s to $11.82 in 1996. Instead of stock market quotes and portfolio management advice, VOP organizers offered their readers a critical perspective on the economic realities they confronted. In Martinsville, Tom Schlesinger of the nonprofit Financial Markets Center joined VOP activists in engaging participants in a wide-ranging discussion of political economy. From state economic development policy to the impact of Federal Reserve Board policies on job creation, wages, and debt, Schlesinger and others untangled the New Economy and the implications of predatory capitalism at the community level.[26]

At the same time, the VOP addressed the "values behind different approaches to organizing economic life." The economic system that enveloped them was not neutral, nor did it function according to immutable laws that only Standard and Poors or the chair of the Federal Reserve Board could discern. Instead, economic life reflected underlying values, convictions about how wealth should be generated and how it should be distributed. Cutting through the rhetoric of entrepreneurial liberation, the VOP cited the Department of Commerce to document the disparity between rising profits and wages. While corporate profits had increased some 64 percent between 1989 and 1995, wages had increased only 18 percent. Distressing enough when considered against the claims that deregulated turbo-capitalism was blazing a path to consumer utopia, VOP editors cited the same report to show that prices had increased by 22 percent, leaving working people behind the cost-of-living curve. In a fascinating exercise in oppositional thought, the VOP encouraged participants to play founding mothers and fathers in establishing the economic guidelines for a mythical "Free State of Henry." Discussing organizing strategies and critically investigating the current economic order, the participants in the Martinsville VOP workshop broke free of the ideological straitjacket that bound average southerners. They engaged in active citizenship, the kind that weighed the merits and liabilities of market-determined social policies.[27]

The VOP wasn't operating in an intellectual vacuum. It was responding to the political climate in Virginia and the nation, but also to the progressive currents of thought emerging from organizations like the Center on Budget and Policy Priorities. When the center produced a report documenting an increasing income gap in Virginia, the VOP pounced on it. Income disparities between the top fifth of families and those on the lower and middle end of the scale had grown in each state. In Virginia in the mid-1990s, the richest 20 percent of families with children enjoyed incomes eleven times larger than those of the poorest 20 percent of families. Between the 1970s and the 1990s, the poorest fifth of Virginia families saw their incomes slide by 11 percent, while the wealthiest fifth saw them grow by 23 percent. What the VOP failed to do was place Virginia's income disparities in relation to that of the South or the rest of the country. What it did do, however, was include the report's recommendations, which directly challenged the orthodoxies of free market fundamentalism. Strong economic growth had not ameliorated growing inequalities. Labor policies and government programs, on the other hand, might "influence the distribution of income" and change tax policies in a fashion that "mitigate[d] the effects on families of the pre-tax income distribution."[28]

The VOP was not alone in the field of social reform in Virginia. Other organizations were active on the economic front as well, including United for a Fair Economy, which opened a Southwest Virginia chapter and which cooperated with the VOP. The Virginia Organizing Project joined a growing stream of grassroots organizations in fostering community-level solutions to the consequences of unrestricted capitalism. Yet the VOP combined thought and action, analysis and grass roots organizing, tapping in to the intellectual critique of corporate globalization that flowed from the pens of writers such as William Greider and organizations such as the Economic Policy Institute. Through the pages of *Virginia.Organizing* and in workshops that attracted Virginians who did not make their living behind leafy-campus walls, the VOP became a conduit of critical thought about the consequences of market liberalization. It provided a forum for commentary and an arena for local democratic action. At the same time, it was a source of insight and ideas about the economic forces that shaped the modern South.

The VOP's oppositional stance toward the market-oriented doctrines flooding the mainstream media was fully evident in its treatment of globalization. Trying at once to educate and agitate, the project's editors outlined the "basics" of market liberalization. Dissecting the "layers" of globalization, they examined international trade and the ramifications of multinational corporations operating "subsidiaries in many countries." This was a development which working-class Virginians were only beginning to understand in the 1990s. The second layer of foreign investment had led to boom and bust in the Southeast Asian market. If that was too remote for readers of *Virginia.Organizing*, the maquiladoras in the northern part of Mexico certainly were not. There, companies operated factories that took "advantage of cheap labor and low costs." Financial speculation had also wreaked havoc in the form of currency devaluation in developing countries. While the mainstream media declared the benign inevitability of international market integration, *Virginia.Organizing* offered its readers another perspective, the one on the receiving end of decisions made by governing elites.[29]

While the VOP was critical, it wasn't curmudgeonly. Economic globalization had advanced productivity, improved the standard of living for many, and rewarded some with enormous profits. More than this, global integration *was* irreversible; there was no way to insulate the United States from the patterns of international exchange facilitated by advances in communications technology. Yet corporate-led global integration was not an unalloyed good. Nor was it simply a matter of innocuous—even beneficent—cultural exchange.

Citing William Greider's analyses of globalization in the *New York Times* and *The Nation*, the editors sounded the cautionary note that would only gain widespread credibility after the market meltdown of 2000. Unlike many southern champions of the New Economy, the VOP drew the connection between globalization and the region's historical experience. While slavery and the textile explosion evaded the magazine's treatment of the subject, the vagaries of the Sunbelt South did not. "Thirty years ago, globalization in the American South occurred as domestic and international corporations moved in to take advantage of corporate welfare, cheap labor and cheap land." The pattern continued throughout the early 1990s, but the transitory character of external investment became crystal clear in that turbulent decade. Modern communications and distribution systems meant that corporations no longer cared "where they are located, as long as their costs are kept low. So many of the factories which the South gained from other areas have now moved on to other countries." Virginians in places like Martinsville and Danville understood very clearly the tenuous, conditional nature of corporate investment. Notions of reciprocal obligation and mutual responsibility counted for little in an era of dwindling profit margins.[30]

The editors of *Virginia.Organizing* pointed to the collapse of Tultex in Martinsville as an illustration of the impact of free trade on the region. The VOP reported that Tultex, which had made Martinsville the "Sweatshirt Capital of the World," had left 1,500 people in that town out of work. (Note: their numbers differed from those reported in the *Virginian-Pilot*.) Altogether, the company laid off 2,600 of its 4,300 workers at plants in North Carolina and Virginia. The decision, which came a week after the historic protests against the WTO in Seattle, illustrated the impact of global capital and labor markets on southerners.[31]

Confronted by inexpensive imports, Tultex decided to shift production to offshore locations where labor costs were considerably lower. According to the editors, the WTO and the International Monetary Fund had presided over the decline of American labor standards, functioning as a "watchdog making sure that the flow of cheap labor from poor countries continues."

That cheap labor undermined American workers, but it also prohibited the working poor of developing nations from achieving economic progress. The key was not to drive wages down in order to make American workers competitive, the solution which seemed to be the "intention of recent welfare reform and the policies of our Federal Reserve Bank." The solution, according to the editors, was to strengthen unions in Virginia, organize workers in foreign export-oriented countries, and forge citizen coalitions that advocated for the reform of the nation's economic policies. Although the VOP failed to coordinate its activities with the state AFL-CIO, it pursued a strategy that at least in principle promoted these objectives.[32]

The VOP's analysis of globalization was not unprecedented or particularly penetrating. The organization was more interested demonstrating the effect of market liberalization on real, living, earning Virginians than in discerning the intricacies of international finance. Unlike many jeremiads on globalization, the VOP also pointed toward solutions. Advocating living wages to "fight against overcapacity and deflation in worker pay," the VOP endorsed the idea of challenging corporate power on home turf and contested the myth that inflation was the central enemy of average Americans. While the federal government relinquished its commitment to organized labor, the VOP called for a coalition of "labor unions, citizens groups, nonprofit agencies and religious institutions" to demand "labor rights, including decent wages and the right to organize."[33] What the VOP championed is what one theorist described as "social movement unionism." In this vision of unionism, the distinction between workplace and the wider community is dissolved in the interest of promoting an integrated space for social reform. Craft distinctions erode but so too do the separations between those trying to achieve racial equality, better housing, and dignity at the point of production.[34] In this vision of unionism, collective bargaining is attached to a broader agenda of social democratic reform.

Cultural liberals had abdicated their alliance to organized labor, but the Virginia Organizing Project returned to the principles of the New Deal era to find solutions for the challenges of economic restructuring. In an atmosphere of corporate anti-unionism and bipartisan enthusiasm for entrepreneurial individualism, the VOP endorsed coalition politics and collective social action.

At the height of the New Economy boom, the VOP bolstered its call for labor rights with the demand for tax reform and federal monetary policies that assisted working Americans. While a few journalists and legislators raised alarms about corporate giveaways, the VOP advocated an end to corporate welfare that "subsidizes the rapid moves of multinational factories from place to place and country to country." Since profit motivated the relocation of capital interests, the VOP called for tax policies that discouraged corporate transience. Challenging the economic orthodoxy that privileged investors over wage earners, the VOP insisted on reduced interest rates that allowed for wage increases. Writing in April 1999, the VOP argued that inflation was negligible "since overcapacity creates the exact opposite, deflation. This will mean lower returns on investments, but stock prices on Wall Street could probably use a healthy dose of realism anyway."[35] Critiquing the big picture of globalized markets, the VOP also took on inflation, the taboo of American monetary policy since the early Reagan administration.

It extended its critique of inflation and free market fundamentalism by running articles from national progressive publications. In the October edition of "Understanding the Economy," the VOP examined inflation fearmongering by reprinting an article by economist Ellen Frank that originally appeared in *Dollars and Sense*. Federal Reserve Board policies reflected the interests of corporate elites and bankers, not average people, Frank argued. The inevitable destruction that flowed from inflation had become "an article of faith" in the mainstream media, but one which "neither history nor logic" supported. Moderate inflation permitted employers to offer pay raises without insisting on a speedup; small businesses enjoyed a reduction of competitive pressure and increased latitude in pricing, and the middle class reaped the benefits of mortgages, loans, and credit card balances that decreased in value. Since inflation redistributes "wealth from the rich to the indebted middle class," it threatened investors and the financial industry. Yet Frank argued that it was "no accident that the moderate inflation of the 1960s and 1970s coincided with more egalitarian distribution of income and wealth, stronger unions, and greater democratic ferment" in the United States.[36]

In the pages of *Virginia.Organizing*, readers encountered thoughtful, rational challenge to the individualistic, supply-side policies that dominated American economic life. Through the expertise of social critics who placed Virginia's experience in a national and global context, the VOP helped erode the regional isolationism that proved distressingly resilient in an era of modern communications. Its attention to issues of macroeconomic significance drove against the grain of social conservatism, which sought to restore boundaries of community control and traditions of subordination against modern egalitarianism. Yet it also challenged mainstream globalizing hype, since it focused on the social consequences of dissolving economic regulations. The VOP's dissidence was all the more significant because it challenged dogmas that found their origin and greatest support in the American South.

Prophetically—both in its social criticism and its prognostications on the stock market—the authors of "Understanding the Economy" called for a reordering of political and economic priorities. Questioning the preemption of social investment by monetary policies designed to assist corporate interests, calling attention to the dangers of overcapacity and deflation, and exposing the social consequences of market liberalization, the VOP outlined a social democratic alternative to the New Economy ideology. Rather than subaltern discourses or retraining rhetoric, the VOP drove at the core of uncertainty afflicting working-class Virginians in the late twentieth century.

The Virginia Organizing Project vigorously exposed the contradictions inherent in free market economic policy, particularly as it was applied in the nettlesome issue of welfare. In effect, conservatives wanted to argue that subsidizing corporations reflected rational economic policy while subsidizing the underprivileged was wasteful utopianism. Signed into law in 1995 during the Allen administration, welfare reform placed a limit of two consecutive years on welfare recipients. It also required recipients to find jobs or engage in community service in order to qualify for benefits. The Virginia Independence Program, as the program was euphemistically labeled, permitted recipients to earn up to the poverty level while still receiving benefits; people who withdrew from the program for work could still be eligible for Medicaid, child-care assistance, and food stamps. Those who exhausted the two years of benefits could also qualify for child-care and transportation subsidies, but for one year only.[37]

Conservatives heralded the program as a cost-savings and character-building measure. Service industry employers—where most of the welfare recipients were headed—welcomed the expansion of the labor pool and the downward pressure on wages. *Virginia Business* allayed fears that working in a fast-food restaurant for $5 an hour meant little improvement over welfare. It assured its business clientele that burger jockeys could "earn promotions and pay raises."[38] Working at minimum wage and learning few of the skills that would qualify them for significant social mobility, former dependents had dim prospects for overcoming the "cycle of poverty, dependency, and hopelessness," as *Virginia Business* described it.[39] While encouraging welfare recipients to return to the workforce harmonized with American traditions of productive self-reliance, abandoning them to the tender mercies of the marketplace without sufficient resources was draconian at best. Editors of *Virginia.Organizing* cut through the rhetoric and clarified the impulse behind the Virginia Independence Program. "The heart of the right wing attack on poor people in recent years has been the myth created around the welfare system. Claims that it creates and underclass of people who feel no personal responsibility for their lives accompany racist depictions of single mothers as 'welfare queens.'"[40]

While Virginia's program preceded the federal overhaul of welfare by a year, the VOP drew the connection to the Republican push for change at the national level. In an article on the myths of welfare reform, Ed Wayland reported on a speech by Republican senator Rick Santorum in 1995. An emerging force in the radical wing of the Republican Party, Santorum attributed poverty, crime, illiteracy, teenage pregnancy, and family decay to the scourge of welfare. The welfare system had created a class of dependents bereft of any sense of individual responsibility.[41]

Wayland was determined to challenge these pernicious misconceptions about welfare. Zeroing in on the chestnut about teenaged mothers on welfare, Wayland observed that the Virginia Department of Social Services had reported that in 1994, approximately 500 mothers in that age-bracket received assistance in the state. That represented about "2/3rds of 1 percent of the 73,000 cases then receiving AFDC [Aid to Families with Dependent Children] benefits." Dismantling myths about welfare as an occasion for illegitimacy and a cause of marriage avoidance ("It is the rare case where people marry, or fail to marry, because of a government policy"), Wayland also challenged the claim that declining welfare rolls meant success. The drop in caseloads was the result of declining unemployment, a trend that began a year before the adoption of welfare reform. For Wayland, the "most shameless lie of all" was that welfare provided a disincentive for work. By virtue of the fact that they raised children, women worked, but raising them on public assistance was also "no picnic." Receiving a check for $291 a month and no more than $300 in food stamps, a mother with two children (the average recipient) struggled simply to survive. The problem was not an aversion to work but the quality of work that was available. According to Wayland, most recipients of TANF (Temporary Assistance for Needy Families—formerly AFDC) could find jobs, but those jobs paid on average $5.50 an hour. With the Virginia Senate Finance Committee reporting that a woman supporting two children would have to earn approximately $9.60

an hour, it was little wonder that women receiving social assistance did not relish the supposed independence of wage work.[42]

Welfare dependency was not the result of character flaws or, as some critics implied, racial traits. The problem was that neither welfare nor low-wage work permitted Virginia's primarily black working poor an avenue out of despair and economic powerlessness. Like the authors of "Understanding the Economy," Wayland posited that unregulated market forces caused poverty. The failure of social assistance reflected the failure of American society to govern economic relations for the common good: "The problem is not motivation; it is market forces and simple budget arithmetic. . . . by focusing on false pictures of the problem, it has allowed policy makers to avoid dealing with the real problems."[43]

Wayland's conclusions enjoyed the support of Patricia McGrath Morris, author of a report titled "The Promise and the Reality: The Outlook for Virginians Leaving Welfare." Sponsored by the Campaign for Virginians in Need and the Social Action Linking Together (SALT), the report discovered that half of the people who used food banks and soup kitchens had held minimum-wage jobs in the previous six months. The description fit former welfare recipients. According to Morris, those jobs simply paid too little for subsistence. More than this, former welfare recipients were compelled to work in low-wage positions that deprived them of subsidized day care, affordable housing, and health insurance. "In effect," Morris somberly observed, "all that welfare reform will achieve is a cut in the rolls and shift people from the ranks of welfare to the ranks of the working poor." Lacking adequate health care, decent housing, and day care assistance to permit reentry to the workforce, the "working poor . . . [would] sink deeper into poverty."[44] The working poor were primarily female and African American, a constituency that was reduced to stereotypes in the minds of many white Americans, if it registered at all.[45]

The VOP's attention to welfare reform was important because it raised public awareness about an issue that Virginia's political elites had all but abandoned. Although state newspapers conducted periodic diagnoses of the program, political leaders of both parties had arrived at a consensus. Quite simply, welfare reform met little resistance from white, affluent voters. If anything, welfare reform gave political elites the chance to prove their toughness and realism in the struggle against "special interests." African Americans and the white working poor were politically vulnerable and dispensable. While the organization spent more time analyzing the problem than solving it, it advocated for the improvement of children's health insurance, decent child care, and affordable housing to supplement low wages.

At the same time, the VOP called for a state-level earned income tax credit. It was not content simply to criticize the failure of welfare reform. Instead of subsidizing dependency, it argued that the state should subsidize low-wage employment. "A state [earned income tax credit] is an important part of welfare reform efforts, since it boosts the income of workers who move from welfare to entry-level, low-wage jobs." The VOP also championed the federal EITC program, which promised as much as $3,756 for families earning less than $30,095 in 1998. While market analysts championed 401Ks and mutual funds, the VOP alerted readers to the benefits of an EITC. The program was particularly valuable for those in need of food stamps, federal housing assistance, and other forms of social support, since the EITC was not considered income when determining eligibility for those programs.[46]

The VOP and its allies, such as the Virginia Coalition for the Homeless, sought concrete solutions to the problem of poverty. Recognizing the core virtue of the conservative argument—that work was better than dependency—it challenged the conclusions that conservatives made about those on welfare. Virginia's poor did not prefer indolence to work, but they did want decent-paying jobs that offered real hope for independence. VOP activists were pragmatic idealists, searching among the few political options available to the disadvantaged in the New Economy era. Its endorsement of the EITC, however, reflected the ambiguous, sometimes contradictory character of its agenda. While the organization championed an increase in the minimum wage and labor activism, it failed to see that the EITC functioned as an alternative to an increase in the minimum wage. Historian Michael Lind points out that the value of the minimum wage declined by 31 percent between 1978 and 1989. This erosion accounted for most of the growing income disparities of the Reagan years. Despite four increases to the minimum wage, which brought it up to $5.15 in 1997, it fell far behind the levels established in the 1960s. Congress also defeated an effort to raise the minimum wage to $6.15 in 2000. In order to lift workers out of the poverty zone, it would have had to establish a minimum wage of $8.00 an hour.[47]

Conservative southern Democrats championed the EITC as a subsidy for business in the region. Senator Russell Long of Louisiana initiated the legislation in 1975, and Texas Democrat Lloyd Bentsen later endorsed it as Clinton's secretary of the treasury. In the absence of organized labor, Democrats were compelled to assist low-wage workers without jeopardizing southern businesses that depended on cheap labor. Lind suggests that the EITC functioned like an "interregional corporate welfare program," subsidizing businesses in a region that paid the lowest benefits, the lowest wages, and maintained the lowest levels of unionization in the country. Since the South accrued a disproportionate share of EITC revenues, it meant that taxpayers in other areas of the country supported the southern low-wage business strategy. While the EITC certainly benefited impoverished workers, it did so without challenging the privileged position of business.[48] It also distracted from the minimum-wage question and failed to promote a national standard that would reduce the destructive impact of the corporate incentives game. In promoting the EITC, the Virginia Organizing Project grasped for lifelines to assist struggling low-wage workers. Yet it reflected both the influence of the market-oriented model in the 1990s and the ambiguities in southern progressive circles.

If the VOP struggled to establish a coherent reform agenda, it convincingly demonstrated that the dominance of business priorities in American life was at the center of working-class insecurity. Tax breaks reflected the assumption that "what is good for the corporations will also be good for the communities in which they are located." State and local governments made risky investments in a well-intentioned, desperate effort to generate jobs. Here, *Virginia.Organizing* linked the defining experience of the early 1990s to the growing sense that the business-first agenda was flawed. The corporate beneficiaries of some of the largest payouts were often the same companies that had been "downsizing like mad for the last 10 years, cutting jobs, factories, and businesses in an effort to become more streamlined and efficient." Virginia's participants in the incentives game were only beginning to realize that companies that received generous giveaways were "also perfectly willing to shut that factory down and move it somewhere with cheaper labor, lower operating costs or higher tax breaks." This was a lesson in the dynamics of global capitalism that rarely appeared in mainstream newspapers. It was certainly absent from the literature produced by the secretary of Virginia's Department of Economic Development.[49]

The editors identified some of Virginia's major beneficiaries of the corporate giveaway program. Volvo-GM had moved out of Ohio and into Pulaski County to take advantage of "lower-paid workers and millions of dollars in economic incentives." Virginia Power, benefiting from deregulation, would be able to write off losses from archaic power plants and pass them on to consumers. Motorola was the most glaring example of development policy gone awry. The state would provide $12 million a year for five years, but the county of Goochland had already spent $60 million to pay for water and sewage upgrades while the state had financed a massive road improvement project to benefit the company.[50]

The VOP's most compelling insight, though, came from its discussion of the illusions of economic development policy. Instead of simply criticizing promiscuous spending on corporate clients, it moved toward a broader commentary on the New Economy. What was galling about the huge payouts to Motorola was that they would be in exchange for factory jobs "paying $9–10 an hour—not exactly high paying, high-tech positions." According to *Virginia.Organizing*, the state and county would pay the company $145 million in incentives to create 2,500 jobs paying an average of $10 an hour. In their estimation, Virginia's taxpayers would absorb $58,000 for each job that Motorola created. Like other high-tech companies, Motorola played on the allure of landing a cutting-edge company delivering futuristic jobs for a post-industrial region. What it provided, though, was a lesson in southern continuity. Low-wage jobs offering little promise of security would be traded for massive state investments.[51]

Against the media current, VOP editors alerted readers to the tenuous character of the high-tech sector. "Considering how computer industry plants all over the country have cut back due to the Asian financial crisis, there is no guarantee that the plant will get built or that the jobs it creates will be permanent." In January of 1999, well over a year before the collapse of the stock market, the VOP was highlighting the dangers of overcapacity and wanton financial speculation. Responding to slackening demand, Motorola was restructuring its business. The consumer chip unit would fold while the semiconductor sector would shed 25 to 30 percent of its workforce. The promise of economic regeneration through corporate incentives was built on sand. The trauma of downsizing that inaugurated the 1990s had not disappeared. It continued throughout the decade, reemerging stunningly at its end to puncture the dreams that had made Motorola the shining hope for Richmond.[52]

Incentives reflected political influence, not sound economic thinking. VOP editors noted that "even . . . conservative economists" objected when huge giveaways privileged larger businesses over small and medium-sized interests. Quoting Randolph Holhut's *The Real Welfare Cheats: Corporate America*, the VOP editors clarified the political implications of the incentive frenzy. Corporate recipients of state and local handouts had "benefited from policies that have eliminated millions of American jobs; who have put the pursuit of ever-higher profits ahead of the public interest." In this seemingly simple formulation, the VOP illuminated the key questions at stake in the 1990s. Did corporate giveaways, trade agreements, regressive taxation, anti-unionism, the dismantling of the social security state, an unregulated economy, and a hype-induced stock market run really serve the public interest?

The larger significance of the VOP's discussion lay in its willingness to posit the existence of a "public interest" against private calculations. The VOP was not calling for a planned economy or reckless social spending. What it did do, however, was identify the core weaknesses of the New Economy. For southerners, this was an economy that flourished on the promise of innovative change but operated on regional traditions of labor suppression, low taxes, and minimal social investment.

The VOP's coverage grew in depth but, fortunately, not stridency as the economy hit turbulence. Through the column "Understanding the Economy," the editors moved toward a comprehensive consideration of the impact of the New Economy on Virginia. With a homespun anecdote about a law school graduate who takes a detour into a technology start-up company, only to land in the stratosphere of material success, *Virginia.Organizing* began an ambitious discussion of the New Economy. The people of Martinsville, who had endured the worst of the collapse of the textile sector, understood what was "new" about the economy. The shift from manufacturing to services, accompanied by the relocation of industrial labor abroad, defined the new order. Technological and communications developments propelled the changes, fostering productivity but also "ruthless competition." Technological advancement meant access to new markets but also tremendous risk, since businesses came head-to-head in marketplaces that often lacked tariff, trade, labor, and environmental regulations. "They move factories, downsize their staff, and rapidly shift their business strategies according to changing markets. They have to, or they won't survive." Capitalism might be predatory and destructive, but it could not be reduced to the machinations of a few ruthless and acquisitive insiders. Southern economic losses in the 1990s were no more the result of greedy New York bankers than they had been in the era of the Populists. Examining the logic of capitalist internationalization, the VOP avoided simplistic moralizing about economic misfortune. It set it sights on understanding what Karl Polanyi had previously discovered: the social costs of market dominance. Like Polanyi, the VOP envisioned a market economy restricted by social institutions and practices that protected human dignity.[53]

In fact, the VOP reported that certain areas of Virginia were faring "relatively well" in the New Economy. Ranking twelfth out of the fifty states in the New Economy Index and high in "so-called Knowledge Jobs," the state looked appealing to high-tech companies. *Virginia.Organizing* may have lost sight of the role of incentives and political culture in drawing investment to the state. Even so, it realized that the New Economy was not simply smoke and mirrors. Investments in telecommunications and computer technology had rewarded some areas of the state quite handsomely.[54]

The blessings were distributed unequally, however. High-tech jobs were clustered in the area from Charlottesville to Hampton Roads and from Richmond to northern Virginia. While Nextel announced a new location in Hampton (establishing a call center offering low-paying jobs facilitated once again by lavish government incentives) and software companies planned for growth in Fairfax, peripheral Virginia languished. "In contrast, Super Sack Bag will be expanding its plant making bulk containers in far southwest Lee County and Martinsville on the Southside will be getting a customer service call center." It was a "poor replacement for Tultex," the editors noted. New prisons in southwest and Southside Virginia added to the insult; the New Economy was leaving vast swaths of Virginia behind.[55]

High-tech investment had not altered the traditional areas of power and poverty in the state. Northern Virginia continued to benefit the most, a point which the VOP might have underscored by noting its proximity to Washington. The irony is that the state which harbored the former capital of the Confederacy and which cherished its southern independence grew wealthy on contracts from the center of national power.

Even here, though, poverty existed amid plenty. The "core city poverty" of Norfolk, Portsmouth, Hampton, and Newport News stood in stark contrast to the dazzling high-tech wealth in Hampton Roads. In Richmond and Petersburg, for example, inner-city poverty had reached an astounding 21.10 percent by 2000. In metropolitan Richmond and Petersburg, median incomes stood at $46,800, while inner-city Richmond and Petersburg reported median incomes of no more than $30,667. In Charlottesville, where VOP activists supported living-wage campaigns at the Marriott Hotel and the University of Virginia, a dual economy flourished, one in which "those on the bottom make minimum wage cleaning the buildings where the New Economy thrives." Northern Virginia was no exception. There, the median household income was $70,000 a year, but over a million families endured the high rents while earning $30,000 a year or less.[56]

As early as 1992, the *Richmond Times-Dispatch* had run an article identifying the high levels of poverty in affluent northern Virginia. That year, reported a lieutenant governor's commission, 62,000 people in the region lived below the poverty line. Almost 25,000 of those people were between the ages of eighteen and thirty-five.[57] Perhaps most importantly, wages in the state had increased only in the last two years of the decade, defying claims about the prosperity of the Roaring '90s. Jim Hite, staff director of the Rural Virginia Prosperity Commission, corroborated the VOP's claims. Hite's research confirmed that the high-tech phenomenon had radically altered northern Virginia. By contrast, Appalachian Virginia had witnessed the implosion of coal mining, the destruction of textiles from international competition, and the continuing decline of the family farm.[58]

Assessing the impact of the New Economy on Virginia in early 2000, the VOP concluded that the real gains had been made in the technology sector, not the service sector, where the majority of the VOP's target audience toiled. An explosive New Economy had led the Federal Reserve Bank to increase interest rates to ward off inflation. Popular among investors, the incremental interest-rate hikes suppressed wages and prices. VOP members discovered that financial policy was not value-neutral. "Whenever economic indicators showed that wages were beginning to rise, the Fed increased rates in order to slow down the economy," in the process punishing "working class" Virginians. It did not simply record the inflexible and inevitable judgments of economic laws; moderate inflation was not the worst enemy of the working class. Globalization was not a strictly benign process, but the source of "competitive pressures" that had left "cities and communities with empty mills and long lines at the Virginia Employment Commission." While the unrestricted pursuit of investment despoiled the environment, it also intensified the campaign for corporate welfare. "States and cities gush tax breaks in order to keep that last textile mill or auto factory in town. The Virginia Economic Development Partnership passes out subsidies like crackers to any high-tech business that looks their way." Taxpayers eventually absorbed the cost.[59]

Virginia Organizing Project activists did more than rail against corporate greed. They explored and critiqued the machinery of the New Economy, unveiling the ideological lubricants that kept its gears moving. The VOP never really did formulate a consistent strategy for managing global integration, but who did? The organization eschewed simpleminded anti-corporatism. However successful the anti-WTO rallies may have been, it did not consider street resistance an effective strategy against the multiple prongs of economic globalization. What it did suggest was that global integration was here to stay. The communications revolution was not an unmitigated disaster. The industrial age, the editors realized, had irrevocably given way to the information economy.

Yet if change was inevitable, and in some cases beneficial, unthinking compliance was not. The global flow of information and capital did not justify dehumanization, economic insecurity, and business control of American social policy. "We have to understand the impact of this new wave on our people," VOP secretary Denise Smith wrote, "its shape, its height, its underlying force, when it will break or whether there are rocks below, who will ride it to shore and who will drown." At the helm of an organization committed to social democratic reform, Smith was interested in how working-class Virginians might achieve a modicum of control over this new reality. "It is not beyond our reach to understand what this means in our lives, nor is it beyond our reach to control it. This economy can control us, or we can organize to control it. The power is in our hands." Southerners did not have to be victims of colonial exploitation or docile recipients of corporate largesse. They could organize, much as they had tried to do during Operation Dixie and successfully did in the civil rights movement, to shape their own destiny.[60]

This message radiated beyond the pages of *Virginia.Organizing* through "Understanding the Economy" workshops in communities such as Cape Charles on the Eastern Shore. With fifteen participants, the VOP and staff from an area housing reform group examined the economic power brokers in the area and the sources of economic influence in their lives. The group discovered that Richmond and Charlottesville had done quite well in the New Economy. By contrast, southwest Virginia, the Southside, the Northern Neck, and the Eastern Shore endured "near double-digit unemployment." (In fact, as *Virginia.Organizing* would later report, the southwest endured the worst. At a time when the state unemployment rate was 2.9 percent, Buchanan County unemployment ran at 14.1 percent and Dickenson County at 15.7 percent. In the Eastern Shore county of Northumberland, 8.7 percent were unemployed, while in Danville, 6.1 percent of the workforce was idle in 1998.)[61] While the VOP overlooked the persistent poverty and joblessness in Richmond's inner-city core, it made an important point. The booming economy had in fact lifted a few boats while leaving many other areas utterly shipwrecked.

Rather than reinforcing the platitudes of entrepreneurial individualism or cultural difference, the group discussed the impact of discriminatory bank lending, housing policies, seasonal unemployment, low wages, and a "local power structure that excludes low-income people and people of color." Organizers also introduced participants to the idea of a living wage, a cause which the VOP vigorously championed in Gilded Age Virginia. Group members agreed that wages would have to reach at least $7.50 an hour before workers could escape poverty.[62]

Instead of a monologue, organizers discussed the economic realities affecting people on the Eastern Shore. They instructed but also learned from the participants. They learned, for example, that food stamps, subsidized housing, and Medicaid were standard fare for those whose wages fell below the living wage. Workshop leaders instructed participants in the history of the Federal Reserve Board and provided an economic analysis that challenged the orthodoxies of the *Richmond Times-Dispatch*. Interest-rate decisions made in Washington directly influenced unemployment, wages, the country's debt, and inflation. Interest rates, they learned, were raised to limit inflation and ensure high returns on stock portfolios. The same decisions, however, translated into unemployment, lower wages, and economic contraction. For Marie Owens, the workshop gave her the questions she needed to ask about the economy. For Denise Worthan, it provided "a lot of insight. I learned things which I didn't know before which I can take back to my community." More than any of the free-market pontificating that appeared in the pages of *The Economist* or on the teleprompters of the evening news, the VOP educated average Virginians in the intersection of politics and economics. They encouraged workshop participants to understand that choices had been made at the highest levels of economic power that affected them directly. They began to grasp that many of those decisions operated in diametrical opposition to their needs.

Those interests privileged investors and business profits over workers. The Federal Reserve Board, economist Ellen Frank points out, operated on the assumption that a 6 percent national unemployment rate was acceptable. According to the theory which Fed chair Alan Greenspan espoused, those 6 percent represented a "natural" unemployment rate, those people who claimed to be looking for work but simply would not accept jobs paying the market price. When the unemployment rate fell below the arbitrarily set 6 percent, the Fed raised interest rates in order to "cool off" the economy.[63] Yet that 6 percent, Frank notes, represented some 9 million jobless Americans. It also included an additional 4 to 7 million more who had abandoned the job search or had taken part-time employment because they could not find full-time work. When wages for the lowest 20 percent of the workforce finally did increase by 2 percent a year in the late 1990s, reducing the poverty level to the post-1945 low of 11 percent, the Fed reacted quickly. Even though inflation remained low at 2.7 percent, the Fed was determined to reduce job and wage growth by raising interest rates six times in the following year. The issue, Frank notes, was not simply the wisdom of Greenspan's monetary policy in a buoyant economy. The issue was that the "Fed chair had taken upon himself responsibility for deciding the proper distribution of income between capital and labor."[64]

This was precisely the point which *Virginia.Organizing*'s editors made in October 2000 when they closely examined wages for Virginians in the New Economy. The economy was strong, as everyone knew. Why, then, had the Federal Reserve Board raised interest rates several times? The Fed feared that "people's wages are going up too fast, and that prices will soon follow. Their priority is to prevent inflation, and working people's paychecks take the back seat." Again, the VOP acknowledged that economic growth had helped to reduce poverty for low-skilled workers, at least those who could work full time, all year long. That excluded single mothers with insufficient child care. It also excluded those who could not afford to move from low-wage to high-wage areas, or those who had to take time off of work to care for sick children or elderly parents. Rosy predictions of growth also failed to account for the increase in the poverty rate in Virginia. Despite the fact that it still fell below national levels, it had increased from 10.0 percent in 1994 to 11.3 percent in 1998. Economic growth certainly helped low-skilled and highly skilled workers, but the decisions of "market-oriented" economists often counteracted these benefits. Eliminating government regulation of business and failing to increase the minimum wage, argued VOP editors, would mean that low-skilled workers would continue to suffer despite economic expansion. Once again, the VOP endorsed an improved EITC and the elimination of discrimination in employment and training. It also waited for the next recession.[65]

The Virginia Organizing Project distinguished itself from the cultural politics that flourished in leftist academic circles by linking economic reform to the improvement of working peoples' lives. From its inception, the VOP spoke to a multiracial constituency. African Americans, Hispanics, Asians, middle-class white liberals, and white working-class Virginians belonged to the group and framed its racial perspective. Its support for a sometimes dizzying array of issues diluted the organization's impact. Nonetheless, the VOP addressed the economic inequalities that afflicted a broad spectrum of working Virginians. It did so without embracing white populism or submerging the reality of racial inequality in the color-blind rhetoric of the 1990s.

The VOP fostered the regeneration of a social democratic movement, the kind that had flourished briefly in the 1930s. This movement returned in the 1960s, as the UAW collaborated with leading civil rights organizations and the federal government to promote an agenda of economic and racial justice. That agenda produced not only the Civil Rights Act of 1964 but also much of the momentum for the Great Society. Broken apart by the Vietnam War, the fragmentation of the civil rights movement, a New Left which attacked the corporate liberalism of establishment elites, the drift of the white working class into conservative ranks, and the devastating violence of 1968, the social democratic impulse of the New Deal era faltered.[66]

The South had not seen a progressive social movement since the black freedom struggle, but the efforts of the Virginia Organizing Project and its allies suggested that its vision of economic democracy and racial justice had returned. In the VOP, African Americans and Hispanics played an active role. Black, white, and Hispanic women were leaders in the organization, serving as coordinators of Dismantling Racism workshops and as director of the organization itself. In the pages of *Virginia.Organizing* and through its multiple grassroots initiatives, the VOP raised the issues of racial inequality which conservatives and neoliberals had desperately tried to ignore.

This fusion of racial egalitarianism and working-class politics was powerfully evident in the VOP's commitment to Virginia's Hispanic immigrants. Drawn by the expansion of low-wage jobs in the New Economy South and pushed by the devastating impact of NAFTA on several sectors of the Mexican economy, Latino workers flooded into the region. In Virginia, the Hispanic population increased 105 percent between 1990 and 2000, from 160,228 to 329,540.[67] Latinos filtered into traditional and developing low-wage manufacturing sectors such as poultry processing, agriculture, and the service industry, gravitating to regions of economic expansion in the South. In Virginia, low-wage service work created a magnet for Hispanic immigration in Fairfax County and Arlington. By 2000, Hispanics made up almost 10 percent of this northern Virginia New Economy nirvana.[68] Contrary to the image of Hispanic workers taking over an agricultural sector abandoned by both working-class blacks and whites, the majority congregated in the urban South. Filling service positions in restaurants, hotels, hospitals, and office buildings, they worked without the benefit of union protection, decent wages, or long-term job security.

Despite the myth of Hispanic workers as contemporary Horatio Algers far too grateful for the opportunity to work in America to challenge the status quo, they did not silently consent to exploitation. In Los Angeles and New York, they organized in the needle trades and joined the Janitors for Justice movement. In Virginia, they supported the Tenants' and Workers' Support Committee (Comité de Apoyo de Inquilinos y Trabajadores). Emerging in Alexandria in 1988 in response to the threat of eviction, African American and Salvadoran residents of Arlandria-Chirilagua established the foundation of a larger democratic campaign. A pocket of low-income people of color in affluent Alexandria, the Arlandria-Chirilagua neighborhood offered a bleak illustration of the limits of the New Economy. With 10,000 residents, 60 percent of whom were Latino and 30 percent black, all of whom were low-wage earners, the Arlandria-Chirilagua district contradicted the glossy images of high-tech northern Virginia. Threatened in the mid-1980s by evictions from developers interested in transforming their neighborhood into upscale condominiums, the immigrant tenants fought back. They adopted a community-based form of direct action modeled on their experiences in El Salvador. By 1996, approximately three hundred families from this low-wage community established an affordable housing cooperative that thwarted the efforts of developers to evict them.[69]

The TWSC then launched a campaign to organize two thousand poorly paid hotel workers in Alexandria and to promote a neighborhood planning project. Affiliating with the Virginia Organizing Project, it became part of a growing reform coalition that synthesized the issues of race and class. The VOP lent its resources and the pages of *Virginia.Organizing* to support the TWSC. By printing almost half of each edition of *Virginia.Organizing* in Spanish and by incorporating Hispanics into the fabric of the organization, the VOP advanced the larger cause of economic justice and cultural acceptance for Hispanic workers.

The TWSC project was a remarkable example of African American and Latino working-class cooperation. Both groups suffered from low-wage work, inadequate and expensive housing, racial or ethnic discrimination. Both understood that race and labor exploitation had a long history in the South. Certainly both grasped the disparity between the rhetoric of a Sunbelt, Silicon, New Economy Virginia and the economic hardship that afflicted them. Instead of exalting the promises of free market individualism, the group endorsed "collective ownership and control of community resources." Through "community education," "self-help initiatives," and the development of their own leaders, the multiracial alliance forged an instrument of democratic action at the grassroots level.

While the Democratic Party endorsed the ethic of competitive globalization, Hispanic workers affected by market liberalization adopted cooperation and collective action. They did so even while mainline unions ignored Hispanic workers or treated them as secondary to the interests of workers in the manufacturing sector. In contrast to a labor movement marred by a history of racial divisions, the TWSC forged a coalition predicated on racial equality and economic democracy. It was a movement that consciously privileged the leadership of women by recognizing such simple but critical issues as child care for female organizers. Through small-group meetings scheduled to accommodate women who worked as housekeepers in area hotels and through designated internships, the TWSC deliberately cultivated women organizers. In the process, it generated grassroots leadership. It also solidified the idea that working-class action required democratic organization. At a time when white and black office workers were expected to relinquish race and gender considerations to a forgotten era of social causes, the middle-class leaders of the VOP confronted them directly. Whether or not the TWSC had the united power to extract a collective bargaining agreement remained to be seen. What was clear was that in the interstices of the New Economy—amid the shimmering office towers and beneath the stainless steel surfaces of American corporate life—black and Latino workers took action.[70]

That action was on display most dramatically in the living-wage movement that broke out across the United States in the 1990s. Beginning with the successful campaign for a living wage in Baltimore in 1994, the movement to require private businesses receiving public funds to pay their workers a decent wage took off. By 2001, as many as sixty-four living-wage campaigns were under way across the country. For most activists, the objective was to extract a wage that would lift a family of four above the poverty line, which would mean at least $8.50 an hour. For companies that failed to provide any health benefits, living-wage proponents demanded $10 an hour.[71] In Virginia, the campaign focused in Charlottesville, both at the University of Virginia and the Courtyard by Marriott Hotel in town.

The most significant, however, took place in northern Virginia, where the TWSC launched a living-wage rally on Labor Day in 1998. By 1997, the living-wage initiative had become the group's central focus. More than an isolated self-help initiative, the TWSC had launched a campaign that united organized labor, community organizations, local residents, and churches. The TWSC had become the linchpin in a broad-based coalition for economic justice. In 1998, the TWSC and several other groups took to the streets in a protest against exploitive wages. Carrying signs reading "Salario Justo Ahora," hundreds of Hispanic workers disrupted the tranquility of corporate Alexandria in a show of strength that exploded the image of the servile Latino immigrant. The Iron Workers Local 5 as well as the Communications Workers 2222, Grace Episcopal Church, the Beverly Hills United Church, and the Virginia Organizing Project joined the TWSC in challenging the consensus that demanded worker flexibility in return for economic insecurity. While Hispanic workers dominated the movement, white liberal Virginians had joined as mediators and organizers. The living-wage campaign galvanized the social democratic energies of the Virginia Organizing Project and expanded the movement beyond workshops and training sessions. Organized labor and organized religion both joined the movement, demonstrating not only the potential to restore the connection between racial equality and economic democracy but social justice and faith.

Christianity did not take an exclusively conservative posture in the 1990s. Despite the rise of militant Christian evangelicalism, which emphasized individual moral purity and personal salvation, a Social Gospel tradition continued, at least in the mainstream churches. Tangible, immediate movements for social reform awakened the moral energies of liberal Christian Reverend Roberto Morales, who proclaimed that "All workers deserve a living wage—enough to put food on the table, a roof over their heads, and to raise a family in dignity." Much as they had in Latin American base communities and through the gospel of liberation theology, local churches aligned themselves with the material needs of their immigrant communities, reminding Christians of a savior who cared about the poor.[72]

The living-wage campaign cut through the New Economy rhetoric and demonstrated the human costs of the northern Virginia miracle. It closed the circuit between low-wage labor, high-tech growth, and public expenditures on capital investment. A Northern Virginia Living Wage Campaign activist clarified the disparity between the South's version of the New Economy ideology and the realities of wage work in modern America:

> Even though our economy is supposed to be doing better than ever, too many workers are working longer hours, running between part-

> time jobs and still struggling to stay afloat. Their employers are paying poverty wages. . . . A cruel irony is that many of these companies are benefiting from our tax dollars: our cities, counties, and states dole out lucrative service contracts, industrial revenue bonds, tax breaks, and other forms of public subsidies.[73]

Living-wage advocates were struggling to recast the "geography" of an increasingly globalized capitalism according to a vision of economic democracy influenced by local interests.[74] Those interests reflected the ethnic traditions that were reshaping the cultural landscape of Virginia. They expressed the religious convictions of working-class Hispanics and progressive white southerners committed to the values of social Christianity. At the same time, they captured the discontent of people who believed that local policymakers had abdicated their responsibility to average workers while enriching the corporations responsible for their predicament. The momentum continued with an interfaith rally on December 10, Human Rights Day, as well a march to city hall on Martin Luther King Day. Using the ideological sanction of ecumenical religion and the symbolism of American protest, the movement achieved strength and credibility. Establishing the common ground of economic justice and self-interest, the participants built a grassroots movement that far outpaced the organizing efforts of mainstream unions.[75]

The streets throbbed with protest the following Labor Day, as Hispanic workers and their allies continued the fight for a living wage. That year the support of the movement from the religious swelled to twenty-five churches. Unionists, poorly paid service workers, and liberal Christians formed delegations and descended on the offices of Arlington's city councilors. They dispatched more than six hundred postcards signed by low-income residents in a door-to-door campaign. They sent living-wage petitions that carried thousands of signatures and phoned the councilors en masse, sometimes directly from the shop floor. Again, unions and community groups joined a campaign that had continued throughout the year through lobbying and legislative pressure.[76] Movements for social reform had few victories to count in the 1990s, but this was one of them. On June 18, 2000, the city council voted 6–0 in favor of a living wage that paid workers $10 an hour.

The connection to organized labor was critical and symbiotic. The TWSC linked arms with the Teamsters who were organizing cleaning workers. They joined forces with the Iron Workers who were struggling against non-unionized construction workers and showed support for airline attendants on strike. Gyula Nagy, coordinator of the living-wage campaign, explained that relations of mutuality were essential. Sharing resources and expertise, building common membership lists, and fostering a united communications front was critical for their success: "Our coalition-building committee met face-to-face with leaders of targeted groups. We pushed leaders to contribute: money, mobilizing members, printing flyers, or (for unions) lending us activists on lost-time pay. We visited leaders monthly, developing relationships, always asking what solidarity they needed from us."[77] When living-wage opponents submitted three bills to the legislature, the AFL-CIO strengthened the coalition by extending it throughout the state. Parking lot employees also testified that the new wage allowed them to quit second jobs and spend time with their families. Organized labor had responded to grassroots activism and offered it the institutional support it needed. Local activists reciprocated by advancing the cause of collective bargaining and supporting a multiplicity of union campaigns. More than this, the TWSC and the Northern Virginia Living Wage Campaign sustained the movement by developing a detailed membership list, establishing communications and research committees, and adopting an ethic of principled commitment.

The market-oriented ideology dominated Virginia and the South in the 1990s, but it did not go unchallenged. If anything, the forces of trade liberalization fostered a response from workers who were able to utilize ethnic traditions of community cohesion, religious commitment, and collective action. They rejected the traditional markers of southern heritage and fostered an alliance with white working-class southerners on the grounds of economic decency. This alliance also included white middle-class liberals and Christian progressives. Their support reflected the moral power of Christian social teachings, the unifying possibilities of economic democracy in the South, and the persistence of a progressive strain in the region. It seemed that the South might evolve into a culturally pluralistic, socially egalitarian region after all. Despite the pervasive insecurity, it seemed like northern Virginia might become a place where economic modernization did not repeat the traditional patterns of southern oppression. *Virginia. Organizing,* which had consistently supported the living-wage movement, captured the sense of hopefulness in a photo on its front page. It featured the El Pulgarcito Salvadoran Dance Troupe whirling in colorful costumes for the crowds attending the Arlandria-Chirilagua Festival. The Tenants' and Workers' Support Committee sponsored the festival, an event which took place on September 9, 2001.

CHAPTER 9

Only Yesterday

Hope and Disillusionment at the End of a Century

The Salvadoran festival signaled a growing sense of working-class confidence. So too did the Richmond youths who joined some 50,000 Americans to protest the World Trade Organization in Seattle two years earlier. Both expressed the advent of alternative visions of Virginia's future. Dreams of Silicon prosperity dominated the state's public life in the 1990s, but they failed to answer nagging questions about the economic hardship that so many Virginians faced. The rhetoric of growth through competitiveness and survival through retraining did not alleviate the sinking feeling of insecurity that gripped so many.

The activism of Hispanic workers and young, anti-globalization Richmonders expressed both discontent and hope. They captured the flourishing of dissent in a period of political conformity. Neither could build a coherent political program that might challenge the market-oriented consensus in Richmond and Washington. Nor could they withstand the dramatic shift in national priorities that followed the tragedy of September 11, 2001. Yet dreams of Silicon liberation faded not because of the trauma of terrorist attacks or the jingoistic patriotism that defined American political culture in the years that followed. They dissolved because the market itself had failed to live up to the claims of its most enthusiastic champions. The stock market hysteria provided the most compelling evidence of the declining fortunes of working Americans. Economist Doug Henwood comments that "The scores of millions of Americans who cheered as the Dow and the NASDAQ made their vertical ascent were really cheering a celebration of their own stagnant incomes and economic insecurity. It was a wonderful confidence trick, and a lot of people still haven't figured it out."[1] The declining stock market and the corporate scandals of the 1990s confirmed what the textile workers of Martinsville already knew: the new economic dispensation brought more despair than deliverance.

The street protests in Seattle seemed astonishingly incongruous for the

1990s. Commentators noted the contrast between black-hooded anarchists and the retail incarnations of New Economy success. Of course, Seattle was also home to Bill Gates, the symbol of New Economy ingenuity and bravado. The disjuncture was not in the fact that protestors had landed in the city of West Coast high-tech cool, but that protestors had shown up at all. In a decade defined by its exaltation of free market individualism, Americans were shocked at the public, disruptive display of discontent.

They should not have been. Organized labor had been regaining strength since John Sweeney became president of the AFL-CIO in 1995. The federation had set out to rejuvenate organizing and repudiate concessionary bargaining. The renewed energy was evident in the successful Teamsters' strike at UPS in 1997, which played out as dramatically in Virginia as it had throughout the rest of the country. Strikes against Verizon Communications in Virginia offered telling evidence of renewed labor militancy. A resurgent labor movement had also started to build alliances with environmental activists, living-wage advocates, community action groups, and anti-globalization groups, many of which benefited from youth support. Policymakers and trade authorities had devoted increasing attention to the "social clause" since the divisive debates over NAFTA. At negotiations for the General Agreement on Tariffs and Trade, in the cloistered circles of the World Bank, and in the unlikely setting of Organisation for Economic Co-operation and Development (OECD) meetings, the impact of international trade agreements on labor standards became a recurring, troubling question.[2]

In the 1990s, then, some southerners were organizing against unrestricted global capitalism. They rejected the claim that an unfettered marketplace distributed equal benefits to all. The evidence of this challenge to business unilateralism was already present in northern Virginia, in the TWSC's campaign for a living wage. While the objective was limited, the motivating conviction was that the market should not uniformly determine wages and working conditions. In that conviction, and in the coalition that Hispanic workers forged, the TWSC anticipated the united front that coalesced in Seattle.

The intricacies of the WTO debate are of less concern here than the fact that Virginians and southerners joined the protests. Precisely how many is uncertain; most Virginians hailed from Richmond, most were white, and almost all were under thirty. Labor unionists from across the South also joined in the protests. Altogether, the actions against the WTO and in 2000 against the IMF illustrated the persistence of democratic sensibilities in an era of market triumphalism. Southerners did not dominate the movement, but their participation suggested the limits of Sunbelt South mythology.

The street protests found their antecedent not in the civil rights movement or the New Left of the 1960s, but in the Populist Movement of the 1890s. Biracial, animated by the sense that industrial consolidation had undermined democratic opportunity for the producing classes, the Populists disrupted the Lost Cause consensus of the New South. Writing shortly after the Seattle protest, historian Michael Kazin drew the connection between the Populists and the WTO protestors. In the 1990s "prosperity convinced many Americans that the free market lifts all boats. But wage inequalities have grown starker too, and to many, the promises of globalization have seemed ephemeral." The amplification of class disparities in a time of boundary-less freedom raised fundamental questions about the new order. "The protests in Seattle should remind us that big business retains its power to enrage as well as to enrich. The brave new marketplace—as represented by the WTO—regards labor rights and environmental protection as 'externalities,' potential impediments to the free flow of goods, bytes and profits." While Kazin felt obligated to pay homage to the benefits of corporate-led globalization, he highlighted the obstacles that confronted this neopopulist movement. Trade unionists and environmentalists did not always agree on how to confront corporate capitalism. Protestors also failed to appreciate the importance of political elites in determining the WTO agenda.[3]

More than this, the protestors fixated on genetically modified foods, the fate of sea turtles, and the preservation of forests in Washington tended to distract attention from the key question of how global market integration affected American citizens. Instead of uniting those issues under an umbrella of social democracy, protestors and organizers allowed a cacophony of competing groups to claim space, time, and energy, ultimately generating more heat than light on global economic integration. At the same time, protestors were at odds over trade policies. Were tariffs necessary to protect American jobs or an obstacle in the way of Third World development through export? Should foreign countries protect against American steel and agricultural goods or reap the benefits of lower-priced products? Could environmental conservation be reconciled with the need for high-paying manufacturing jobs?

Not surprisingly, the *Richmond Times-Dispatch* dismissed the protestors as the "Luddite Veto," mindless opponents of progress and prosperity. According to the editors, the anti-globalization protestors championed "autocratic government decrees" against free trade and capitalism.[4] The *Times-*

Dispatch failed to acknowledge the glaring contradictions inherent in its argument. If market integration represented freedom, then why did international business require the WTO at all? Why the need for an unelected, undemocratic organization to enforce trade agreements that compromised the national sovereignty of more than one country? The "regulatory state" that the paper condemned was fully manifest in the WTO and the IMF. If "free trade and capitalism" were what "happen[ed] when you leave people alone," the divisive NAFTA debate and the subsequent efforts to enforce the Washington Consensus would never have been necessary.[5] In a glaring example of red-herring abuse, the editors linked the anti-globalization protestors to Friedrich Engels, who pointed out that industrial capitalism had fostered market integration. Quoting Engels, the paper suggested that the protestors believed that this development "ensured that whatever happens in [one country] will have repercussions in all other countries."[6] Oddly enough, the conservative *Times-Dispatch* had quoted one of the leading proponents of modern communism to explain a point which advocates of corporate globalization had been making all along: the economic actions of one country did indeed have repercussions elsewhere. The paper was not interested in countering Engels's argument. It was enough to discredit the protestors simply by pointing to the parallel between the critique of economic globalization and the famed author of the *Manifesto*.

The paper's coverage of the events in Seattle also demonstrated how the champions of marketplace dominance had captured the idiom of freedom. In the paper's estimation, the Seattle protestors opposed "economic freedom," the only force that could alleviate worldwide poverty.[7] The freedom which the *Times-Dispatch* championed, however, excluded the freedom to protect labor standards, to defend vulnerable domestic industries (as had the United States in the nineteenth century), or protect a fragile environment. It did not include the freedom of governments to repudiate onerous International Monetary Fund debts that made a mockery of economic development. It certainly did not include the freedom to establish trade unions or to question whether or not corporate freedom came at the expense of workers in America and abroad. For the mainstream media, freedom meant an unrestricted marketplace. Yet this vision had little in common with the nineteenth-century ideal of small producers competing in a robust, expansive market. It accepted corporate consolidation as the norm and imagined that lower prices were the only standard for measuring American well-being. Missing from this discussion was an appreciation for the work ethic that continued to define American life. Missing was any sense that a decent wage, a reliable income, and steady work meant more to Virginians than shopping at Wal-Mart.

Writing for *Virginia.Organizing*, Russell Mokhiber and Robert Weissman offered a decidedly different interpretation of the events in Seattle. For them, democracy "was in the streets of Seattle last week" as 40,000 protestors challenged the legitimacy of the WTO. For Mokhiber and Weissman, the 10,000 or so students and young people who engaged in direct action protests at the Seattle convention center were "extraordinarily well-organized and highly-disciplined."[8] Their discipline did not extend to the notorious Black Bloc, the hooded, pseudo-anarchists who believed that breaking windows in a Nike store equaled revolution. The hooliganism was limited to a disaffected minority, and the destruction of property was minimal. Even so, the student protestors failed to control the anarchist minority, and the conservative, mainstream media had a field day with that minority's wanton destruction of property. Images of angry young vandals destroying storefront windows eclipsed the image of courageous protestors challenging corporate power.

Moreover, the 10,000 or so protestors who disrupted the WTO meetings did not include organized labor. It was willing to march but unwilling to engage in sit-ins. The failure to attract African American and Hispanic youth to the movement, the amorphous character of the Seattle coalition ("Teamsters and Turtles, together at last"), and the random foolishness of the "anarkids" did not bode well for the anti-globalization struggle. While the protestors opposed corporate globalization, they did not construct a plausible alternative program. That may very well have evolved over the next few years, but few spoke about establishing a political agenda at the time. Beyond organized labor, few protestors made a connection between WTO-style globalization and the deterioration of the American working class. That political agenda would have to combine the immediate needs of American workers and the interests of developing nations. And that was a large part of the problem. The Seattle protestors had forged a "stunning coalition of teamsters, consumers, sea turtle protection activists, religious people, women's groups, environmentalists, students, and anti-corporate youth,"[9] but diversity could not substitute for clarity. What did they want to accomplish beyond disrupting the WTO? What ideological convictions did they hold in common? What specific program of reform did they advance? What principles would galvanize such a diverse coalition into action? That remained unclear beyond the events of Seattle, even as Richmond's veterans of the protest took on the IMF meetings in Washington and the Republican National Convention in 2000. Unlike the TWSC, the unwieldy Seattle protestors struggled to fashion a political platform that crossed the race and class divide. The effort to contest falling wages and outsourcing could not be easily reconciled to the interests of Asian farmers or African exporters.

The protests in Seattle were important not simply because young radicals of the Richmond Anti-Globalization Protest Network joined in. Protestors from Georgia joined Stuart Acuff, president of the Atlanta Central Labor Council, and converged on Seattle along with activists from North Carolina and other Dixie states. The significance of the Seattle protests, suggested Chris Kromm in the pages of *Southern Exposure*, was that the South had emerged as "the most 'globalized' region of the country today." Southerners—like those who joined the Virginia Organizing Project—were starting to question the wisdom of a "corporate-driven agenda" that damaged working families, the environment, and democracy itself.[10]

Kromm reminded readers that the South had been on the forefront of global economic integration since the "days of King Cotton's reign." It was only in the previous twenty years, however, that southern states had adopted a strategy to propel the South into the forefront of the global economic system. Through lucrative tax incentives and the intensification of the export trade, the South had won some benefits from market integration. Attracting more foreign investment than any other region, winning investment deals from Asian and German car manufacturers, and expanding southern exports, the former Confederacy had excelled in the globalization "game." The success, however, came at a cost, one which was born largely by working- and middle-class southerners. While governors went on high-intensity trade trips abroad to recruit "migrating multinationals to set up shop in their state," taxpayers absorbed the cost, measured not only by increasing property taxes but also by the failure to invest in schools and social infrastructure. Manufacturing interests did bring jobs, but they paid one-third of what workers would have made in their home countries, offered little to no security, and subscribed to a vicious form of anti-unionism. Virginians had been learning the same lesson as people throughout the region: "Globe-trotting corporations often have little loyalty to the region—and in many areas, they are heading out of the South just as fast as they are coming in." As Kromm noted, the Economic Policy Institute reported that the South had experienced more than a third of all American job losses resulting from NAFTA.[11]

The people of Martinsville, Chilhowie, and Dickenson County had learned this hard and painful lesson. The people of Richmond and Hampton also understood the capricious nature of global capitalism. Promises of jobs facilitated by huge state and municipal tax giveaways evaporated as the stock market declined. At the same time, companies felt the intensifying pressure of declining or nonexistent profitability, which the speculative hysteria of the 1990s had only masked. Plagued by overcapacity and slackening demand, they extricated themselves from places like southwest Virginia and Hampton Roads, seeking out lower operating costs and even more favorable business climates.

By 2000, that pattern of instability had merged with a general economic collapse that saw Virginia's technology sector plummet and business failures skyrocket. Job losses continued to accelerate in the areas most vulnerable to capital mobility. In Martinsville, the town that had suffered the devastating loss of Tultex in 2000, the economic disintegration continued. In 2002, VF Knitwear announced that it would dismiss 2,600 workers. Even *Virginia Business* had to admit the economic catastrophe that global trade and the recession had visited upon the manufacturing sector in Virginia. The recession of 2001 had crippled textiles, furniture, personal computers, semiconductors, chemical processing, auto parts, metals, telephones, and related electrical industries. Some Virginia manufacturers were facing job losses that matched the devastating recession of 1990/1991.[12]

The information technology companies that had been the shining hope for the Silicon Dominion were not profitable after all. Thirty of the leading, publicly traded companies had lost almost $5.8 billion in revenue in 2000. Companies like PSINet, Nextel Communications, and Telligent, stars in the firmament of the New Economy, plummeted in value, revealing precisely how illusory their profitability had always been. In April 2001, thirteen of the leading publicly traded high-tech companies in Virginia were trading at approximately a dollar a share. Financial misfortune forced layoffs of a magnitude that reminded Virginians of how little had really changed since 1991. Network Access Solutions laid off 145 people in September 2000 and shut down 400 network operation centers to manage costs. The most shocking of high-tech implosions occurred in the South, and Virginia was not immune. When the telecommunications giant WorldCom revealed that its earnings were but a house of cards, the company dismissed 6,000 workers, 400 of whom were in northern Virginia.[13]

Ironically, while the federal government became the nemesis of southern conservatives in the 1990s, it was the principal customer for high-tech business in Virginia. In many respects, it was the economic savior of the region during the recession. Federal contracts in the Washington area amounted to $70 billion in 1999, double the value of government deals in Silicon Valley. With President George Bush calling for a $2.6 billion injection into research and development, Virginia defense contractors stood to weather the storm. Like the recession of 1990/1991, the massive job losses provided the silver lining for business. Now, according to *Virginia Business*, the 25,000 "unfilled jobs" would have desperate applicants. The "costly perks and sign-up bonuses" would disappear while the limited opportunities would squash "job hopping," a phenomenon which an earlier generation would have described as occupational mobility. In other words, the brief period of rising wages and expanding opportunities for young, technologically skilled workers had come to an end. The Insecurity Economy had returned.[14]

In Martinsville, Lynchburg, and communities throughout Southside Virginia, workers were sliding inexorably into economic ruin. In Chilhowie and Martinsville, Virginians who had depended on textiles for decent-paying manufacturing jobs since the 1970s watched helplessly as Buster Brown, Spring Ford, American, Natalie Knitting Mills, and Tultex shut down.[15] In Smyth County alone, ten factories went out of business after 1988. Chilhowie alone lost five of these, which eliminated 1,430 jobs in a population of 1,827. In the Martinsville area, more than 9,000 textile jobs had evaporated between 1993 and 2000. A surging economy in northern Virginia had not translated into general prosperity for the Old Dominion[16]

The recession once again sharpened class lines in Virginia. It highlighted the conflict between an ideology which posited that globalization was a function of natural law and a critical perspective which identified the economic suffering it caused. Curiously enough, Hugh D. Keogh, the Virginia economic development official who had claimed in 1992 that the recession was a "helpful background" to corporate restructuring, returned to the pages of *Virginia Business* to justify the latest recession. Now the president of Virginia's Chamber of Commerce, Keogh smugly asserted that "the old line manufacturing industries have been deteriorating for many years. . . . they would diminish with or without NAFTA." Not all business leaders dismissed the misfortunes of hundreds as the inevitable churning of the business cycle. Some acknowledged the connection between international trade agreements and the massive job losses. Noel Chitwood, president of American of Martinsville, admitted that trade agreements had convinced his company to reduce its workforce in Chilhowie and import materials from China. "I'm forced to change the business model at American of Martinsville to include production from overseas. . . . Unfortunately the cost of that is eliminating jobs in the United States." Chitwood, however, was considerably less comfortable with that development: "Is it regrettable? Sure it is. *Do I understand the greater good? Not really*" (emphasis added).[17]

The question of the greater good or the common wealth of Virginia's citizens remained a remote abstraction in most economic development discussions. Virginia's policy elite were not indifferent to the social consequences of trade agreements and corporate relocations. Like their Washington counterparts, however, they filtered these massive economic dislocations through a framework of market primacy that afforded few alternatives. They privileged the supply side over the demand side, imagining that incentives for exciting high-tech ventures would invariably translate into jobs and prosperity. Like Keogh, they believed that restructuring was inevitable; those unfortunately displaced would retrain for high-paying positions in the service sector. They applauded job growth, regardless of its quality or endurance. Job creation in the information technology sector was morally equivalent to the hiring of new cashiers at a Wal-Mart in Colonial Heights. Political elites deposited these job gains in their political savings accounts. They assumed that what was good for Motorola or Gateway was good for the residents of Richmond and Hampton. Speaking for Chilhowie's despondent citizens, journalist Warren Vieth questioned the basic assumption underlying New Economy thinking in the South: "In Chilhowie, the greater good seems unfathomable. How can Americans be better off when so many people are losing their jobs? Where are the new U.S. jobs that global trade is supposed to create? The textbook answer is that layoffs are being offset by job growth in other parts of the economy, such as service industries. But few of those jobs are finding their way to Smyth County." In the long run, as John Maynard Keynes once suggested, we all die. Working-class Virginians were beginning to conclude that economic policies which failed to address immediate needs, reflect democratic principles, or advance some semblance of the common good, failed as well.

In the pages of a journal for which no claim about the wonders of the New Economy for Virginia had been too extravagant, economist Christine Chmura reported that appearances had been deceiving. Virginia's economy had grown moderately, not explosively, between 1991 and 2001. "Despite its booming tech economy," the journal confessed, the state had grown at the rate of "26.6 percent, ranking it only No. 19 in the country." Virginia's growth was "above average," but Chmura informed readers that the state's economic performance was more "robust" in the 1980s because of the Reagan administration defense spending.[18] More than this, northern Virginia was preventing the state from slipping into a more intense recession. Chmura claimed that the northern Virginia engine generated 20,000 jobs in 2001–2002, more than making up for the 19,400 jobs lost in the rest of the state. Chmura, like most mainstream economists, was silent on the character of those jobs. Part-time, contract, benefit-paying or not, they offered little consolation to those mired in the economic morass of southwest Virginia. Chmura also conceded that northern Virginia was not insulated from the recession. Distilling the Richmond economist's conclusions, *Virginia Business* reported that "The broad employment numbers obscure wrenching transitions within Northern Virginia's tech-intensive economy. The sector that includes telecommunications shows a disturbing 7.4 percent drop in employment. This drop is due in part to the glut of phone equipment and the demise of such marquee name firms as Telligent and PSINet after the tech bubble popped in 2000."[19] Arlington and Fairfax were shedding high-paying jobs and contributing to the labor surplus in the technology sector. Overproduction, underutilized capacity, the instability in the technology sector, and the shock of market readjustment quickly dissolved the idea that northern Virginia was invincible.

As for Roanoke and western Virginia, its labor-intensive, manufacturing-oriented economy was moving nowhere quickly. Dependent on textiles, furniture, clothing, and wood products, the region had fallen victim to the economic realignment that was decimating the manufacturing sector. According to another report by economist Christine Chmura, western Virginia had more in common with the declining cities of Ohio and Pennsylvania than with northern Virginia. It was an economy that had experienced "no growth" while the national economy was in its "greatest expansion ever." Deprived of new jobs during the robust 1990s, western Virginia had grown stagnant. Chmura concluded that "We're seeing declining industries, we're seeing less opportunity, and an aging work force which ultimately could lead to a dwindling tax base and a deteriorating infrastructure that would cause further decline."[20] That diagnosis could have applied to any number of regions that fell outside of the Golden Crescent of New Economy growth. With the exception of Richmond, northern Virginia, Charlottesville, and Hampton, the Old Dominion had every reason to question the claim that the New Economy had just transformed the commonwealth. Even *in* those charmed areas like northern Virginia, insecurity and inequality were constant companions of many, and not just those who agitated for a living wage.

Americans had good reason to question the claim that the New Economy had improved their lives. It's instructive to remind ourselves that, beyond questions of foreign investment, Sunbelt growth, the relocation of the financial industry to places like Atlanta, and the expansion of job opportunities in the service sector, the liberated free market failed to deliver social stability. While the economy benefited from stock market-induced growth, the wages for nonsupervisory workers and people on the lower end of the wage scale continued to deteriorate. They remained below the wage rates of the 1970s and considerably below those established during the Reagan and Bush administrations. For example, the average wage for nonsupervisory workers between 1969 and 1976 was $15.03; from 1993 to 2000, it was $13.60. The descent of wages from a high of $15.70 in 1973 to a low of $13.27 in 1993 happened at the same time that productivity was increasing annually. Despite business lamentations about indolent American workers and obstructionist unions, productivity was increasing in the Carter to Bush years. Wages, however were not. When Bill Clinton took office, wages were at a forty-year low and the disparity between average real wages and productivity at an all-time high. According to British journalist Godfrey Hodgson, the "most shocking single statistic is that in 1999 average wages, discounted for inflation, had still not caught up with the level they had reached in 1973. Indeed, as late as the spring of 1999, average wages were actually 10 percent *lower* than in 1973."[21] Wages stabilized between 1993 and 1996 but remained stagnant even while productivity increased from 1993 to 1996.[22]

That situation changed briefly between 1996 and 1999, when real wages rose significantly. The business demand for labor drew more people into the economy which drove down the unemployment rate below five percent for the first time since 1969. In Virginia, the unemployment rate was lower than the national average, declining to 3.1 percent in 1998. While it might be comforting to imagine that labor had regained its bargaining strength, the reality was that the stock market explosion and the production of new computer equipment lay behind the increase.[23] Economist Michael Yates puts wage decline in a larger historical framework. According to his findings, workers in manufacturing and nonsupervisory positions benefited from real hourly earning increases of 2.3 percent between 1947 and 1967. Real wages had doubled in these years of what has been described as the capital-labor accord. Between 1979 and 1999, the situation changed drastically, as real wages declined by 0.2 percent a year. Wages were significantly lower in 1999 than twenty years before. Benefits, health care, and pensions had also been aggressively reduced. These were the years of Reaganite hope and prosperity, the years of the Sunbelt South, the years of the New Economy.[24]

According to economists at the Economic Policy Institute, the South did not endure the worst of the 1990s. In fact, between 1989 and 1999, median hourly wages grew the fastest there and in the Midwest. Unemployment and poverty rates declined most significantly in these two regions as well. Low-wage workers also benefited more in the South than in the West or Northeast. In the South, hourly wages increased by 7.5 percent, while wages declined by 2.3 percent in the Northeast and 0.2 in the West. It was a similar story for white-collar employees and workers in the middle ranks. Southerners in this bracket saw their incomes grow by 4.7 percent while northeastern office dwellers found their salaries decrease by 2.4 percent. At 13.7 percent, poverty remained the highest in the South, but even here improvements were made, falling 1.7 percent between 1989 and 1998.[25] And for economist John Knapp, Virginia's economic performance in the Second Gilded Age was stellar. Unemployment remained low, new jobs were being added, and the state's per capita income exceeded the national average during the 1990s. However, while median household income grew from $35,073 to $42,957, the inflation-adjusted income level for 1990 stayed the same as in 1997.[26]

Knapp was reporting in 1999, two years before the economic bottom fell out in Virginia and the nation. Even so, the South and Virginia had made some progress during a period of increasing class polarization and negligible real wage growth for the nation. The overwhelming majority of that progress was concentrated in the counties surrounding Washington, and much of it would prove ephemeral when the new millennium arrived. Moreover, relative regional improvement hardly compensated for the job losses, the steady casualization of labor, the inequalities of wealth, and the sheer precariousness that characterized the lives of so many southerners in the New Economy era. Traveling down I-95 into South Carolina on his way to an academic conference, historian Peter Coclanis captured the disparity between the rhetoric of New Economy liberation and the reality that most working-class southerners lived: "No frissons of excitement regarding tech transfer here, nor bullish rhetoric on the promise of globalization. Rather, billboards condemning free trade and offshore outsourcing" alongside injunctions to Christian conversion. "From the look of things, the key businesses in this desolate region are pawnshops and trailer sales lots, strip bars, bail bondsmen, and party shops, junkyards and purveyors of payday-advance loans." Only the evangelical churches disrupted this depressing scene, a "landscape characteristic of this part of the hard-scrabble South in the early twenty-first century, a South that never had much and now has less, a South that has received little, if anything from globalization."[27]

Marginally increased wages and job growth did not insulate the South from the economic dislocations that gripped the United States in this critical decade. Instead, as previous chapters have argued, the South was at the forefront of economic globalization and all of the uncertainties that accompanied it. There was little question that Virginians had come to share in the wider American experience of working longer hours, managing more than one job to make a living, the caprices of contract labor, and the pervasive job insecurity that kept wages low despite economic expansion. The southerners who experienced the wrenching insecurity of the post-war twentieth century were not only textile workers but insurance salespeople, pharmaceutical company executives, data entry clerks, and middle managers. The South was no exception.

The region continued to be distinctive, however, on several disconcerting fronts, and these strongly challenged the EPI's findings that the South was still rising. Per capita personal income continued to trail national standards (Virginia being a notable exception, where the city of Alexandria and Loudoun and Fairfax Counties pushed the state ahead of the nation). Poverty rates exceeded those of most northern states, and de-industrialization shredded the jobs of thousands of southerners and Virginians. Economist Alfred Eckes reminds us that between 1994 and 2000, 31.3 percent of the jobs lost as a result of trade deals were lost in the South.[28] Investment in education failed to match national standards, while the much-celebrated job growth of the 1980s and 1990s was in the low-wage service sector. Even while some southern workers benefited from the relocation of automobile manufacturing to the region, particularly in states like Tennessee and South Carolina, they bore the burden of economic development deals that cost the state in social investments. Many of those workers were (and probably still are) happy with the deal. Comparatively high-paying jobs employing literally thousands of southerners can hardly be considered the evidence of economic despair. By 1995, the South employed 156,281 people in auto- and parts-manufacturing plants. While by no means an insignificant sector in the region's economy, it still employed fewer than the total number in Michigan alone. Auto industry employees also tended to work in relatively small undertakings in predominantly rural areas, which perpetuated the pattern of southern rural industrialization inherited from the New South era.[29]

More telling than the continuation of the tradition of rural manufacturing was the combination of factors that brought auto manufacturing to the South in the first place. From the establishment of the first Nissan plant in 1980 to Nissan's 2005 decision to shift its headquarters from Los Angeles to Franklin, Tennessee, foreign auto makers were drawn to the region for its low wages, low taxes, and corporate incentive packages. Nissan considered rural white Tennesseans the ideal candidates for its automotive operations. Culturally "homogenous," lacking industrial training (and thus bargaining leverage or craft traditions) and traditionally anti-union, they were malleable enough for lean production.[30] Southern policymakers had deliberately followed a pattern of low-skilled, anti-union manufacturing facilitated by exorbitant giveaway schemes. That development strategy deprived communities of revenue for schools, training, health care, and the social infrastructure necessary to overcome the legacy of an underdeveloped labor market.[31] Short-term gains might very well develop into long-term gains should those companies stay in the region. Yet the South's experience of capital flight should make it wary of promises about the future. In the meantime, those who are not employed in the car-manufacturing sector have good reason to wonder whether the economic planning that brought foreign car companies to the region has benefited them. Lacking the leverage of collective bargaining and democratic representation in the workplace, employees in the automobile sector may begin to see the socioeconomic order in the same way that Be-Lo workers did in the early 1990s.

If democratic vitality could be measured by statistics, then the question of where Virginia and the South stood at the beginning of the twenty-first century would be a simple matter of reading a balance sheet. On that account, the region would be divided into areas of prosperity and rural decay, high wages and low wages, economic growth and social decline. Economist Gavin Wright has suggested that even this distinction needs to be qualified. Instead of an urban, dynamic, almost "northern" New Economy South versus a typically de-industrializing rural South, the region demonstrated a "surprisingly persistent regionalism in some of the most robust southern industries." Beyond specific industries, Wright suggests that the "political economy of industrial recruitment" qualifies as one of the strongest indications of southern economic continuity.[32] Sociologist Richard Tardanico agreed, placing southern economic deficiencies in the context of a history of inadequate social investment. Enumerating the indications of southern economic continuity, he included "underdeveloped public infrastructure and social services; excessive percentage of undereducated people, low-wage workers, branch manufacturing plants . . . still substantial legacies of deeply rooted racial exploitation; and economic subordination to external ownership, linkages, and control."[33] The legacy of southern economic distinctiveness was evident, but the important point is that the South was on the leading edge of the transformations overtaking the United States. The southern past was becoming the American future.

Yet economic issues were inseparable from political decisions. They were inextricably tied to questions of power, ideology, and economic self-interest. Class disparities and racial inequalities figured prominently in the lives of average Virginians, even when they were not aware of them, even when they actively denied them. A new sense of rootlessness and social drift, of vulnerability to decisions made in remote locations and against their interests, afflicted Virginians in this last decade of the twentieth century. Inscrutable forces were not at work. What was happening was that Americans were experiencing the disorienting, atomizing effects of the kind of unrestrained market expansion that sociologist Karl Polanyi had once warned against. The "great transformation" that he had detected in the form of union mobilization and government regulation had never advanced as far in the South as it had in the rest of the United States. It was no surprise, then, that the reaction against market restraints advanced as powerfully as it did south of the Mason-Dixon line. Yet the South was not the exception in this experience. Rather, it was on the leading edge in this movement to revitalize market dominance in the United States in the late twentieth century. That movement was not the product of disembodied economic forces but the result of political decisions designed to restore profitability and maximize the return on capital investment. While new communications and transportation technology had indeed dissolved barriers between previously distant countries, they did not ineluctably sweep away the existing political order. Quite simply, there was nothing inevitable or irreversible about the collapse of the American social responsibility state. There was nothing ineluctable about the dissolution of the social contract.

The decisions of power brokers in the United States had the most dramatic impact on Americans, southerners included. For a variety of reasons, few of which can be separated from considerations of material self-interest, political and economic elites dismantled or discredited institutions that protected Americans from the caprices of unregulated market competition. It is worth recalling, as Gavin Wright does, that during the same time that African Americans benefited in social terms from the civil rights movement, "average real wages for unskilled labor have stagnated or declined, and income inequality has steadily increased—among blacks as well as whites, in the North as well as the South, for the population as a whole and within every sizable demographic subgroup." The South did not stand outside of modern economic change: "These trends are national or global in character, beyond the control of southern state politics with or without the Voting Rights Act. But they have hit the South with unusual force, and they have coincided historically with the demise of New Deal labor market institutions and policies."[34] Factors beyond the South had eroded wage levels for all Americans and undermined the New Deal social responsibility state. Yet the South had played a paradoxically critical role in advancing the political and ideological forces behind market dominance. It offered decisive leadership in fashioning the notion that untrammeled private enterprise best served the interests of a globalizing America.

These were not impartial "trends," nor were they completely beyond the control of state governments. By dissolving trade barriers erected in the 1940s without sufficient protections for American workers, by forging trade agreements that did not protect American and foreign workers against economic free-fall, governing elites set in motion the forces that would erode the social contract. By advocating a neo–states' rights agenda that actively resisted federal government action, Virginia conservatives of both parties deprived Virginia's citizens of the resources, leadership, and political allies required for managing the crisis of the 1990s. By enthusiastically embracing the competition model, Virginia and its southern counterparts canceled any hope for regional economic cooperation. By endorsing the idea that New Deal protections against unfettered business competition stifled individual freedom, southern conservatives cut the ground from under working people who could rely on little else.

Mirroring the economic agenda set by the White House and conservative Democrats, Governor George Allen, Governor Jim Gilmore, and others championed the forces of market competition. In an era of economic balkanization, southern corporate and political leaders accelerated the process. They did so, however, at a time when the implications of an ideology of market fundamentalism had become clear. The strategy of liberating capitalism had been given "a massive ideological and material fillip by the fall of communism," writes economist Robert Brenner. The entrepreneurial potential that had supposedly been "restrained by high taxes, inflexible labor markets, too large a welfare state, and too much state regulation of business" would finally be realized. Yet policymakers should have asked whether "after more than two decades of wage-cutting, tax-cutting, reductions in the growth of social expenditure, deregulation and 'sound finance,' the ever less fettered free market" really did deliver the benefits that its champions claimed.[35] Since the economy was not performing even as well as it did in the 1960s, the era of Big Government Spending, political leaders had even more reason to question their favored assumptions. Certainly, this realization should have been stronger for political elites of the late 1990s. At least they *had* the resources to spend on social investment. Virginia's political leaders were not defenseless, and they were not incidental to national economic policy. They were, in effect, the harbingers of a business-dominated social order. A political and economic program, neither conspiratorial in intent nor entirely unconscious of its consequences, lay behind the crisis of the 1990s.

This mood of social anxiety transcended traditional distinctions of class and race. Middle-class southerners felt troubled by job insecurity and the continuing threat of corporate downsizing. Poorly paid African American workers in Richmond, downsized textile workers in Chilhowie, and out-of-luck bank tellers in Roanoke felt the crushing sense of distress at a time when television screens and billboard ads assured them that their prospects were bright. That does not mean that the South had become an oasis of racial egalitarianism. If anything, the official color blindness of the era made the burden of racial discrimination even heavier. African Americans endured the resegregation of schools, the persistent limitations on corporate upward mobility, and the nagging income inequalities that confirmed the limits of racial amelioration after the civil rights movement.

This was no longer an exclusively southern story, however. African American working-class insecurity and underclass poverty continued to defy claims that a rising tide had lifted all boats. Those frustrations were felt as strongly in south central Los Angeles as south of the James River in Richmond. The Hispanic workers who struggled to gain a foothold in Alexandria through poorly paying janitorial jobs shared the experience of Hispanic service workers in Chicago and San Diego. What they had in common was a profound sense that the economic order was largely indifferent to their suffering. They shared the belief that political and business elites had abandoned any commitment to average people. Instead, they promoted an abstract, inscrutable "market" that rewarded only the most flexible. Being socially conscious now meant selfless sacrifice to market competitiveness. Thinking of one's standard of living, family needs, mental health, or dignity was compelling proof that one had not sufficiently reengineered for the challenges of global competition. The Competition Era gripped Americans in the working and eroding middle class; living in southwest Virginia or Southern California determined how well one would negotiate those challenges.

Reasserting boundaries of ethnic, racial, geographic, and religious identity offered a promising way of navigating a homogenous consumer culture. It seemed to offer a defense against the disorienting forces of radical self-interest and marketplace anomie. It seemed to offer shelter from the storm of a social consensus that denied persistent racial inequality. Hip-hop music, the rise of violent urban gangs, the proliferation of drug use, and the chronic unemployment in the nation's decaying cities offered stunning testimony to the intensification of despair among African Americans and Hispanics. Civil rights accomplishments aside, the dream remained deferred. Difference replaced equality as the defining ethic of the post–civil rights era, and the South was no exception. Celebrating one's Celtic roots, African origins, or linguistic heritage provided a defense against rootlessness, a protective shell of empowerment in an era that had lost the idiom of mutuality, cooperation, and industrial democracy. It offered a feeling of control in a world where decisions were made by anonymous technocrats and where the governing forces were seemingly relentless and often unforgiving. It gave participants access to a series of fictional golden eras, when group cohesion was supposedly unassailable and social values were crystalline. It gave them the myth of simpler times.[36]

What it did not provide was an effective counterpoint to the very forces that were eroding their independence. Addressing the impact of cultural politics on the South after the 1960s, historian James Cobb concluded that it undermined the momentum of the movement for racial justice while simultaneously making southerners vulnerable to dominant interests: "Regardless of its radical-populist trappings, identity politics typically redounds to the ultimate benefit of elites, who can use it to divert and divide the masses and even exploit them economically." While donning the trappings of one identity or another reflected the consumer reflex of post-war America, it carried more sinister implications. With its dedication to preserving an Anglo-Saxon southern identity from "ethnic cleansing," the League of the South echoed the chauvinistic nationalists of Eastern Europe who manipulated subterranean prejudices to launch murderous political campaigns.[37] In either manifestation, identity politics could not offer a set of ideals or a political program that challenged the drift. If anything, it represented a repudiation of the democratic ideals that had redeemed a slaveholding, colonizing, and exploitive America. The irony is that at a time when ethnic, racial, and gender differences defined political discourse, black and white southerners, male and female, working and middle class, had more in common than ever. Evidently, they had more in common than they could imagine.

Despite the persistence of some of the most distinguishing features of economic "regionalism," as Gavin Wright puts it, the South and the rest of the country had converged. It is not too much of an exaggeration to say that, after a brief respite of New Deal liberalism, the rest of the nation rejoined it. Just as the southern experience of economic realignment mirrored the national experience—albeit in a fashion that intensified traditional southern liabilities—its political conservatism harmonized with the national mood. Cobb reminds us that, although Republicans like Ronald Reagan effectively manipulated white southern racism to solidify political gains, they were not utterly dependent on the region for their success. "The South remained a citadel of political conservatism by anybody's standard," Cobb conceded, but "the GOP's presidential successes in the 1980s were so sweeping and national in scope that the Republicans could have claimed the White House in each election without carrying a single southern state." The South did not produce Ronald Reagan, Barry Goldwater, or Richard Nixon. Cobb argues that commentators have so thoroughly absorbed the "southernization of America" argument—the idea that since the 1970s the South has been extending its cultural and political values to the rest of the nation—that they overlook how conservative the rest of America already was. "American culture has always been more southern than many contemporary liberals are willing to admit, but the national embrace of so many of the activities and traits once deemed distinctly southern raises questions about how much longer they can be legitimately identified with the South."[38] Cobb underestimates the leading position which southern Republicans have taken in legitimizing the conservative ideology at the national level. That tradition of political influence stretches back to the period of the Slave Power and the infamous Dred Scott decision, forward to congressional acquiescence in lynching and Jim Crow, and into the 1990s assault on the liberal welfare state.

Even so, Cobb's central position is correct. The low-tax, decentralizing, anti-working-class, racially regressive position associated with the South has so often been the American norm since before a musket was fired on Lexington Green. Liberalism, republican governance, and the Enlightenment ideals that generated it are the exceptionalisms that have made the United States, from time to time, a beacon of moral leadership and political virtue for the world. What happened in the 1990s had been happening since the 1960s: the effort to return the United States to the social hierarchies and laissez-faire doctrines of the Gilded Age. What Cobb overlooks is that southern legislators and business pundits played a leading, even decisive, role in validating that agenda. Southern conservatives were able to articulate their agenda more effectively not because they were drastically more right-wing than their northern Reaganite counterparts. Rather, southern conservatives gained influence because they met so little resistance. In the North and West, conservatives had to contend with organized labor (albeit weakened), environmental and anti-nuclear activists, a viable women's movement, and a Democratic Party that maintained a marginal commitment to liberal democratic ideals. Southerners, and in particular Virginians, played a decisive role in updating and modernizing conservatism for the New Economy Era.

If inequality and exploitation clouded the American scene far too often, it never eclipsed American egalitarianism. Inherited from the Enlightenment, the rationalist principles of equality, freedom, compassion, humanity, decency, and genuine human liberty became the conscience of the nation. Those ideals, articulated by slaveholders and New England merchants alike at the constitutional convention, were the inheritance of both regions. This American conscience, which balanced social responsibility against the demands of libertarian freedom, had never been the monopoly of northerners. Jeffersonian minimalism was not only the South's ideological legacy. Through the Populist movement, the social democratic reform movement of the New Deal era, and the civil rights movement of the post-war period, the South demonstrated its purchase on the American conscience. Visions of a cooperative commonwealth, of racial equality, and positive government action were not entirely alien to the South.

In the 1990s, a majority of Americans reached the last stage in a long process of stripping away the institutional manifestations of those egalitarian ideals. Deprived of the tradition of civic virtue, a perverted form of Jeffersonian minimalism became dogmatic. Leading elites exalted Jeffersonian decentralization in the belief that individual self-interest provided an anchor against the tidal waves of economic and political change. Collective considerations became impediments to individual freedom, though market-oriented legislators of both parties made concession after concession to the corporate entities that dominated American public life.

Those waves of social change had risen dramatically in the years following Vietnam and Watergate, threatening to swamp the leaky vessel of

New Deal liberalism. White southerners and many blue-collar northerners returned to the entitlements of racial privilege that had comforted their predecessors in an era of Jim Crow. This was the American norm, one of racial exclusion, the exploitation of relatively powerless groups, and atomistic individualism. It warred, however, against the egalitarian and democratic strains in the nation's tradition, which transformed the Civil War into a crusade against racial servitude. That same enlightened conscience turned the logic of the Cold War on its head in a movement for racial equality. It expressed itself not only in collective movements for social change but in the defense of individual rights, personal freedom, and cultural values that countered the ethic of unrestrained consumption. That imperative was never the exclusive monopoly of liberals, Democrats, or others on the left of the political spectrum.

What was at stake in the 1990s was whether or not that Enlightenment inheritance, expressed through imperfect but rational institutions of social responsibility, would endure. Could the Enlightenment inheritance, strengthened by religious traditions that periodically reminded us of the better angels of our nature, restrain the ethic of unenlightened self-interest that Adam Smith condemned as much as Eugene Debs did? That was the issue in the drive for unilateral control on the shop floor; so too was it the issue in the movement to impose a trade agreement that working Virginians opposed. Putting it in those terms might sound artificially grandiose, but a discussion that fails to move beyond per capita income ignores what was at stake for average Americans in the age of market dominance. Ultimately, it ignores the largest questions that faced the United States in the era of global integration.

Lacking the language of class inequality and economic democracy, Virginians struggled to make sense of what was happening to them. By the end of the decade, the Virginia Organizing Project was advancing an alternative analysis of working- and middle-class despair. The VOP fostered a set of organizational tools and a critical perspective that reawakened the possibility of collective, democratic reform. Understanding the critical importance of political economy, the VOP promoted a social agenda that connected racial egalitarianism and fundamental workplace justice. It advanced the social democratic aspirations of people like Thomas R. McNutt and the UFCW in Hampton Roads.

Most importantly, the VOP and a small coterie of social activists rekindled the idea of democratic citizenship in the South. As philosopher Mark Kingwell writes, "Citizenship is a role now in danger of losing its privileged position in human life, through various forms of withdrawal from the political realm; into consumerist fetishism, into cultural separatism, into self-regarding isolation."[39] This is what market dominance and the individualistic business ethos of the 1990s threatened. Living-wage advocates, southern participants in the WTO protests, and VOP organizers of community action initiatives challenged the decline of citizenship. They reignited the idea that southerners were Americans endowed with certain inalienable rights, however fragile. They were citizens, not simply consumers limited to the choices that multimedia conglomerates and "box store" retailers could offer them. They restored the notion that negative liberty was not the best that America had to offer but only a check against totalizing control. In the organizing efforts of workers at Be-Lo, in the writings of adjunct professors like Eileen Huey, in the work of Hispanic activists in northern Virginia, and in the racial egalitarianism and social democratic consciousness of the Virginia Organizing Project, the entire notion of active citizenship returned. This form of citizenship confronted the self-absorbed individualism and self-defeating identity separatism that passed for social consciousness in the 1990s. Again, Mark Kingwell suggests that individualism could not solve the fundamental social crises of the advanced capitalism:

> Without a background of commonality, without some form of civic responsibility, autonomy degenerates into mere special pleading. Without a strong commitment to other people and our shared undertakings, without a sense that we are together creating a just world, a world not ruled by cheap acceptance of inevitability or the easy superiority of wealth, our hard-won individualism loses its deeper significance.[40]

Against a neo–states' rights philosophy that condemned government activism on behalf of the least powerful, the Virginia Organizing Project advocated bonds of community responsibility. It sought to "submerge" the economic system—as Karl Polanyi once described it—in a web of social relationships and cultural norms that would protect human dignity. They did not accept the New Economy argument that the competitive marketplace was normal, natural, and benevolent. Like Polanyi, they believed that it distorted human nature, distributed its benefits inequitably, and disrupted social bonds. It should be controlled, they submitted, not in the interest of denying Americans the fruits of their labor but in ensuring that the chimera of marketplace freedom did not extinguish the possibility for a more authentic form of freedom. In that vision of freedom, economic security, democratic citizenship, ties of mutual responsibility, and uncompromising honesty about the nation's tragic history of racial intolerance were front and center. Despite its nebulous program for reform, the VOP unequivocally acknowledged the persistence of racial inequality and gender discrimination but embedded them in a framework of economic democracy. Quite simply, it recognized the moral obligation to act on behalf of those persons most vulnerable to unenlightened self-interest.[41]

Undertaking this project, the VOP called on southerners to rejuvenate the traditions of collective action that had briefly threatened the New South order in the 1890s. It regenerated the democratic energies of New Deal liberalism. At the same time, it insisted that racial equality and minority leadership were key ingredients of any humane social movement. In the end, reformers failed to articulate a program of political reform that would bind together a diverse coalition. They could not answer the problem of American participation in the global competition era.

What they did do, however, was point the way toward the regeneration of American social democracy. That way would lead to decent wages, revitalized labor unions, trade policies that protected the rights of workers and the environment, investment in social infrastructure that benefited communities rather than simply corporations, a vigorous social safety net, and an education system that encouraged democratic citizenship rather than occupational retraining. That direction included a regeneration of the Keynesian, redistributionist arguments that had made so much sense to working-class Americans in the post-war era. Decent wages, reasonable health care, and personal benefits had helped individual workers. No less important, these supports had raised the spending power of consumers, who in turn helped local businesses and paid local taxes. The direction that reformers pointed included a political system that addressed the interests of the disadvantaged and defeated.

In effect, they were reaching for a counternarrative to the conservative story of liberal malfeasance and special interest politics. They were also searching for an alternative to the neoliberal ideology of market dominance and entrepreneurial liberation. Republicans, conservative Democrats, and prominent business leaders responded to the crisis of the early 1990s by advocating radical individualism and corporate stewardship of American society. By the beginning of the twenty-first century, Virginians were questioning that dogma and imagining an alternative. When the justified retaliation for the terrorist attacks of September 11, 2001, degenerated into a crusade for conformity at home and dubious military intervention abroad, that alternative went into dormancy. Progressive southerners were left wondering if the American conscience that had burned brightly in the twilight of the second Gilded Age would revive again.

Notes

Chapter 1. The South in the Era of Market Dominance

Epigraph source: Greider, "The Future Is Now," 24.

1. Polanyi, *The Great Transformation*, 29.

2. Ibid., 67.

3. Ibid., 69.

4. Ibid.

5. Ibid., 216. For example, economist Robert Brenner points to higher net profit rates, output, labor productivity, and real wages for the post-war period of 1950 to 1970 in comparison to the period of 1970 to 1993. Brenner, "The Economy of Global Turbulence," 5. According to economist D. M. Gordon, the real rate of growth in real GNP was higher (3.8 percent) during the period of 1948 to 1966 than it was between 1973 and 1979. Productivity was also higher for the earlier period in comparison to the later, while unemployment was lower. Gordon, "Chickens Home to Roost," 37. Examining social and economic decline in the 1990s, economist Robert Pollin postulated an "alternative policy approach" based on the idea of "full employment at decent wages," the foundation of the more egalitarian economic order of the post-war period. "The corollary to a policy of full employment at decent wages is that workers can afford to spend money, which then maintains overall spending in the economy at a high level. This creates the further benefit of businesses wanting to increase their investment to meet the demands of an expanding market." Pollin, *Contours of Descent*, 177–78.

6. Bullock and Deitz, "Transforming the South," 261.

7. Polanyi, *The Great Transformation*, 163.

8. Wright, *Old South, New South*, 64–80.

9. Michael Lind has suggested that the "tragedy of the New Deal . . . was that Franklin Roosevelt and his successors industrialized the South without liberalizing it." While the observation overlooks the democratizing impact of the civil rights movement, it highlights the limited impact that federal social programs had on the political culture of the region. Despite its considerable achievements, the civil rights movement did not transform southern political culture. Lind, "Conservatives and the Counterrevolution against the New Deal," 285.

10. Black and Black, *The Rise of Southern Republicans*, 222, 237–38.

11. Several studies of historical memory and the South now crowd the bookshelves. The most important and provocative of these is Fitzhugh Brundage's, *The Southern Past*. For more on the Confederate history month debate in Virginia, see pages 316, 337–38.

12. A representative example of the argument that the South was leading the nation and had overcome the burden of its past was "The American South: For Whom

the Belle Tolls," 3–18. For journalistic coverage of the persistence of racial disparities despite increasing prosperity, see Peter Applebome, "In Selma, Everything and Nothing Changed," *New York Times*, August 2, 1994, and "A Suburban Eden Where the Right Rules," ibid., August 1, 1994. For a journalistic inquiry that combined the traditional preoccupation with southern identity and regional economic backwardness, see "South's Identity Challenges Potent—Still, It Stubbornly Refuses to Be 'Anyplace,' but Its Classic Problems Also Endure," *Richmond Times-Dispatch*, July 13, 1997. For a discussion of the rise of the conservative right, its connection to reactionary racism, and its capture of the Republican Party, see Carter, *The Politics of Rage*. James Cobb examines the fixation on enduring southern distinctiveness and questions it by pointing, for example, to the conservatism in the rest of the country during the period of Republican ascendancy—see *Away Down South*, 318–40.

13. See for example K. Michael Prince, *Rally 'Round the Flag, Boys!*, David W. Blight, *Race and Reunion*, and James C. Cobb, *Away Down South*.

14. As James Cobb points out in a collection on the modern South, "We live in an age of rapid economic and cultural globalization, where even distinctions among nations seemed to be fading by the day. Does it really make sense, therefore, to continue to talk so much about 'southern distinctiveness,' especially when much of what now passes for it is little more than the caricatured creation of the crafty folks who have found an economic bonanza in marketing a commodified version of southernness to those who feel they have lost sight of what being southern really means?" Cobb, "From the First New South to the Second," 10.

15. Gitlin, *The Intellectuals and the Flag*, 97–98, 100.

16. J. Jones, "The History and Politics of Poverty in Twentieth-Century America," 144.

17. Peacock, "The South in a Global World," 585.

18. Peacock, "The South and Grounded Globalism," 272.

19. Margolies, "One New World Order and Many New Souths."

20. See for example Robert Zieger, ed., *Southern Labor in Transition, 1940–1995* (Knoxville: University of Tennessee Press, 1997), and Glenn T. Eskew, ed., *Labor in the Modern South* (Athens: University of Georgia Press, 2001), the latter of which does not address labor or industrial history beyond the 1970s.

21. Perhaps the most influential and provocative from this school has been Benjamin Barber's *Jihad vs. McWorld: How Globalism and Tribalism Are Reshaping the World* (New York: Ballantine Books, 1996); no less important and no less insightful on the deleterious implications of what has been described as the "Washington Consensus" in favor of unrestricted free markets is Joseph E. Stiglitz's *Globalization and Its Discontents* (New York: Norton, 2003).

22. Cobb and Stueck, *Globalization and the American South*, xv.

23. On the cooperative, compassionate values that briefly dominated American life in the 1930s and which continued to pulsate through movements for social democratic change, see McElvaine, *The Great Depression*, introduction and chapter 9.

24. Tabb, "Neoliberalism and Anticorporate Globalization as Class Struggle," 63.

25. Faux, *The Global Class War*, 5.

26. G. Wright, "Afterword," 299.

27. Goldfield, *Still Fighting the Civil War*, 273–97.

28. Thomas F. Jackson, *From Civil Rights to Human Rights*, 1–24, 216–17, 256–75, 351–53.

29. Edward N. Luttwak, "Will Success Spoil America? Why the Pols Don't Get Our Real Crisis of Values," *Washington Post*, November 27, 1994.

30. Zweig, *The Working-Class Majority*, 1–3.

31. Ibid., 39–57. The following discussion borrows extensively from this important work.

32. Ibid., 4–5, 10.

33. Ibid., 5.

34. Zweig, *What's Class Got to Do with It?*, 4–6.

35. Fonseca, "The Nine Regions of Virginia."

36. Wood, "The Demise of Virginia Democrats," 2.

37. Judis, "Sneak Preview," 9.

38. Strictly on the basis of gross national product in the twentieth century, growth was most aggressive in the 1948 to 1973 period, when it averaged 4.0 percent a year. In the free market period of 1919–1929, it was 3.5 percent; in the free market period of 1979 to 2000, it was 3.0 percent a year. In terms of productivity, the short period of expansion between 1995 and 2000 registered a 2.5 percent growth rate, while the annual productivity rate between 1948 and 1973 was 2.9 percent. The relatively vibrant productivity rate in the latter part of the 1990s probably also reflected the exaggerated impact of computer equipment replacement. In reality, the productivity rate was probably closer to 2.2 percent per year. Kotz and Wolfson, "Déjà Vu All Over Again," 32–33. In terms of wages, the dominant pattern was decline. While the trend of declining wages stretches back to 1979 (others suggest 1973), the lack of advancement in the 1990s during a period of improving productivity was particularly distressing. From 1989, the median male wage declined by 1 percent until 1996, while female wages grew by 0.1 percent between 1989 and 1997. At the same time, productivity increased by 9 percent between 1989 and 1997, but the gains from it were not equitably distributed. According to one study, the decline from 1979 until 1999 was attributable to "a general shift to a more deregulated, laissez-faire economy that has weakened the bargaining power of workers, both union and non-union, white- and blue-collar." Mishel, Bernstein, and Schmitt, "Is It a New Economy for Working America?" 6.

Chapter 2. Reengineered and Rewired

1. Henwood, *After the New Economy*, 3–5.

2. As James Cobb points out, this anti-union strategy made pragmatic sense from the standpoint of economic development. Opposition to unions—much of it illegal—solidified the power of management and maintained low regional wage rates. The southern union exception also tended to undermine the strength of union organization throughout the rest of the nation, a reminder that the South's economic fortunes were inextricably tied to those of the rest of the nation. Cobb, *The Selling of the South*, 260.

3. Kotz and Wolfson, "Déjà Vu All Over Again," 25–27.

4. Ibid., 26–29.

5. Ibid., 29–31.

6. Harrison, "The Dark Side of Flexible Production," 39–45.

7. Henwood, *After the New Economy*, 37–38.

8. Sheikers, "Fairfax," 54.

9. "Virginia Building High-Tech Center: State Spending $30 Million on Research Hub Linking Colleges and Industry," *New York Times*, September 16, 1984; J. A. Bacon, "The Fairfax Revolution," 30; Taylor, "Eat Your Heart Out, D.C.," 31–37.

10. Sheikers, "Fairfax," 54–56; Paul Bradley, "Identity in the Making: Northern Virginia Wants to Be Another Silicon Valley," *Richmond Times-Dispatch* November 19, 1995; "Virginia Building High-Tech Center: State Spending $30 Million on Research Hub Linking Colleges and Industry," *New York Times*, September 16, 1984; Odin, "From Milch Cow to Cash Cow," 38–39.

11. J. A. Bacon, "The Fairfax Revolution," 30; Taylor, "Eat Your Heart Out, D.C.," 31–37. The boosterism was still under way at the turn of the century, and the rest of Virginia was still trying to catch up or benefit from northern Virginia's exponential growth. See "Virginia Is among Tech Leaders: Northern Virginia Business Helping to Drive the Numbers," *Norfolk Virginian-Pilot*, May 17, 2000.

12. Sheikers, "Fairfax," 52.

13. Odin, "From Milch Cow to Cash Cow," 45.

14. Taylor, "Eat Your Heart Out, D.C.," 34–35.

15. Ibid., 34–35, quote on 35.

16. White, "The Fairfax Formula," 58. The effort in Virginia to forge connections between high-tech industries and the public sector mirrored developments at the national level. See "The Birth of Silicon Statesmanship: The High-Tech Companies that Once Shunned Washington Now Seek Its Help," *New York Times*, February 27, 1983; in the South, North Carolina was at the forefront of the effort to substitute high-wage, high-tech jobs for low-wage positions in the declining textile industry. See "Going After High Tech," *New York Times*, July 19, 1981.

17. J. A. Bacon, "The Fairfax Revolution," 30.

18. Frederick, "Do You Hear a Giant Sucking Sound?" 81.

19. Ibid.

20. As one report pointed out, the wage rate in the Hampton Roads area as late as 2000 was at least $6,000 less than the national wage level. The high-paying jobs in the technology sector also tended to spin off jobs that were not nearly as well-paying and usually concentrated in the service sector. But it's important to balance this out against the fact that the expansion of high-paying jobs in northern Virginia spurred a per capita income increase from 98 percent of the national average to 103 percent in 1997. This gave Virginia the distinction of being the only state in the South with a higher than national average for per capita income. This overlooks the question of who was filling the low-end jobs in northern Virginia, what they were being paid, and the quality of economic growth in the rest of the state, which for the most part failed to benefit from high-tech development. Wage rates in southwestern, central, and southern Virginia lagged behind the northern region throughout the period. Still, Virginia was not the

worst of southern states, at least in terms of per capita income and job creation. See Karen Weintraub, "Region's Wages Have Far to Go to Hit U.S. Average," *Virginian-Pilot*, August 17, 2000; MDC, *State of the South 2000*, 103–105; by the end of the decade, southwest Virginia—with Roanoke as its center—was still suffering economic stagnation. The diagnosis, at least according to economist Christine Chmura, whom the city of Roanoke and Virginia Tech had commissioned to conduct an economic report—reinforced existing assumptions with a New Economy twist. The problem was declining, labor-intensive industries, an aging workforce, and weak business infrastructure. The solution: pursue the high-tech option through retraining and skills development. Like many analyses influenced by the New Economy ideology, this prescription failed to address tax policies, the impact of technology on labor, and the contingent quality of jobs for those people who were not engineers and computer programmers. See "Western Virginia's Economy Headed Nowhere, Study Says," *Roanoke Times*, November 19, 2000.

21. Cobb, *The Selling of the South*, 14–15, 22–25, 280–81.

22. On the importance of Virginia as the South's most northerly "right to work" state—one in which compulsory membership in a union that had secured a union shop was prohibited—to economic development strategy, see Woodlief, "What Sets Virginia Apart?" 5–6, and Micas, "The Changing Face of Manufacturing in Virginia," 45–50.

23. Cobb, *The Selling of the South*, chapters 1, 3, 10; Crocket, Binta, and Orton, "No Escape from History," 28–29.

24. Frederick, "Do You Hear a Giant Sucking Sound?" 84.

25. Ibid., 84–85.

26. Jim Gallant, "Counting the Costs," *Virginia Business* (July 1992): 36.

27. Ibid., 82.

28. Ibid., 82. The role of the state government in providing financial incentives for corporate relocation will be discussed in chapter 3.

29. Bacon, "Economic Exodus," 54 and previous quotes.

30. Ibid., 55.

31. Ibid., quotes on 56 and 59. A survey by the Virginia Foundation for Research and Economic Education seemed to confirm that business leaders echoed *Virginia Business*'s conservative sentiments. A survey of 761 corporate leaders found that most had disliked the state's unions (even though no more than 12.2 percent of workers were unionized), did not care for the governor or attorney general, thought that Virginia's lax environmental regulations were too strict, supported aggressive privatization and—paradoxically—believed that Virginia's "business climate" was better than surrounding states. See C. Jones, "Virginia Is the Perfect Place for Business," 13–18.

32. Fraser, *White Collar Sweatshop*, 17–38, 191–98.

33. Stiglitz, *The Roaring Nineties*, 180–85; Luttwak, *Turbo Capitalism*, 44–46; Mandel, *The High-Risk Society*, 102–5; Uchitelle, *The Disposable American*, 6–9. For a study that identifies the transformative impact of technology on work—its demand for greater "flexibility" (longer hours), adaptability (insecurity and lack of control over workplace environment), temporary work, "networking" (extensive monitoring and pressure to be more productive), and constant skills upgrading (threat that inability to adjust to new

demands will mean extinction)—and defends it as a positive good, see Conroy, *Sustaining the New Economy*, chapter 3.

34. Moody, *Workers in a Lean World*, 85–86. Moody stresses the point that, despite the modern human resources ideology of worker empowerment and teamwork, lean production represents an extension of Fordist mass production and Taylorite time-motion rationalization. The governing idea is to reduce the cost of production and ensure that workers do not have the institutional or procedural resources to control the manufacturing process. The following two paragraphs borrow extensively from this important work.

35. Ibid., 86–88.

36. Ibid., 87; Moody attributes this expression to Mike Parker and Jane Slaughter of *Labor Notes*.

37. Nonini, "Critique," 256.

38. Mandel quotes a study by Thomas Kochan and Paul Osterman suggesting a "relatively high attrition rate for workplace innovations." The same study asserted that only 13 percent of companies participating in the survey had continued production reforms for more than five years. Mandel, *The High-Risk Society*, 134.

39. Moody, *Workers in a Lean World*, 92.

40. Ibid., 89–96.

41. Mandel, *High-Risk Society*, 135–36, quote on 135.

42. Moody, *Workers in a Lean World*, 97–101.

43. "Trade Climate Changes Fast Now, Executive Says," *Richmond Times-Dispatch*, June 10, 1996.

44. "Schools Overhaul: Gearing Up for a Strong Economy," *Richmond News-Leader*, January 3, 1991.

45. Daniel Nelson, "Virginia's Next Governor Must Lead the State into the Global Marketplace," *Virginian-Pilot*, August 22, 1993. The *Newport News Daily Press* made the same urgent case in 1992: "Better skills translate into higher-paying jobs. Businesses raise their competitiveness if they can perform more complex functions. If more incentives are provided business to create lucrative jobs, the next decade should see more workers earning their way to the good life." This argument became standard fare in Virginia as well as national newspapers covering the changing economy. The argument was consistent: the business climate was changing, becoming increasingly technological and demanding higher skills levels from employees; the changes were ineluctable and required immediate action by government in cooperation with business. The failure to adjust, to raise skill levels as dictated by transnational, information technology businesses would result in economic disaster. The key and unquestioned assumption was that the state and society had no power to control or modify these forces. See "Changing Fortune: Businesses, Educators Should Upgrade Work Force," *Newport News Daily Press*, September 6, 1992.

46. "Final Report of the Joint Subcommittee Studying the Labor Force Needs of the 1990s to the Governor and the General Assembly of Virginia," 1–10.

47. Governor's Advisory Committee, "The Virginia Plan for Strengthening the Commonwealth's 21st Century Workforce," 1–2.

48. Penn, "Take This Job . . . And Love It!" 38.

49. Ibid., 39.

50. Ibid., 41.

51. Ibid., 44.

52. Penn, "Productivity Pros," 58.

53. Frederick, "Magnum Work Force," 57.

54. Penn, "Take This Job and . . . And Love It!" 38.

55. Ibid., 41, 44, both quotes on 41.

56. Penn, "Productivity Pros," 54, 56.

57. Ibid., 54–56, quotes on 56.

58. Anderson, "Hidden Valley," 24.

59. Gerring, "Counting the Costs," 38.

60. Frederick, "Magnum Work Force," 59.

61. Ibid., 25.

62. Ibid., 25, 21.

63. Penn, "Take This Job . . . And Love It!" 41.

64. Penn, "Productivity Pros," 52.

65. Anderson, "Hidden Valley," 21.

66. Ibid., 25.

67. Frederick, "Magnum Work Force," 57–58.

68. Ibid., 57–59.

69. Uchitelle, *The Disposable American*, 13.

70. Anderson, "Quest for Quality," 28–29, 36.

71. Ibid., 36.

72. Frederick, "Magnum Work Force," 59.

73. Larance, "The Comeback Trail," 18.

74. Chip Jones, "Retraining Revolution: How Richmonders Are Staying One Step Ahead of a Pink Slip," *Richmond Times-Dispatch*, September 6, 1993.

75. "At Dupont, Global Economic Math Equals Local Pain: Bitter Union Says Workers Being Sacrificed as Company Says It Has to Recognize Realities," *Richmond Times-Dispatch*, July 18, 1993.

76. "Team-Building Is on the Wane—Downsizing Discourages It, Expert Says," *Richmond Times-Dispatch*, May 25, 1998.

77. Rinehart, Huxley, and Robertson, *Just Another Car Factory?*, 58–62, quote on 57.

78. Ibid., 87; Lewchuk and Robertson, "Production without Empowerment," 37–64.

79. Rinehart, Huxley, and Robertson, 85–107, quote on 107.

80. Ibid., 124–56, quotes in sequence on 128 and 203–4.

81. Paul Bradley, "Northern Virginia's Poor Defined," *Richmond Times-Dispatch*, August 13, 1992.

82. Conway, "Welcome to the Real World," Southern Growth Policies Board, October 11, 2002, available at www.southern.org/pubs/realworld.

83. "Northern Virginia's Poor Defined," *Richmond Times-Dispatch*, August 13, 1992; in celebrating the possibilities that Richmond might become "Silicon South" journalist

Elizabeth Corcoran pointed out the chronic need for additional investment in education and in coordinating business. Interestingly, Corcoran's exaltation of Virginia's high-tech potential was cased in an announcement of Motorola's plan to build a $3 billion semiconductor plant close to Richmond, a deal that never materialized but which cost the state millions in incentives. See "Planting a Seed of Silicon: Experts See High-Tech Nurturing Role for Virginia," *Washington Post*, April 13, 1995.

84. Knapp, "Virginia's Economy in the 1990s," 2–3. Lon Wagoner pointed out that job growth in Roanoke and entire state came primarily in "business and health care service jobs," which are often disparaged as "low pay positions." See "Va. Job Growth Most Robust in 90s," *Roanoke Times*, July 14, 1994.

Chapter 3. After the Deluge

1. "VA. Recession Rated the Worst," *Newport News Daily Press*, March 2, 1992.

2. Knapp, "Virginia's Economy in the 1990s," 2.

3. Reich, *I'll Be Short*, 14–15. As Steven Pearlstein explained it in the *Washington Post*, "Prevailing norms of behavior that had tied employees to their firms—and to one another—have been swept aside: Partnerships have crumbled, and loyalty has become a deeply discounted commodity. In the jargon of professional sports, everyone is now a free agent." See "New Economy Gives Work a Hard Edge," *Washington Post*, November 14, 1995.

4. Harrison and Bluestone, *The Great U-Turn*, 22–26.

5. Uchitelle, *The Disposable American*, 7.

6. "The R Word Hit Home in Area in 1990," *Richmond Times-Dispatch*, December 31, 1990; Galbraith, *A Journey Through Economic Time*, 228–31. Unemployment figures for Virginia in Knapp, "Recent Developments in the Virginia Economy," 5.

7. "Va., U.S. Economies Get More Bad News: State Is Lagging Behind Nation, Crestar Index Says," *Richmond Times-Dispatch*, September 4, 1993.

8. "Is the Recession Over? Economists Say 'Yes,' but Richmonders Aren't So Sure. Maybe," *Richmond Times-Dispatch*, December 28, 1992.

9. Ibid.

10. "Dominion Bank Cuts 500 Jobs—About 50 in Roanoke to Lose Out," *Roanoke Times*, January 16, 1992.

11. John Levin, "It'll Take Time to Fill the Seats," *Roanoke Times*, November 15, 1992.

12. Thomas Silvestri, "This Job Market Isn't for the Meek," *Richmond Times-Dispatch*, September 15, 1991. William J. Baumol, Alan S. Blinder, and Edward N. Wolff—all of whom are economists—suggest that the ever-increasing subjection of American society to marketplace forces may have played a role in advancing corporate downsizing. Although they attribute corporate downsizing to other economic forces, they admit that "the elevation of shareholder value to primacy among a firm's possible goals" has influenced attitudes toward labor. Labor is increasingly considered another exchangeable commodity "whose price and conditions of employment are determined by supply-demand conditions and nothing else." Baumol, Blinder, and Wolff, *Downsizing in America*, 20–21.

13. Gerring, "Surviving the Workforce Famine," 41–42.

14. Lane, Mikelson, Sharkey, Wissoker, "Low-Income and Low-Skilled Workers' Involvement in Nonstandard Employment."

15. Gerring, "Surviving the Workforce Famine," 41.

16. Bruce Potter, "Dealers Have All the Aces in This Game: Job Seekers Are Beggars, Employers Are Choosers in Competitive Job Market," *Richmond Times-Dispatch*, September 20, 1992.

17. Jann Malone, "The Severing of Deep Roots after the Layoff: Six Jobs, Three Cities," *Richmond Times-Dispatch*, May 31, 1998.

18. Pearlstein, "New Economy Gives Workers a Hard Edge."

19. Ibid.

20. Harrison and Bluestone, *The Great U-Turn*, 22–26.

21. Ibid.; R. Brenner, "The Economy of Global Turbulence," 190–200.

22. Cohen, *The Politics of Globalization in the United States*, 109.

23. Luttwak, "Will Success Spoil America?"

24. Baumol, Blinder, and Wolff, *Downsizing in America*, 261–62.

25. R. Brenner, 199–200.

26. Ibid.

27. Levin, "It'll Take Time to Fill the Seats." This is a point which economist R. A. Blecker corroborates. The recovery in 1992 was decidedly sluggish, as the economy registered an abysmal 2.6 percent GDP growth rate in comparison to the 3.9 percent rate logged in 1983 following the Reagan recession. In this recovery, workers who had been dismissed were not invited back. Their jobs had been downsized or outsourced. While government spending was eliminated to control the deficit, private sector spending stagnated and exports declined. Virginia was not immune to what Blecker described as "the most prolonged contraction since the 1930s." See Blecker, "The New Economic Stagnation and the Contradictions of Economic Policy Making."

28. Silvestri, "This Job Market Isn't for the Meek."

29. C. Jones, "Retraining Revolution: How Richmonders Are Staying One Step Ahead of a Pink Slip," *Richmond Times-Dispatch*, September 6, 1993.

30. Jeremy Rifkin illustrated this bleak but compelling picture in *The Age of Access*, chapter 2. Rifkin has been criticized for exaggerating the obsolescence of manufacturing and manual labor, but his larger point is convincing. What was emerging was not so a "virtual" economy but one oriented almost exclusively to service, which rendered people, work traditions, and the dignity of labor inconsequential. What mattered was providing an "experience" for paying customers, even if that involved webs of degradation and exploitation hidden by the smooth surfaces and artificial smiles of customer service. Rifkin's important point is not the disappearance of the corporation, but the advent of a service economy predicated on outsourcing, tenuous employment, customer sovereignty, and the commodification of almost all human relationships.

31. Steven Pearlstein, "Job Losses Likely to Continue—Business Upheaval Hobbles Recovery," *Washington Post*, November 6, 1992.

32. "The South at Work," 14–18.

33. Ibid.

34. Quoted in Silvestri, "This Job Market Isn't for the Meek."

35. Tom Kazas, "Coping with Career Change: Middle Managers Faced with Layoffs Find Help in Looking for Employment Alternatives," *Richmond Times-Dispatch*, December 30, 1991; see also Gardner, "The 1990–1991 Labor Market," 3–11.

36. John Levin, "It'll Take Time to Fill the Seats."

37. Quoted in Kromm, "The Globalization Game," 24.

38. George Kegley, "This Recession Catches Those in the Middle," *Roanoke Times*, June 30, 1991.

39. Ibid.

40. Kazas, "Coping With Career Change."

41. Ibid. Thomas Silvestri certainly admitted that the job market was "tough" and that the "bean-counter theory" had reduced workers to "costs" that should be eliminated in the interest of business competition. But in suggesting that the Virginia job market was not for the "disorganized," the "meek," and the easily discouraged, Silvestri subconsciously reflected the dominant values of the ruthless brand of capitalism that gained ascendancy in the 1990s. What few journalists were willing to do, and what evidently workers were ready to articulate, was conscious opposition to a system that commodified and disposed of people while claiming that "trimming the fat" and "right sizing" served the public interest. See also "After Layoff, Consulting Firm Steps In," *Richmond Times-Dispatch*, October 14, 1991.

42. Daniel J. Curtain, Bureau of Labor Statistics, "Extended Mass Layoff Events and Separations for Virginia, Private Non-Farm, 1996–2006," table included in e-mail to author, Tuesday, April 10, 2007, 10:07 a.m.; data on 1995 included in e-mail to author, Tuesday, April 10, 2007, 11:46 a.m.

43. Bob Rayner, "Why Me? What's Next? After Shock Subsides, Some Find Opportunity," *Richmond Times-Dispatch*, May 26, 1998.

44. Mary Beausoleil, "'Community' Is Gone: Ex–Bank Workers Feel Loss of One Another," *Richmond Times-Dispatch*, May 25, 1998.

45. Rayner, "Why Me? What's Next?"

46. Quoted in ibid.

47. Robin Farmer, "A Loss of Purpose: Depression, Frustration Become Companions," *Richmond Times-Dispatch*, May 27, 1998.

48. Helwig, "Worker Displacement in a Strong Labor Market," 13–28.

49. Ilg and Haugen, "Earning and Employment Trends in the 1990s," 21–33.

50. Statistics quoted in Johnson, *The Best of Times*, 465.

51. Beausoleil, "'Community' Is Gone."

52. Newman, "Troubled Times," 337.

53. Chip Jones, "Surviving a Layoff: How One Man Copes with Job Loss," *Richmond Times-Dispatch*, December 27, 1993.

54. Kazas, "Coping with Career Change."

55. Silvestri, "This Job Market Isn't for the Meek."

56. Tom Kazas cites at least two cases where people took advantage of downsizing to launch their own businesses. What we don't know is how successful these ventures were in the long run and precisely how many displaced workers had the resources to go

into business for themselves. Certainly many turned to "consulting," a glamorous name for working on a contract with no long-term prospects.

57. Levin, "It'll Take Time to Fill the Seats."

58. Henwood, *After the New Economy*, 152–53.

59. Levin, "It'll Take Time to Fill The Seats."

60. Piven, "Neoliberal Social Policy and Labor Market Discipline," 120–21.

61. Taylor-White, "Hugh D. Keogh on How and Why We Have the Ability to Meet the Needs of Prospects," 8.

62. Potter, "Dealers Have All the Aces in This Game."

63. C. Jones, "Retraining Revolution."

64. Head, *The New Ruthless Economy*, 14, 6.

65. Ibid., 14, 68–71.

66. Ibid., 14, 68–69.

67. Ibid.

68. Uchitelle, *The Disposable American*, 64–67, quote on 66; "A Difficult Lesson: Job Retraining, though Touted, Often Fails the Test," *Washington Post*, April 16, 2004.

69. Tilly, *Monthly Labor Review*, 10–18, quotes on 10 and 16.

70. C. Jones, "Retraining Revolution."

71. Gene Marlowe, "Era Reinvents Careers: With Up to 7 Moves Likely, Workers Need New Thinking, Flexibility," *Richmond Times-Dispatch* April 3, 1994. All quotes in this paragraph.

72. As Beausoleil points out, the team building that became popular in the 1970s ran headlong into the efficiency-minded downsizing assault of the 1990s. Corporate restructuring undermined any sense of loyalty to the company, encouraged an environment of anomie driven by reckless intra-office competition, and discouraged those employees who remained. See "Team-Building Is on the Wane: Downsizing Discourages It, Expert Says," *Richmond Times-Dispatch*, May 25, 1998.

73. In one of the better management-advice-type books that crowded the shelves in the 1990s, Lesley Wright and Marti Smye discussed, among other topics, the "culture of sacrifice" that encouraged employees to consistently subordinate personal interests and career objectives to the needs of the corporation. "In the Culture of Sacrifice, people are driven by feelings of responsibility to the company. This is particularly true for those who link loss of performance with loss of self-esteem." The authors use the hackneyed term "workaholic" to describe a situation that had little to do with subjective mental conditions. What they were identifying was a hegemonic arrangement whereby employees were trained to equate independence, moderately paced work, time off from the office, and resistance to petulant customer demands with indolence and ineffectiveness. As the authors write, "If they slow down or relax, they worry they will be seen as slackers or incompetents. In their quest to be 'good enough,' they draw themselves and others into a working frenzy that focuses on quantity rather than quality, aggressively pushing the company and fellow workers to the point of collapse." Of course, the New Economy, corporate downsizing, Total Quality Management, and the other ingredients of lean production had already made quantitative measurements the standard for assessing productivity. Wright and Smye, *Corporate Abuse*, 81–82.

74. Marlowe, "Era Reinvents Careers."

75. Ibid.

76. Van Costen, "Global Capitalism Victimizes Many," *Norfolk Virginian-Pilot*, September 21, 1994.

77. "After the Downsizing, Who Will Buy? Labor Today," *Norfolk Virginian-Pilot*, September 4, 1995.

78. Greider, "The Future Is Now," 25.

79. John Cunniff, "Trickledown Theory Trickling Out," *Roanoke Times*, May 12, 1992.

80. "Workers' Year Ending in Carnage of Layoffs," *Roanoke Times*, November 16, 1995.

81. Cunniff, "Trickledown Theory Trickling Out."

82. As Julie Hatch and Angela Clinton demonstrate, low inflation and consumer confidence sparked monumental job growth throughout the 1990s. At least in their analysis, productivity increased and real wages showed some improvement. Yet they also suggest that the service industry, with business services leading the way, accounted for over 90 percent of the job development in this era. Construction growth helped to balance out the devastating losses in manufacturing and mining. The average wages of workers in insurance, finance, real estate, and wholesale trade exceeded those of employees in manufacturing, yet this was as much an expression of how bad things had gotten in manufacturing as how good they had become in those other fields. Only workers in retail trade and services earned less on average than manufacturing workers. Yet here is the key: business services led the way in job creation, with "personnel supply services" (temporary agencies) the most robust. Hatch and Clinton, "Job Growth in the 1990s," 3–18. Yet even if we allow for the greatest growth in highly skilled temporary workers, the greatest proportion of them were working for less than full time and with fewer benefits. As Ken Hudson pointed out in a study for the Economic Policy Institute, "Employers argue that these jobs (also called contingent work) provide the flexibility needed to be competitive. But these perceived advantages notwithstanding, as of 1997, most nonstandard workers, on average, were paid less, were less likely to receive health insurance or a pension, and had less job security than workers in regular full-time jobs. The disparities between nonstandard and regular full-time persist even when comparing workers with similar personal, educational, and job characteristics." Job growth in the tenuous business services area did not necessarily lead to secure positions that equitably remunerated workers. K. Hudson, "No Shortage of 'Nonstandard' Jobs."

83. Mollie Gore, "The Other Economy: Area Job Growth Obscures Pain of Thousands Put Out of Work," *Richmond Times-Dispatch*, May 24, 1998

84. Ibid.

85. Howard Owen, "Readers Reply: We're Stressed, Anxious about Holding Onto Jobs," *Richmond Times-Dispatch*, June 7, 1998.

86. Ibid.

87. Luttwak, "Will Success Spoil America?"

Chapter 4. Wealth against Commonwealth

1. For more on the Pittston Strike, particularly on the way in which it highlighted a network of labor laws designed to protect corporate interests and state prerogatives, but also on the year-long action as an example of labor's ability to exploit political opportunities to achieve considerable gain, see Brisbin, *A Strike Like No Other Strike,* particularly chapter 11, titled "The Power of Law and the Effectiveness of Resistance." Of course, Pittston was not the only strike of significance in the early years of the decade. For the conditions of the settlement, which once again highlighted the difficulties facing both workers and corporations in managing the rising costs of a private health insurance system, see "A Healthy Settlement for Mine Workers: Pittston Strikers Won Big, but the Fight over Retiree Benefits Has Just Begun," *U.S. News and World Report,* January 15, 1990. Of course, the Pittston Strike was not the only major work action in the early years of the 1990s. A United Steelworkers' strike at the Ravenswood Aluminum Plant in 1989 which lasted for almost two years produced a contract that resolved most of the issues that precipitated the strike, foremost of which was corporate restructuring in the interest of greater employee flexibility. According to authors Tom Juravich and Kate Bronfenbrenner, this strike succeeded where others did not because of the "connections between rank-and-file militancy and participation, strategic pressure, and top union support." With this winning combination, the Steelworkers contributed immeasurably to the rejuvenation of labor in the 1990s. See Juravich and Bronfenbrenner, *Ravenswood,* as well as Draper, "No Retreat, No Surrender."

2. "The South at Work: An Institute Report," 19; Lichtenstein, *State of the Union,* 238–45. Michael Zweig explains the drive for labor-management cooperation as part of the corporate movement to persuade organized workers to accept concessions in the first place. In other words, claims of democracy and participation in the workplace eased the transition toward reduced wages and reduced union power: "Management had another goal for these cooperative programs: to smooth the way for the concessions capitalists were demanding from unions at the time. Management used the offer of cooperation . . . to sweeten their demands for wage-cuts, changes in work rules that weakened worker protections, stepped-up subcontracting, and other steps that reversed decades of union gains." Zweig, *The Working Class Majority,* 117.

3. "Can Labor Unions Rebound? In Hampton Roads and Across the U.S., the Labor Movement Has Been Fading," *Virginian-Pilot,* October 29, 1995.

4. Larry J. Sabato, "Chuck Robb Faces a Defining Vote on the Striker Replacement Bill," *Richmond Times-Dispatch,* July 26, 1993.

5. Ibid.

6. Thomas R. McNutt, "Another View: Labor Not Wild about Wilder," *Virginian-Pilot,* May 3, 1991.

7. Spears, "Nissan Is Not the Norm," 40.

8. Ibid., 42.

9. Grim, "So You Thought Unions Were Dead in Virginia?" 54.

10. Glasmeier and Leichenko, "From Free-Market Rhetoric to Free-Market Reality," 30–31, quote on 19.

11. Ibid., 31.

12. Eckman et al., "Job Equity in the Downsized South," 9.

13. Ibid.

14. Ibid., 10.

15. Neil Cornish, "Grocery Union Comes Back for Seconds: UFCW Tries Again to Make an Inroad into Hampton Roads," *Newport News Daily Press*, October 22, 1990.

16. Jay Hancock, "Fighting Over the Grocery Store Workers, Union Face Off Like Never Before," *Virginian-Pilot*, October 22, 1990.

17. Ibid.

18. Peter T. Kilborn, "Union Testing Its Strength against Grocers," *Roanoke Times*, October 28, 1990.

19. Joe Taylor, "Union Vows to Appeal Be-Lo Vote," *Richmond Times-Dispatch*, March 22, 1991.

20. "Jackson Says 'Rise Together': Organizing Grocery Workers Addressed," *Roanoke Times*, May 13, 1990.

21. Ibid.

22. John Witt, "At Rally, Jackson Urges Grocery Workers to Unite," *Richmond Times-Dispatch*, May 12, 1990.

23. Neil Cornish, "Jackson Lends Support to Union Drive: Grocery Official, Activist Confer," *Newport News Daily Press*, May 12, 1990.

24. Witt, "At Rally, Jackson Urges Grocery Workers to Unite." Supermarket mergers and the growth of "superstores" was characteristic of the industry in the early 1990s. The total number of supermarkets in the United States fell from 26,815 in 1980 to 24,548 in 1993. Kaufman, "Fewer but Larger Supermarkets," 26–29.

25. Ibid.

26. Kilborn, "Union Testing Its Strength against Grocers."

27. Cornish, "Grocery Union Comes Back for Seconds."

28. Zweig, *The Working Class Majority*, 123–125, quote on 125.

29. Hancock, "Fighting Over the Grocery Store Workers."

30. Ibid.

31. Cornish, "Grocery Union Comes Back for Seconds."

32. Ibid.

33. Kilborn, "Union Testing Its Strength against Grocers."

34. Hancock, "Fighting Over the Grocery Store Workers."

35. Ibid.

36. Windham, "Will Unions Organize the South?" 22–24.

37. Hancock, "Fighting Over the Grocery Store Workers."

38. "Union Claims Area Groceries Harassing Workers, Organizers," *Newport News Daily Press*, May 11, 1990.

39. Cornish, "Grocery Union Comes Back for Seconds."

40. Kilborn, "Union Testing Its Strength against Grocers."

41. Jay Hancock, "Be-Lo Workers Voting on Union Today—Election Viewed As Test of Organized Labor Strength," *Virginian-Pilot*, March 21, 1991.

42. Ibid.

43. Jay Hancock, "Be-Lo Workers Turn Away Union," *Virginian-Pilot*, March 22, 1991.

44. Hancock, "Be-Lo Workers Turn Away Union."

45. Ibid.

46. "Union Vows to Appeal Be-Lo Vote," *Richmond Times-Dispatch*, March 22, 1991.

47. Neil Cornish, "Be-Lo Workers Refuse Union—UFCW's Effort to Represent 800 Employees Fails 377–220," *Newport News Daily Press*, March 22, 1991.

48. Hancock, "Food Workers' Union Campaign Turns Bitter," *Virginian-Pilot*, May 9, 1991.

49. Ibid.

50. Eleena de Lisser, "Be-Lo Asks Judges to Let Pickets Back on Property," *Virginian-Pilot*, December 11, 1991.

51. Joann Frohman, "Pickets to Be Back at Be-Lo Stores," *Newport News Daily Press*, December 11, 1991.

52. Hancock, "Food Workers' Union Campaign Turns Bitter."

53. While the Reverend Rudolph Smith claimed that Be-Lo sold out-of-date products, and while two Be-Lo workers corroborated Smith's accusations by admitting that they had removed expired products prior to a Department of Agriculture inspection, the department itself found nothing unusual to report. Smith believed that managers had been notified of the inspection and cleared away out-of-date product before the inspection took place. Hancock, "Food Workers' Campaign Turns Bitter." In any case, the allegations of higher prices—which the store could probably justify because of the higher rent and operating costs of a downtown location versus the economy of scale enjoyed in larger, newer suburban locations—and sub-par food only confused the issues at stake in the union organizing drive.

54. See "Hampton Roads' 2001 Year in Business," *Virginian-Pilot*, December 30, 2001, which details Be-Lo's inability to compete against Food Lion and Farm Fresh, part of a much larger story of consolidation in the grocery and retail industry.

55. Ibid.

56. "National Labor Relations Board Decision and Order, Be Lo Stores and United Food and Commercial Workers Union, Local 400, AFL-CIO," July 31, 1995, p. 16, available at http://www.nlrb.gov/shared_files/Board%20Decisions/318/318-1.pdf, accessed May 11, 2008, 3:20 p.m. (hereafter cited as NLRB Be-Lo Decision).

57. Ibid., 14.

58. Ibid., 15.

59. Ibid., 15.

60. Ibid., 15–17.

61. Bronfenbrenner, "We'll Close!" 51.

62. Ibid., 52.

63. Peckenham, "Confessions of a Union Buster," 35.

64. Ibid.

65. Minchin, *Fighting Against the Odds*, 150–51.

66. NLRB Be-Lo decision, 20.

67. Ibid.

68. Ibid., 3.

69. Ibid., 15.

70. Stephanie Stoughton, "National Labor Relations Board Rules Against Be-Lo," *Virginian-Pilot*, August 5, 1995.

71. *Be-Lo Stores v. National Labor Relations Board*, United States Court of Appeals, Fourth Circuit Court, in *Labor Relations Reference Manual: The Law of Labor Relations, Volume 156* (Washington, D.C.: Bureau of National Affairs, 1998) 2274–75, (hereafter abbreviated as U.S. Court of Appeals Be-Lo Decision and cited as 156 LRRM).

72. Ibid., 156 LRRM 2275.

73. Ibid., 156 LRRM 2277.

74. Ibid., 156 LRRM 2277–156 LRRM 2278.

75. Ibid., 156 LRRM 2278.

76. Ibid., 156 LRRM 2270.

77. Ibid., 156 LRRM 2264.

78. Ibid., 156 LRRM 2278.

79. Ibid., 156 LRRM 2279.

80. Ibid., 156 LRRM 2280.

81. Ibid., 156 LRRM 2289, first quote; 156 LRRM 2277, second quote.

82. Ibid., 156 LRRM 2295.

83. Bronfenbrenner, "We'll Close!" 53.

84. Compa, "Unfair Advantage."

85. Abramson, "The Uncertain Fate of *Gissel* Bargaining Orders in the Circuit Court of Appeals."

86. U.S. Court of Appeals Be-Lo Decision, 156 LRRM 2293, footnote #14.

87. Brody, *Labor Embattled*, 152.

88. Compa, "Unfair Advantage," 26.

89. Brody, *Labor Embattled*, 152.

90. Ibid., 143.

91. Grim, "So You Thought Unions Were Dead in Virginia?" 57.

92. Stephanie Stoughton, "Meatland, Food City Workers Reject Union Representation," *Virginian-Pilot*, April 15, 1995.

93. Jeff Sturgeon, "UMW Accuses Dupont, Workers Testify to Intimidation," *Roanoke Times*, January 6, 1995.

94. Stephanie Stoughton, "Union Says Supermarkets Have 'Threatened' Workers in Weeks Leading Up to Vote," *Virginian Pilot*, April 12, 1991.

95. "Food Workers' Union Vows to Try Again," *Richmond Times-Dispatch*, March 23, 1991.

96. As Thom Hartmann pointed out, mergers and acquisitions drove one-third of the Fortune 500 companies listed for 1980 out of existence by 1990. Between 1990 and 1995, two-fifths of the Fortune 500 companies disappeared for the same reason. As for economic influence, the 200 largest corporations, which employ fewer than 0.8 percent of the world's workers, are responsible for more than 27 percent of global economic activity. As for the political influence of corporations versus labor unions, Hartmann

offers the following: "The 82 largest American corporations contributed $33,045,832 to political action committees in the year-2000 election cycle . . . outspending labor unions 15 to 1." This concentration of corporate wealth parallels the maldistribution of wealth in the United States. In 1976, the wealthiest 10 percent of Americans owned 50 percent of the nation's resources. By 1997, they controlled 73 percent. As Hartmann points out, this shift of wealth from the middle and working to the upper class was not simply a product of economic growth. Americans are working longer hours and performing multiple jobs for less money. Between 1973 and 1998, the hourly wages of nonsupervisory employees dropped by 9 percent, from $14.09 to $12.77. For a stark illustration of this polarization of wealth, Hartmann points to this statistic: in 2000, the leading 1 percent of American households had accrued more wealth "than that of the bottom 95 percent combined." Hartmann, *Unequal Protection*, 204–5.

97. Dave Mayfield, "Labor: Leverage in New Lines?" *Virginian-Pilot*, April 1, 1991.

98. Grim, "So You Thought Unions Were Dead in Virginia?" 57.

99. Michael Buettner, "Getting Organized after a Lull, Unions Are Back," *Richmond Times-Dispatch*, April 15, 1991.

100. Ibid.

101. Moberg, "Labor Faces the Twenty-First Century," 22.

102. Babson, *The Unfinished Struggle*, 158.

103. Ibid.

104. Nicholson, *Labor's Story in the United States*, 322.

105. "Labor Wants More Effort on Striker Bill," *Roanoke Times*, February 24, 1994.

106. "Striker Bill Is Bad for Business—Robb Should Vote No," *Virginian-Pilot*, May 15, 1994.

107. "Striking Out," *Richmond Times-Dispatch*, July 14, 1994.

108. Lichtenstein, *State of the Union*, 174.

109. Ibid., 176–77.

110. "The Union Label," *Richmond Times-Dispatch*, May 18, 1994.

111. Greg Edwards, "Union Research Found That While the Average Pay for U.S. Industrial Workers Increased 2.6 percent Last Year, the Pay for Chief Executive Officers of Fortune 500 Companies Was Up 35 Percent," *Richmond Times-Dispatch*, September 7, 1998.

112. Duncan Adams, "Western Virginia's Economy Headed Nowhere, Study Says," *Roanoke Times*, November 19, 2000.

113. Mylene Mangalindan, "Hampton Roads Residents Say the Middle Class Has Taken a Beating," *Virginian-Pilot*, September 24, 1995.

114. "Widening Income Gap Poses Problems Ahead for the Working Class," *Virginian-Pilot*, August 19, 1990.

115. G. D. Lewis, "Assessing Jesse Jackson's Union Plea," *Virginian-Pilot*, May 26, 1990.

116. Thomas R. McNutt, "Why Unions Are Needed," *Virginian-Pilot*, June 6, 1990.

117. Jerry L. Hufton, "Unions Aid Workers," *Virginian-Pilot*, June 6, 1990.

118. Metzgar, *Striking Steel*, 142–48.

119. Ibid.

120. Rosa P. White, "Union Helps Workers," *Virginian-Pilot*, June 5, 1990.

121. Ibid.

122. Bernard F. Hopkins, "Unions Make Sense," *Virginian-Pilot*, June 11, 1990.

123. Brody, *Labor Embattled*, 86–87.

124. Thomas McNutt, "Striker Bill Would Help Labor and U.S.," *Virginian-Pilot*, May 20, 1994.

125. Lauch Faircloth, "Labor's Strike Bill: 'Pure Economic Poison,'" *Virginian-Pilot*, June 13, 1994.

126. Bruce Woolridge, "Striker Bill Would Protect Dignity," *Virginian-Pilot*, June 25, 1994.

127. "Bill Barring Replacement of Strikers Fails in Senate," *Richmond Times-Dispatch*, July 13, 1994.

128. Andrew Herod, *Labor Geographies: Workers and the Landscapes of Capitalism* (New York: Guilford Press, 2001), 259–60.

129. Arthur R. Poskocil, "Right-to-Work Laws Don't Exist to Benefit Workers," *Roanoke Times*, July 10, 1999.

130. Philip Hawks, "Unions Bring Justice to the Workplace," *Roanoke Times*, July 22, 1999.

131. Eileen Huey, "Another View: VA. Workers Treated as Second-Class Citizens," *Virginian-Pilot*, August 3, 1998.

132. Ibid.

Chapter 5. Trading in Southern Futures

1. As Mark Rupert explains, this tendency to assert the normative and objective character of market forces represents the "hegemony of abstract individualism among American economists and those under their intellectual influence." This belief in the apolitical, absolute character of the marketplace gave defenders of NAFTA additional legitimacy, since they could position themselves as scientific experts interpreting the plan according to the inexorable tendencies of the free market economy rather than as political partisans. Opponents were conversely considered soft-headed neophytes who operated according to "emotion" rather than "reason." Rupert, *Ideologies of Globalization*, 56–57.

2. Cohen, *The Politics of Globalization in the United States*, 96–97.

3. Ibid., 100.

4. Ibid.

5. Ibid., 102.

6. "Emotional Battle Brewing Over U.S.-Mexico Trade Pact," *Washington Post*, April 21, 1991.

7. This coalition also included most state governors. Doug Wilder, governor of Virginia, initially expressed reservations about the agreement, then reversed himself, and then condemned the agreement in late August 1993 in an apparent bid for union support in a future senate race. See "Wilder Assails Free Trade Agreement," *Washington Post*, August 28, 1993. Governor Ann Richards of Texas captured the sentiments of most state executives: "NAFTA is being used as a whipping boy to express fears . . . about

jobs leaving America. They . . . want to strike out at something. . . . They say if you're against NAFTA, you will stop jobs from leaving America. Nothing can be further from the truth." According to a Heritage Foundation report, 41 of 50 governors supported the agreement. See " . . . And Not Just South of the Border," *Washington Post*, August 19, 1993.

8. Rupert, *Ideologies of Globalization*, 58.

9. Gerald Meadows, "Trade Agreement Condones Corporate Misbehavior," *Roanoke Times*, August 16, 1993.

10. Dreiling, "The Class Embeddedness of Corporate Political Action," 42–43.

11. "How Do You Spell NAFTA? In Virginia, It's Jobs," *Richmond Times-Dispatch*, November 16, 1993.

12. Ibid.

13. "A Tough Sell: NAFTA Promises to Bring Greater Prosperity to All," *Roanoke Times*, November 11, 1993.

14. Ibid.

15. Ibid.

16. Steven Pearlstein, "Trade Tales: But Biggest Effect May Be on Low-Skill Workers' Pay," *Washington Post*, October 31, 1993.

17. Marsha Mercer, "Showdown over NAFTA: Clinton Courts GOP, Labor Threatens Ill Will," *Richmond Times-Dispatch*, November 17, 1993.

18. "Down to the Wire: A Vote for NAFTA Reaffirms American Strengths," *Newport News Daily Press*, November 16, 1993.

19. "Embrace the Future: Free Trade Agreement in Nation's Best Interests," *Newport News Daily Press*, November 7, 1993.

20. Gene Marlowe, "NAFTA: Here's a Look at What It Is and What It Isn't," *Richmond Times-Dispatch*, November 14, 1993.

21. Rupert, *Ideologies of Globalization*, 59.

22. "Al Gore vs. Ross Perot: NAFTA's the Winner," *Norfolk Virginian-Pilot*, November 6, 1993.

23. "A Tough Sell: NAFTA Promises to Bring Greater Prosperity to All."

24. Mercer, "Showdown over NAFTA."

25. "Embrace the Future: Free Trade Agreement in Nation's Best Interest."

26. Ross Mackenzie, "Economics and Politics: A Major Clinton Movement," *Richmond Times-Dispatch*, November 21, 1993.

27. Ibid.

28. Hawkins, "The Wreck of the Free Trade Model Engenders Myths and Falsehoods."

29. "Past as Prologue," *Richmond Times-Dispatch*, November 16, 1993.

30. Moody, "NAFTA and the Corporate Redesign of North America," 103. Political scientists Stephen D. Morris and John Passe-Smith make the point that Mexican political and ideological alignments closely followed American developments in the 1980s. "Just as deep structural economic changes in Mexico during the past decade correspond closely to the needs of the U.S. economy and the demands of global capital . . . the ideological shift championed by Salinas reflects a renewed cultural/ideological hege-

mony on the part of the United States." This "hemispheric consensus" included "the importance of (1) maintaining a cheap labor supply to draw foreign direct investment (new factor mixing), (2) creating new and uninhibited financial opportunities for global capital (emerging capital markets), (3) reorienting the role of the state away from social needs or Keynesian policies toward greater attention to the protection of private property" and countenancing the resulting social inequalities. What is important to realize, though, is that this hemispheric and "Washington" consensus continued to apply to the American South, the original destination for American corporate outsourcing. So while American policymakers claimed to promote communications and information systems as the substitute for lost manufacturing jobs, they collaborated with southern politicians and business leaders from both regions in maintaining Virginia's status as a low-wage, tax-free, unregulated sanctuary for corporate capital. Morris and Passe-Smith, "What a Difference a Crisis Makes," 127.

31. Gerald L. Baliles, "NAFTA Would Help Americans," *Virginian-Pilot*, October 18, 1993.

32. "Fighting the Past, Economist Says of NAFTA," *Roanoke Times*, November 18, 1993.

33. Cohen, *The Politics of Globalization in the United States*, 103.

34. Ibid., 103–4, quote on 104.

35. Bruce Potter, "Push Support for NAFTA, Forum Urged," *Richmond Times-Dispatch*, November 6, 1993.

36. Ibid.

37. Lon Wagoner, "Salem GE Leader Spreads the Word," *Roanoke Times*, November 13, 1993.

38. Potter, "Push Support for NAFTA, Forum Urged."

39. Wagoner, "Salem GE Leader Spreads the Word."

40. George Grayson, "Free Trade Means More Business for VA.," *Virginian-Pilot*, September 10, 1993.

41. Gitlin, *Media Unlimited*, 8–11, 165, 175.

42. "NAFTA: State Lawmakers' Opinions Mixed," *Richmond Times-Dispatch*, September 18, 1993.

43. Ibid.; "Boucher to Oppose NAFTA Out of Concern for Jobs," *Roanoke Times*, November 6, 1993.

44. "Payne for NAFTA," *Richmond Times-Dispatch*, October 28, 1993.

45. "Vow Came on Heels of Payne's Decision: He Denies NAFTA Support Prompted Clinton 'Reward,'" *Richmond Times-Dispatch*, November 12, 1993.

46. Ibid.; see also "Payne Withholding Judgment on North American Trade Deal," *Richmond Times-Dispatch*, September 8, 1993.

47. "Payne's Behind Free-Trade Pact," *Roanoke Times*, October 26, 1993.

48. "Vow Came on Heels of Payne's Decision."

49. "White House Offers Deals, Wins Converts," *Washington Times*, November 17, 1993.

50. "Payne's Behind Free Trade Pact."

51. "Payne for NAFTA."

52. "Payne's Behind Free Trade Pact."

53. "Residents Voice Disapproval of NAFTA: A Local Branch of United We Stand America Demonstrated against Pact," *Virginian-Pilot*, November 14, 1993.

54. Moody, *Workers in a Lean World*, 95.

55. "Labor Sees 'Fast Track' to Oblivion," *Roanoke Times*, June 2, 1991; "Union Video Stars Fairlawn AT&T: CWA Says Plant Closing Illustrates Worries about Free Trade Agreement," *Roanoke Times*, March 18, 1993.

56. "What NAFTA Could Do to You: Global Goals Give Locals Job Jitters," *Roanoke Times*, October 14, 1993.

57. The literature on this is expansive, but one of the more intriguing entries is from Bennett Harrison, a political economist at Carnegie Mellon. In the interests of minimizing labor costs, multilayered corporations like Nike stratified their workforce into core and periphery workers, the latter being the outsourced, subcontracted employees who worked part-time for abysmal wages and no benefits in Thailand, Indonesia, Malaysia, China, and other developing nations. Core employees, on the other hand, were whittled down to the bare necessities. As Harrison noted, the same principles of outsourcing work to temporary employees was being applied to back-office operations in the effort to achieve maximum flexibility. Advocates of efficiency might celebrate the company's capacity to shed labor costs, "But the growing use of outside subcontractors linked in varying degrees of dependence to the core firms sharpens the divisions between insiders and outsiders and reinforces the long-term trend toward the polarization of American earnings." The pattern, as Harrison pointed out early on in the decade, was to shift production from high-wage, often unionized workers to contingent and relatively tenuous employees. The reality of continued de-industrialization and capital transplantation to developing nations would trigger labor's response to the proposed NAFTA. Harrison, "The Dark Side of Flexible Production," 43–45, quote on 45.

58. Daniel G. LeBlanc, "No to NAFTA: It's Our Jobs, Stupid," *Virginian-Pilot*, November 12, 1993.

59. Ibid.

60. Ibid. According to LeBlanc, real wages for American workers declined by 7 percent between 1987 and 1990. The Economic Policy Institute provides a less dramatic but equally grim portrait of real wages in the early 1990s. For the period 1989 to 1995, the average hourly wage did grow, but at the abysmal rate of 0.6 percent annually. It was the incomes of low-wage men that registered steady deterioration. Between 1989 and 1995, the hourly wages of low-wage men declined by 0.9 percent a year. See "State of Working America 2000–2001: Introduction and Executive Summary," available at http://www.epi.org/content.cfm/books_swa2000_swa2000intro, accessed July 14, 2008. As Michael Dunkerley pointed out in 1996, computer circuit boards can be transported easily by air and produced inexpensively in developing nations such as India, where highly qualified employees perform the tasks that were allegedly nontransferable. "Graduates from universities on the Indian subcontinent are just as clever as graduates from Oxford or Harvard, and they work for a fraction of the wage that their western counterparts expect. British Airways has located a significant part of its computerized ticketing system in India. It is just one of a growing number of companies relocating

their data-processing operations to the subcontinent." This, of course, was a trend that would accelerate dramatically over the next ten years. It suggested the emptiness of the claim that NAFTA defenders consistently made about sacrificing low-wage jobs in return for a high-tech monopoly. Dunkerley, *The Jobless Economy.*

61. Tom Cadorette, "NAFTA Bad for U.S. Workers," *Virginian-Pilot,* November 2, 1993. The type of trade that Cadorette described is "intrafirm trade of outsourced work," as Kim Moody explains, "including maquiladora and other production for reexport to the United States." Proponents' claims that NAFTA would generate jobs in the United States were erroneous, since "export-linked jobs in the United States are not new jobs at all. Furthermore, the outsourced work now done in Mexico is producing job-displacing imports of greater value than the exports that went into them." With Mexico paying the costs of World Bank debts, government austerity programs, and export-oriented production, its citizens would not develop the buying power to purchase American goods and offset the losses from outsourcing. Moody, "NAFTA and the Corporate Redesign of North America," 104.

62. Cadorette, "NAFTA Bad for U.S. Workers."

63. David A. Whitt, "Perot, Not Clinton, Is Friend of Worker," *Roanoke Times,* October 25, 1992.

64. Roger Ethier, "NAFTA: A Giveaway," *Washington Post,* July 16, 1993.

65. E. Alfred Picardi, "NAFTA: Harmful or Helpful to Virginia?" *Virginian-Pilot,* November 11, 1993.

66. John P. McAllister, "To Help Workers, Just Say No to NAFTA," *Virginian-Pilot,* November 17, 1993. McAllister and Picardi were not alone in these sentiments. On the same day that the McAllister article appeared, the *Virginian-Pilot* printed letters expressing concern about the implications of the NAFTA agreement. In both of these letters, the writers focused on the ramifications of competing with a low-wage nation and used the disparity between Mexican and American wage rates to refute claims that the agreement would lead to job creation in the United States. See letters by Howard Mathias and Mark A. Bazemore, page A18, *Virginian-Pilot,* November 17, 1993.

67. Dick Austin, "A Poor Bargain—Workers Beware: NAFTA Is Not Free Trade," *Roanoke Times,* November 1, 1993. See also Garry L. Ashburn's letter to the editor, "Don't Send Jobs South of the Border," *Roanoke Times,* November 7, 1993.

68. As John D. French explains, the resurgence of workers' rights as a social issue—evidenced by the street protests at the World Trade Organization meeting—can be attributed in part to the intense political dispute that NAFTA generated. The "inclusion of labor and environmental side accords as part of this unprecedented trade and investment pact between the U.S., Canada, and Mexico seemed to provide a compelling and influential precedent for the future." French, "From the Suites to the Streets," 285.

69. "Unions Rally to Protest Trade Pact," *Roanoke Times,* April 30, 1993.

70. "Residents Voice Disapproval of NAFTA."

71. "200 Protest NAFTA at Boykins Mill," *Richmond Times-Dispatch,* November 11, 1993.

72. "Getting Hot Under Those Blue Collars," *Roanoke Times,* March 30, 1992.

73. C. de N. Smith, "Unions and NAFTA," *Newport News Daily Press*, November 22, 1993.

74. "Virginians Appear Wary about Health Plan," *Virginian-Pilot*, October 3, 1993.

75. Louis Harris and Associates, 1995, "Harris 1993 November Omnibus Public Opinion Survey, Study no. 931107," hdl: 1902.291H-931107; Louis Harris and Associates, 1995, "Harris 1993 December Omnibus Public Opinion Survey, Study no. 931108," hdl: 1902.291H-931108. Both polls available through the Odum Institute online database at http://www.irss.unc.edu/data_archive/pollsearch.html, accessed June 7, 2008, 10:01 p.m.

76. Rupert, *Ideologies of Globalization*, 62.

77. "Trade Pact's Side Deals Are Worrisome," *Roanoke Times*, September 15, 1993.

78. Gerald W. Meadows, "Who's 'Us'? Free-Trade Pact Continues to Devastate American Workers," *Roanoke Times*, April 7, 1996.

79. Karl E. Balliet, letter to editor, *Roanoke Times*, February 19, 2000.

80. T. Frank, "The Rise of Market Populism," 14, 18–19.

81. Burfisher, Robinson, and Thierfelder, "The Impact of NAFTA on the United States," 129–30, 141–42, quote on 141.

82. Scott, "The High Price of 'Free' Trade," 1–3.

83. Ibid., 7–8, quote on 8.

84. Ibid., 8.

85. As Burfisher, Robinson, and Thierfelder delicately put it, "Recently, U.S. trade policy has become a much more politically sensitive topic" (p. 141). Yet others less interested in administration policy arrive at the same conclusion, pointing to domestic factors such as the attack on unions, automation, deregulation, the dismantling of welfare, and corporate restructuring as equally important determinants of real wage decline and worker insecurity. See Cohen, *The Politics of Globalization in the United States*, 108.

86. Glasmeier and Leichenko, "From Free-Market Rhetoric to Free-Market Reality," 37.

87. Thomas B. Edsall, "Divided We Brawl: Age of Irritation—the New Bitter, Politics of Fear," *Washington Post*, November 28, 1993.

88. Anne S. Evans, "NAFTA: 'The Working People Lost,'" *Virginian-Pilot*, November 26, 1993.

Chapter 6. Virginia Is for Business

1. As David Carlton points out, the textile industry exemplified the kind of industrial growth that the peripheral South attracted in the late nineteenth century. Although it defied the pattern of export production, it reinforced a system of low-grade, low-skilled manufacturing. While tobacco, pig iron, and lumber flourished, "leading-sector industries such as machinery and machine tools scarcely appeared at all in the former Confederacy, their absence both an effect and a cause of the region's small machinery industry." As Carlton deftly points out, southern underdevelopment was tied to the advanced industrial and capital-intensive character of growth in the Northeast and Midwest. It was not, in other words, a reflection of southern character or values. See

Carlton, "The American South and the American Manufacturing Belt," in *The South, the Nation, and the World*, 173–74, quote on 173.

2. It's important to reiterate the character and quality of jobs generated during the 1990s boom period. While boosters and growth-oriented governors championed the addition of each new job—overwhelmingly to northern Virginia, it should be recalled—they offered no insight into the kind of jobs created under the broad and ambiguous umbrella of "high tech." As Jill Andresky Fraser reported after interviewing hundreds of high-tech and New Economy employees, long hours and the subtle expectation that company prerogatives came before personal needs became the norm in the 1990s. "If they want to hold on to their paychecks and benefits packages," she observed, "if they want to keep rising within the corporate hierarchy, if they still care about their careers, they will put in whatever hours are necessary to handle their workloads. And they require neither timekeepers nor shop-floor supervisors to crack the whip, since they will self-impose whatever work schedule . . . is necessary to get the job done." Fraser, *White-Collar Sweatshop*, 24. See also Ross, *No Collar*, 43–44. More than overwork, "job spill" into weekends and evenings, and the constant threat of dismissal for "underperformance," white-collar workers—and these were precisely the jobs that Virginia's growth advocates celebrated most—saw their incomes grow modestly at best. When considering that much of the alleged growth in productivity came through longer hours at the office, it is hardly a signal achievement that, as Fraser notes by citing a report by the Center on Budget and Policy Priorities, family incomes for the middle 20 percent of Americans increased by $780 between 1988 and 1998 (p. 39). Lawrence Mishel, Jared Bernstein, and Jon Schmitt arrive at much more grim conclusion. They suggest that productivity grew by 9 percent between 1989 and 1997, a development which historically had translated into significant income gains for working Americans. "Instead," they observe, "the income of the median family, despite this increase in productivity and despite a large increase in hours worked per year, grew a scant $285, or less than 1%." Mishel, Bernstein, and Schmitt, "Is It a New Economy for Working America?" 6. In addition, proponents of high-tech growth in Virginia rarely commented on the contingent nature of many of the new IT sector jobs. As Bernstein and Mishel pointed out in "*The State of Working America 1998–1999*," nearly 30 percent of workers occupied jobs that were not regular full-time positions. Of course, many of these jobs afforded workers desirable latitude in determining work hours and conditions, but "nonstandard workers generally earn less than workers with comparable skills and backgrounds who work in regular full-time jobs." Nonstandard workers also have a decidedly lower level of pension and benefit coverage. Bernstein and Mishel, "*The State of Working America 1998–1999*." Again, sober economic analysis also challenged some of the claims made by New Economy pundits, which Virginia spawned in the dozens during the 1990s. Against the assertion that the information technology sector was the main engine of job growth and that wages in the IT sector were escalating dramatically, Bernstein and Mishel concluded in "The State of Working America, 2000–2001" that "the IT sector has not played a leadership role in the labor market," contributing no more than 7.5 percent of new jobs between 1992 and 1999. In addition, the authors conclude that "IT sectors were not wage leaders: among men, IT wages were stable relative to those of

comparable workers since the mid-1980s; among women, IT wages fell relative to similar workers. Thus, the IT sector apparently is not experiencing any labor shortage and has not contributed directly (except through the overall productivity effect) to wage acceleration." Bernstein and Mishel, "The State of Working America, 2000–2001." Yet there were important regional variations on this theme, and the South was one of the beneficiaries. As the authors point out, median hourly wages and family incomes grew most quickly in the South and the Midwest (7.5 percent in the South between 1989 and 1999), a statistic that needs to balanced against the comparatively higher poverty rates in the region (13.7 percent in the South versus 12.3 percent in the Northeast). Over the course of the 1990s, the South enjoyed greater employment growth than any other region, reaching 25.7 percent versus an abysmal 4.1 percent in the Northeast. How much of this was in the low-paying service sector and as a result of northern out-migration to the anti-union South is the key question.

3. Carlton, "Smokestack Chasing and Its Discontents," 118–19.

4. Ibid., 118–19; Cobb, *The Selling of the South*, 5–34.

5. Knapp et al., *The People and Economy of Southwest Virginia*, 14–16, 84–87, 90–93.

6. "Our Jobs, Our Kids, Our Future: Can't Anyone Play This Game?" *Roanoke Times*, June 19, 1993.

7. Bookser-Feister and Wise, "The Politics of Economic Development," 3.

8. Minchin, *Fighting Against the Odds*, 152.

9. Ibid.

10. A. Brenner, "International Rank-and-File Solidarity."

11. Citing a Southern Growth Policies Board study, Amy K. Glasmeier and Robin M. Leichenko argue that the South's "historic emphasis on building a low-cost business environment has resulted in poorly funded school and infrastructure systems. The region's basic human and social infrastructure will seriously impede its ability to compete globally." The fact that additional investments in public services were imperative at a time when business was facing increasing price competition—which would only make it more resistant to taxation—only exacerbated the issue. See Glasmeier and Leichenko, "From Free-Market Rhetoric to Free-Market Reality," 36.

12. Minchin, *Fighting Against the Odds*, 155.

13. "Parts Makers Resist U.A.W.: Shifts of Plants to South Slow Organizers," *New York Times*, April 8, 1981; "Low Wages Persist in North Carolina," *New York Times*, January 2, 1981.

14. "Going After High Tech," *New York Times*, July 19, 1981; "New Infusion of State Funds Brightening Job Prospects," *New York Times*, March 28, 1982.

15. "Virginia Building High-Tech Center: State Spending $30 Million on Research Hub for Linking Colleges and Industry," *New York Times*, September 16, 1984.

16. C. Jones, "The Giveaway Game," 43–44. As Robert Guskind pointed out as early as 1990, the lavish deals included low-interest and interest-free loans, tax abatements, direct grants, land contributions, and million-dollar packages for employee training. Quoting management professor Donald Haider, Guskind described it as a "war of all against all"; Haider also suggested that state and local incentives amounted at that time

to $30 billion a year. Faced with the prospect that tax abatements were insufficient for attracting corporate relocations, municipalities have borrowed profligately in the hope that that tax revenues would cover the loans. The leading concerns of all corporate incentive critics included the belief that companies made decisions about relocating regardless of financial incentives, that incentives and abatements did not always translate into jobs and economic growth, that companies would take state handouts without making a long-term commitment to the community, and that social infrastructure and public investment would suffer as a result. Guskind, "The Giveaway Game Continues," 5–6. Examining 22 states with energetic large industry recruitment plans—11 of which are southern—economists William Fox and Matthew Murray conclude that corporate incentives do little to improve regional economic prospects. "One thing seems clear," they say, after considering prestige and political rewards as motives for a program that yields so few results, "recruitment does not lead to more rapid regional growth. In all likelihood, the absence of significant growth impacts means that large companies simply displace other sources of job and income growth in the regional economy." According to these analysts and a considerable body of literature on corporate incentives, "typical business recruitment strategies focused on larger enterprises along with the liberal granting of tax and other incentives to the same firms is simply not a cost-effective economic development strategy." Fox and Murray, "Do Economic Effects Justify the Use of Fiscal Incentives?" 91.

17. "Introduction," in *The Almanac of Virginia Politics*, xv; "Maryland, Virginia Tighten Budget Belts Another Notch: Wilder Slashes $150 Million More to Make Up Revenue Shortfall," *Washington Post*, December 29, 1990.

18. Rubino, "The Promise of Progress," 10–12

19. Ibid., quotes on 12.

20. Ibid., 13.

21. According to "industry experts," Virginia's decision to include corporate executives in formulating development strategy and in fact executing it through trade missions was "the right way to go." It certainly suggested that the Allen administration was pursuing an aggressive strategy to privatize government functions and contract out to private enterprise those operations which provided high-paying, secure jobs to Virginia citizens. The objective was to reduce taxes wherever possible and include business in the political decision-making as much as possible. Allen mapped out this strategy early on in the administration. In the Executive Summary for "Opportunity Virginia: A Strategic Plan for Jobs and Prosperity," Beverly H. Sgro, secretary of education, and Robert T. Skunda, secretary of commerce and trade, called for a coordinated response to "global competition and defense downsizing," which included an economic development strategy premised on significant private sector involvement. As the two officials put it, "This plan, to be known as Opportunity Virginia, represents a departure from previous attempts in that it will be guided by and be responsive to the needs of the private sector and local communities." Executive Summary, "Opportunity Virginia: A Strategic Plan for Jobs and Prosperity," p. 1, Governor George Allen Executive Office Files, Box 1, accession #35861, folder titled "Secretary of Commerce and Trade—General Correspondence, 1994–1995." The rhetorical nod to "lo-

cal communities" aside, the Virginia Economic Development Partnership operated in the interests and according to the dictates of business interests. For example, no community member accompanied a foreign trade mission. See "Governor's Pitch Paid Off for State—12 Days, 4 Deals Worth $43 Million," *Richmond Times-Dispatch*, June 18, 1995.

22. "Opportunity Virginia," 13, 15.

23. "Final Report: Virginia Economic Development Competitiveness Study," 9, National Association of State Development Agencies and Virginia Chamber of Commerce, April 1993, Governor George Allen, Governor's Working Papers, 1994–1997, box 2, folder 43, "Opportunity Virginia," accession #35864.

24. Ibid., 44.

25. Ibid., 10.

26. Ibid., 10–11.

27. Ibid., 48.

28. "State's Plans to Attract Industry May Need Make-Over—Report Suggests Virginia's Reliance on Its Traditional Assets May Not Be Enough," *Richmond Times-Dispatch*, April 8, 1993.

29. "Allen Pitches Less Government, New Priorities," *Richmond Times-Dispatch*, January 12, 1995.

30. Quoted in Hudson and McCue, "Virginia for Sale," 11.

31. "Allen Pitches Less Government, New Priorities."

32. Chi Chi Sileo, "Governor Grapples with 'Genteel' State Politics," *Insight*, April 17, 1995.

33. "Virginia Politics: Poor George," *Economist* 334 (March 4, 1995): 31.

34. "Tax Plan: Questions, Few Answers—Budget Cut Fallout Could Damage VA.'s Image, Senate Democrats Say," *Richmond Times-Dispatch*, December 3, 1994.

35. "Opponents Tear at Allen Program—Business Leaders Blast Plan to Cut Income Taxes," *Roanoke Times*, January 31, 1995.

36. "Virginia Gov. George Allen Suffers Defeat Yesterday," transcript, NPR program "All Things Considered," February 3, 1995; "Assembly Repudiates Allen's Budget—Governor, Agenda in Ruins, Threatens to Rewrite the Plan," *Richmond Times-Dispatch*, February 10, 1995.

37. "The Year of Turmoil—Events Thrust Virginia Business into the National Spotlight," *Richmond Times-Dispatch*, December 19, 1994.

38. "State's Plan to Attract Industry May Need Make-Over." For Virginia's media's generally favorable attitude toward business incentives, see for example "Tax Dollars at Work: Incentives to Lure Businesses Come at a Price, but the Payoff May Be in the Jobs They Create," *Roanoke Times*, June 30, 1996.

39. "Motorola Has Marks of Winner—State Incentives Seem to Have Broad Support," *Richmond Times-Dispatch*, April 13, 1995.

40. "New Ventures for the Old Dominion: State and Business Leaders Strive for Technological Attention," *Newport News Daily Press*, November 19, 1995.

41. "New Ventures for the Old Dominion"; "Tax Dollars at Work."

42. Higgins, "Keeping Up with Carolina," 16.

43. "Sell Va., Local Governments Urged Catering to Business Is Key, Beyer, Skunda Say," *Richmond Times-Dispatch,* November 5, 1994.

44. Kathryn Larin and Elizabeth McNichol, "Virginia's Income Gap," *Virginian-Pilot,* March 13, 1998.

45. "How Much Is Too Much When the Need Is Great?" *Virginian-Pilot,* October 8, 1995. Oddly enough, this declaration came in an article that tentatively questioned the business subsidy program, but did so safely from within a neoliberal framework that grappled with the problem of creating "the right business climate."

46. Larin and McNichol, "Virginia's Income Gap."

47. "A Legacy of Reform: Allen Rekindled GOP by Picking, Winning His Fights," *Virginian-Pilot,* January 11, 1998.

48. "Tax Dollars at Work."

49. For the Allen administration's desperate attempt to recruit the Nucor Steel Corporation, which involved the state in an intense bidding war with South Carolina, see "The Choice: VA. or S.C.," *Richmond Times-Dispatch,* February 12, 1995.

50. "Virginia's Incentives," *Roanoke Times,* October 8, 1995.

51. "Is Virginia Next Silicon State?" *Norfolk Virginian-Pilot,* September 3, 1995.

52. Ibid; "State's 'Silicon Crescent' Evolving: Can High-Tech Sectors Become Cohesive Whole?" *Richmond Times-Dispatch,* August 27, 1995.

53. Higgins, "Keeping Up with Carolina," 14–15.

54. "PC Maker Heads Here: Gateway 2000 to Bring 1,000 Jobs to Hampton—City Beat York, JCC, Chesterfield to Snare Company," *Newport News Daily Press,* September 29, 1995.

55. "How Much Is Too Much When the Need Is Great?"

56. McClenahen, "Selective Pursuit."

57. "Challenging Corporate Incentives: Consumer Watchdog Questions How We Court Companies," *Roanoke Times,* March 29, 1998; "State to Evaluate Business Incentives Plan—Virginia Spends Millions to Lure Companies," *Newport News Daily Press,* June 11, 1995.

58. "Challenging Corporate Incentives."

59. Ibid.

60. "What's the Attraction? Regional Wooing Paying Off with Influx of New Companies," *Richmond Times-Dispatch,* July 1, 1998.

61. "Governor's Pitch Paid Off for State."

62. "Can't Anyone Here Play This Game?" *Roanoke Times,* June 19, 1993.

63. "How Much Is Too Much When the Need Is Great?"

64. "State to Evaluate Business Incentives Plan—Virginia Spends Millions to Lure Companies," *Newport News Daily Press,* June 11, 1995.

65. "Panel: Stay Stingy—State Incentives Downplayed," *Roanoke Times,* September 28, 1995.

66. Ibid.

67. "Incentives Carry a Cost," *Roanoke Times,* June 4, 1995.

68. Ibid.

69. "Industry Tax Breaks: Who Profits? State's Wooing of Texas Steel Recycler Raises Questions," *Virginian-Pilot*, November 29, 1999.

70. Turner, "The Political Economy of Gubernatorial Smokestack Chasing," 270–93.

71. Ibid., quotes on 273 and 289.

72. Brunori, "Principles of Tax Policy and Targeted Tax Incentives," 50–61, quotes on 54, 55, 58, 59.

73. "Talking Points for Governor Allen: VDED Marketing and Governor Whitman's Response"; "Virginia and New Jersey: A Comparison," Governor George Allen, Secretariat of Commerce and Trade Subject Files, 1994–1997, accession #35862, box 1 (4/G/1/76/6), folder 8, Competition for Economic Development. Attorney James D. Demetrakis of Fort Lee, New Jersey, also wrote to Allen at this time complaining of a state administration that failed to "understand the needs of business and the time table to secure permits and approvals," which in his mind were the principal reasons businesses were leaving New Jersey. What the Allen administration seemed to do then was produce the image of state in which business would face very little regulation—exemplified in the governor's laissez-faire attitude toward environmental regulations—and the presumption that what was good for business was good for the state. Demetrakis to Allen, May 30, 1996, ibid.

74. "Money Talks, Companies Walk: States Are Playing Tug of War—N.J. Fights to Replace Lost Firms," *Bergen County (N.J.) Record*, May 30, 1996.

75. "Don't Unilaterally Disarm Virginia in the Jobs War," *Richmond Times-Dispatch*, March 2, 1996, in, Secretariat of Commerce and Trade, box 1, folder 8, Allen Papers.

76. Higgins, "Keeping Up with Carolina," 12–13.

77. "Ex-Gov. Allen Says Sales Pitch Helped Land Frito-Lay Factory—He Tells Council Southern States Must Stress Their Strengths," *Newport News Daily Press*, October 21, 1998.

78. Ibid.

79. Memorandum, "Response to Robert T. Barrata on August 3 Washington Post Article," John Mahone to Bob Benton, August 7, 1996; Memorandum, "Various Inquiries," Robert T. Skunda to George Allen, August 6, 1996 (including quote); "Comparison of Virginia and Maryland Employment Trends, August 7, 1996"; "Va. Economy Falters as Md. Shows Gains—Both Have Big Leads over D.C. in Jobs Data," *Washington Post*, 1996, Governor George Allen, Secretariat of Commerce and Trade Subject Files, 1994–1997, box 1, folder 8. The tooth-and-nail competition with Maryland continued during the Gilmore administration, which saw the governor and Maryland quarreling over which state's economy was growing the fastest, whose was the most growth-oriented, and whether or not Virginia could draw water from the Potomac—in Maryland territory—for its multiplying suburbs. "Gilmore: VA., MD. Philosophies Different—Neighbor's Approach Is Not 'Growth,'" *Richmond Times-Dispatch*, May 24, 2000.

80. Noland, "United We Stand, Divided We Fall?" 4, 10; text in Governor Allen Papers.

81. "Allen's Fingerprint All Over Southwest VA.," *Roanoke Times*, September 24, 2000.

82. Lawrence L. Schack, "Grading Governor Allen on Economic Development," *Virginian-Pilot*, February 4, 1998.

83. Ibid.

84. "Allen's Pro-Growth Legacy Still Clouded," *Washington Post*, October 5, 2000.

85. "A Record $40 Billion Budget: Allen's Two-Year Plan Spreads the Wealth for Education, Tax Cuts," *Richmond Times-Dispatch*, December 20, 1997; "Allen Budget Would Freeze College Tuition—$24 Million Aimed At W&M Library," *Newport News Daily Press*, December 18, 1997.

86. "Gov. Allen's 1998–2000 Virginia Budget: A Little Something for Everyone," *Virginian-Pilot*, December 20, 1997.

87. "Teachers Uneasy about New Standards—State Tests Begin in the Spring," *Roanoke Times*, November 24, 1997.

88. Ibid.

89. "Training Essential to Success: Schools, Businesses Are Partners in Effort to Prepare Workers," *Richmond Times-Dispatch*, June 8, 1994.

90. J. Wade Gilley, "Education and the New Economy: Colleges Must Restructure to Absorb Economic Change," *Richmond Times-Dispatch*, December 29, 1993. For similar thinking and prescriptions, see "Spend More on Colleges, South Urged: Report Cites Growing Global Competition," *Richmond Times-Dispatch*, February 22, 1994; "Universities Urged to Work with Industry to Create Jobs—Union Called Key in Economic Development," *Richmond Times-Dispatch*, May 3, 1994; "Tie Educational Investments, Economy, Casteen Says," *Richmond Times-Dispatch*, November 22, 1994.

91. "Education and the New Economy: Colleges Must Restructure to Absorb Economic Change," *Richmond Times-Dispatch*, December 29, 1993; "Vision of Future Colleges Sparks Lively Debates," *Newport News Daily Press*, October 6, 1989; "Retraining, if Not Retaining: Downsizers Report Gains with Education Programs," *Washington Post*, February 29, 1996.

92. "Lost in the Job Market: There's Work to Be Had—And an Awful Lot of People Who Aren't Being Educated to Do It," *Washington Post*, September 9, 1997.

93. "Labor Search Leads Abroad," *Virginian-Pilot*, September 7, 1998.

94. Tonelson, *Race to the Bottom*, 51, 28–29.

95. "Labor Search Leads Abroad," *Virginian-Pilot*, September 7, 1998..

96. As Alfred E. Eckes has recently pointed out, the period between 1994 and 2002 saw the South produce millions of new service jobs while manufacturing positions continued to decline. As Eckes relates, trained professionals and educated workers were not immune to the forces of capital mobility. "In efforts to remain competitive, many large transnational firms have begun to move research and backroom operations . . . offshore in search of well-trained, English-speaking professionals prepared to work for a fraction of American wages. Foreign engineers, scientists, accountants, software designers, and even lawyers are benefiting from global cost cutting." Eckes, "The South and Economic Globalization, 1950 to the Future," 57.

97. "Unemployment," *Virginian-Pilot*, October 8, 1997.

98. "Virginia Sees Jobs Increase—Service Sector Fuels Local Economy," *Roanoke Times*, May 27, 1995.

99. Henwood, *After the New Economy*, 72–73.

100. "Polluters Go Free, Critics Say," *Roanoke Times*, January 8, 1995.

101. "Environment Entrusted to Private Sector—State Natural Resource Agencies See Their Mission to Cut Red Tape, with Corporations and Citizens Left to Combat Pollution and Protect Wildlife," *Roanoke Times*, October 23, 1995.

102. "Polluters Go Free, Critics Say."

103. "Environment Entrusted to Private Sector" and "Polluters Go Free, Critics Say." See also "Allen Foes Say State Is Too Easy on Industry—They Warn That Pollution Will Hurt Business as well as the Environment," *Virginian-Pilot*, January 10, 1995; "Critics Say Environment Office Too Kind to Industry," *Roanoke Times*, January 11, 1995; "An Environmental Question Mark: Allen, Opponents Dispute His Legacy in Va.," *Washington Post*, October 14, 2000.

104. Hudson and McCue, "Virginia for Sale," 11.

105. "Environment Entrusted to Private Sector" and "Polluters Go Free, Critics Say." See also "Allen Foes Say State Is Too Easy on Industry";"Critics Say Environment Office Too Kind to Industry"; "An Environmental Question Mark."

106. "Motorola Pulls the Plug on VA Chip Plant," *Washington Post*, September 17, 1998.

107. G. Wright, "Persisting Dixie," 87.

108. "Gateway Cashed In at City's Expense: Computer Maker Fought Hampton for Years over Repaying Incentive Money after Failing to Hire Enough Workers," *Newport News Daily Press*, March 27, 2005, available at http://www.dailypress.com/news/specials/; "Gateway to Trim 1,500 More Jobs by Year's End," *Newport News Daily Press*, April 30, 2004.

109. "Broken Promises," *Newport News Daily Press*, March 27, 2005, http://www.dailypress.com/news/specials/

110. "Allen's Fingerprints All Over Southwest Virginia."

111. "Nexus Communications Has Laid Off 166 of its 188 Call Center Employees," *Bristol Herald Courier*, November 10, 2000, available at http://www.sullivan-county.com/nfo/nov_2000/nexas.htm.

112. "Advancing the Issue: A Fragile Job Market—A Company Can Quickly Outsource Its Office Work Force to Another State or Country Via the Internet. Virginia Town's Loss is India's Gain," *Newport News Daily Press*, March 31, 2004.

113. "Call Center to Close, Cutting 300 Jobs," *Roanoke Times*, February 13, 2004.

114. "Travelocity to Move 250 VA. Jobs Overseas—Online Travel Service Is Closing Its Center in Dickenson County," *Richmond Times-Dispatch*, February 13, 2004.

115. "Advancing the Issue: A Fragile Job Market."

116. Carlton, "The American South and the American Manufacturing Belt," 165.

Chapter 7. Dreams of Revolution

1. Larry Sabato, "Chuck Robb Faces a Defining Vote on the Striker Replacement Bill," *Richmond Times-Dispatch*, July 26, 1993; Black and Black, *The Rise of the Southern Republicans*, 98–99.

2. Atkinson, *The Dynamic Dominion*, 451–56.

3. Wood, "The Demise of Virginia Democrats," 2; Judis, "Sneak Preview," 9; Atkinson, *The Dynamic Dominion*, 417; "In Virginia, 'Conservative' Doesn't Mean What It Used To," *New York Times*, August 23, 1981.

4. Atkinson, *The Dynamic Dominion*, 459.

5. William Schneider, "The Suburban Century Begins," 33–44.

6. Atkinson, *The Dynamic Dominion*, 457.

7. Meyerson, "Low-Tax Liberal," 28; Jeffries, *Virginia's Native Son*, 112.

8. Jeffries, *Virginia's Native Son*, 86–93.

9. Crater et al., *The Almanac of Virginia Politics*, xxi; "Worker Issues Will Be Touchy for Election-Year Assembly, Wilder's Last Year as Governor," *Richmond Times-Dispatch*, January 17, 1993; "Maryland, Virginia Tighten Budget Belts Another Notch—Wilder Slashes $150 Million More to Make Up for Revenue Shortfall," *Washington Post*, December 29, 1990.

10. Meyerson, "Low-Tax Liberal," 29.

11. Jeffries, *Virginia's Native Son*, 87.

12. Kilgore, "Making Corrections Work for Us in Virginia," 34–36.

13. As late as 1994, for example, the unemployment rate in predominantly black Petersburg was 9.4 percent, while textile-plagued Martinsville featured a 9.7 percent unemployment rate and Dansville, 8.2. While the state's unemployment rate for 1994 was 4.9 percent, Richmond's was 6.0, which meant that 6,332 workers in the city had been idled by unemployment. Presumably at least some of those would have been able and willing to take advantage of public works projects sponsored by the state and from wages that would have exceeded what the average convict would have been paid. See "Labor Force Status for Virginia's Counties and Cities, 1993 and 1994."

14. Thomas R. McNutt, "Another View: Labor Not Wild about Wilder," *Norfolk Virginian-Pilot*, May 30, 1991.

15. "Interview: L. Douglas Wilder," *Europe* 310 (October 1991): 33.

16. McNutt, "Another View: Labor Not Wild about Wilder"; "Democrats: An Aye for Business," *New York Times*, March 1, 1981.

17. Atkinson, *The Dynamic Dominion*, 452–57.

18. "Commonwealth Conversation: Richard Cranwell," *Norfolk Virginian-Pilot*, October 16, 1996; "Where the Candidates Stand on Jobs," *Roanoke Times*, October 9, 1995.

19. Montgomery, "The Silicon Dominion Skews Right."

20. Crater et al., *The Almanac of Virginia Politics, 1996*, Vol. 10., xii–xiii.

21. Ibid., xiv.

22. "Allen Abandons Income Tax Cut: New Budget Plan Restores Funds to Education, Social Programs," *Newport News Daily Press*, December 19, 1995.

23. Ibid.

24. Ibid.

25. Rozell and Wilcox, "Joining the Mainstream," 27–28.

26. Rozell and Wilcox, *God at the Grass Roots*, 112.

27. Ibid., 29–30.

28. Rozell and Wilcox, "Joining the Mainstream," 28.

29. Rozell, "Virginia: The New Politics of the Old Dominion."

30. Ajene Quillin, "Culture Referendum: The Contract Won't Cure What Is Ailing the Country," *Roanoke Times*, March 15, 1995.

31. Wiener, "Working-Class Republicans and 'False Consciousness,'" 56–57.

32. Cowie, "From Hard Hats to the NASCAR Dads," 11–12.

33. T. Frank, *What's the Matter with Kansas?* 5–6.

34. Ross McKenzie, "The People Are Applauding George Allen Wildly, and for Good Reason," *Richmond Times-Dispatch*, December 28, 1997.

35. Warren Fiske, "A Legacy of Reform: Allen Rekindled GOP by Picking, Winning His Fights," *Virginian-Pilot*, January 11, 1998.

36. McKenzie, "The People Are Applauding George Allen Wildly."

37. Fiske, "A Legacy of Reform."

38. McKenzie, "The People Are Applauding George Allen Wildly." A State Senate Finance Committee found that welfare recipients were expected to take minimum wage, dead-end jobs that only exacerbated the impoverishment of their families. See Fiske, "A Legacy of Reform."

39. Frank Atkinson, "George Allen Changed Way State Operates," *Richmond Times-Dispatch*, January 11, 1998.

40. Cowie, "From Hard Hats to the NASCAR Dads," 12.

41. Borosage, "The Turning?" 14.

42. Wiener, "Working-Class Republicans and 'False Consciousness,'" 57.

43. Sileo, "Republican Revolution in Miniature," 14–15. This piece was one of the first to suggest that Allen's governorship represented a stepping-stone to national politics and perhaps the presidency. More to the point, it suggested that the Republican "revolution" was advancing in states like Virginia, Louisiana, and Mississippi.

44. "Voters Divided on Allen Policies: Poll Shows No Clear Move to Dump Democrats," *Richmond Times-Dispatch*, September 24, 1995.

45. "Soundbites or Real Issues: Building a Citizens' Agenda," *Norfolk Virginian-Pilot*, July 16, 1995.

46. Ibid.

47. Barone and Ujifusa, *Almanac of American Politics 1998*, 1439.

48. Miller, "Conservative of the Future?" 26–28; Walter and Bovenizer, "'Live' with TAE: George Allen," accessed July 4, 2006, 12:43 p.m.

49. Scully, "Taking the Tenth," 28.

50. "Governors: Leave Us Alone—GOP Group Tells Feds to Back Off the Control," *Richmond Times-Dispatch*, November 21, 1994.

51. Ibid.; "Allen Urges States to Retake Power—In Speech, He Blasts Federal Government Intrusion," *Richmond Times-Dispatch*, May 20, 1995.

52. "Allen Urges States to Retake Power," May 20, 1995.

53. "Gov. Allen's 1998–2000 Virginia Budget: A Little Something for Everyone," *Norfolk Virginian-Pilot*, December 20, 1997.

54. Plaisance, "Cutting Taxes," 142–44; Taylor-White, "Governor James S. Gilmore," 13–19; "Beyond the Tax-Repeal: Gilmore Espouses Pro-Business Agenda, Low-Tax Agenda," *Norfolk Virginian-Pilot*, January 25, 1998.

55. Wood, "The Demise of Virginia Democrats," 3–4.

56. Walter, "'Live' with TAE: George Allen."

57. Medvic, "Forging 'Debatable Ground,'" 90.

58. "Gridlock and Padlocks," *Norfolk Virginian-Pilot*, August 3, 1999.

59. Montgomery, "The Silicon Dominion Skews Right."

60. "Business as Usual: Industry Leaders Pleased with Results from Legislative Session," *Richmond Times-Dispatch*, March 27, 2000; "Off-Year Elections Give GOP the Virginia House," 5.

61. "Business as Usual."

62. Judis, 8–9; Sileo, "Governor Grapples with 'Genteel' State Politics," 15–16; Miller, "Conservative of the Future?" 28; Rozell and Wilcox, *Second Coming*, 216–21.

63. Shafer and Johnston, *The End of Southern Exceptionalism*, 173–75; Lamis, "The Emergence of a Two-Party System," 242–43.

64. Lamis, "The Emergence of a Two-Party System," 243.

65. Rozell, "Virginia: The New Politics of the Old Dominion," 137.

66. Edds and Morris, "Virginia: Republican Surge in the Competitive Dominion," 164. Edds and Morris's chapter, like Atkinson's homage to the rise of the Republicans, exults in the arrival of a "competitive," even "dynamic," Dominion. For Republican partisans, there was certainly reason to cheer. For those eager for genuine political alternatives and ideological debate, cheer was in short supply. Partisan competition may limit what an incumbent can achieve, but it cannot inject new intellectual or philosophical content into the political life of a democracy. With two pro-business, low-tax, antilabor parties, working Virginians had reason to be skeptical about the claim that the commonwealth had been emancipated from its politically stagnant past.

67. Edward N. Luttwak, "Will Success Spoil America? Why the Polls Don't Get Our Real Crisis of Values," *Washington Post*, November 27, 1994.

Chapter 8. Democratic Vistas in the Old Dominion

1. "What Is the Virginia Organizing Project?" *News from the Virginia Organizing Project* 1 (December 1995): 4, 5; "Building Public Relationships: the Cornerstone of Our Approach," ibid. 1 (February 1996): 1.

2. "VOP Holds Successful Founding Convention," News from the Virginia Organizing Project 2 (August 1997): 1–2.

3. "Virginia Organizing Project—Statement of Beliefs," ibid., 5.

4. "Lee Co. Chapter Works on Racism," *Virginia.Organizing* 3 (January 1998): 4.

5. "Building Public Relationships: The Cornerstone of Our Approach," News from the Virginia Organizing Project 1 (February 1996): 1–2, 7.

6. Ibid.

7. "Virginia Organizing Project Calls on Governor to Restore Felons' Rights," *Virginia.Organizing* 7 (July 2002): 6.

8. Huey, "Voting in Virginia Is 'For Whites Mostly,'" 20.

9. Ibid.

10. "Virginia Organizing Project Calls on Governor to Restore Felons' Rights," 1, 6; "Teens Speak Out on Restoration of Voting Rights," ibid., 9.

11. Maxwell, "Silence and Denial Are Dangerous for Anti-Racism Efforts," 12.

12. Ibid.

13. Ibid., 13.

14. Ibid.

15. Goldfield, *Still Fighting the Civil War*, 290.

16. Brown et al., *Whitewashing Race*, 1–9.

17. Ibid., 15–22.

18. Goldfield, 294.

19. Goldfield, 291.

20. Brown, 13.

21. Gitlin, *The Intellectuals and the Flag*, 98–99.

22. "VOP Hosts Tour for Richmond Federal Reserve Bank President," *Virginia.Organizing* 3 (January 1998): 1, 9.

23. "A Change of Fortune: Loss of Biggest Employer Unravels Lives in Textile Town," *Virginian-Pilot*, February 20, 2000; "We're Rebounding: Jobless Rate Helps Martinsville Area Attract Businesses," *Richmond Times-Dispatch*, June 18, 2000.

24. "Understanding the Economy," *Virginia.Organizing* 3 (January 1998): 26.

25. E. Frank, *The Raw Deal*, 6.

26. "Understanding the Economy," 26.

27. Ibid., 27.

28. "Report Finds Income Inequality Growing," *Virginia.Organizing* 3 (July 1998): 10–11.

29. "Some Basics of Economic Globalization," ibid., 4 (April 1999): 6–7.

30. Ibid., 7.

31. "Tultex a Virginia Victim of Free Trade," *Virginia.Organizing* 5 (January 2000): 8.

32. Ibid.

33. Ibid.

34. Herod, *Labor Geographics*, 268.

35. "Some Basics of Economic Globalization," 7.

36. E. Frank, "What's Wrong with Inflation?" *Virginia.Organizing* 4 (October 1999): 6.

37. "Welfare Reform Has VA. Shifting Its Focus on Aid to Working Poor," *Virginian-Pilot*, December 27, 1997.

38. Phalen, "Hospitable to Hiring," 40.

39. Ibid.

40. "Corporate Welfare: Who Benefits?" *Virginia.Organizing* 4 (January 1999): 8.

41. Ed Wayland, "Welfare Reform: Myths, Lies, and Realities," *Virginia.Organizing* 3 (April 1998): 11.

42. Ibid., 11–13.

43. Ibid.

44. "New Report Casts Doubt on Promises of Welfare Reform in Virginia," ibid., 10.

45. The SALT report, "The Promise and the Reality: The Outlook for Virginians Leaving Welfare," was also covered by the *Richmond Times-Dispatch*. The paper re-

ported that the state social services commissioner objected to the findings, claiming that "that the goal was to get people on the road to self-sufficiency. We are doing that in great numbers." What the commissioner's observations suggest is the ideological motivation behind the reform, not the improbability of SALT's findings. See "From Welfare Roll to Poverty Roll?" *Richmond Times-Dispatch*, March 4, 1998. The mainstream media largely neglected the consequence of welfare reforms, but not entirely. The *Norfolk Virginian-Pilot* ran an extensive story that included interviews with former welfare recipients struggling to make ends meet in low-wage employment. See "Welfare Reforms Likely Will Put Society's Framework to the Test," September 29, 1997. The *Washington Post* also gave periodic coverage to the problem, including a piece that questioned the program's key assumptions but also provided evidence that suggested the majority were "better off" since finding work. See "From Welfare to Worse: Va. Has Cut Rolls, but Few Becoming Self-Sufficient," July 10, 2000.

46. "Earned Income Credit Can Mean Extra Dollars for Millions of Working Families," *Virginia.Organizing* 3 (October 1998): 8; "Virginia Taxes Punish the Working Poor," *Virginia.Organizing* 6 (April 2001): 11.

47. Lind, "Conservative Elites and the Counterrevolution against the New Deal," 274–75.

48. Ibid., 275–76.

49. "Corporate Welfare: Who Benefits?" 9.

50. Ibid., 8.

51. Ibid., 9.

52. Ibid.

53. "Virginia Rides the New Economy," *Virginia.Organizing* 5 (April 2000): 4.

54. Ibid., 5.

55. "Considerations for Call Center Development: A Case History," available at http://www.tmcnet.com/articles/ccsmag/0100/0100staubach.htm, accessed May 25, 2006.

56. MDC, "The State of the South 2002: Shadows in the Sunbelt Revisited," 20.

57. "Northern Virginia's Poor Defined," *Richmond Times-Dispatch*, August 13, 1992.

58. "Boom Skirted Va. Rural Areas: Economists Work for Solution," ibid., December 24, 2000.

59. "Virginia Rides the New Economy," 6.

60. Ibid.

61. "Virginia Wages: Are We All Better Off?" *Virginia.Organizing* 5 (October 2000): 7.

62. "Understanding the Economy Workshop Held on Eastern Shore," *Virginia.Organizing* 4 (July 1999): 19.

63. E. Frank, *The Raw Deal*, 136–39.

64. Ibid., 139–42.

65. "Virginia Wages: Are We All Better Off?" 6, 17.

66. Kevin Boyle examines the UAW's role in sustaining the Social Democratic agenda through the dark night of the 1950s and fusing it to the civil rights movement in

the 1960s. See in particular chapters 7 and 8 in *The UAW and the Heyday of American Liberalism, 1945–1968.*

67. U.S. Bureau of the Census, 2000, quoted in Barbara Ellen Smith, "The New Latino South: An Introduction," 7.

68. Ibid., 8.

69. "New Chapter, Affiliate Join VOP," News from the Virginia Organizing Project 2 (August 1997): 6.

70. Jon Liss, "Tenants' and Workers' Support Committee: Lessons of the Chirilagua Community," *Virginia.Organizing* 3 (January 1998): 24.

71. Reynolds and Kern, "Labor and the Living-Wage Movement," 17–18.

72. "Living Wage Campaign Rocks Northern Virginia," *Virginia.Organizing* 3 (October 1998): 1, 4.

73. Ibid.

74. Gyula Nagy, "Winning a Living Wage Ordinance from the Grassroots," Labor Notes 274 (January 2002), available at http://labornotes.org/archives/2002/0102/0102d.html.

75. Herod, *Labor Geographies*, 260–63.

76. Nagy, "Winning a Living Wage Ordinance from the Grassroots."

77. Ibid.

Chapter 9. Only Yesterday

1. Henwood, "The New Economy and After," *Left Business Observer* 106 (January 2004), available at http://www.leftbusinessobserver.com/NewEcon.html, accessed June 29, 2006, 9:19 am.

2. French, "From the Suites to the Streets," *Labor History* 43 (2002): 285–86.

3. Michael Kazin, "Battle of Seattle Echoes Similar Cries from the 1890s," *Seattle Post-Intelligencer*, December 7, 1999.

4. "The Luddite Veto," *Richmond Times-Dispatch*, December 1, 1999.

5. Ibid.

6. "Battle in Seattle," *Richmond Times-Dispatch*, December 12, 1999.

7. Ibid.

8. Mokhiber and Weissman, "A Whiff of Democracy in Seattle," *Virginia.Organizing* 5 (January 2000): 10.

9. Ibid.

10. Kromm, "Southerners Should Remember Seattle," *Southern Exposure* 27 (Winter 1999–2000): 18.

11. Ibid.

12. Galuszka, "How Bad?" *Virginia Business* (February 2002): 8.

13. Burke, "It Really Is That Bad," *Virginia Business* (April 2001): 9–17.

14. Ibid., quotes on 17.

15. Warren Vieth, "A Town Out of Work: Globalization Takes Toll on Industries," *Seattle Times*, May 11, 2002.

16. Eckes, "The South and Economic Globalization, 1950 to the Future," 54; "Draped in Prosperity: For Seven Decades, Martinsville and Henry County's Textile Industry Clothed America and Employed One in Five Workers," *Roanoke Times*, August 17, 2002.

17. Ibid.

18. Galuszka, "How Bad?" 11.

19. Ibid.

20. "Western Virginia's Economy Headed Nowhere, Study Says," *Roanoke Times*, November 19, 2000.

21. Godfrey Hodgson, *More Equal Than Others*, 93.

22. Pollin, *Contours of Descent*, 42–44; Blecker, "The New Economic Stagnation and the Contradictions of Economic Policy Making," 286–87.

23. Pollin, *Contours of Descent*, 44, 61.

24. Yates, *Naming the System*, 113.

25. Economic Policy Institute, "State of Working America, 2000–2001: Introduction and Executive Summary," available at http://www.epi.org/content.cfm/books, accessed April 10, 2005, at 8:27 am.

26. Knapp, "Virginia's Economy in the 1990s," 4.

27. Peter Coclanis, "Down Highway 52: Globalization, Higher Education, and the Economic Future of the American South," *Journal of the Historical Society* 5 (Fall 2005): 333–34.

28. Eckes, "The South and Economic Globalization, 1950 to the Future," 56. On the issue of per capita income, Eckes reports that the former Confederacy posted an average of $26,531 in 2001 versus the national average of $30,472. Virginia was ahead of the national curve that year and for much of the 1990s, listing $32,431 as its average per capita income. The closest southern counterpart was Texas, at $28,581. In the 1970s, approximately 38 million jobs were lost to plant shutdowns and relocations. Almost half of these occurred in the Sunbelt South and West. See Barry Bluestone, "Foreword," ix.

29. Hulsemann, "Greenfields in the Heart of Dixie," 236–37.

30. Ibid., 228.

31. Gavin Wright recapitulates the South as isolated labor market theory in "Persisting Dixie," 79–82. David Carlton suggests that "the showpieces of the modern industrial South—the auto complexes of Smyrna, Spring Hill, Tuscaloosa, and Spartanburg, and the Research Triangle of North Carolina—remain essentially branch-plant economies, and have yet to develop vital, self-propelling entrepreneurial cultures of the most advanced sort." Carlton, "The American South and the American Manufacturing Belt," in *The South, the Nation, and the World*, 178.

32. Wright, "Persisting Dixie," 85–86.

33. Tardanico, "Poverty or Development?" 265.

34. G. Wright, "Afterword," 299.

35. R. Brenner, "The Economy of Global Turbulence," 238.

36. Goldfield, *Still Fighting the Civil War*, 292–94.

37. Cobb, *Away Down South*, 334–35, quote on 334.

38. Ibid., 318–23, quotes on 319 and 323.

39. Kingwell, *The World We Want*, 15.

40. Ibid.

41. Ibid., 113; Polanyi, *The Great Transformation*, 69.

Bibliography

Primary Sources

Allen, George F., Executive Office Files, 1994–1997, Library of Virginia Manuscript Collections.

Allen, George, Governor's Working Papers, 1994–1997, Library of Virginia Manuscript Collections.

Allen, George F., Secretariat of Commerce and Trade Papers Subject Files, 1994–1997, Library of Virginia Manuscript Collections.

"Final Report of the Joint Subcommittee Studying the Labor Force Needs of the 1990s to the Governor and the General Assembly of Virginia." *Senate Document No. 32*, Commonwealth of Virginia, Richmond. 1991. 1–10.

Gilmore, James, Policy Office, Policy Office Files, Secretary of Commerce and Trade, 1998–2000, Library of Virginia Manuscript Collections.

Governor's Advisory Committee, Workforce Virginia 2000. "The Virginia Plan for Strengthening the Commonwealth's 21st Century Workforce." 1991. 1–47.

Knapp, John, et al., and Appalachian Regional Commission. "The People and Economy of Southwest Virginia: A Study Prepared for the Southwest Virginia Economic Development Commission," Center for Public Service, 1986.

National Labor Relations Decision and Order, Be-Lo and United Food and Commercial Workers Union, Local 400, AFL-CIO, July 31, 1995, available at http://www.nlrb.gov/shared_files/Board%20Decisions/318/318-1.pdf accessed May 14, 2008, p. 1–42.

United States Court of Appeals for the Fourth Circuit versus National Labor Relations Board, Section 9, subsection IV, November 4, 1997, available at http://pacer.ca4.uscourts.gov/opinion.pdf/961575.P.pdf, accessed on May 4, 2005, 5:25 p.m.

Books

Atkinson, Frank B. *The Dynamic Dominion: Realignment and the Rise of Virginia's Republican Party since 1945*. Fairfax: George Mason University Press, 1992.

Babson, Steve. *The Unfinished Struggle: Turning Points in American Labor, 1877–Present*. New York: Rowman and Littlefield, 1999.

Barone, Michael, and Grant Ujifusa, eds. *Almanac of American Politics 1998*. USA: United Book Press, 1997.

Baumol, William J., Alan S. Blinder, and Edward N. Wolff. *Downsizing in America: Reality, Causes, and Consequences*. New York: Russell Sage Foundation, 2003.

Black, Earl, and Merle Black. *The Rise of Southern Republicans*. Cambridge, Mass.: Belknap Press of the Harvard University Press, 2002.

Blecker, Robert. "The New Economic Stagnation and the Contradictions of Economic

Policy Making." In *Understanding American Economic Decline*, ed. Michael A. Bernstein and David E. Adler. Cambridge: Cambridge University Press, 2004.

Blight, David W. *Race and Reunion: The Civil War in American Memory*. Cambridge: Belknap Press of the Harvard University Press, 2001.

Bluestone, Barry. "Foreword." In *Beyond the Ruins: The Meanings of Deindustrialization*, ed. Jefferson Cowie and Joseph Heathcott. Ithaca: ILR Press, 2003.

Boyle, Kevin. *The UAW and the Heyday of American Liberalism, 1945–1968*. Ithaca: Cornell University Press, 1995.

Brisbin, Richard A., Jr. *A Strike Like No Other Strike: Law and Resistance during the Pittston Coal Strike of 1989–1990*. Baltimore: Johns Hopkins University Press, 2002.

Brody, David. *Labor Embattled: History, Power, Rights*. Urbana and Chicago: University of Illinois Press, 2005.

Brown, Michael K., et al. *Whitewashing Race: The Myth of a Color-Blind Society*. Berkeley: University of California Press, 2003.

Brundage, W. Fitzhugh. *The Southern Past: A Clash of Race and Memory*. Cambridge, Mass.: Belknap Press of the Harvard University Press, 2005.

Bullock, Charles S., III, and Janna Deitz. "Transforming the South: The Role of the Federal Government." In *The American South in the Twentieth Century*, ed. Craig S. Pascoe, Karen Trahan Leathem, and Andy Ambrose. Athens: University of Georgia Press, 2005.

Carlton, David. "Smokestack Chasing and Its Discontents: Southern Development Strategy in the Twentieth Century." In *The American South in the Twentieth Century*, ed. Craig S. Pascoe, Karen Trahan Leathem, and Andy Ambrose. Athens: University of Georgia Press, 2005.

Carlton, David, and Peter Coclanis. *The South, the Nation, and the World: Perspectives on Southern Economic Development*. Charlottesville: University of Virginia Press, 2003.

Carter, Dan T. *The Politics of Rage: George Wallace, the Origins of the New Conservatism, and the Transformation of American Politics*. New York: Simon and Schuster, 1995.

Cobb, James. *Away Down South: A History of Southern Identity*. New York: Oxford University Press, 2005.

———. "From the First New South to the Second: The Southern Odyssey through the Twentieth Century." In *The American South in the Twentieth Century*, ed. Craig S. Pascoe, Karen Trahan Leathem, and Andy Ambrose. Athens: University of Georgia Press, 2005.

———. *The Selling of the South: The Southern Crusade for Industrial Development, 1936–1990*. 2nd ed. Urbana and Chicago: University of Illinois Press, 1993.

Cobb, James C., and William Stueck, eds. *Globalization and the American South*. Athens: University of Georgia Press, 2005.

Cohen, Edward S. *The Politics of Globalization in the United States*. Washington, D.C.: Georgetown University Press, 2001.

Conroy, Martin. *Sustaining the New Economy: Work, Family, and Community in the Information Age*. Cambridge, Mass.: Harvard University Press, 2000.

Crater, Flora, et al. *The Almanac of Virginia Politics*, 1990, vol. 8. Alexandria, Va.: Woman Activist Fund, 1991.

———. *The Almanac of Virginia Politics*, 1992 Supplement, vol. 8. Alexandria, Va.: Woman Activist Fund, 1992.

———. *The Almanac of Virginia Politics*, 1996, vol. 10. Alexandria, Va.: Woman Activist Fund, 1995.

Dunkerley, Michael. *The Jobless Economy? Computer Technology in the World of Work*. Cambridge: Polity Press, 1996.

Eckes, Alfred E. "The South and Economic Globalization, 1950 to the Future." In *Globalization and the American South*, ed. James C. Cobb and William Stueck. Athens: University of Georgia Press, 2005.

Edds, Margaret, and Thomas R. Morris. "Virginia: Republican Surge in the Competitive Dominion." In *Southern Politics in the 1990s*, ed. Alexander P. Lamis. Baton Rouge: Louisiana State University Press, 1999.

Faux, Jeff. *The Global Class War*. Hoboken: Wiley, 2006.

Frank, Ellen. *The Raw Deal: How Myths and Misinformation about the Deficit, Inflation, and Wealth Impoverish America*. Boston: Beacon Press, 2004.

Frank, Thomas. *What's the Matter with Kansas? How Conservatives Won the Heart of America*. New York: Henry Holt, 2004.

Fraser, Jill Andresky. *White-Collar Sweatshop: The Deterioration of Work and Its Rewards in Corporate America*. New York: W. W. Norton, 2001.

Galbraith, John Kenneth. *A Journey through Economic Time: A Firsthand View*. Boston: Houghton Mifflin, 1994.

Gitlin, Todd. *The Intellectuals and the Flag*. New York: Columbia University Press, 2006.

———. *Media Unlimited: How the Torrent of Images and Sounds Overwhelms Our Lives*. New York: Metropolitan Books, 2001.

Glasmeier, Amy K., and Robin Leichenko. "From Free-Market Rhetoric to Free-Market Reality: The Future of the U.S. South in an Era of Globalization." In *Poverty or Development? Global Restructuring and Regional Transformations in the U.S. South and the Mexican South*, ed. Richard Tardanico and Mark. B. Rosenberg. New York: Routledge, 2000.

Goldfield, David R. *Still Fighting the Civil War: The American South and Southern History*. Baton Rouge: Louisiana State University Press, 2002.

Gordon, David M. "Chickens Home to Roost: From Prosperity to Stagnation in the Postwar U.S. Economy." In *Understanding American Economic Decline*, ed. Michael A. Bernstein and David E. Adler. Cambridge: Cambridge University Press, 2004.

Harrison, Bennett, and Barry Bluestone. *The Great U-Turn: Corporate Restructuring and the Polarizing of America*. New York: Basic Books, 1988.

Hartmann, Thom. *Unequal Protection: The Rise of Corporate Dominance and the Theft of Human Rights*. New York: Rodale Books, 2002.

Head, Simon. *The New Ruthless Economy: Work and Power in the Digital Age*. New York: Oxford University Press, 2003.

Henwood, Doug. *After the New Economy*. New York: New Press, 2003.

Hodgson, Godfrey. *More Equal Than Others: America from Nixon to the New Century.* Princeton: Princeton University Press, 2004.

Hulsemann, Karsten. "Greenfields in the Heart of Dixie: How the American Auto Industry Discovered the South." In *The Second Wave: Southern Industrialization from the 1940s to the 1970s*, ed. Philip Scranton. Athens: University of Georgia Press, 2001.

"Introduction." In *The Almanac of Virginia Politics*, ed. Flora Crater et al. vol. 7. Alexandria, Va.: Woman Activist Fund, 1991.

Jackson, Thomas F. *From Civil Rights to Human Rights: Martin Luther King, Jr., and the Struggle for Economic Justice.* Philadelphia: University of Pennsylvania Press, 2007.

Jeffries, J. L. *Virginia's Native Son: The Election and Administration of Governor L. Douglas Wilder.* West Lafayette: Purdue University Press, 2000.

Johnson, Haynes. *The Best of Times: America in the Clinton Years.* New York: Harcourt, 2001.

Jones, Jacqueline. "The History and Politics of Poverty in Twentieth-Century America." In *Perspectives on Modern America: Making Sense of the Twentieth Century*, ed. Harvard Sitkoff. New York: Oxford University Press, 2001.

Juravich, Tom, and Kate Bronfenbrenner. *Ravenswood: The Steelworkers' Victory and the Revival of American Labor.* Ithaca: ILR Press, 1999.

Kingwell, Mark. *The World We Want: Virtue, Vice, and the Good Citizen.* Toronto: Penguin Books, 2000.

Knapp, John L., et al. *The People and Economy of Southwest Virginia: A Study Prepared for the Southwest Virginia Economic Development Commission Under the Sponsorship of the Appalachian Regional Commission.* Charlottesville: Center for Public Service, 1986.

"Labor Force Status for Virginia's Counties and Cities, 1993 and 1994." In *Virginia Statistical Abstract, 1996–1997 Edition*, ed. Michael Spar. Charlottesville: Weldon Cooper Center for Public Service, 1996.

Lamis, Alexander P. "The Emergence of a Two-Party System: Southern Politics in the Twentieth Century." In *The American South in the Twentieth Century*, ed. Craig S. Pascoe, Karen Trahan Leathem, and Andy Ambrose. Athens: University of Georgia Press, 2005.

———. *Southern Politics in the 1990s.* Baton Rouge: Louisiana State University Press, 1999.

Lichtenstein, Nelson. *State of the Union: A Century of American Labor.* Princeton: Princeton University Press, 2002.

Lind, Michael. "Conservatives and the Counterrevolution against the New Deal." In *Ruling America: A History of Wealth and Power in a Democracy*, ed. Steve Fraser and Gary Gerstle. Cambridge, Mass.: Harvard University Press, 2005.

Luttwak, Edward. *Turbo-Capitalism: Winners and Losers in the Global Economy.* London: Weidenfeld and Nicolson, 1998.

Mandel, Michael J. *The High-Risk Society: Peril and Promise in the New Economy.* New York: Random House, 1996.

McElvaine, Robert. *The Great Depression: America, 1929–1941*. New York: Three Rivers Press, 1984. Reprint, New York: Three Rivers Press, 1993.

Medvic, Stephen K. "Forging 'Debatable Ground': The Transformation of Party Politics in Virginia." In *Government and Politics in Virginia: The Old Dominion at the 21st Century*, ed. Quentin Kidd. Needham Heights: Simon and Schuster, 1999.

Metzgar, Jack. *Striking Steel: Solidarity Remembered*. Philadelphia: Temple University Press, 2000.

Minchin, Timothy J. *Fighting Against the Odds: A History of Southern Labor since World War II*. Gainesville: University Press of Florida, 2005.

Moberg, David. "Labor Faces the Twenty-First Century." In *Which Direction for Organized Labor? Essays on Organizing, Outreach, and Internal Transformations*, ed. Bruce Nissen. Detroit: Wayne State University Press, 1999.

Moody, Kim. *Workers in a Lean World: Unions in the International Economy*. London: Verso, 1997.

Newman, Katherine S. "Troubled Times: The Cultural Dimensions of Economic Decline." In *Understanding American Economic Decline*, ed. Michael A. Bernstein and David E. Adler. Cambridge: Cambridge University Press, 1994.

Nicholson, Philip Yale. *Labor's Story in the United States*. Philadelphia: Temple University Press, 2004.

Nonini, Donald M. "Critique: Creating the Transnational South." In *The American South in a Global World*, ed. James L. Peacock, Harry L. Watson, and Carrie R. Matthews. Chapel Hill: University of North Carolina Press, 2005.

Pascoe, Craig S., Karen Trahan Leathem, and Andy Ambrose. *The American South in the Twentieth Century*. Athens: University of Georgia Press, 2005.

Peacock, James L. "The South and Grounded Globalism." In *The American South in a Global World*, ed. James L. Peacock, Harry L. Watson, and Carrie R. Matthews. Chapel Hill: University of North Carolina Press, 2005.

Piven, Frances Fox. "Neoliberal Social Policy and Labor Market Discipline." In *What's Class Got to Do with It? American Society in the Twenty-First Century*, ed. Michael Zweig. Ithaca: Cornell University Press, 2004.

Plaisance, Patrick Lee. "Cutting Taxes: Good Public Policy or Political Expediency?" In *Government and Politics in Virginia: The Old Dominion at the 21st Century*, ed. Quentin Kidd. Needham Heights: Simon and Schuster, 1999.

Polanyi, Karl. *The Great Transformation: The Political and Economic Origins of Our Time*. Boston: Beacon Press by arrangement with Rinehart and Company, 1944, 1957.

Pollin, Robert. *Contours of Descent: U.S. Economic Fractures and the Landscape of Global Austerity*. London: Verso, 2003.

Prince, K. Michael. *Rally 'Round the Flag, Boys!: South Carolina and the Confederate Flag*. Columbia: University of South Carolina Press, 2004.

Reich, Robert. *I'll Be Short: Essentials for a Decent Working Society*. Boston: Beacon Press, 2002.

Rifkin, Jeremy. *The Age of Access: The New Culture of Hypercapitalism, Where All of Life Is a Paid-For Experience*. New York: Penguin Putnam, 2000.

Rinehart, James W., Christopher Huxley, and David Robertson. *Just Another Car Factory? Lean Production and Its Discontents*. Ithaca: ILR Press, 1997.

Ross, Andrew. *No Collar: The Humane Workplace and Its Hidden Costs*. Philadelphia: Temple University Press, 2004.

Rozell, Mark. "Virginia: The New Politics of the Old Dominion." In *The New Politics of the Old South: An Introduction to Southern Politics*, ed. Charles S. Bullock III and Mark J. Rozell. Lanham, Md.: Rowman and Littlefield, 1998.

Rozell, Mark, and Clyde Wilcox, eds. *God at the Grass Roots, 1996: The Christian Right in the American Elections*. Lanham, Md.: Rowman and Littlefield, 1997.

———. *Second Coming: The New Christian Right in Virginia Politics*. Baltimore: Johns Hopkins Press, 1996.

Rupert, Mark. *Ideologies of Globalization: Contending Visions of a New World Order*. London: Routledge, 2000.

Scranton, Philip, ed. *The Second Wave: Southern Industrialization from the 1940s to the 1970s*. Athens: University of Georgia Press, 2001.

Shafer, Byron E., and Richard Johnston. *The End of Southern Exceptionalism: Class, Race, and Partisan Change in the Postwar South*. Cambridge, Mass.: Harvard University Press, 2006.

Stiglitz, Joseph. *The Roaring Nineties: A New History of the World's Most Prosperous Decade*. New York: W. W. Norton, 2003.

Tabb, William K. "Neoliberalism and Anticorporate Globalization as Class Struggle." In *What's Class Got to Do with It? American Society in the Twenty-First Century*, ed. Michael Zweig. Ithaca: ILR Press, 2004.

Tardanico, Richard, and Mark B. Rosenberg, eds. *Poverty or Development? Global Restructuring and Regional Transformations in the U.S. South and the Mexican South*. New York: Routledge, 2000.

Tonelson, Alan. *Race to the Bottom: Why a Worldwide Worker Surplus and Uncontrolled Free Trade Are Sinking American Living Standards*. New York: Westview Press, 2000.

Uchitelle, Louis. *The Disposable American: Layoffs and Their Consequences*. New York: Alfred A. Knopf, 2006.

Wright, Gavin. *Old South, New South: Revolutions in the Southern Economy Since the Civil War*. Baton Rouge: Louisiana State University Press, 1986.

———. "Afterword." In *The Second Wave: Southern Industrialization from the 1940s to the 1970s*, ed. Philip Scranton. Athens: University of Georgia Press, 2001.

———. "Persisting Dixie: The South as an Economic Region." In *The American South in the Twentieth Century*, ed. Craig S. Pascoe, Karen Trahan Leathem, and Andy Ambrose. Athens: University of Georgia Press, 2005.

Wright, Lesley, and Marti Smye. *Corporate Abuse: How "Lean and Mean" Robs People and Profits*. Toronto: Key Porter Books, 1996.

Yates, Michael D. *Naming the System: Inequality and Work in the Global Economy*. New York: Monthly Review Press, 2003.

Zweig, Michael, ed. *What's Class Got to Do with It? American Society in the Twenty-First Century*. Ithaca: ILR Press, 2004.

———. *The Working-Class Majority: America's Best Kept Secret.* Ithaca: ILR Press, 2000.

Articles

"The American South: For Whom the Belle Tolls." *Economist*, December 10, 1994, 3–18.

Anderson, Belinda. "Hidden Valley." *Virginia Business* (March 1993): 21–25.

———. "Quest for Quality." *Virginia Business* (March 1991): 28–36.

Bacon, James. "Economic Exodus." *Virginia Business* (July 1991): 53–60.

Bacon, James A. "The Fairfax Revolution." *Virginia Business* (January 1990): 30.

Bookser-Feister, John, and Leah Wise. "The Politics of Economic Development." *Southern Exposure* 14 (September–October, 1986): 2–13.

"The Boom and the Bubble." *New Left Review* 6 (November–December 2000): 5–43.

Borosage, Robert L. "The Turning? Populist Influence Is Growing, but Big Money Still Rules the Democratic Party." *The Nation*, June 26, 2006.

Brenner, Aaron. "International Rank-and-File Solidarity: Labor's Democratic Response to Globalization," paper presented at International Studies Association Meeting, February 1999, in author's possession.

Brenner, Robert. "The Economy of Global Turbulence." *New Left Review* 229 (May–June 1998): 1–265.

Bronfenbrenner, Kate. "We'll Close!" *Southern Exposure* (Summer–Fall 1998): 50–54.

Brunori, David. "Principles of Tax Policy and Targeted Tax Incentives." *State and Local Government Review* 29 (Winter 1997): 50–61.

"Building Public Relationships: The Cornerstone of Our Approach." *News from the Virginia Organizing Project* 1 (February 1996): 1–7.

Burfisher, Mary E., Sherman Robinson, and Karen Thierfelder. "The Impact of NAFTA on the United States." *Journal of Economic Perspectives* 15 (January 2001): 125–44.

Burke, Robert. "It Really Is That Bad." *Virginia Business* (April 2001): 8–17.

Coclanis, Peter. "Down Highway 52: Globalization, Higher Education, and the Economic Future of the American South." *Journal of the Historical Society* 5 (Fall 2005): 331–45.

"Corporate Welfare: Who Benefits?" *Virginia.Organizing* 4 (January 1999): 8–9.

Cowie, Jefferson. "From Hard Hats to the NASCAR Dads." *New Labor Forum* 13 (Fall 2004): 9–17.

Crocket, Hasan, Ashaki Binta, and Dennis Orton. "No Escape from History: A Short History of Globalization in the South." *Southern Exposure* 26 (Summer–Fall, 1998): 26–30.

"A Democratic Revival in Virginia." *Virginia News Letter* 78 (February 2002): 1–11.

Draper, Alan. "No Retreat, No Surrender: Concessions, Resistance, and the End of the Postwar Settlement." *Labour/Le Travail* 51 (Spring 2003): 251–64.

Dreiling, Michael C. "The Class Embeddedness of Corporate Political Action: Leadership in Defense of the NAFTA." *Social Problems* 47 (February 2000): 21–48.

"Earned Income Credit Can Mean Extra Dollars for Millions of Working Families." *Virginia.Organizing* 3 (October 1998): 8.

Eckman, Anne, et al. "Job Equity in the Downsized South: A Special Report on Work in the 1990s." *Southern Exposure* 25 (Fall–Winter 1997): 7–11.

"Ex-Gov. Allen Says Sales Pitch Helped Land Frito-Lay Factory—He Tells Council Southern States Must Stress Their Strengths." *Newport News Daily Press*, October 21, 1998.

Fox, William, and Matthew Murray. "Do Economic Effects Justify the Use of Fiscal Incentives?" *Southern Economic Journal* 71 (2004): 78–92.

Frank, Ellen. "What's Wrong with Inflation?" *Virginia.Organizing* 4 (October 1999): 6–7.

Frank, Thomas. "The Rise of Market Populism: America's New Secular Religion." *The Nation* (October 30, 2000): 13–19.

Frederick, Mary Helen. "Do You Hear a Giant Sucking Sound?" *Virginia Business* (November 1995): 79–89.

———. "Magnum Work Force." *Virginia Business* (February 1991): 57–59.

French, John D. "From the Suites to the Streets: The Unexpected Re-Emergence of the 'Labor Question,' 1994–1999." *Labor History* 43 (2002): 285–304.

Galuszka, Peter. "How Bad? Manufacturers Take Hits, but Overall Virginia Fares Well during the Recession." *Virginia Business* (February 2002): 8–17.

Gardner, Jennifer M. "The 1990–1991 Labor Market: How Bad Was the Labor Market?" *Monthly Labor Review* 117 (June 1994): 3–11.

Gerring, Jane. "Counting the Costs." *Virginia Business* (July 1992): 34–40.

———. "Surviving the Workforce Famine." *Virginia Business* (April 1994): 41–43.

Greider, William. "The Future Is Now: With the Reigning Economic Ideology Discredited, the Way Is Clear for New Ideas." *The Nation*, June 26, 2006, 24.

Grim, Michael P. "So You Thought Unions Were Dead in Virginia?" *Virginia Business* (April 1990): 52–59.

Guskind, Robert. "The Giveaway Game Continues." *Planning* (February 1990): 4–8.

Harrison, Bennett. "The Dark Side of Flexible Production." *Technology Review* 97 (May–June 1994): 39–45.

Hatch, Julie, and Angela Clinton. "Job Growth in the 1990s: A Retrospect." *Monthly Labor Review* 123 (December 2000): 3–18.

Helwig, Ryan T. "Worker Displacement in a Strong Labor Market." *Monthly Labor Review* 124 (June 2001): 13–28.

Higgins, Jackson. "Keeping Up with Carolina." *Virginia Business* (April 1997): 12–17.

Hudson, Mike, and Cathy McCue. "Virginia for Sale." *Southern Exposure* 24 (Spring 1996): 10–14.

Huey, Eileen. "Voting in Virginia Is 'For Whites Mostly.'" *Virginia.Organizing* 5 (October 2000): 20.

Ilg, Randy E., and Steven Haugen. "Earning and Employment Trends in the 1990s." *Monthly Labor Review* 123 (March 2000): 21–33.

"Interview: L. Douglas Wilder." *Europe* 310 (October 1991): 33.

"Is It a New Economy for Working America?" *EPI Journal* (Winter 1999): 1–8.

Jones, Chip. "The Giveaway Game." *Virginia Business* (February 1992): 43–48.

———. "Virginia Is the Perfect Place for Business." *Virginia Business* (February 1992): 13–18.

Judis, John. "Sneak Preview." *The American Prospect* (July 2–July 16, 2001): 8–9.

"June 10, 1997: What If Virginia Held an Election and Nobody Came?" *Virginia News Letter* 73 (August 1997): 1–6.

Kaufman, Phil. "Fewer but Larger Supermarkets." *Food Review* (May–August, 1995): 26–29.

Kilgore, Jerry W. "Making Corrections Work for Us in Virginia." *Virginia Review* (May–June 1996): 34–36.

Knapp, John L. "Recent Developments in the Virginia Economy." *Virginia News Letter* 77 (March 2001): 1–7.

———. "Virginia's Economy in the 1990s: Some Caution Is Warranted." *Virginia News Letter* 75 (February 1999): 1–7.

Kotz, David M., and Martin H. Wolfson. "Déjà Vu All Over Again: The 'New' Economy in Historical Perspective." *Labor Studies Journal* 28 (Winter 2004): 25–44.

Kromm, Chris. "The Globalization Game: Going for Broke." *Southern Exposure* 26 (Summer/Fall 1998): 21–25.

———. "Southerners Should Remember Seattle." *Southern Exposure* 27 (Winter 1999–2000): 18.

Larance, Leigh Anne. "The Comeback Trail." *Virginia Business* (March 1995): 18–25.

"Lee Co. Chapter Works on Racism." *Virginia.Organizing* 3 (January 1998): 4.

Lewchuk, Wayne, and David Robertson, "Production without Empowerment: Work Reorganization from the Perspective of Motor Vehicle Workers." *Capital and Class* 63 (Autumn 1997): 37–64.

Lind, Michael. "Conservative Elites and the Counterrevolution against the New Deal." In *Ruling America: A History of Wealth and Power in a Democracy*, ed. Steve Fraser and Gary Gerstle. Cambridge, Mass.: Harvard University Press, 2005.

Liss, Jon. "Tenants' and Workers' Support Committee: Lessons of the Chirilagua Community." *Virginia.Organizing* 3 (January 1998): 24.

"Living Wage Campaign Rocks Northern Virginia." *Virginia.Organizing* 3 (October 1998): 1, 4.

Maxwell, Bill. "Silence and Denial Are Dangerous for Anti-Racism Efforts." *Virginia.Organizing* 6 (July 2001): 12–13.

McClenahen, John. "Selective Pursuit." *Industry Week* 7 (October 1996): 35–38.

Meyerson, Adam. "Low-Tax Liberal: Governor Douglas Wilder Calls for Fiscal Responsibility with Compassion." *Policy Review* 55 (Winter 1991): 26–31.

Micas, Steven L. "The Changing Face of Manufacturing in Virginia." *Virginia Review* 74 (September–October 1996): 45–50.

Miller, John J. "Conservative of the Future? George Allen Rises in Virginia." *National Review* 52 (November 6, 2000): 26–28.

Mishel, Lawrence, Jared Bernstein, and Jon Schmitt. "Is It a New Economy for Working America?" *EPI Journal* (Winter 1999): 1, 6.

Mokhiber, Russell, and Robert Weissman. "A Whiff of Democracy in Seattle." *Virginia.Organizing* 5 (January 2000): 10–11.

Moody, Kim. "NAFTA and the Corporate Redesign of North America." *Latin American Perspectives* 22 (Winter 1995): 95–116.

Morris, Stephen D., and John Passe-Smith. "What a Difference a Crisis Makes: NAFTA, Mexico, and the United States." *Latin American Perspectives* 28 (May 2001): 124–49.

"New Chapter, Affiliate Join VOP." *News from the Virginia Organizing Project* 2 (August 1997): 6.

"New Report Casts Doubt on Promises of Welfare Reform in Virginia." *Virginia.Organizing* 3 (April 1998): 10–11.

Noland, Terrance. "United We Stand, Divided We Fall? The State Doesn't Think So, but Some Say Regionalism Has Diminished North Carolina's Value as a Brand Name." *Business North Carolina* (February 1997): 4, 10.

Odin, Paula. "From Milch Cow to Cash Cow." *Virginia Business* (January 1990): 38–47.

"Off-Year Elections Give GOP the Virginia House." *State Legislatures* 25 (December 1999): 5.

Peacock, James. "The South in a Global World." *Virginia Quarterly Review* 78 (Autumn 2002): 581–94.

Peckenham, Nancy. "Confessions of a Union Buster." *Southern Exposure* 18 (Fall 1990): 34–36.

Penn, Ann C. "Productivity Pros." *Virginia Business* (July 1992): 50–59.

———. "Take This Job . . . And Love It!" *Virginia Business* (March 1991): 38–44.

Phalen, Kathleen F. "Hospitable to Hiring." *Virginia Business* (January 1996): 40–44.

"Report Finds Income Inequality Growing." *Virginia.Organizing* 3 (July 1998): 10–11, 28.

Reynolds, David, and Jen Kern. "Labor and the Living-Wage Movement." *Working USA* 5 (Winter 2001–2002): 17–18.

Rozell, Mark, and Clyde Wilcox. "Joining the Mainstream: The New Christian Right in Virginia," *Spectrum* (Winter 1996): 26–32.

Rubino, John. "The Promise of Progress." *Virginia Business* (February 1994): 9–16.

Sabato, Larry. "A Century in the Making: The 1997 Republican Sweep." *Virginia News Letter* 74 (February 1998): 1–12.

Schneider, William. "The Suburban Century Begins." *Atlantic Monthly* 270 (July 1992): 33–44.

Scully, Matthew. "Taking the Tenth." *National Review* 46 (December 19, 1994): 26–28.

Sheikers, Hale V. "Fairfax: Hotbed of High-Tech Growth." *Virginia Business* (September 1997): 52–61.

Sileo, Chi Chi. "Governor Grapples with 'Genteel' State Politics." *Insight* 11 (April 1995): 14–16.

———. "Republican Revolution in Miniature." *Insight* November 20, 1995): 14–15.

"Some Basics of Economic Globalization." *Virginia.Organizing* 4 (April 1999): 6–8.

"The South at Work: An Institute Report." *Southern Exposure* 18 (Fall 1990): 14–19.

Spears, Ellen. "Nissan Is Not the Norm." *Southern Exposure* 18 (Fall 1990): 40–44.

Taylor, Andy. "Eat Your Heart Out, D.C." *Virginia Business* (January 1990): 31–37.

Taylor-White, Alyson Lindsey. "Governor James S. Gilmore, III: No Car Pledge Leads to Historic Win." *Virginia Review* 76 (March–April 1998): 13–19.

———. "Hugh D. Keogh on How and Why We Have the Ability to Meet the Needs of Prospects." *Virginia Review* 76 (September 1992): 7–10.

"Teens Speak Out on Restoration of Voting Rights." *Virginia.Organizing* 7 (July 2002): 9.

Tilly, Chris. "Continuing Growth of Part Time Employment." *Monthly Labor Review* 114 (March 1991): 10–18.

"Tultex a Virginia Victim of Free Trade." *Virginia.Organizing* 5 (January 2000): 8.

Turner, Robert C. "The Political Economy of Gubernatorial Smokestack Chasing: Bad Policy and Bad Politics?" *State Politics and Policy Quarterly* 3 (Fall 2003): 270–93.

"Understanding the Economy." *Virginia.Organizing* 3 (January 1998): 26–27.

"Understanding the Economy Workshop Held on Eastern Shore." *Virginia.Organizing* 4 (July 1999): 19.

"Virginia Organizing Project—Statement of Beliefs." *News from the Virginia Organizing Project* 2 (August 1997): 5.

"Virginia Organizing Project Calls on Governor to Restore Felons' Rights." *Virginia. Organizing* 7 (July 2002): 1, 6.

"Virginia Politics: Poor George." *Economist* 334 (March 4, 1995): 31.

"Virginia Rides the New Economy." *Virginia.Organizing* 5 (April 2000): 4–6.

"Virginia Taxes Punish the Working Poor." *Virginia.Organizing* 6 (April 2001): 11.

"Virginia Wages: Are We All Better Off?" *Virginia.Organizing* 5 (October 2000): 6–9, 17.

"VOP Holds Successful Founding Convention." *News from the Virginia Organizing Project* 2 (August 1997): 1–2.

Wayland, Ed. "Welfare Reform: Myths, Lies, and Realities." *Virginia.Organizing* 3 (April 1998): 11–13.

"What Is the Virginia Organizing Project?" *News from the Virginia Organizing Project* 1 (December 1995): 1–2, 6.

White, Jason. "The Fairfax Formula." *Virginia Business* (September 1994): 57–63.

Wiener, Jon. "Working-Class Republicans and 'False Consciousness.'" *Dissent* (Spring 2005): 55–58.

Windham, Lane. "Will Unions Organize the South?" *Southern Exposure* 23 (Winter 1999–2000): 22–24.

Wood, William H. "The Demise of Virginia Democrats." *The Virginia News Letter* 77 (April 2001): 1–4.

Woodlief, Milton C. "What Sets Virginia Apart?" *Virginia Review* 70 (April 1992): 5–6.

Sources Online

Abramson, Gil A. "The Uncertain Fate of *Gissel* Bargaining Orders in the Circuit Court of Appeals." American Bar Association Committee on Development of the Law under the National Labor Relations Act. www.bnabooks.com/ababna/nira/2002/gissel.doc.May 16, 2005.

"Broken Promises." Daily Press. http://www.dailypress.com/news/specials/. March 27, 2005.

Compa, Lance. "Unfair Advantage: Workers' Freedom of Association in the United States under International Human Rights Standards." Human Rights Watch. http://www.hrw.org/reports/2000/uslabor/. May 16, 2005.

Conway, Carol. "Welcome to the Real World: Educators in Industry." Southern Growth Policies Board. www.southern.org/pubs/realworld. October 11, 2002.

"Considerations for Call Center Development: A Case History." http://www.tmcnet.com/articles/ccsmag/0100/0100staubach.htm. May 25, 2006.

Bernstein, Jared, and Lawrence Mishel. "The State of Working America 1998–1999: Executive Summary." Economic Policy Institute, available at http://www.epinet.org/content.cfm/books_swa98.

Economic Policy Institute. "The State of Working America, 2000–2001: Introduction and Executive Summary." Economic Policy Institute, available at http://www.epinet.org/content.cfm?id=839.

Economic Policy Institute. "State of Working America, 2000–2001: Introduction and Executive Summary." Economic Policy Institute, available at http://www.epi.org/content.cfm/books.

Fonseca, Jim. "The Nine Regions of Virginia." http://www.zanesville.ohiou.edu/geography/virginia/index.htm. July 11, 2006.

"Gateway Cashed In at City's Expense: Computer Maker Fought Hampton for Years over Repaying Incentive Money after Failing to Hire Enough Workers." Daily Press. http://www.dailypress.com/news/specials/. March 27, 2005.

Hawkins, William R. "The Wreck of the Free Trade Model Engenders Myths and Falsehoods." http://www.americaneconomicalert.org. August 1, 2005.

Henwood, Doug. "The New Economy and After." *Left Business Observer* 106 (January 2004), available at http://www.leftbusinessobserver.com/NewEcon.html.

Hudson, Ken. "No Shortage of 'Nonstandard' Jobs." Economic Policy Institute Web site, 1999. http://www.epi.org/content.cfm/briefingpapers_hudson_hudson.

Lane, Julia, Kelly S. Mikelson, Patrick T. Sharkey, and Douglas Wissoker. "Low-Income and Low-Skilled Workers' Involvement in Nonstandard Employment." Urban Institute Report for U.S. Department of Health and Human Services. http://aspe.hhs.gov/hsp/temp-workers01/index.htm.

Margolies, Daniel S. "One New World Order and Many New Souths." Review of *Globalization and the American South*, ed. James C. Cobb and William Stueck, H-Net, June 2006, http://www.h-net.org/reviews/showrev.cgi?path=78351160772984 .

MDC (formerly Manpower Development Corporation). *State of the South 2000*, September 2000, http://www.mdcinc.org/knowledge.

Montgomery, Alicia. "The Silicon Dominion Skews Right." Salon.com http://archive.salon.com/news/feature/1999/11/03/virginia/index.html.

Nagy, Gyula. "Winning a Living Wage Ordinance from the Grassroots." Labor Notes. http://labornotes.org/node/1083.

"National Labor Relations Board Decision and Order, Be Lo Stores and United Food and Commercial Workers Union, Local 400." AFL-CIO. http://www.nlrb.gov/shared_files/Board%20Decisions/318/318-1.pdf. May 11, 2005.

"Nexus Communications Has Laid Off 166 of Its 188 Call Center Employees." Bristol Herald Courier. http://www.sullivan-county.com/nfo/nov_2000/nexas.htm.

Scott, Robert E. "The High Price of 'Free' Trade: NAFTA's Failure Has Cost the United States Jobs across the Nation," 1–13, Economic Policy Institute Briefing Paper, November 2003. Available at http://www.epinet.org/briefingpapers/147/epi_bp147.

Smith, Barbara Ellen. "The New Latino South: An Introduction," 1–13. A Joint Project of the Center for Research on Women at the University of Memphis, the Highlander Research and Education Center, and the Southern Regional Council. Available at http://www.highlandercenter.org/pdf-files/new_latino_south_intro.pdf.

Walter, Scott. "'Live' with TAE: George Allen." The American Enterprise. Available at http://proquest.umi.com/pqdweb.

Index

Michael Dennis is an associate professor of history at Acadia University. He is author of *Luther P. Jackson and a Life for Civil Rights* (University Press of Florida, 2004) and *Lessons in Progress: State Universities and Progressivism in the New South* (University of Illinois Press, 2001).